Popular Complete Smart Series

Complete Canadian Curriculum

Grade 7

Contents

Mathematics

English

History

New France and British North America, 1713 – 1800

Canada, 1800 – 1850: Conflict and Challenges

Geography

Physical Patterns in a Changing World

Natural Resources around the World: Use and Sustainability

Science

Answers

MATHEMATICS

* The Canadian penny is no longer in circulation. It is used in the units to show money amounts to the cent.

Exponents

- identify the base and exponent in a power
- write powers in exponent form, expanded form, and standard form
- compare powers
- identify a power as a perfect square or perfect cube

Write each power in expanded form.

1. 3^8 ___
2. 4^5 ___
3. 8^7 ___
4. 12^4 ___
5. 9^6 ___
6. 7^8 ___

Fill in the missing numbers.

7. $\_\_^5 = 3 \times 3 \times 3 \times 3 \times 3$
8. $9^{\_\_} = 9 \times 9 \times 9 \times 9 \times 9 \times 9$
9. $2^3 = \_\_ \times \_\_ \times \_\_$
10. $\_\_^4 = 7 \times 7 \times 7 \times 7$
11. $4^{\_\_} = 4 \times 4 \times 4 \times 4$
12. $\_\_^7 = 8 \times 8 \times 8 \times 8 \times 8 \times 8 \times 8$
13. $11^4 = \_\_ \times \_\_ \times \_\_ \times \_\_$
14. $3^{\_\_} = 3 \times 3 \times 3$

Find the base and exponent for each power.

15. 5^3 ___ base ___ exponent
16. 7^5 ___ base ___ exponent
17. 22^{10} ___ base ___ exponent
18. 13^6 ___ base ___ exponent
19. 39^2 ___ base ___ exponent
20. 1^{100} ___ base ___ exponent

Write each in exponent form and standard form.

	Expanded Form	Exponent Form	Standard Form
21.	8 x 8	8^2	64
22.	3 x 3 x 3 x 3	3^4	81
23.	7 x 7 x 7	7^3	343
24.	5 x 5 x 5 x 5 x 5	1^5	3125
25.	9 x 9 x 9	9^3	729
26.	2 x 2 x 2 x 2 x 2 x 2	2^6	64
27.	1 x 1 x 1 x 1 x 1 x 1 x 1 x 1	1^8	1

Read what the children say. Write each power in exponent form, expanded form, and standard form.

28.

5 to the power of 4

5^4 ; 5 x 5 x 5 x 5 ; 20

29.

the sixth power of 7

7^6 ; 7 x 7 x 7 x 7 x 7 x 7 ~~6 x 6 x 6 x 6 x 6 x 6 x 6~~ ; 64

30.

the base of the power is 2 and its exponent is 8

2^8 ; 2 x 2 x 2 x 2 x 2 x 2 x 2 x 2 ; 16

A Product of Powers:

e.g. $3 \times 7 \times 7 \times 7 \times 3$

$= 3 \times 3 \times 7 \times 7 \times 7$ ← Rearrange the order to group the numbers.

$= 3^2 \times 7^3$

3 and 7 are the bases of the powers; and 2 and 3 are their exponents respectively.

Comparing Powers:

- If the powers have the same base, the one with the greater exponent is greater.

  e.g. $7^3 < 7^4$ ← same base (7) ; 7^4 is greater

- If the powers have the same exponent, the one with the greater base is greater.

  e.g. $5^3 < 6^3$ ← same exponent (3) ; 6^3 is greater

Write each as a product of powers.

31. $2 \times 2 \times 5 \times 5 \times 5 =$ ________

32. $6 \times 4 \times 6 \times 4 \times 4 =$ ________

33. $9 \times 9 \times 5 \times 9 \times 9 =$ ________

34. $8 \times 1 \times 8 \times 8 \times 1 \times 8 =$ ________

35. $7 \times 7 \times 2 \times 2 \times 7 \times 2 \times 7 \times 7 \times 2 =$ ________

36. $8 \times 3 \times 3 \times 8 \times 3 \times 3 \times 3 \times 8 \times 3 =$ ________

Evaluate each power. Compare the powers with the help of their standard form. Then put ">", "<", or "=" in the circles.

37. $3^3 =$ ______ $6^4 =$ ______

$5^3 =$ ______ $2^5 =$ ______

$4^5 =$ ______ $7^3 =$ ______

$9^3 =$ ______ $8^4 =$ ______

a. 7^3 ◯ 5^3

b. 3^3 ◯ 7^3

c. 4^5 ◯ 2^5

d. 8^4 ◯ 6^4

Put ">", "<", or "=" in the circles.

38. 7^3 ◯ 7^2

39. 8^4 ◯ 9^4

40. 5^4 ◯ 5^6

41. 6^5 ◯ 4^5

42. x^5 ◯ x^8

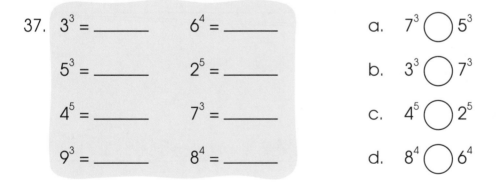

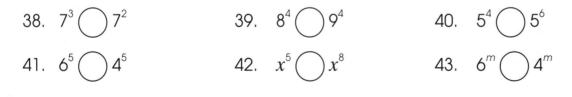

43. 6^m ◯ 4^m

A Perfect Square – a number that is the square of an integer

e.g. $\frac{1}{1 \times 1}, \frac{4}{2 \times 2}, \frac{9}{3 \times 3}, \frac{16}{4 \times 4}, \frac{25}{5 \times 5}, \frac{36}{6 \times 6}, \ldots$ ← perfect squares

A Perfect Cube – a number that is the cube of an integer

e.g. $\frac{1}{1 \times 1 \times 1}, \frac{8}{2 \times 2 \times 2}, \frac{27}{3 \times 3 \times 3}, \frac{64}{4 \times 4 \times 4}, \frac{125}{5 \times 5 \times 5}, \ldots$ ← perfect cubes

Rewrite each power as another power with an exponent of 2 or 3. Then evaluate the power and tell whether the number is a perfect square or perfect cube.

44. $5^4 = 5 \times 5 \times 5 \times$ ____

$= 25 \times$ ____

$= 25$

$=$ ________

So, ______ is a ________________.

45. $8^6 = 8 \times 8 \times 8 \times 8 \times$ ______

$= 64 \times$ _____ $\times$ _____

$= 64$

$=$ ________

So, ______ is a ________________.

46. $7^4 = 49 \quad =$ ________

So, ______ is a ________________.

47. $3^9 = 27 \quad =$ ________

So, ______ is a ________________.

Simplify each group of powers. Then describe the pattern that you can see in the answers.

48. **A**

$8^1 =$ ____ $\quad 15^1 =$ ____

$415^1 =$ ____ $\quad 67^1 =$ ____

B

$9^0 =$ ____ $\quad 42^0 =$ ____

$7^0 =$ ____ $\quad 125^0 =$ ____

A *If the exponent of a power is 1, then the answer will be the number ________ (itself / multiplied itself).*

B ____

2

Squares and Square Roots

- find the square of a number
- find the square root of a number
- draw squares with a given area
- solve problems involving squares and square roots

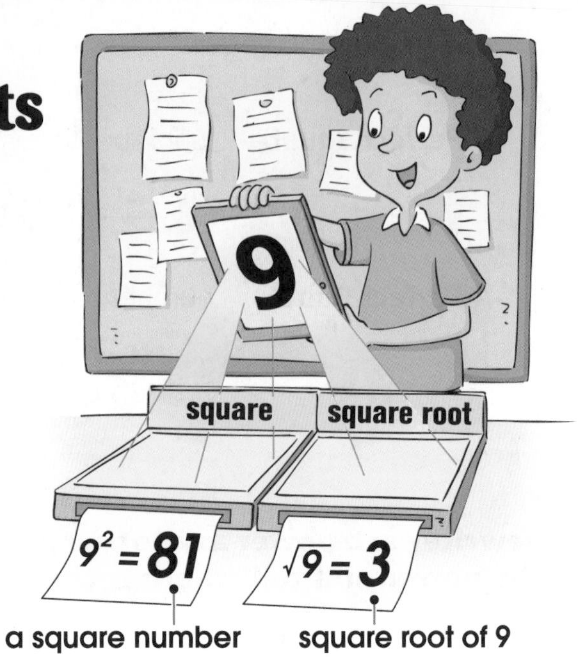

Complete the list of square facts. Then find the square roots with the help of the square facts.

1. **Square Facts**

$1^2 =$ ______	$6^2 =$ ______
$2^2 =$ ______	$7^2 =$ ______
$3^2 =$ ______	$8^2 =$ ______
$4^2 =$ ______	$9^2 =$ ______
$5^2 =$ ______	$10^2 =$ ______

2. $\sqrt{49} =$ ______
3. $\sqrt{36} =$ ______
4. $\sqrt{81} =$ ______
5. $\sqrt{4} =$ ______
6. $\sqrt{100} =$ ______
7. $\sqrt{16} =$ ______

Find the missing digit in the ones column of each number.

8. $19^2 = 36\square$
9. $37^2 = 136\square$
10. $54^2 = 291\square$
11. $23^2 = 52\square$
12. $32^2 = 102\square$
13. $75^2 = 562\square$
14. $42^2 = 176\square$
15. $57^2 = 324\square$
16. $29^2 = 84\square$
17. $18^2 = 32\square$

Hint

When you square the digit in the ones column of any number that has two or more digits, the ones digit of the product must be the same as the ones digit of the square of the number that you started with.

e.g. 18^2 ← The square of 8 is 64; 4 is the digit in the ones column.

= 324 ← 4 in the ones column

Fill in the blanks to complete the sentences. Then translate each sentence into a mathematical expression.

A Mathematical Expression

18. 16 is the square of ______ . $16 = \square^2$ ____________

19. 49 is the square of ______ . ____________

20. 8 squared is ______ . ____________

21. 25 squared is ______ . ____________

22. 7 to the power of 2 is ______ . ____________

23. 9 to the power of 2 is ______ . ____________

24. 10 is the square root of ______ . ____________

25. 12 is the square root of ______ . ____________

Find the answers. Then write a matching fact.

26. $\sqrt{225} =$ ______
$15^2 =$ ______

27. $\sqrt{400} =$ ______
____

28. $\sqrt{121} =$ ______
____

29. $16^2 =$ ______
____

30. $17^2 =$ ______
____

31. $\sqrt{441} =$ ______
____

32. The square root of 64 is ______ . ____________

33. 20 to the power of 2 is ______ . ____________

Find the area or side length of each square.

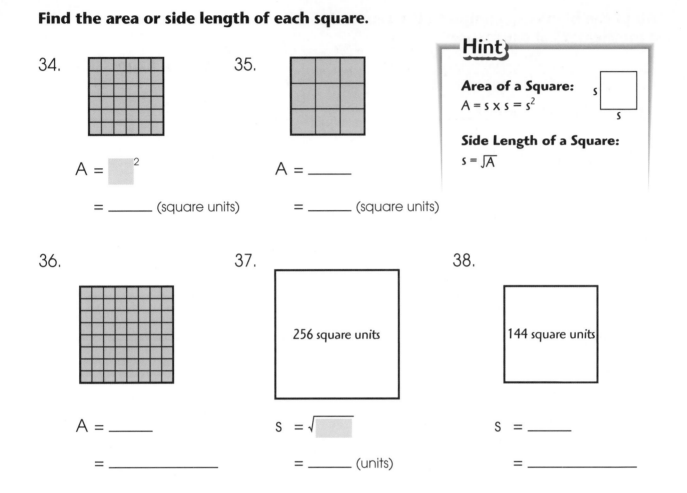

34.

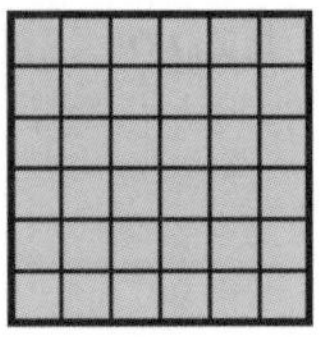

A = ▢^{2}

= ______ (square units)

35.

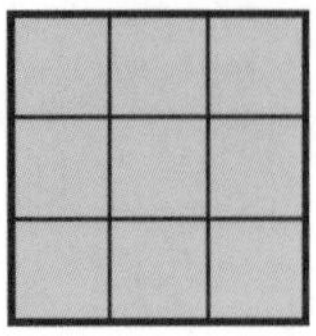

A = ______

= ______ (square units)

Hint

Area of a Square:

A = s x s = s^2

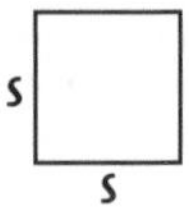

Side Length of a Square:

$s = \sqrt{A}$

36.

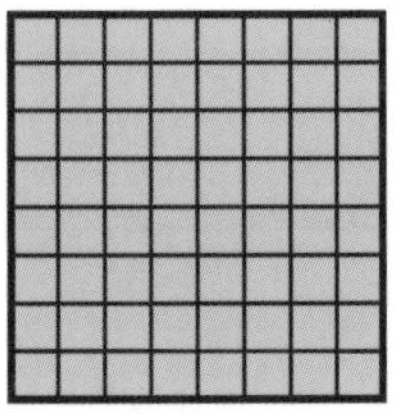

A = ______

= ______________

37.

s = $\sqrt{}$

= ______ (units)

38.

s = ______

= ______________

Find the areas and side lengths of the squares.

39. The big square is formed by a small square and 4 congruent isosceles right triangles.

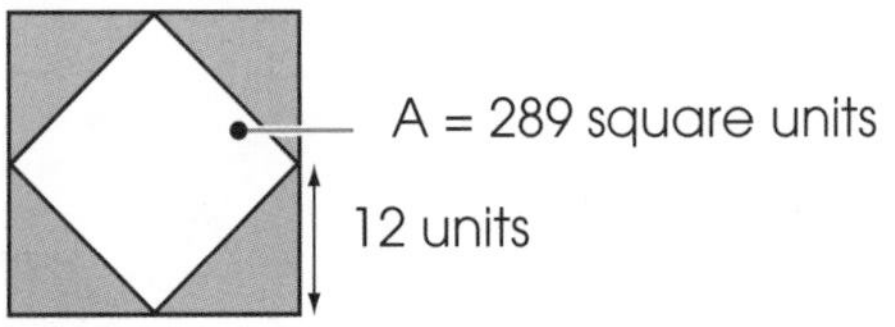

	Small Square	Big Square
Area (square units)		
Side Length (units)		

40. This figure is formed by 2 congruent rectangles and 2 squares of different sizes.

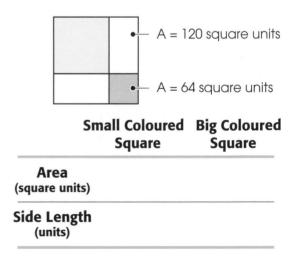

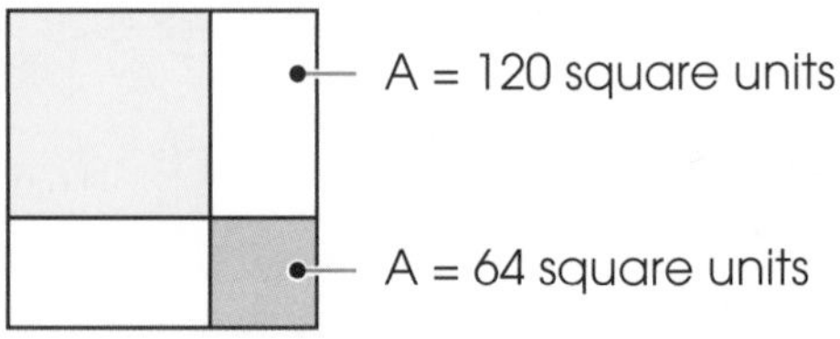

	Small Coloured Square	Big Coloured Square
Area (square units)		
Side Length (units)		

Draw and label the squares on the grid with the given areas.

41. **Area of Squares**

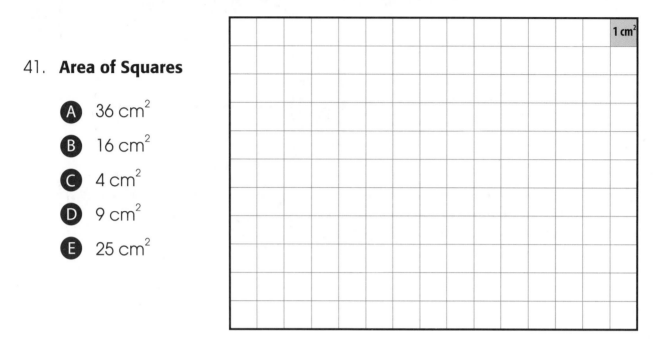

- **A** 36 cm^2
- **B** 16 cm^2
- **C** 4 cm^2
- **D** 9 cm^2
- **E** 25 cm^2

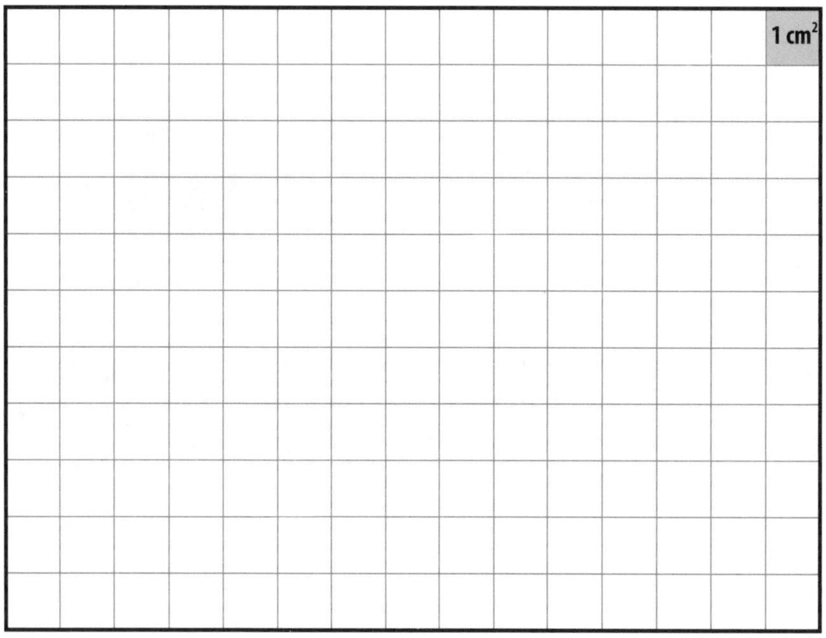

Solve the problems.

42. The areas of the big and small squares are 169 cm^2 and 49 cm^2 respectively.

a. What are the side lengths of the two squares?

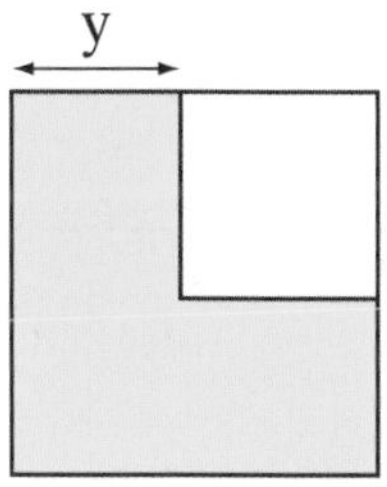

The side lengths are ____________________ .

b. What is the value of y?

The value of y is __________ .

43. Jason cuts a square cardboard with an area of 576 cm^2 into 4 identical small squares. What is the side length of each small square?

The side length of each small square is ______ cm.

Factors and Multiples

- list out the factors of a number
- find the G.C.F. of a set of numbers
- list out the multiples of a number
- find the L.C.M. of a set of numbers

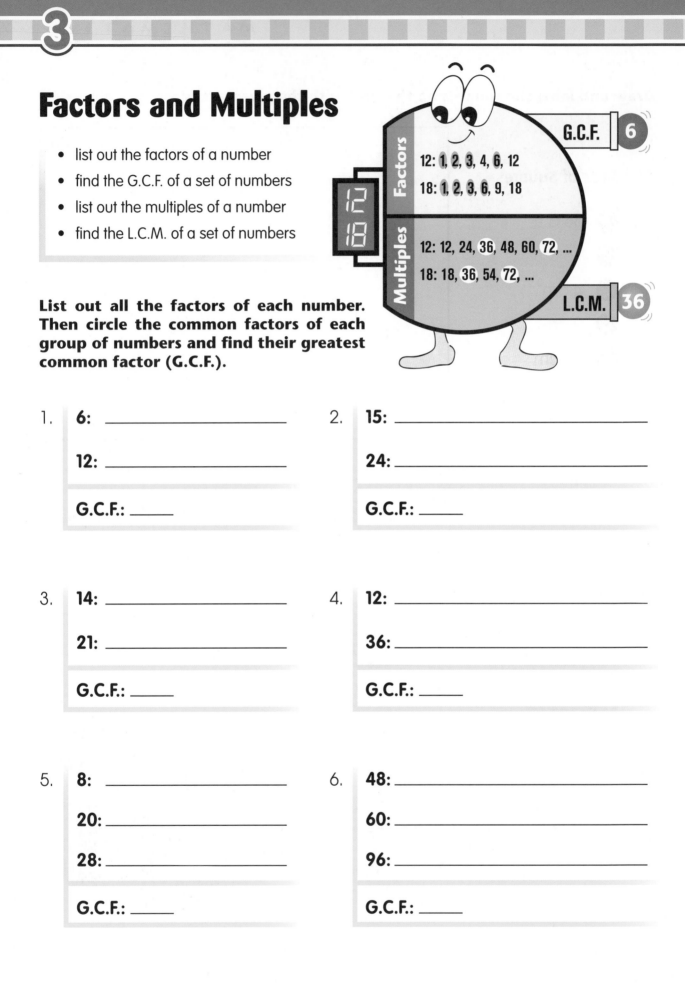

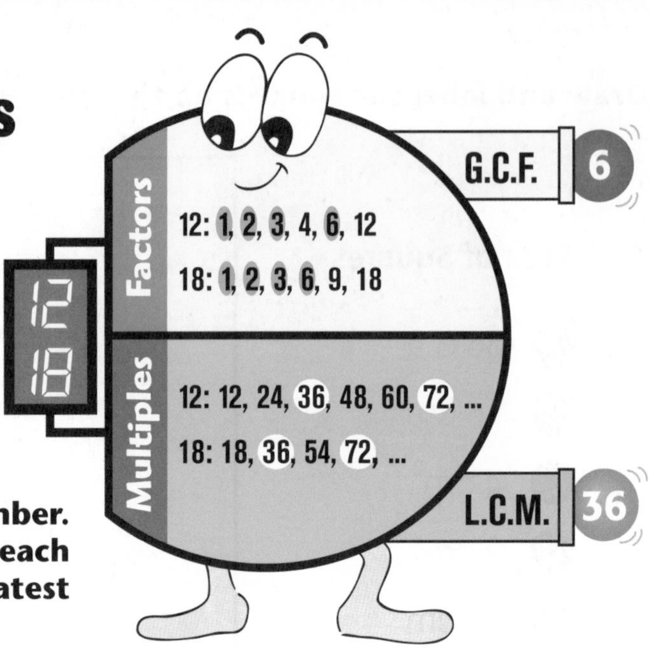

List out all the factors of each number. Then circle the common factors of each group of numbers and find their greatest common factor (G.C.F.).

1. **6:** ____________________

   12: ____________________

   G.C.F.: _____

2. **15:** ____________________

   24: ____________________

   G.C.F.: _____

3. **14:** ____________________

   21: ____________________

   G.C.F.: _____

4. **12:** ____________________

   36: ____________________

   G.C.F.: _____

5. **8:** ____________________

   20: ____________________

   28: ____________________

   G.C.F.: _____

6. **48:** ____________________

   60: ____________________

   96: ____________________

   G.C.F.: _____

Look at the Venn diagram. Find the common factors of each group of numbers and their G.C.F.

7. **24 & 40** ____________________ ; ______

8. **40 & 60** ____________________ ; ______

9. **24 & 60** ____________________ ; ______

10. **24, 40, & 60** ____________________ ; ______

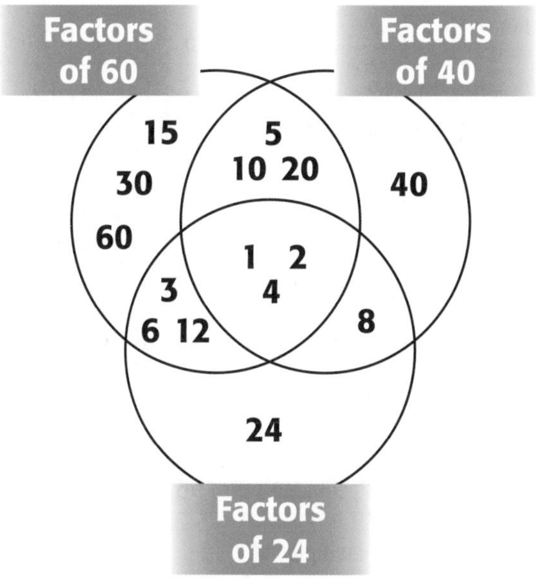

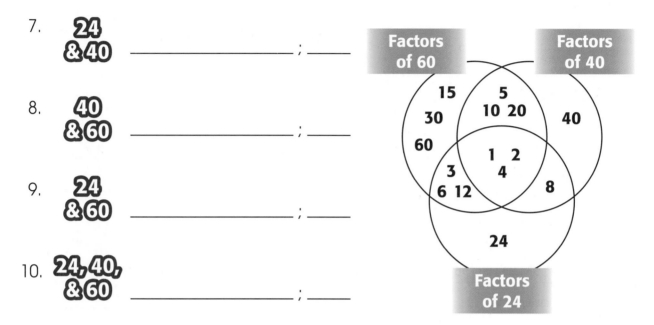

List out the factors of the numbers using Venn diagrams. Then find the G.C.F.

11. 30 and 42

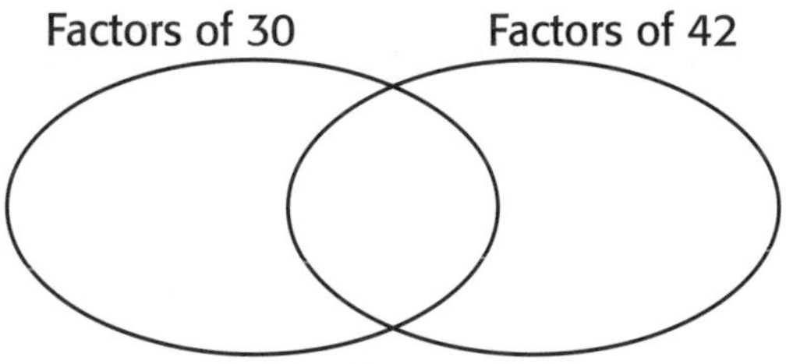

G.C.F. = ______

12. 28 and 35

G.C.F. = ______

13. 12, 20, and 36

G.C.F. = ______

14. 10, 45, and 60

G.C.F. = ______

Make a legend to mark the multiples of the numbers in the hundreds chart. Find the least common multiples (L.C.M.) of the numbers. Then answer the questions.

15.

1	2	3	4	5	6	7	8	9	10
11	12	13	14	15	16	17	18	19	20
21	22	23	24	25	26	27	28	29	30
31	32	33	34	35	36	37	38	39	40
41	42	43	44	45	46	47	48	49	50
51	52	53	54	55	56	57	58	59	60
61	62	63	64	65	66	67	68	69	70
71	72	73	74	75	76	77	78	79	80
81	82	83	84	85	86	87	88	89	90
91	92	93	94	95	96	97	98	99	100

☐ : multiples of 2 ☐ : multiples of 3

☐ : multiples of 4 ☐ : multiples of 10

a. common multiples of 3 and 10:

____

L.C.M.: ______

b. common multiples of 3 and 4:

____

L.C.M.: ______

c. common multiples of 4 and 10:

____

L.C.M.: ______

16. a. common multiples of 2 and 10:

____

b. Describe the pattern that you can see in the common multiples of 2 and 10.

____

c. Follow the pattern to find the next 5 common multiples of 2 and 10.

____

Write the first 12 multiples of each number. Circle the common multiples. Then fill in the blanks.

17. **4:** ______, 8, 12, ____________________

6: ______, 12, 18, ____________________

L.C.M. of 4 and 6: ______

The first 4 common multiples of 4 and 6: ____________________

List the first 12 multiples of each number. Then find the L.C.M. of each pair of numbers.

18.

Multiples	L.C.M.
3: ______________________	• 3 & 4: _____
4: ______________________	• 5 & 6: _____
5: ______________________	• 6 & 7: _____
6: ______________________	• 5 & 7: _____
7: ______________________	

Solve the problems. Show your work.

19. Tina has a sandwich for lunch every 4 days and Joe has one every 6 days. If they both have a sandwich for lunch today, how many days after will they both have sandwiches for lunch again?

Hint

List the multiples. The L.C.M. is the least number of days that the two children will have sandwiches again.

Tina (multiples of 4): ______________________

Joe (multiples of 6): ______________________

They will both have sandwiches again after _____ days.

20. Farmer Jack puts the eggs into the fewest cartons. Each carton holds the same kind and the same number of eggs. How many eggs does each carton hold? How many cartons are needed for each kind of egg?

factors of 18: ______________________

factors of 12: ______________________

Each carton holds _____ eggs.

We need _____ cartons for 18 brown eggs and _____ cartons for 12 white eggs.

This problem can be solved by finding the G.C.F.

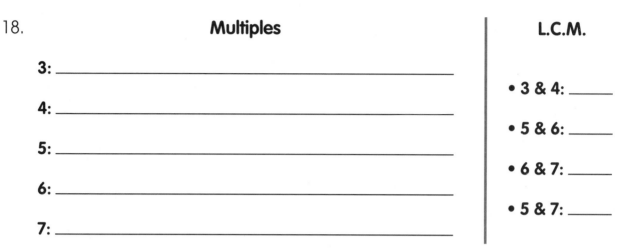

4

Integers

- locate integers on a number line
- relate integers to day-to-day activities
- compare and put integers in order
- add and subtract positive and negative integers

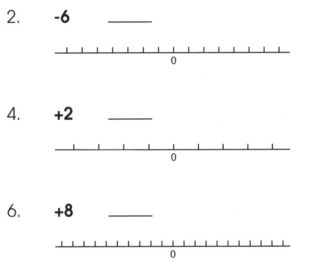

You haven't won this game yet. Don't you know that -2 is the opposite of +2? They are the same distance from 0.

Write the opposite of each integer and mark both integers on the number line.

1. **+3** ______

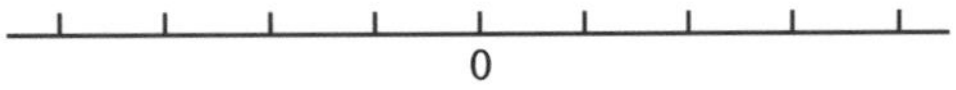

2. **-6** ______

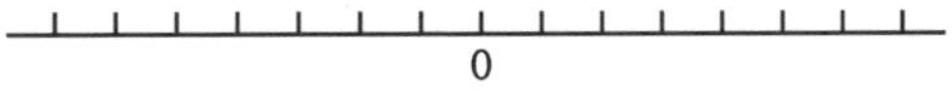

3. **+7** ______

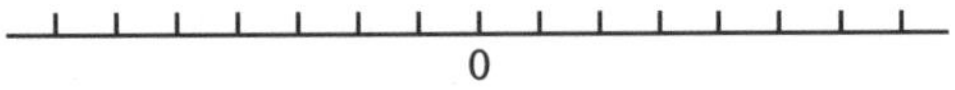

4. **+2** ______

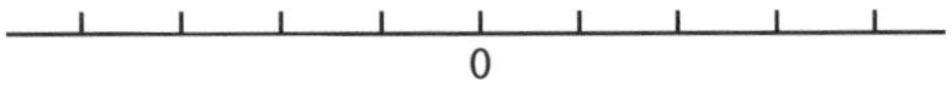

5. **-5** ______

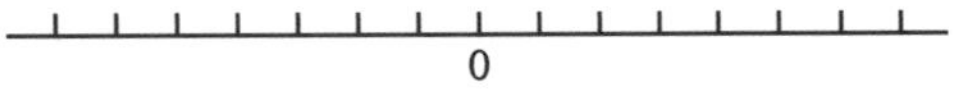

6. **+8** ______

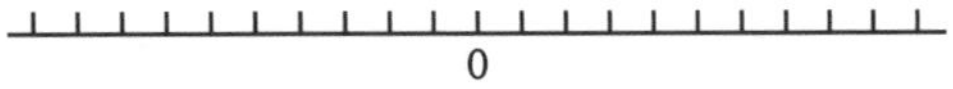

Write an integer to represent each situation.

7. Today's temperature has risen by 5°C. ________
8. Louise's cat gained 2 kg. ________
9. Peter is 3 cm taller than last year. ________
10. The company lost $273. ________
11. Jason's wage has increased by $4/hour. ________
12. After the expansion, the park is 18 km^2 larger. ________

Locate the integers on the number line with arrows. Then compare them and put ">", "<", or "=" in the circle.

13. -4 ◯ 3

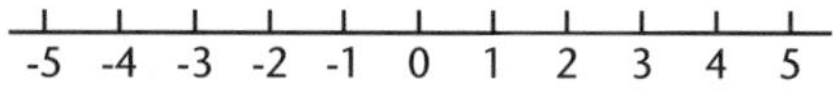

14. 2 ◯ -5

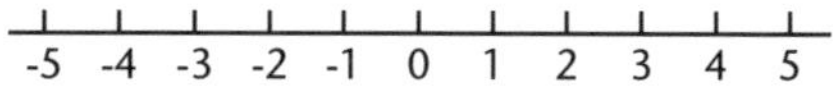

15. -3 ◯ 6

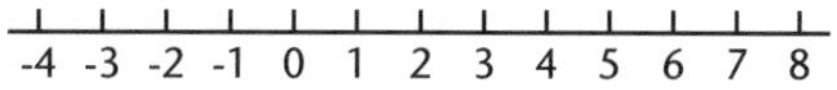

16. 0 ◯ -5

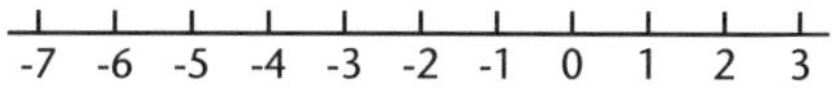

Hint

Comparing Integers:

An integer is always greater than the integers on its left. Similarly, an integer is always smaller than the integers on its right.

e.g. 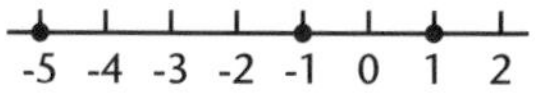

- -5 is on the left of -1.
  -1 (>) -5
- 1 is on the right of -1.
  -1 (<) 1

Circle the greatest integer in each group.

17. +2 -3 +5

18. -3 -5 -8

19. -9 -2 -4

20. -1 -10 0

Put each group of integers in order from least to greatest.

21. +6 -2 +8 -4

____

22. +5 -3 -5 +2

____

23. -9 -1 0 -7

____

24. -11 +3 +12 -8

____

25. 0 -4 4 -2

____

26. -3 -15 -9 -6

____

Do each addition with the help of the number line.

27. (+3) + (+4) = ______

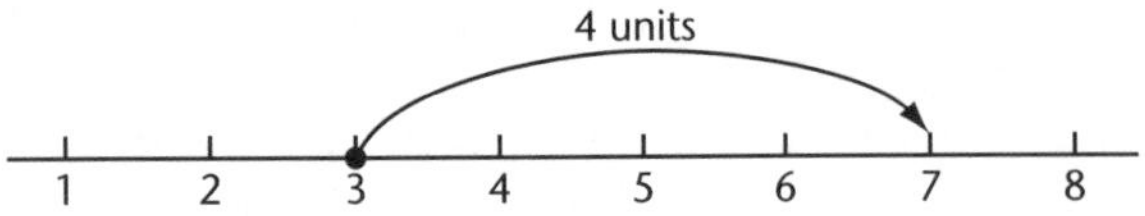

28. (+4) + (-5) = ______

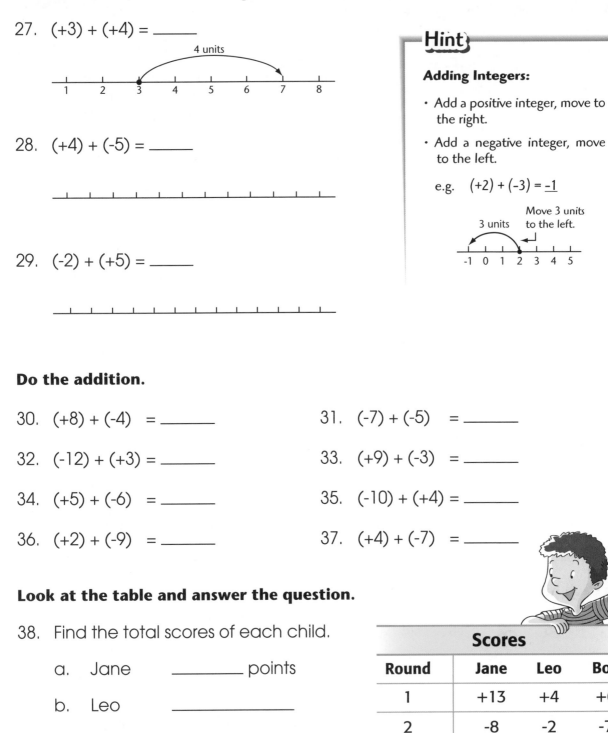

29. (-2) + (+5) = ______

Hint

Adding Integers:

- Add a positive integer, move to the right.
- Add a negative integer, move to the left.

e.g. (+2) + (-3) = <u>-1</u>

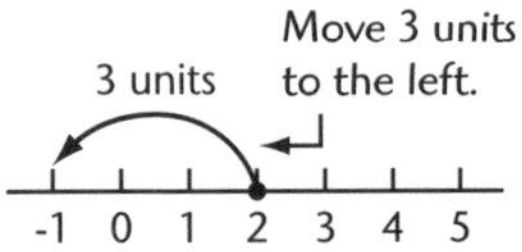

Do the addition.

30. (+8) + (-4) = ______
31. (-7) + (-5) = ______
32. (-12) + (+3) = ______
33. (+9) + (-3) = ______
34. (+5) + (-6) = ______
35. (-10) + (+4) = ______
36. (+2) + (-9) = ______
37. (+4) + (-7) = ______

Look at the table and answer the question.

38. Find the total scores of each child.

 a. Jane ________ points

 b. Leo ________

 c. Bob ________

Scores

Round	Jane	Leo	Bob
1	+13	+4	+6
2	-8	-2	-7

39. If Leo teams up with Bob to race against Jane, can they beat Jane in these two rounds? If not, how many more points are needed?

____

Subtracting Integers:

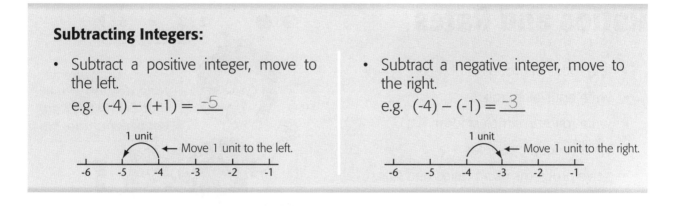

- Subtract a positive integer, move to the left.
  e.g. (-4) – (+1) = <u>-5</u>

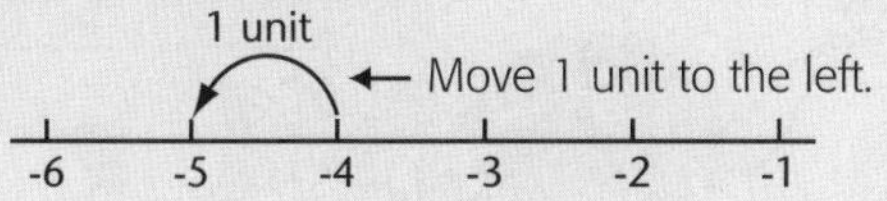

- Subtract a negative integer, move to the right.
  e.g. (-4) – (-1) = <u>-3</u>

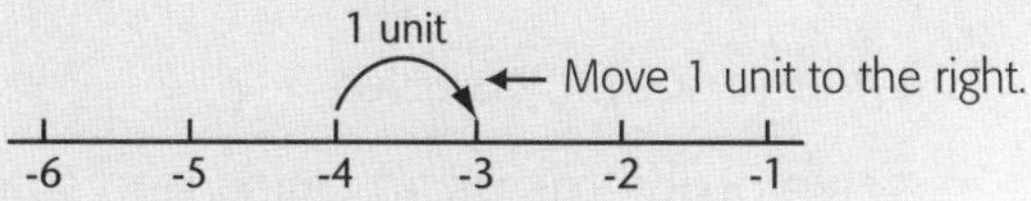

Do the subtraction with the help of the number line.

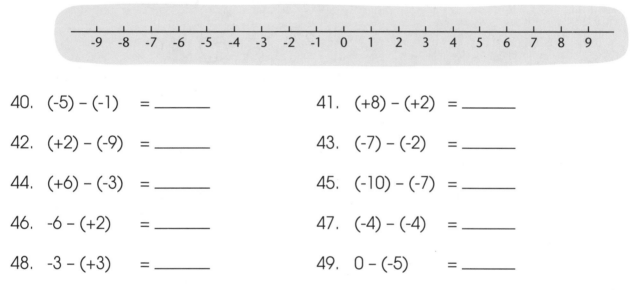

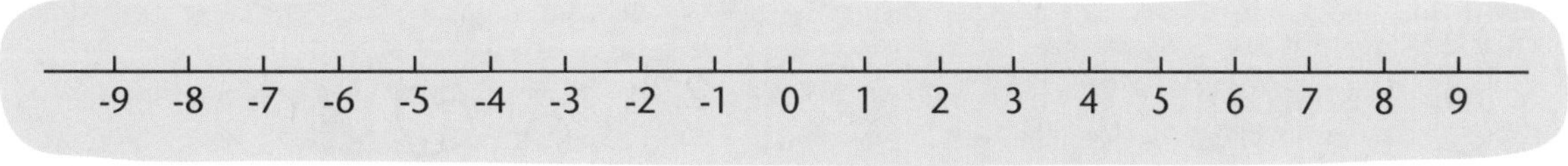

40. (-5) – (-1) = ______
41. (+8) – (+2) = ______
42. (+2) – (-9) = ______
43. (-7) – (-2) = ______
44. (+6) – (-3) = ______
45. (-10) – (-7) = ______
46. -6 – (+2) = ______
47. (-4) – (-4) = ______
48. -3 – (+3) = ______
49. 0 – (-5) = ______

Read what Susan says. Help her complete the table.

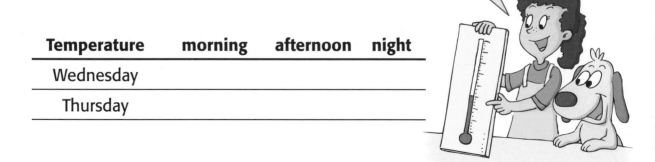

50. *On Wednesday, the morning temperature was 4°C. It dropped 3°C in the afternoon and then another 4°C at night. On Thursday, the afternoon temperature was 5°C lower than the morning temperature. The temperature at night was -3°C and it was 8°C higher than the afternoon temperature.*

Temperature	morning	afternoon	night
Wednesday			
Thursday			

5

Ratios and Rates

- find ratios of groups of objects
- write equivalent ratios
- write ratios in simplest form
- write amounts as rates
- solve problems using ratios and rates

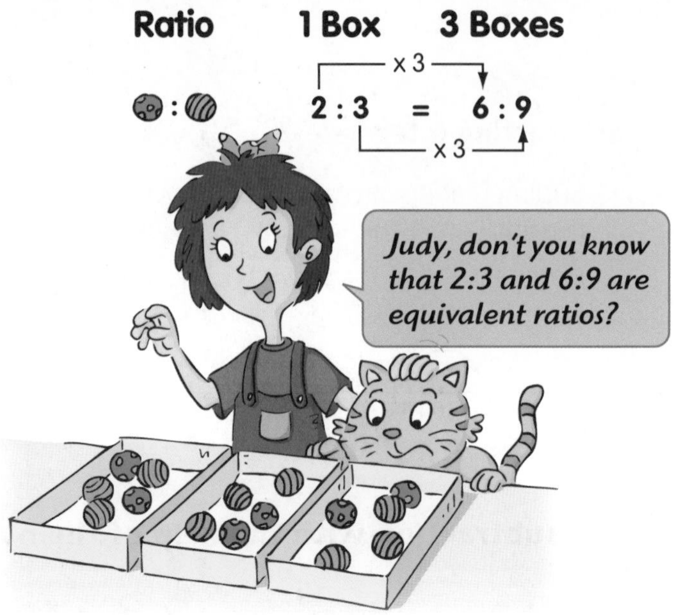

Ratio
1 Box
3 Boxes
x 3
2 : 3 = 6 : 9
x 3
Judy, don't you know that 2:3 and 6:9 are equivalent ratios?

Write the ratios for each group.

1.

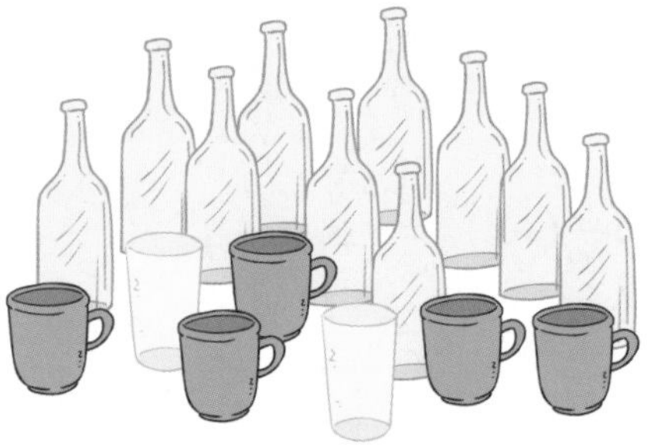

a. cups to mugs = ____ : ____

b. cups to bottles = ________

c. mugs to bottles = ________

d. bottles to all = ________

2.

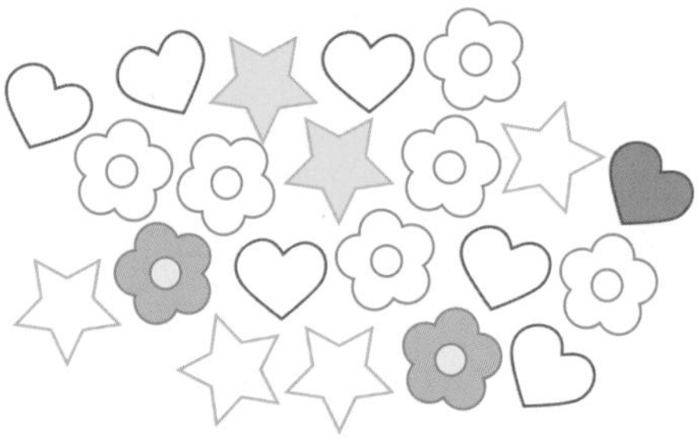

a. hearts to stars = ________

b. flowers to hearts = ________

c. shaded shapes to unshaded shapes = ________

Colour the shapes to match the given ratios. Then find the ratios.

3. green circles to all shapes = 5:16
red rectangles to all shapes = 3:8

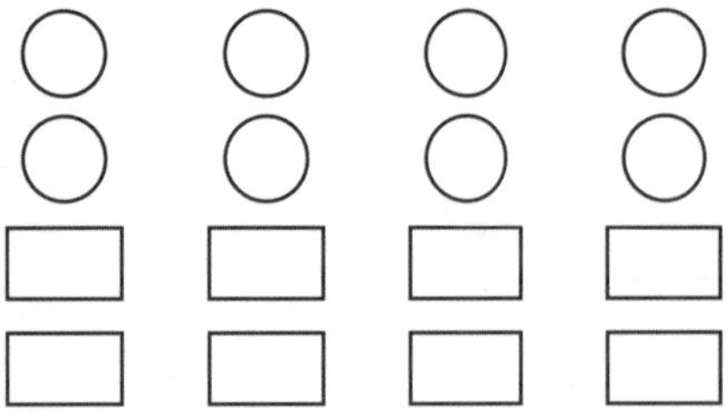

green ○ : red ▭ = ______

4. red squares to blue stars = 3:3
red triangles to yellow stars = 3:2

red □ : red △ = ______

Jane has a collection of marbles. Read what she says. Then help her complete the table.

5. *If my sister gives me 4 blue marbles and 1 red marble, what will the new ratios be?*

Marbles	Ratio	Ratio (New)
green : blue	3:2	
red : green		
blue : all		
red : all		

Find the equivalent ratios.

6. (x 2) 3 : 5 = ____ : ____ (x 2)

7. (x 4) 2 : 7 = ____ : ____ (x 4)

8. (÷ 2) $\frac{8}{6}$ = ____ (÷ 2)

9. (÷ 5) $\frac{15}{25}$ = ____ (÷ 5)

10. 4:12 = ______

11. 10:20 = ______

12. 30:8 = ______

13. 6:15 = ______

Hint

Finding Equivalent Ratios:

You may multiply or divide each term in a ratio to find an equivalent ratio.

e.g. (x 4) 2 : 3 = 8 : 12 (x 4) (x 4) $\frac{2}{3} = \frac{8}{12}$ (x 4)

* Multiply both terms by 4.

Equivalent ratios: 2:3 and 8:12

Write two equivalent ratios for each.

14. 6:4 ____________

15. 4:10 ____________

16. 8:5 ____________

17. 10:25 ____________

18. 12:15 ____________

19. 1:7 ____________

Fill in the missing numbers.

20. 3:8 = ____ : 24

21. 6:4 = 3 : ____

22. ____ : 3 = 4:12

23. 7 : ____ = 21:6

24. 12:20 = ____ : 10

25. 24 : ____ = 8:6

Ratio in Simplest Form:

Divide both terms in the ratio by their G.C.F.

e.g. Write 6:9 in simplest form.

Think: The G.C.F. of 6 and 9 is _3_.

$6:9 = \underline{2} : \underline{3}$ (÷ 3 both terms)

The simplest form of 6:9 is _2:3_.

There are 3 muffins and 4 doughnuts in a box. If there are 20 doughnuts, how many muffins are there?

Think: It is a ratio problem. Write as a ratio.

muffins : doughnuts = 3:4

$3:4 = \underline{15} : 20$ (x 5 both terms) ← Multiply both terms by 5 to figure out the answer.

There are _15_ muffins.

Find the G.C.F. of the terms. Then write each ratio in simplest form.

26. 9:27 = ________
G.C.F. = ______

27. 18:45 = ________
G.C.F. = ______

28. 35:14 = ________
G.C.F. = ______

29. 30:18 = ________
G.C.F. = ______

30. 15:24 = ________
G.C.F. = ______

31. 42:18 = ________
G.C.F. = ______

Solve the problems.

32. The ratio of the height of a triangle to its base is 2:3. If the height of the triangle is 18 cm, what is the length of the base?

____

33. *The number of candies that Tom has to the number that I have is in the ratio of 4:5. If I have 35 candies, how many candies does Tom have?*

____

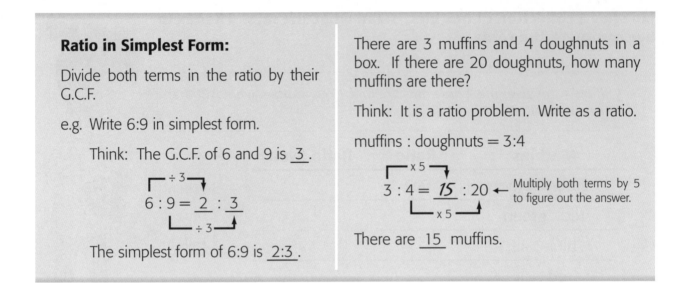

Rate:

a comparison, or a type of ratio, of two measurements with different units

e.g. It takes Sue 10 days to build 15 models.

Rate = 15 ÷ 10 = 1.5

Sue's rate is 1.5 models/day.

Unit Rate:

a rate with the second term being one unit

e.g. The cost of 8 pizzas is $63.92.

Unit rate = $63.92 ÷ 8 pizzas
= $7.99/pizza

The unit rate of a pizza is $7.99.

Write each as a rate.

34. travelling 82.4 km in 6 hours ____________

35. 8 chicken balls for $4.72 ____________

36. reading 36 pages in 4 days ____________

37. assembling 15 bicycles in 3 hours ____________

Find the unit rates. Then check the one with a higher unit rate in each group.

38. (A) type 378 words in 9 minutes
unit rate: ______ words/min

(B) type 990 words in 15 minutes
unit rate: ____________

39. (A) travel 382.6 km in 5 hours
unit rate: ____________

(B) travel 32.44 km in 0.5 hour
unit rate: ____________

40. *I can finish 326 g of food in 4 days and Sam can finish 39.25 g of food in half a day.*

	Unit Rate
(A) Judy the Cat	
(B) Sam the Cat	

6

Fractions

- write equivalent fractions
- add, subtract, and multiply fractions
- solve problems that involve the addition, subtraction, and multiplication of fractions

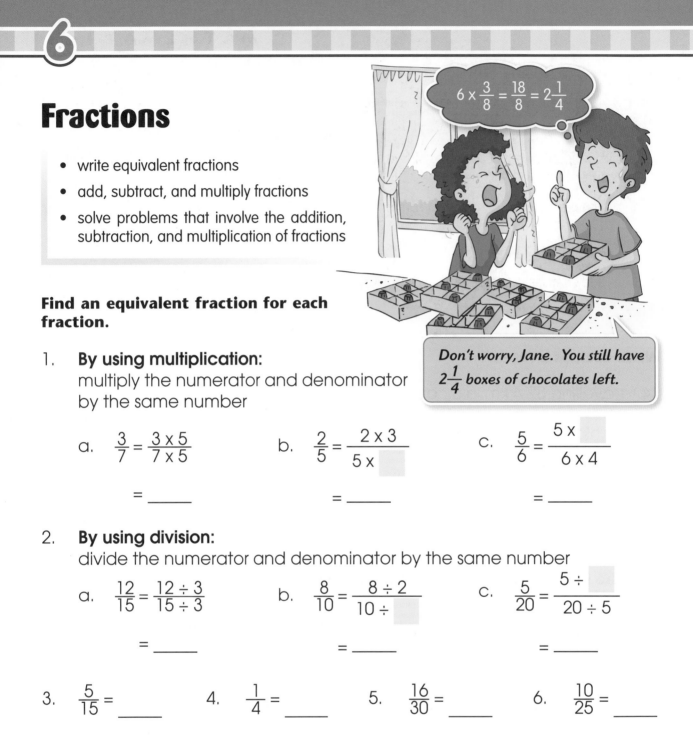

Find an equivalent fraction for each fraction.

1. **By using multiplication:**
   multiply the numerator and denominator by the same number

   a. $\frac{3}{7} = \frac{3 \times 5}{7 \times 5}$

   $= \_\_\_\_\_$

   b. $\frac{2}{5} = \frac{2 \times 3}{5 \times \square}$

   $= \_\_\_\_\_$

   c. $\frac{5}{6} = \frac{5 \times \square}{6 \times 4}$

   $= \_\_\_\_\_$

2. **By using division:**
   divide the numerator and denominator by the same number

   a. $\frac{12}{15} = \frac{12 \div 3}{15 \div 3}$

   $= \_\_\_\_\_$

   b. $\frac{8}{10} = \frac{8 \div 2}{10 \div \square}$

   $= \_\_\_\_\_$

   c. $\frac{5}{20} = \frac{5 \div \square}{20 \div 5}$

   $= \_\_\_\_\_$

3. $\frac{5}{15} = \_\_\_\_\_$

4. $\frac{1}{4} = \_\_\_\_\_$

5. $\frac{16}{30} = \_\_\_\_\_$

6. $\frac{10}{25} = \_\_\_\_\_$

Find the equivalent fractions for each pair of fractions so that the equivalent fractions have the same denominator. Then colour the correct number of parts to find the sum.

7. $\frac{1}{2}$ and $\frac{2}{5}$

   $\frac{1}{2} = \_\_\_\_\_$ | $\frac{2}{5} = \_\_\_\_\_$

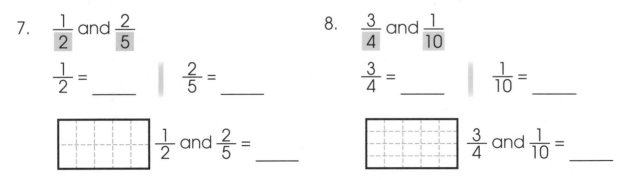

   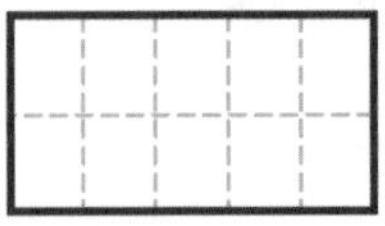

   $\frac{1}{2}$ and $\frac{2}{5} = \_\_\_\_\_$

8. $\frac{3}{4}$ and $\frac{1}{10}$

   $\frac{3}{4} = \_\_\_\_\_$ | $\frac{1}{10} = \_\_\_\_\_$

   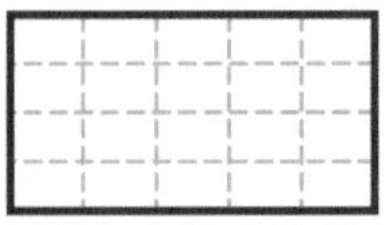

   $\frac{3}{4}$ and $\frac{1}{10} = \_\_\_\_\_$

Adding fractions with different denominators:

1st Find the least common denominator (L.C.D.) and equivalent fractions.

2nd Add the numerators and keep the denominator the same.

3rd Write the answer in simplest form.

Add the numbers.

e.g. $\frac{1}{4} + \frac{7}{12} = \frac{3}{12} + \frac{7}{12} = \frac{10}{12} = \frac{5}{6}$

The L.C.M. of 4 and 12 is 12. So, 12 is the L.C.D.

Fractions in Simplest Form:

A fraction is in its simplest form if the greatest common factor of the numerator and denominator is 1.

e.g. $\frac{2}{7}$ ← in simplest form

Do the addition. Write the answers in simplest form.

9. $\frac{3}{5} + \frac{1}{10}$

$= \_\_\_\_ + \frac{1}{10}$

$= \_\_\_\_$

10. $\frac{3}{4} + \frac{1}{5}$

$= \frac{}{20} + \_\_\_\_$

$= \_\_\_\_$

11. $\frac{3}{10} + \frac{8}{15} = \frac{}{30} + \_\_\_\_$

$= \_\_\_\_$

$= \_\_\_\_$ ← in simplest form

12. $\frac{5}{9} + \frac{7}{36} = \_\_\_\_\_\_\_\_ = \_\_\_\_$

13. $\frac{2}{7} + \frac{5}{14} = \_\_\_\_\_\_\_\_ = \_\_\_\_$

14. $\frac{3}{4} + \frac{4}{5} = \_\_\_\_\_\_\_\_ = \_\_\_\_$

Write the answer as a mixed number.

15. $\frac{1}{2} + \frac{17}{18} = \_\_\_\_\_\_\_\_ = \_\_\_\_$

Solve the problems.

16. What is the total weight of one bag and one box of cookies?

________ = ____ ________

17. Sue has $\frac{5}{6}$ kg of cookies. If she buys a bag of cookies, how many kg of cookies will she have in all?

________ = ____ ________

Subtracting fractions with different denominators:

1st Find the least common denominator and equivalent fractions.

2nd Subtract the numerators and keep the denominator the same.

3rd Write the answer in simplest form.

e.g. $\frac{5}{6} - \frac{1}{3}$ ← L.C.D. = 6

$= \frac{5}{6} - \frac{2}{6}$

$= \frac{3}{6}$ ← Subtract the numerators; keep the denominator the same.

$= \frac{1}{2}$ ← in simplest form

Do the subtraction. Write the answers in simplest form.

18. $\frac{9}{10} - \frac{1}{2}$ ← L.C.D. = ____

$= \frac{9}{10} - \_\_\_\_$

$= \_\_\_\_$

19. $\frac{5}{6} - \frac{11}{15}$ ← L.C.D. = ____

$= \_\_\_\_ - \_\_\_\_$

$= \_\_\_\_$

20. $\frac{2}{3} - \frac{1}{6} =$ ____

21. $\frac{3}{10} - \frac{2}{15} =$ ____

22. $\frac{3}{4} - \frac{5}{12} =$ ____

23. $\frac{4}{5} - \frac{3}{10} =$ ____

24. $\frac{17}{20} - \frac{3}{5} =$ ____

25. $\frac{8}{15} - \frac{1}{3} =$ ____

Solve the problems. Write the answers in simplest form.

26. How much farther does Billy the Dog go than Ted in one minute?

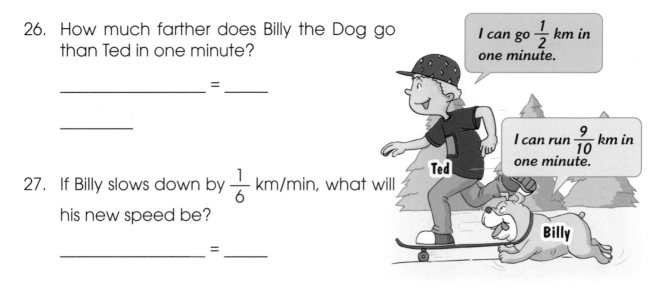

________ = ____

____

27. If Billy slows down by $\frac{1}{6}$ km/min, what will his new speed be?

________ = ____

____

Do the multiplication using addition. Write the answers in simplest form.

28. $3 \times \frac{5}{8} = \frac{5}{8} + \_\_\_\_ + \_\_\_\_$

$= \frac{\_\_}{8}$

$= \_\_\_\_$

29. $4 \times \frac{5}{6} = \frac{5}{6} + \_\_\_\_\_\_\_\_$

$= \frac{\_\_}{6}$

$= \_\_\_\_$

Do the multiplication. Write the answers in simplest form.

30. $6 \times \frac{4}{9} = \_\_\_\_$

31. $3 \times \frac{2}{7} = \_\_\_\_$

32. $8 \times \frac{3}{10} = \_\_\_\_$

33. $5 \times \frac{4}{15} = \_\_\_\_$

34. $\frac{3}{8} \times 6 = \_\_\_\_$

35. $\frac{5}{7} \times 4 = \_\_\_\_$

36. $\frac{7}{10} \times 5 = \_\_\_\_$

37. $3 \times \frac{7}{12} = \_\_\_\_$

Hint

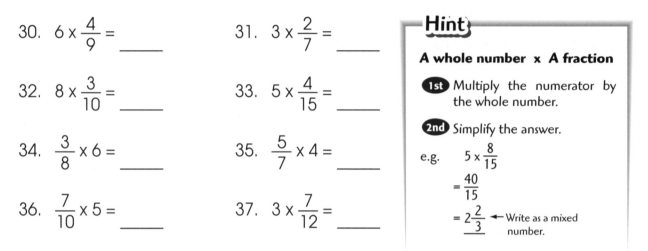

A whole number x A fraction

1st Multiply the numerator by the whole number.

2nd Simplify the answer.

e.g. $5 \times \frac{8}{15}$

$= \frac{40}{15}$

$= 2\frac{2}{3}$ ← Write as a mixed number.

38. Joe drinks $\frac{3}{5}$ L of milk every day. How much milk does Joe drink in a week?

________ = ____ ______

39. A basket of apples weighs $\frac{11}{12}$ kg. What is the total weight of 3 baskets of red apples and 5 baskets of green apples?

________ = ____ ______

40. *If it takes us $\frac{5}{6}$ h to make 3 models, how many hours will it take to make 24 models?*

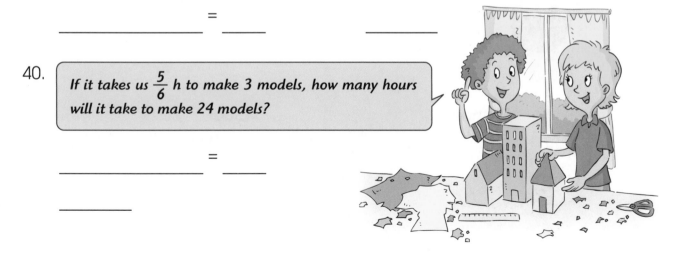

________ = ____

______

Decimals

- round decimals to thousandths
- estimate and find sums and differences
- follow the order of operations on decimals
- solve problems with decimals involving different operations

Round the decimal to the nearest ones, tenths, hundredths, and thousandths.

1. 2.8037
2. 11.5491
3. 4.0675
4. 25.8023

Estimate the sum and difference of each pair of decimals by rounding the decimals to the nearest ones. Then find the actual sums and differences.

5. 17.62 8.193

Estimate		Actual	
sum	difference	sum	difference
+			

6. 9.087 24.3

Estimate		Actual	
sum	difference	sum	difference

Estimate the product. Then put a decimal point in the correct place of the given product with the help of the estimated answer.

7. 2.6 x 5 = 130

   Estimate: 3 x ______ = ______

8. 4.38 x 2 = 876

   Estimate: ____________

9. 5.4 x 0.6 = 324

   Estimate: ____________

10. 7.9 x 2.3 = 1817

    Estimate: ____________

Do the multiplication.

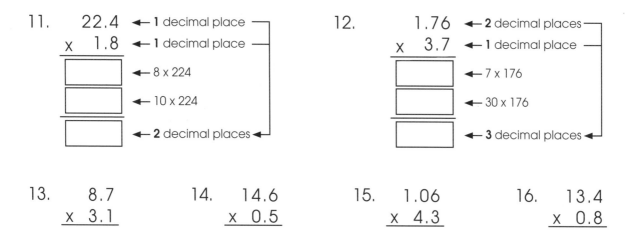

11.
   22.4 ← **1** decimal place
   x 1.8 ← **1** decimal place
   [ ] ← 8 x 224
   [ ] ← 10 x 224
   [ ] ← **2** decimal places

12.
   1.76 ← **2** decimal places
   x 3.7 ← **1** decimal place
   [ ] ← 7 x 176
   [ ] ← 30 x 176
   [ ] ← **3** decimal places

13. 8.7 x 3.1

14. 14.6 x 0.5

15. 1.06 x 4.3

16. 13.4 x 0.8

Solve the problems.

17. Distance travelled

   a. in 1.6 h: ____________ = ______

   b. in 2.3 h: ____________ = ______

   c. in 3.5 h: ____________ = ______

   d. in 4.7 h: ____________ = ______

Our average speed is 82.46 km/h.

Decimals ÷ Decimals

1st Change the divisor into a whole number by moving the decimal point to the right end, and move the decimal point of the dividend the same number of places.

2nd Divide as "Decimals ÷ Whole numbers".

1.3 $\overline{)8.32}$ → Rewrite. → 13 $\overline{)83.2}$

Move 1 decimal place to the right.

```
    6.4
13 )83.2
    78
     52
     52
```

8.32 ÷ 1.3 = 6.4

Estimate. Then do the division.

18. 41.76 ÷ 5.8 = ______

Estimate: 42 ÷ ______ = ______

5.8 $\overline{)41.76}$ → $\overline{)\quad}$

19. 32.24 ÷ 2.08 = ______

Estimate: ______

2.08 $\overline{)32.24}$ → $\overline{)\quad}$

20. 12 ÷ 6.25 = ______

Estimate: ______

6.25 $\overline{)12}$ → $\overline{)\quad}$

21. 21.6 ÷ 1.5 = ______

Estimate: ______

1.5 $\overline{)21.6}$ → $\overline{)\quad}$

Do the division.

22. 39.52 ÷ 1.6 = ______

23. 15.036 ÷ 2.8 = ______

24. 9.66 ÷ 2.3 = ______

25. 19.18 ÷ 3.5 = ______

26. 15.6 ÷ 2.4 = ______

27. 35.524 ÷ 4.15 = ______

Find the answers.

28. (1.6 + 2.3) x 4

29. 7.5 – 5 ÷ 2.5 x 1.25

30. 4.6 x 1.3 – 1.05 ÷ 0.5

31. 8.4 + 2.73 ÷ 1.3 = ______

32. 11.85 ÷ (3.21 + 6.27) x 5 = ______

33. 3.5 x 4.2 – 5.42 = ______

34. 10.32 ÷ 3.44 + 1.3 x 3.6 = ______

35. 29.61 ÷ (1.73 + 2.97) = ______

36. (8.96 + 1.8) x (10.54 – 6.09) = ______

Check the correct number sentence that describes each situation. Then solve it. Show your work.

37. Mrs. Kay bought 4 bags of 2.83-kg flour and used 3.07 kg of it to make bread. Then she put the rest of the flour equally into 5 jars. How much flour is there in each jar?

(A) (2.83 x 4 – 3.07) ÷ 5

(B) (3.07 – 2.83) x 4 ÷ 5

There are ______ kg of flour in each jar.

38. Tommy the Mouse ran at a speed of 30.6 km/h in the first 0.35 h and 25.2 km/h in the next 0.25 h. What was his average speed?

(A) (30.6 + 25.2) ÷ (0.35 + 0.25)

(B) (30.6 x 0.35 + 25.2 x 0.25) ÷ (0.35 + 0.25)

____

8

Fractions, Decimals, and Percents

- describe parts of a whole using fractions, decimals, and percents
- shade diagrams to match the given percents
- do conversions between fractions, decimals, and percents
- solve word problems involving conversions

= 75% = 0.75 = 75/100
75%
7
0.75
75/100
Actually, all three of us got the same score on the test. But why does he think that his is higher than ours?

Write the fraction, decimal, and percent for each coloured part.

1. 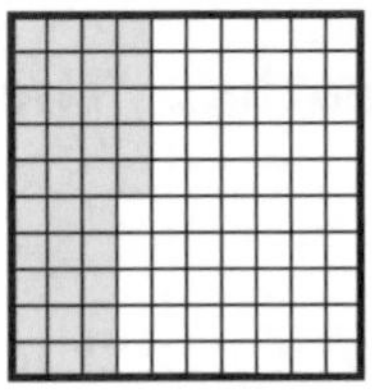

____ ____ ____

2. 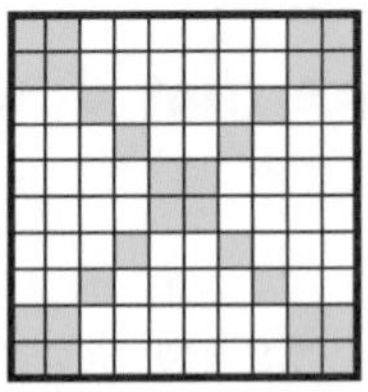

____ ____ ____

3. 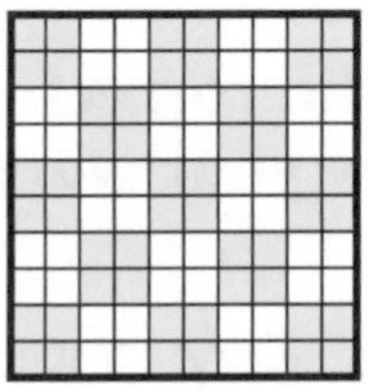

____ ____ ____

4. 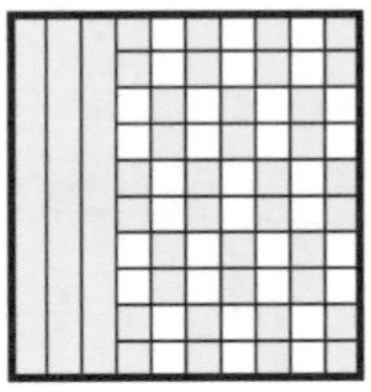

____ ____ ____

5. 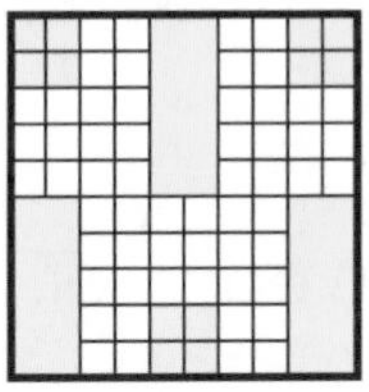

____ ____ ____

6. 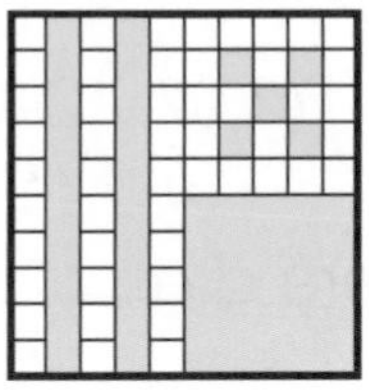

____ ____ ____

Colour the diagram to match each percent.

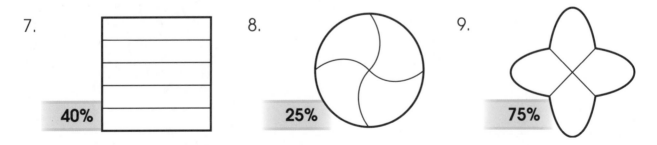

7. 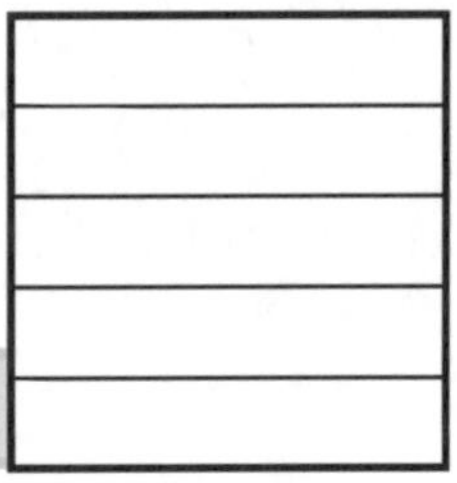

40%

8. 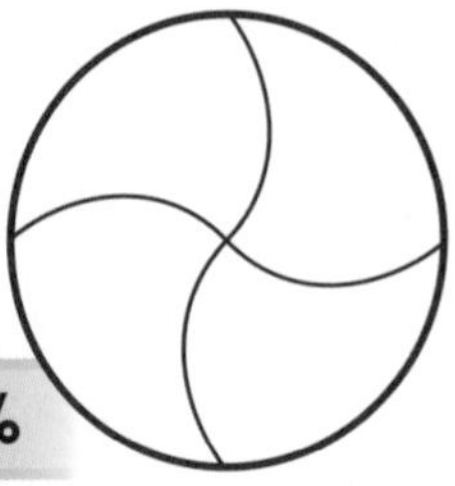

25%

9. 

75%

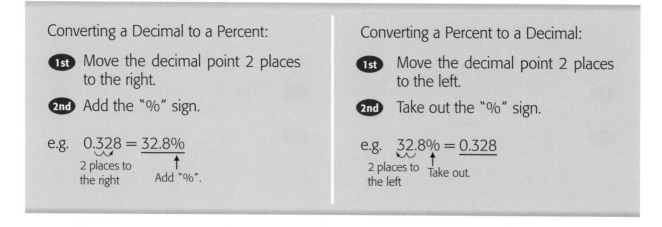

Converting a Decimal to a Percent:

1st Move the decimal point 2 places to the right.

2nd Add the "%" sign.

e.g. 0.328 = 32.8%
2 places to the right — Add "%".

Converting a Percent to a Decimal:

1st Move the decimal point 2 places to the left.

2nd Take out the "%" sign.

e.g. 32.8% = 0.328
2 places to the left — Take out.

Do the conversions.

10. **Decimal ⟶ Percent**

a. 0.48 = ____________

b. 0.8 = ____________

c. 2.15 = ____________

d. 0.279 = ____________

e. 0.082 = ____________

f. 1.05 = ____________

11. **Percent ⟶ Decimal**

a. 52% = ____________

b. 15.4% = ____________

c. 200% = ____________

d. 0.5% = ____________

e. 8.9% = ____________

f. 7% = ____________

Write a decimal and a percent to match the coloured part of each diagram, or colour the diagram to match the given decimal or percent.

12.
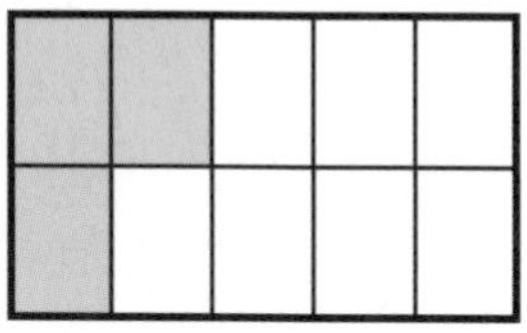

_____ _____

13.
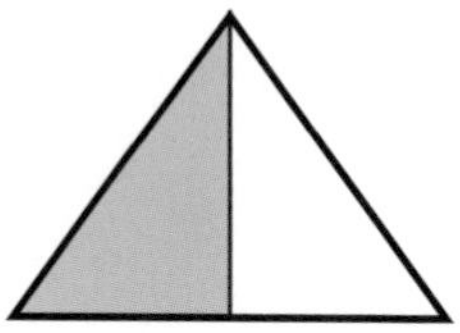

_____ _____

14.
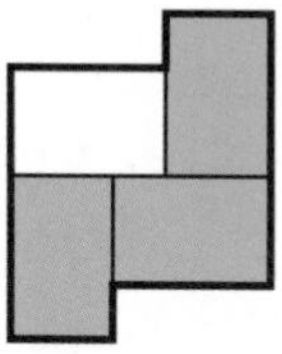

_____ _____

15.

0.9

_____

16.
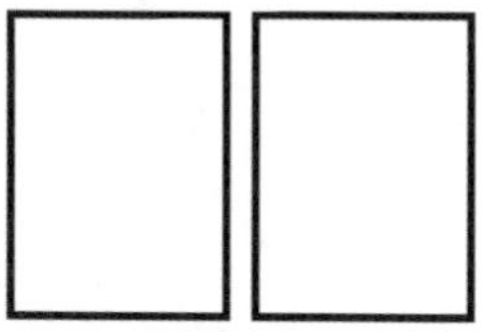

_____

120%

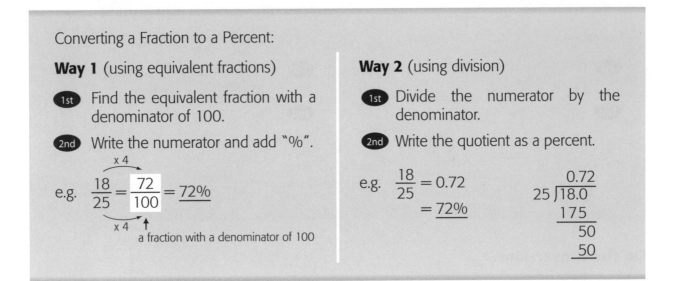

Converting a Fraction to a Percent:

Way 1 (using equivalent fractions)

1st Find the equivalent fraction with a denominator of 100.

2nd Write the numerator and add "%".

e.g. $\frac{18}{25} = \frac{72}{100} = \underline{72\%}$ (× 4 numerator and denominator; $\frac{72}{100}$: a fraction with a denominator of 100)

Way 2 (using division)

1st Divide the numerator by the denominator.

2nd Write the quotient as a percent.

e.g. $\frac{18}{25} = 0.72$

$= \underline{72\%}$

$$\begin{array}{r} 0.72 \\ 25\overline{)18.0} \\ \underline{175} \\ 50 \\ \underline{50} \end{array}$$

Find the equivalent fraction with a denominator of 100 for each fraction. Then write it as a percent.

17. $\frac{3}{10} = \frac{}{100} = \_\_\_\_\%$

18. $\frac{9}{50} = \_\_\_\_ = \_\_\_\_$

19. $\frac{16}{25} = \_\_\_\_ = \_\_\_\_$

20. $\frac{3}{4} = \_\_\_\_ = \_\_\_\_$

21. $\frac{19}{20} = \_\_\_\_ = \_\_\_\_$

22. $\frac{3}{5} = \_\_\_\_ = \_\_\_\_$

Write each fraction as a percent using division.

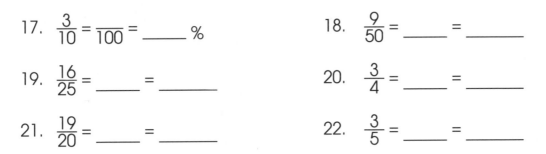

23. $\frac{8}{50}$ $50\overline{)8}$

$= \_\_\_\_$

$= \_\_\_\_\%$

24. $\frac{9}{25}$

$=$

25. $\frac{17}{20}$

$=$

Write each percent as a fraction in simplest form.

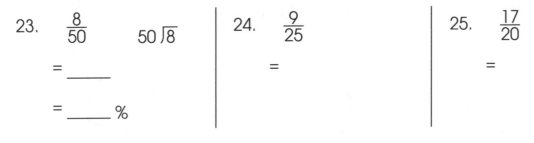

26. 24% = ____

27. 52% = ____

28. 78% = ____

29. 83% = ____

30. 36% = ____

31. 62% = ____

Hint

Percent ⟶ Fraction

e.g. 35%

$= \frac{35}{100}$ ← Drop the "%". Write as a fraction with a denominator of 100.

$= \frac{7}{20}$ ← Simplify.

Write a fraction, a decimal, and a percent to match the coloured part in each shape.

32.

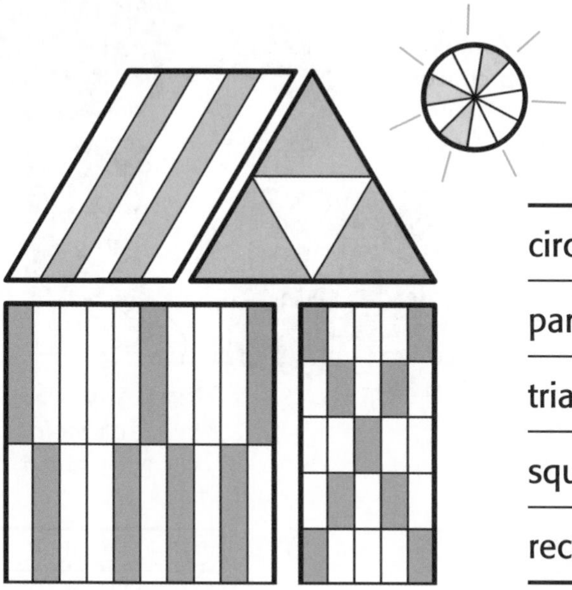

	Fraction	Decimal	Percent
circle			
parallelogram			
triangle			
square			
rectangle			

Solve the problems. Show your work. You may draw diagrams to illustrate your answers.

33. Jason has $\frac{4}{5}$ cup of raisins, George has 0.7 cup, and 75% of Tim's cup is filled with raisins. Who has the most raisins?

__________ has the most.

34. 25% of the buttons in a box are black, 0.1 are green, and the rest are red. What fraction of the buttons in the box are red?

____

35. *Look at my record. Which one is my best subject?*

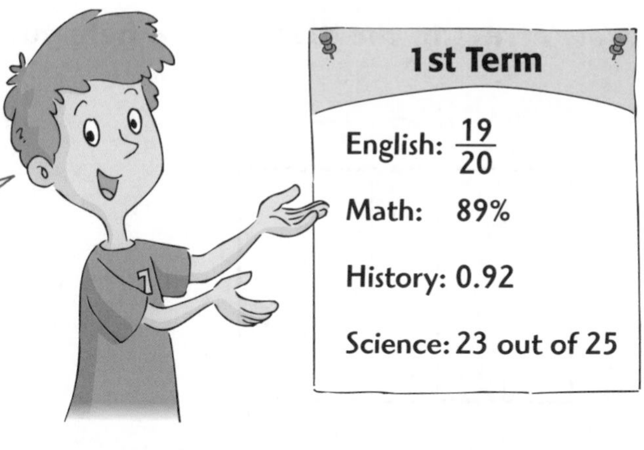

____

Percents

- find the percent of an amount
- find the whole with the given amount of a percent
- solve problems related to finding amount and the amount of one whole

Don't cry, Erica. There are 5 columns of chocolates in this box. I'll give you 40%.
40% of 20
= 40% x 20
= 0.4 x 20
= 8
Each column contains 20% of a box of chocolates; 2 columns contain 40%, which means 8 chocolates.
Thank you. So, I'll have 8 chocolates.

Colour the diagram. Then find the amount.

1. 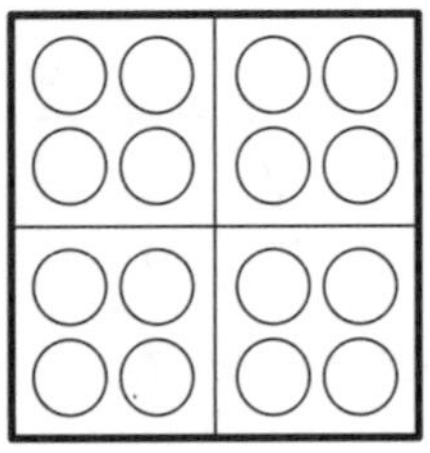

25% of 16 = ______

2. 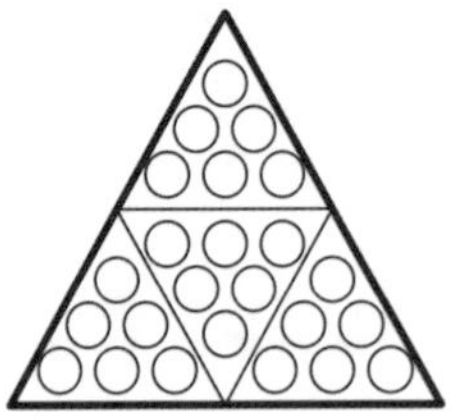

75% of 24 = ______

3. 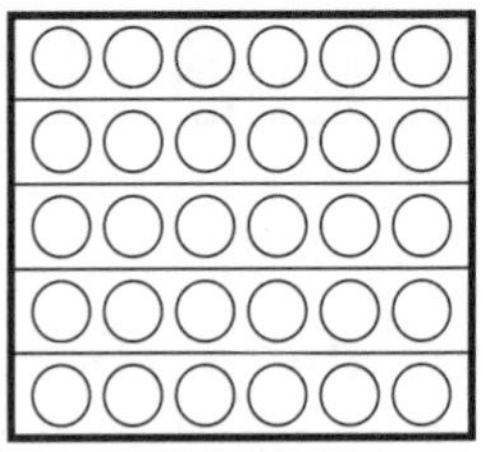

60% of 30 = ______

4. 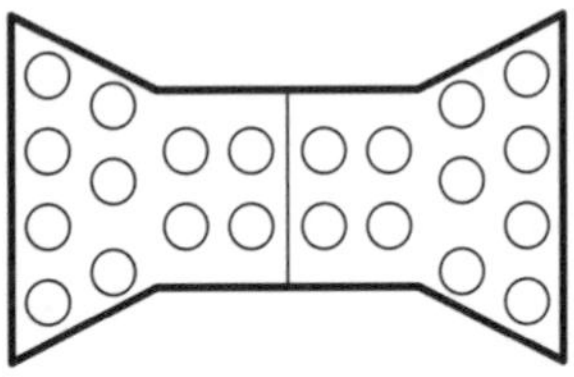

50% of 22 = ______

5. 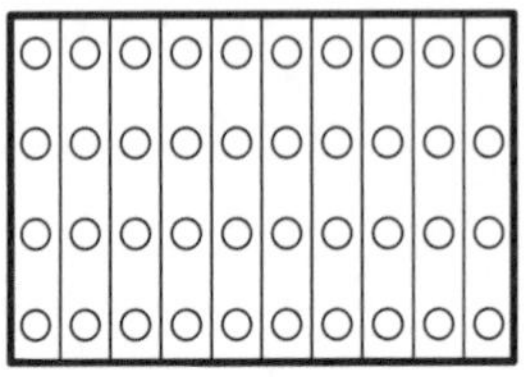

80% of 40 = ______

6. 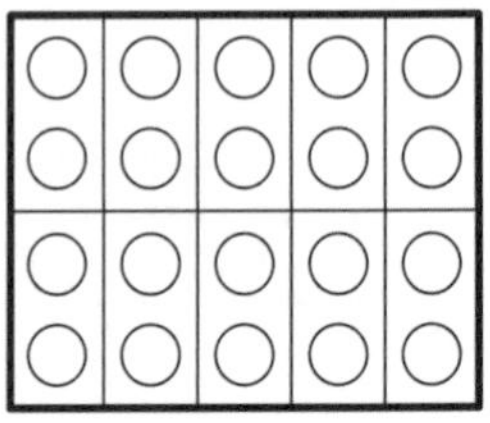

70% of 20 = ______

Draw arrays in the diagrams to help you find the amounts.

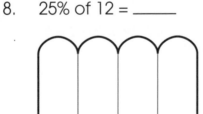

7. 40% of 25 = ______

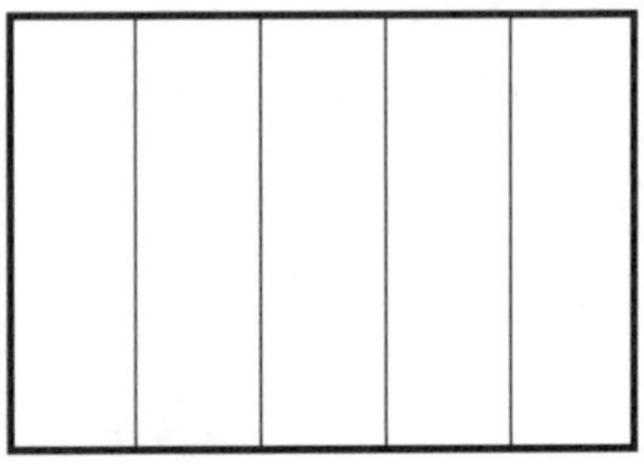

8. 25% of 12 = ______

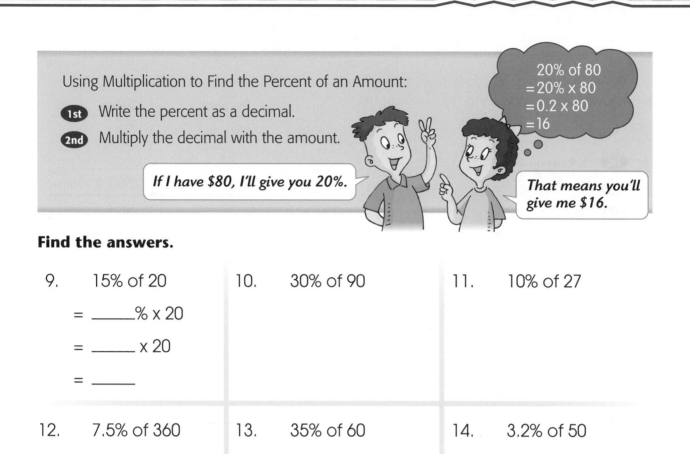

Using Multiplication to Find the Percent of an Amount:

1st Write the percent as a decimal.

2nd Multiply the decimal with the amount.

If I have $80, I'll give you 20%.
20% of 80
= 20% x 80
= 0.2 x 80
= 16
That means you'll give me $16.

Find the answers.

9. 15% of 20
   = _____% x 20
   = _____ x 20
   = _____

10. 30% of 90

11. 10% of 27

12. 7.5% of 360

13. 35% of 60

14. 3.2% of 50

Read what Erica says. Find how many children like each colour. Then answer the questions.

I've surveyed 80 children. 20% of the children like yellow, 25% like green, 30% like blue, 10% like red, and the rest of the children like orange.

15.

Colour	No. of Children
Yellow	20% x =

16. If 70% of the children who like green are boys, how many boys like green?

_____

When the percent and the value of the percent are known, use proportion to find the number.

Steps:

1st Set up a proportion.

2nd Find the value of 1% using division.

3rd Find the value of 100% using multiplication.

e.g. 5% of a number is 10.

Percent	Value
5%	10
1% ($\frac{5\%}{5}$)	2 ($\frac{10}{5}$)
100% (1% x 100)	200 (2 x 100)

So, the number is 200.

Find the numbers.

17. 3% of a number is 18.

3% → ____

1% → ____

100% → ____

So, the number is ____ .

18. 12% of a number is 24.

12% → ____

1% → ____

100% → ____

So, the number is ____ .

19. 4% of a number is 5, so the number is ____ .

20. 30% of a number is 21, so the number is ____ .

21. 15% of a number is 9.6, so the number is ____ .

Solve the problems.

22. 28% of the jar is filled with water. What is the capacity of the jar?

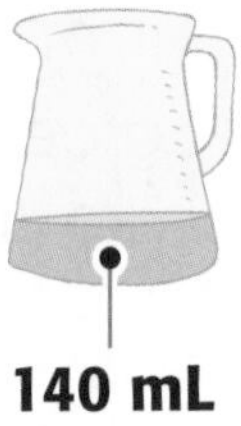

____

23. Jane uses 25% of her savings to buy a doll for her sister. What were Jane's savings?

____

Solve the problems.

24. Find the number of marbles that each child has.

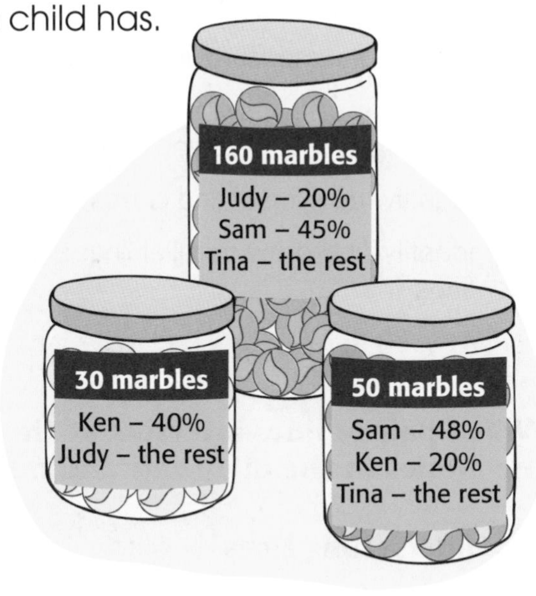

 Judy

____

 Ken

____

 Sam

____

 Tina

____

25. If Sam gives 25% of his marbles to his sister Pamela, how many marbles will Pamela get from Sam?

____

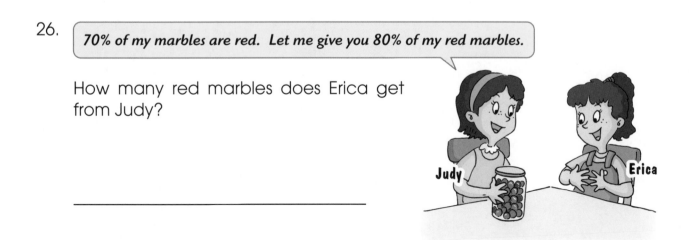

26. *70% of my marbles are red. Let me give you 80% of my red marbles.*

How many red marbles does Erica get from Judy?

____

10

Angles

- identify and measure angles formed by intersecting lines
- draw lines with the given measures of angles
- identify transversal and corresponding angles
- identify and draw parallel lines and perpendicular lines

Which pair of lines intersect at the given angles? Mark the angles in the diagrams and name the lines.

1. **Intersecting Lines**

   a. 80°: ____________

   b. 105°: ____________

   c. 35°: ____________

   d. 55°: ____________

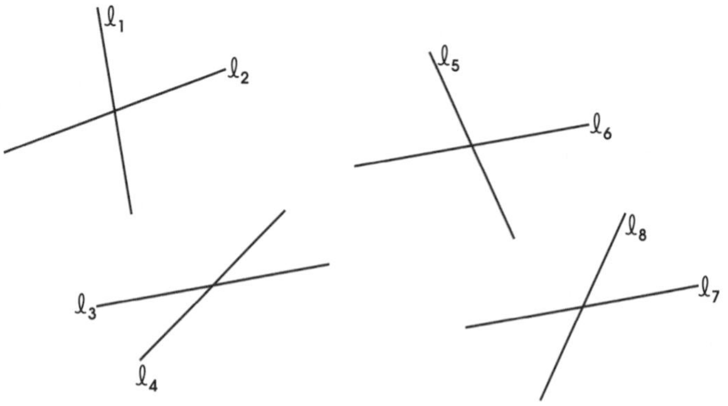

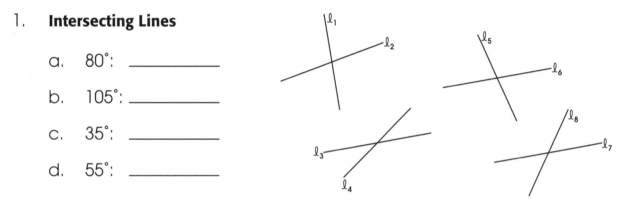

Draw lines that intersect at the given angles. Then mark the angles.

2. 65°

3. 110°

4. 97°

5. 83°

Transversal:
a line intersecting 2 or more lines

Parallel lines:
2 or more lines that never intersect

Corresponding angles:
angles in the matching corners that are formed when a transversal crosses 2 lines

e.g.

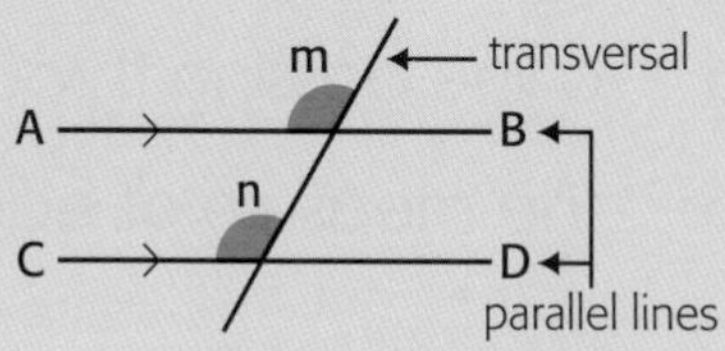

m and n are corresponding angles.
Since AB//CD, so ∠m = ∠n.

If a transversal crosses two lines that are parallel, then the measures of the corresponding angles are the same.

Name the transversal and find the corresponding angles for each set of lines.

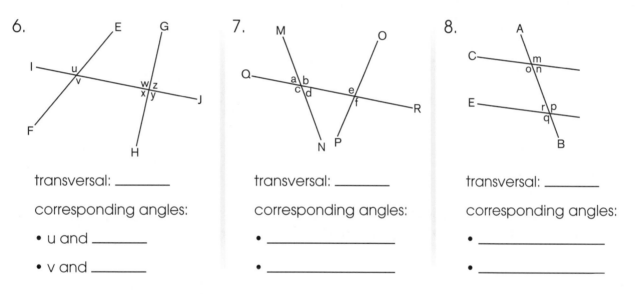

6.

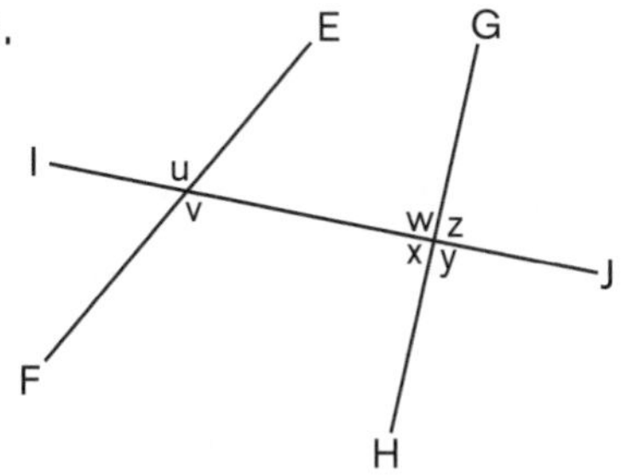

transversal: ______

corresponding angles:

- u and ______
- v and ______

7.

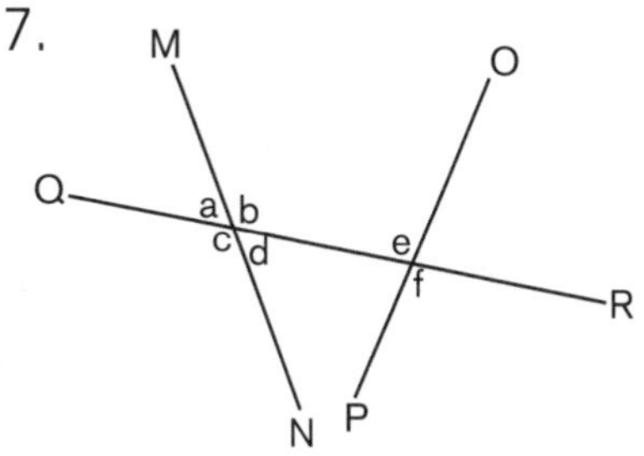

transversal: ______

corresponding angles:

- ______
- ______

8.

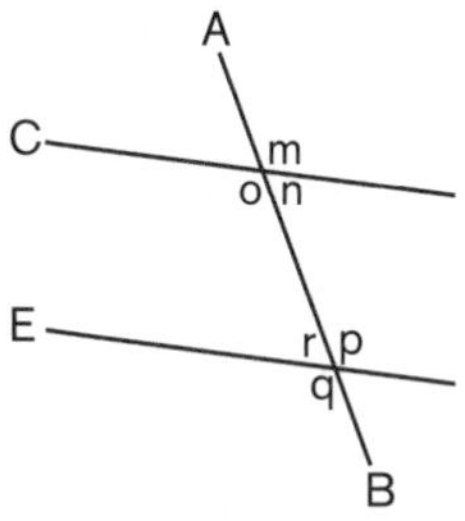

transversal: ______

corresponding angles:

- ______
- ______

Measure and record the marked angles. Then find the parallel lines.

9.

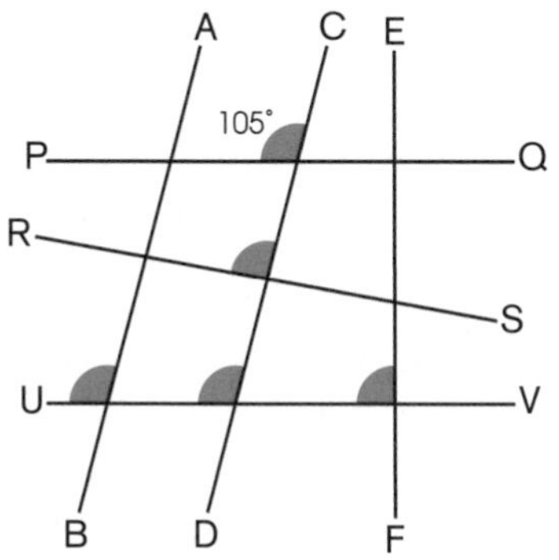

- ______ // ______
- ______ // ______

10.

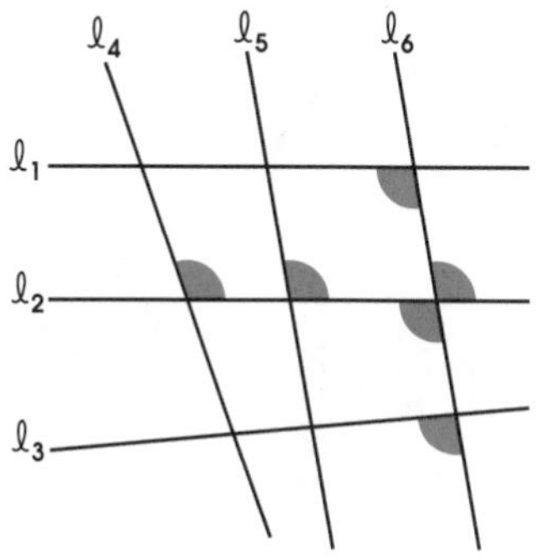

- ______
- ______

Draw lines as described. Then find and label one pair of corresponding angles.

11. a. a line passing through A and parallel to IJ

    b. the measure of each corresponding angle:

    ____

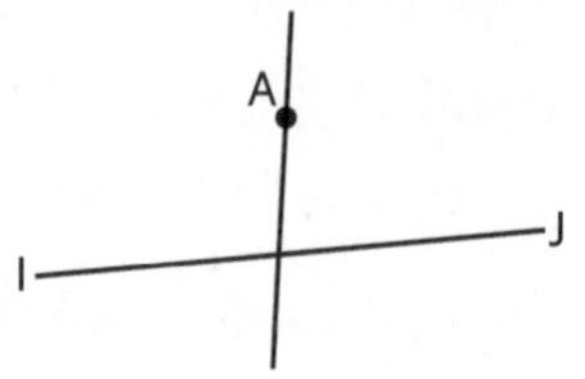

12. a. a line passing through points A and B

    b. the measure of each corresponding angle:

    ____

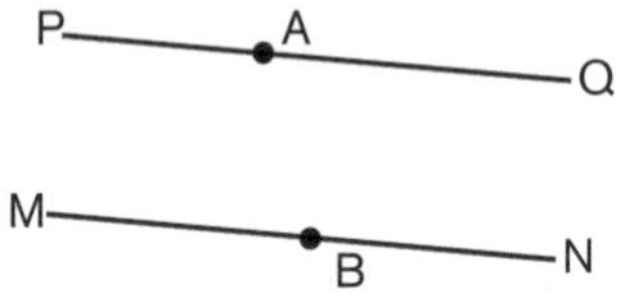

13. a. a line parallel to AB and intersecting XY

    b. the measure of each corresponding angle:

    ____

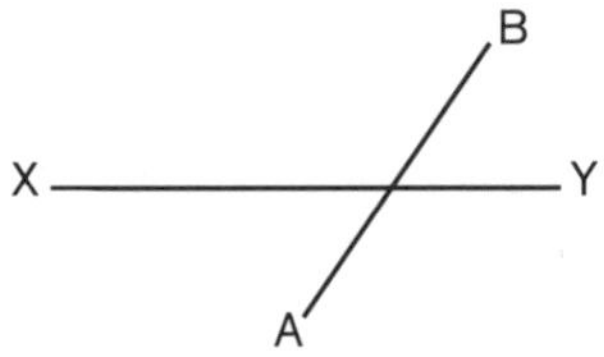

Fill in the blanks to complete what Jimmy says. Look at each highlighted angle. Then put a check mark in the circle if the lines are perpendicular.

14.

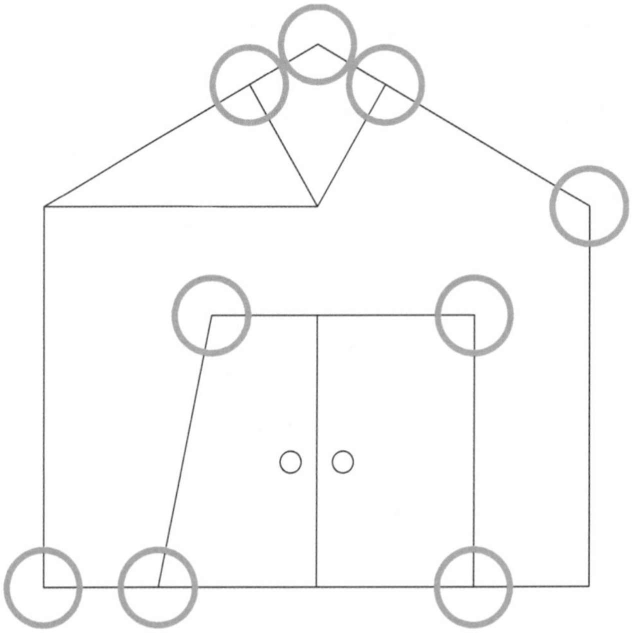

Steps to draw a perpendicular bisector to bisect a line segment with a compass and a ruler:

1st Draw a line AB.

2nd Take A and B as centres and a compass with radius longer than half the length of AB. Draw two arcs intersecting at the points C and D.

3rd Join C and D.

Bisect means "to cut in half". CD is perpendicular to and bisects AB.

Draw a perpendicular bisector to each given line with a compass and a ruler.

15.

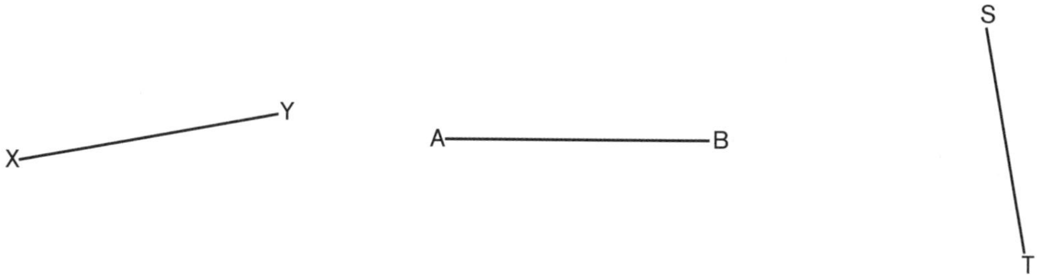

Draw the perpendicular bisector. Then find the measure of the angles and fill in the blanks.

16. Draw a perpendicular bisector to AB.

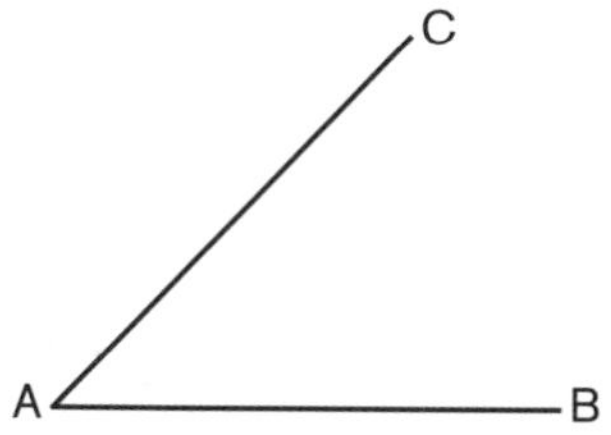

The measures of the adjacent angles formed by AC and the bisector are ______ and ______ .

17. *Draw a perpendicular bisector to MN. Mark a point K on the bisector. Then draw two lines from K to M and N.*

The measures of the angles of the triangle NKM are ____________ .

It is a/an ____________ triangle.

Angles and Lines in Shapes

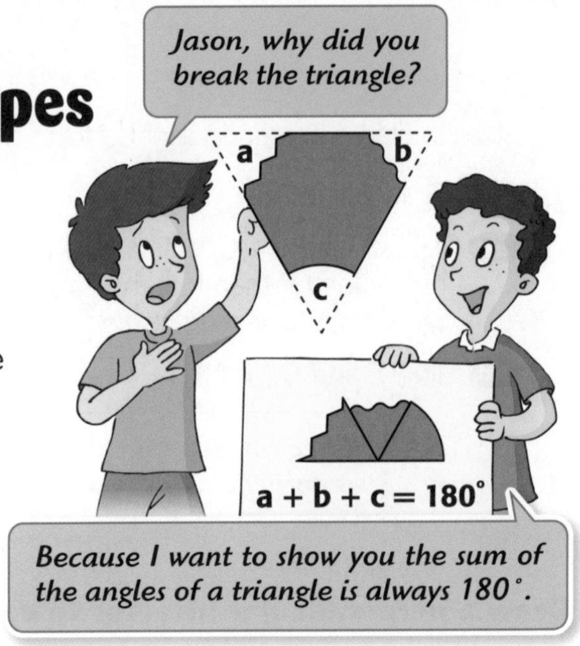

- identify properties of quadrilaterals
- identify and mark equal angles and sides
- identify convex and concave figures
- find the size of an angle using the sum of the angles in a triangle
- draw angle bisectors

Read each sentence. Write "T" for true and "F" for false.

1. A quadrilateral with 4 angles is a rectangle. _____
2. All triangles are symmetrical. _____
3. All the angles of a rectangle must be equal. _____
4. A parallelogram always has two pairs of parallel sides. _____
5. A trapezoid has no obtuse angles. _____

Measure and mark the equal angles and sides in each figure if there are any. Then colour the regular polygons.

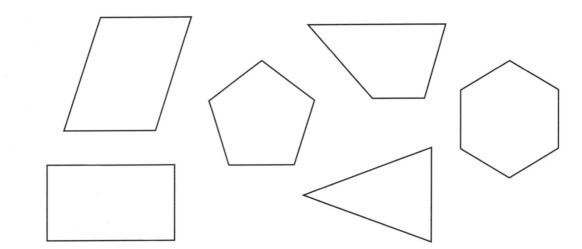

6.

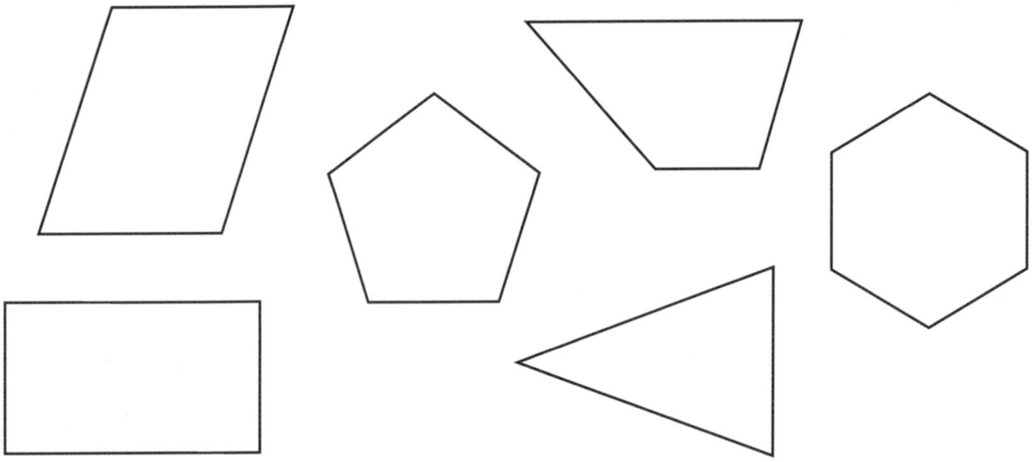

We can name a triangle in two ways.

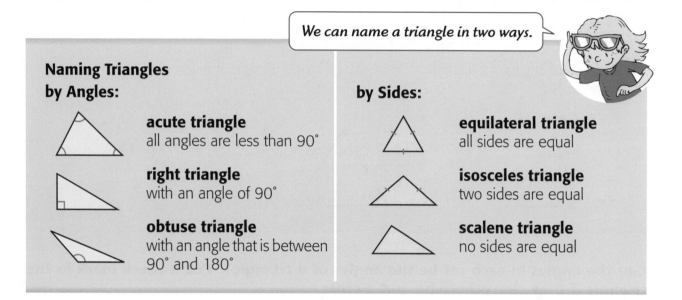

Naming Triangles

by Angles:

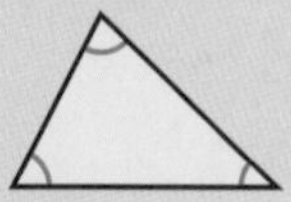

acute triangle
all angles are less than 90°

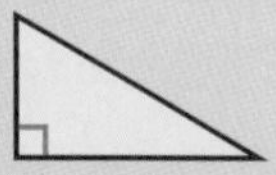

right triangle
with an angle of 90°

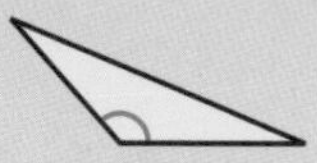

obtuse triangle
with an angle that is between 90° and 180°

by Sides:

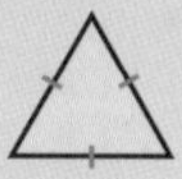

equilateral triangle
all sides are equal

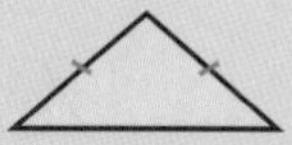

isosceles triangle
two sides are equal

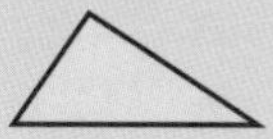

scalene triangle
no sides are equal

Mark the equal sides and angles in each triangle. Then name each triangle in two ways.

7.

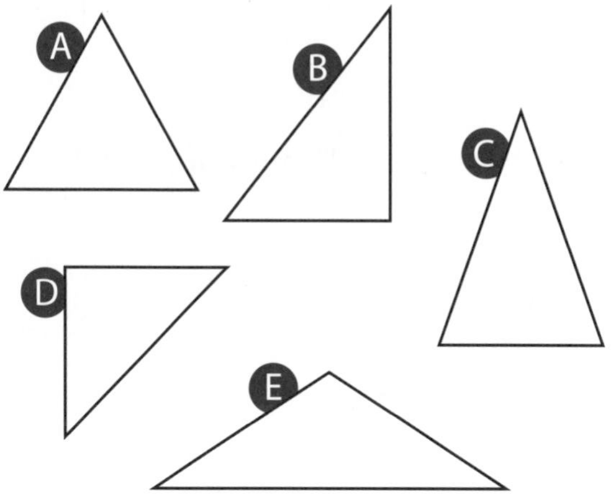

Name

A ____________________

B ____________________

C ____________________

D ____________________

E ____________________

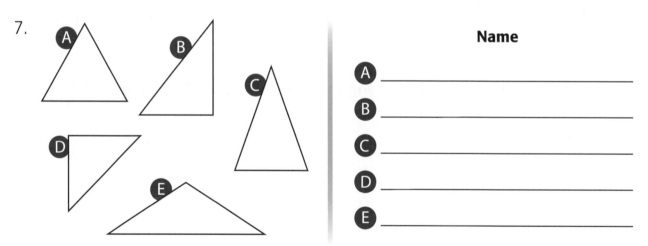

Colour the convex shapes yellow and the concave shapes red.

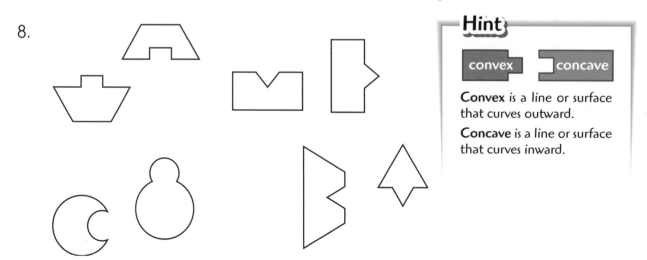

8.

Hint

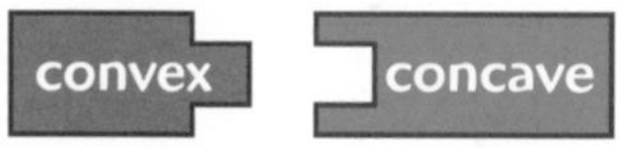

Convex is a line or surface that curves outward.

Concave is a line or surface that curves inward.

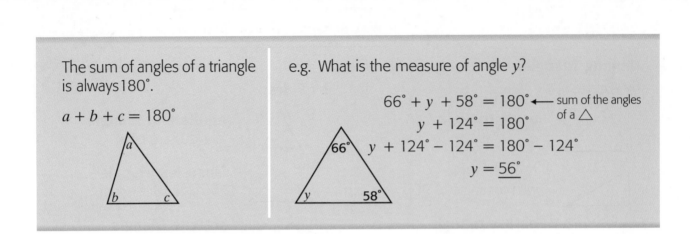

The sum of angles of a triangle is always 180°.

$a + b + c = 180°$

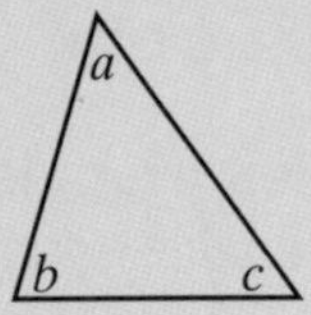

e.g. What is the measure of angle y?

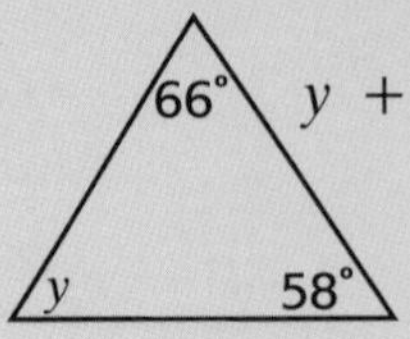

$$66° + y + 58° = 180° \leftarrow \text{sum of the angles of a } \triangle$$
$$y + 124° = 180°$$
$$y + 124° - 124° = 180° - 124°$$
$$y = \underline{56°}$$

Can the angles in each set be the angles of a triangle? Put a check mark in the triangle if they can; otherwise, put a cross.

9. 60°, 36°, 94° △
10. 47°, 82°, 52° △
11. 36°, 98°, 46° △
12. 15°, 15°, 150° △
13. 85°, 80°, 20° △
14. 64°, 52°, 64° △

Find the measures of the marked angles in the triangles. Show your work.

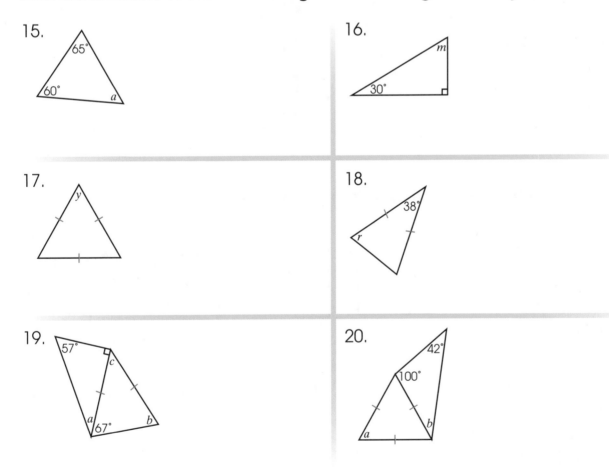

15.

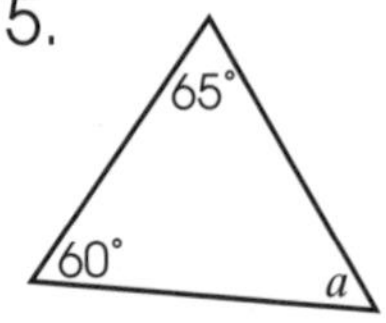

16.

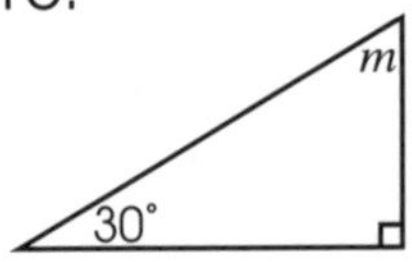

17.

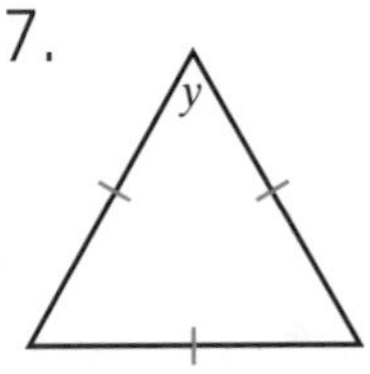

18.

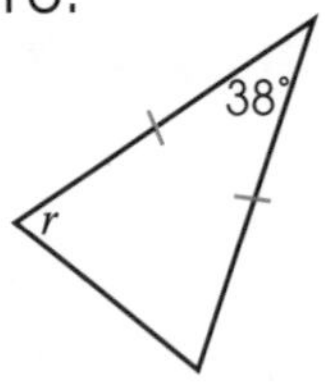

19.

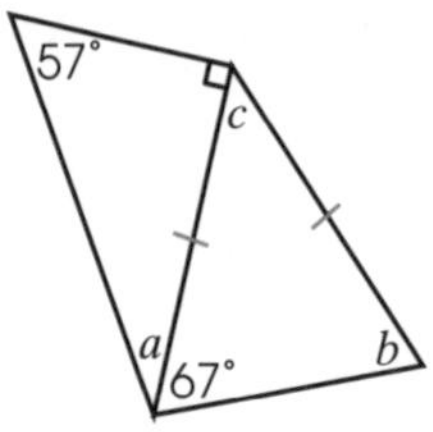

20.

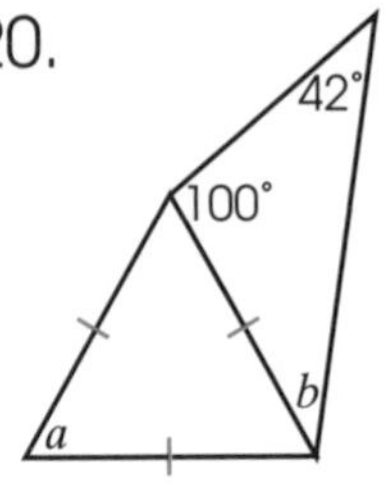

Steps to draw an angle bisector with a compass and a ruler:

1st Take A as centre and draw an arc that intersects the arms of the angle at B and C.

2nd Take B and C as centres and draw 2 arcs that intersect at D.

3rd Join A and D. Line AD is the angle bisector of ∠A.

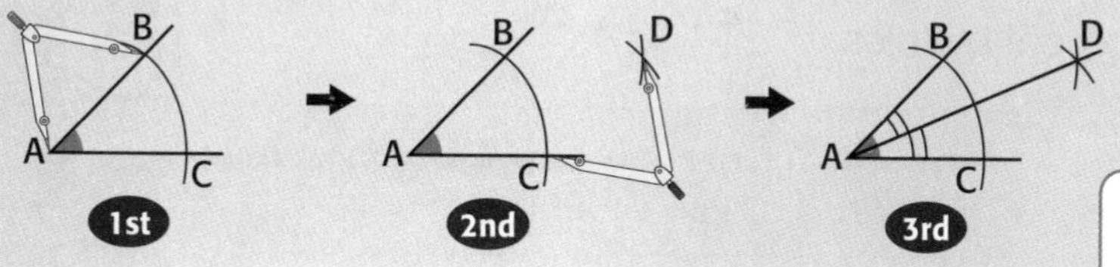

Draw the angle bisector for each marked angle.

21.

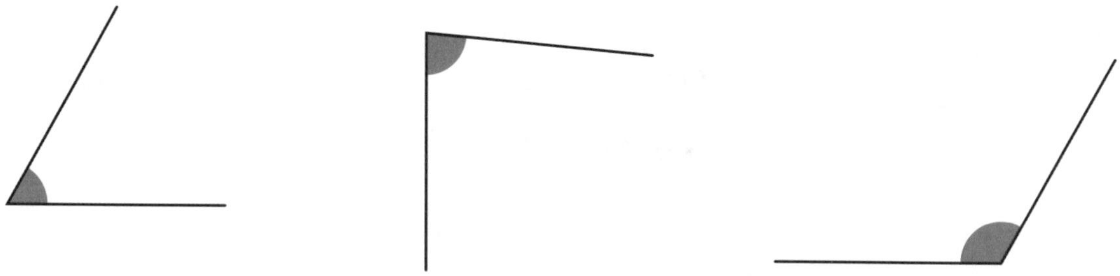

Look at Justin's straws. Draw the triangle that can be built with Justin's straws and name it in two ways. Then bisect one of the angles in the triangle and answer Justin's question.

22.

Name: ______________________

23. *If the long straws make an angle of 40°, what are the measures of the other two angles?*

____

Congruent and Similar Figures

- name equal sides and angles
- identify and name congruent triangles
- show how triangles are congruent by rules
- identify similar figures

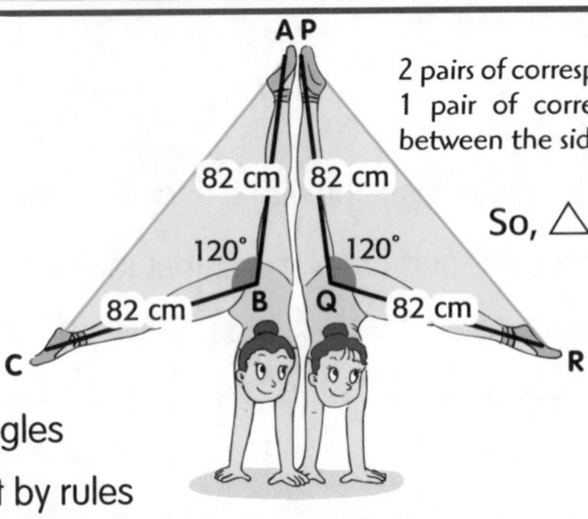

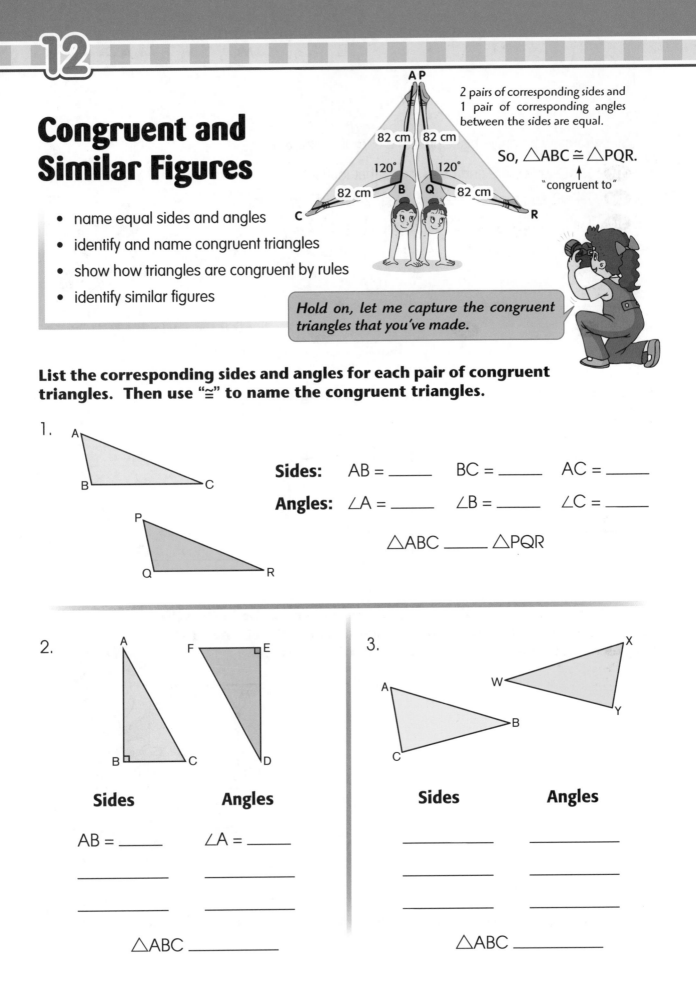

2 pairs of corresponding sides and 1 pair of corresponding angles between the sides are equal.

So, △ABC ≅ △PQR.
"congruent to"

List the corresponding sides and angles for each pair of congruent triangles. Then use "≅" to name the congruent triangles.

1.

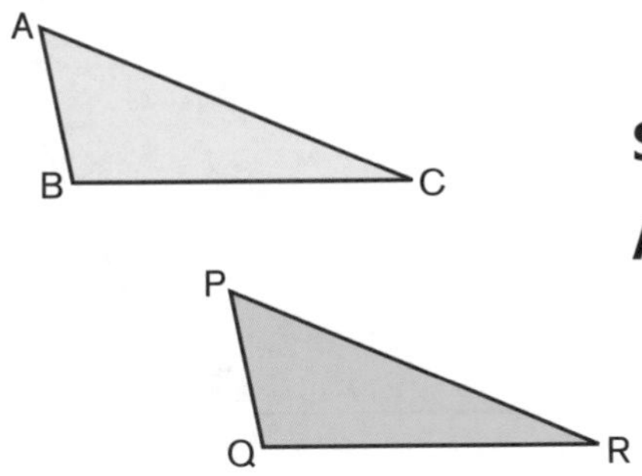

Sides: AB = ______ BC = ______ AC = ______

Angles: ∠A = ______ ∠B = ______ ∠C = ______

△ABC ______ △PQR

2.

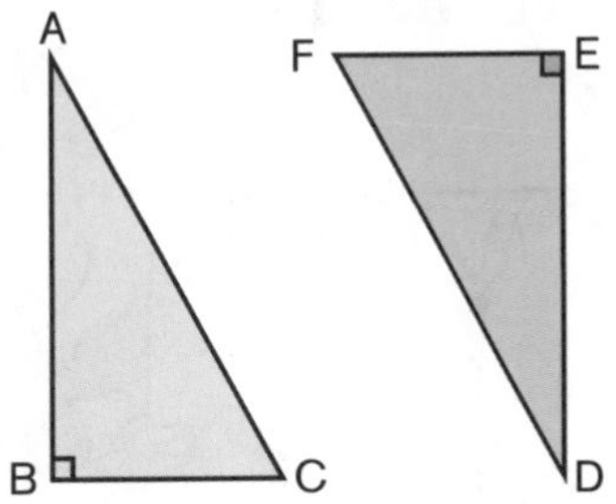

Sides	**Angles**
AB = ______	∠A = ______
______	______
______	______

△ABC ______

3.

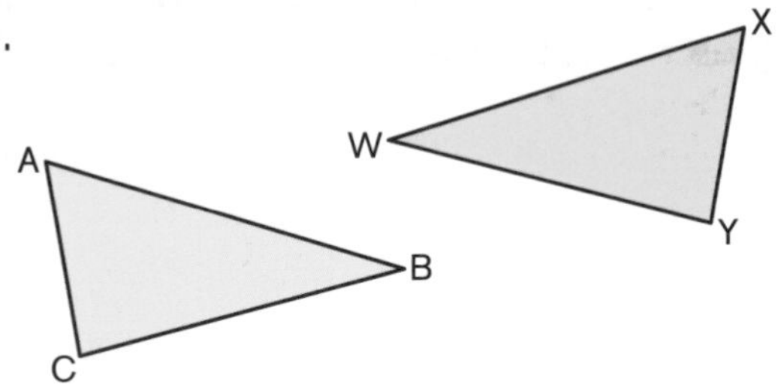

Sides	**Angles**
______	______
______	______
______	______

△ABC ______

Rules to prove that two triangles are **congruent**:

side-side-side

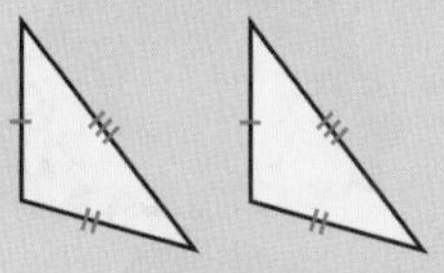

3 pairs of corresponding sides are equal

side-angle-side

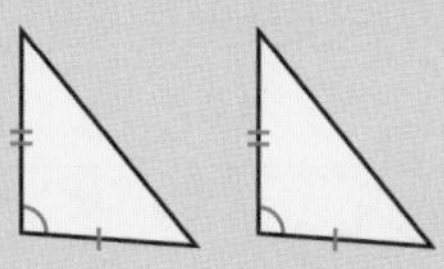

2 pairs of corresponding sides and 1 pair of angles between the sides are equal

angle-side-angle

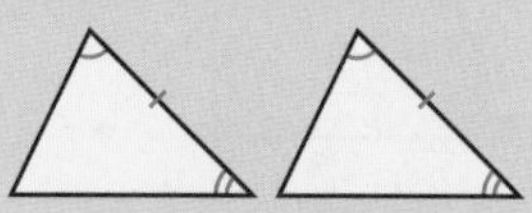

2 pairs of corresponding angles and 1 pair of sides between the angles are equal

angle-angle-side

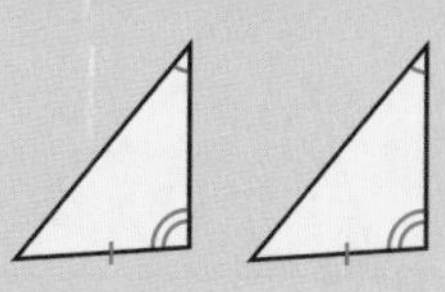

2 pairs of corresponding angles and 1 pair of corresponding sides are equal

Look at the markings on each pair of congruent triangles. Then write which rule can be used to prove that they are congruent.

4.

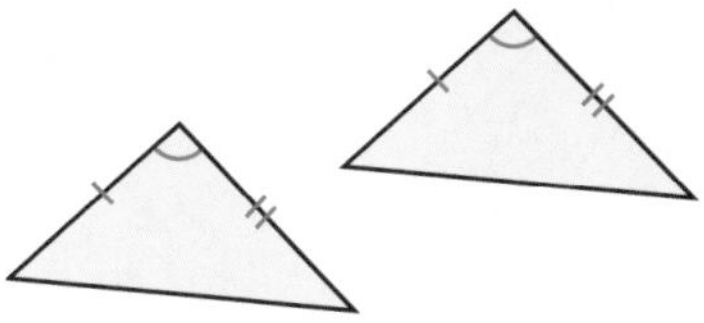

____

5.

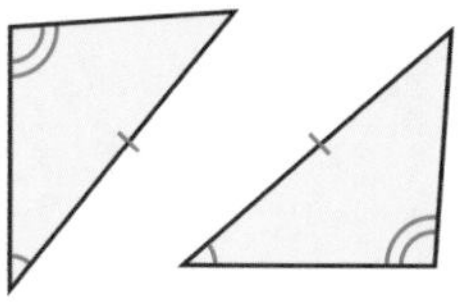

____

6.

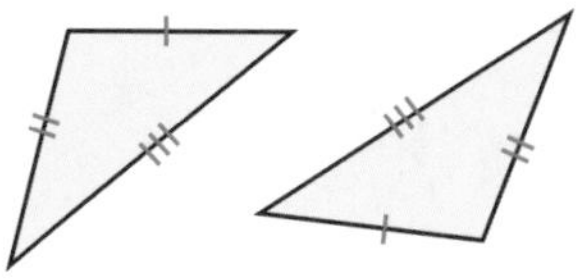

____

7.

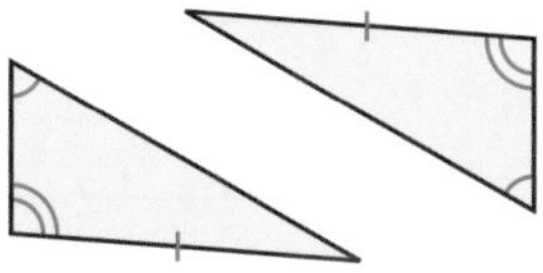

____

8.

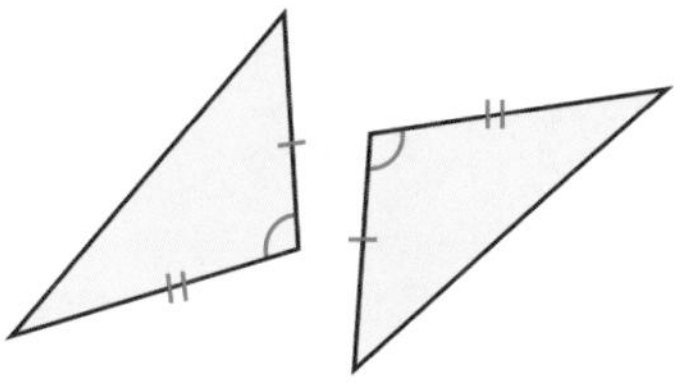

____

9.

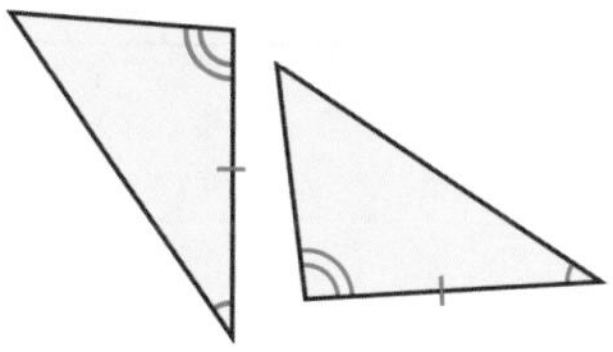

____

For each pair of congruent triangles, label the measurements on the coloured triangle the same as the other one. Then write the rule that proves they are congruent.

10.

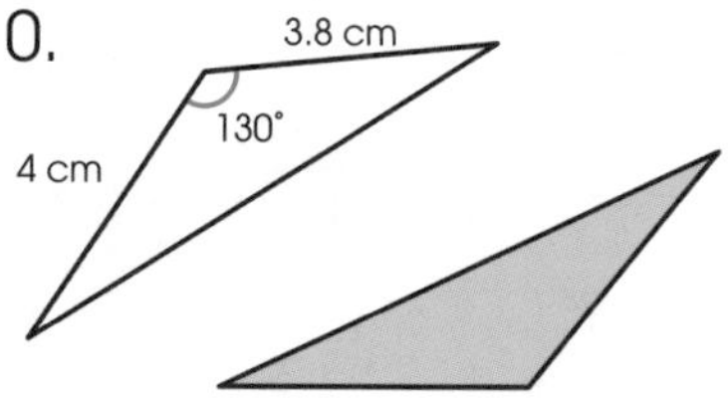

____

11.

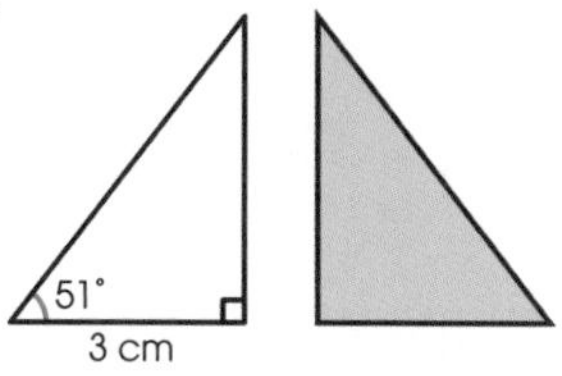

____

12.

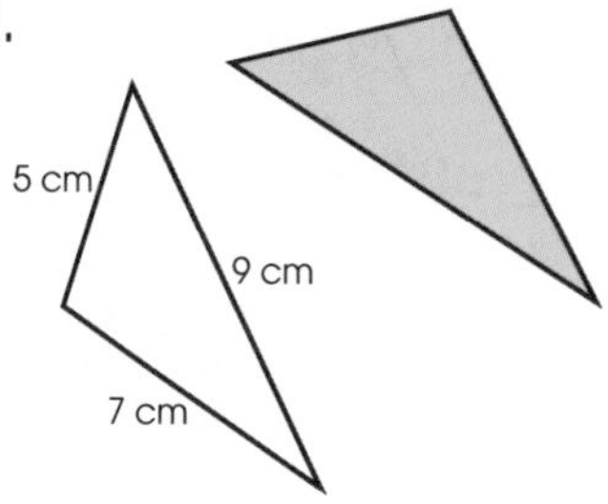

____

Complete each list to show how the two triangles are congruent.

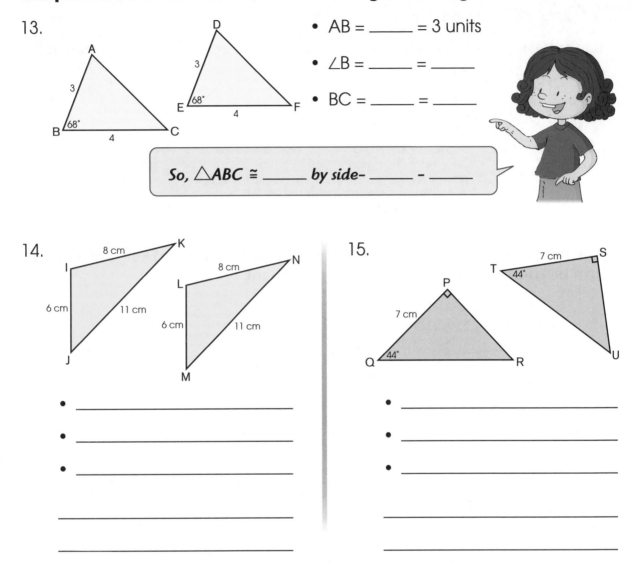

13.

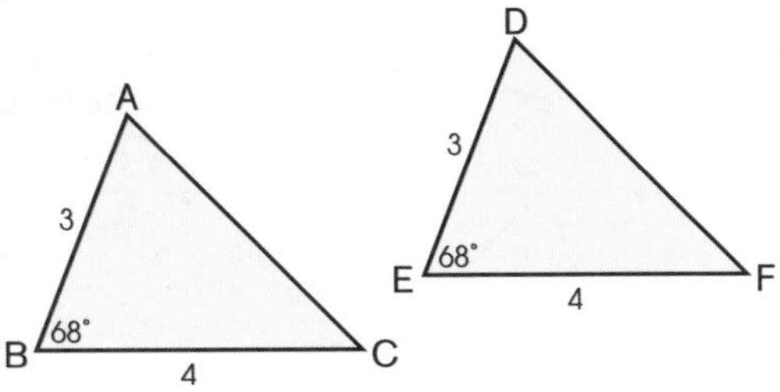

- AB = ______ = 3 units
- ∠B = ______ = ______
- BC = ______ = ______

So, △ABC ≅ ______ by side- ______ - ______

14.

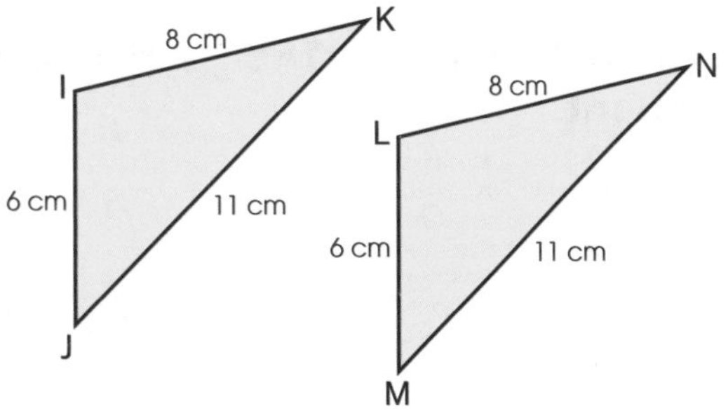

- ________________________
- ________________________
- ________________________

____

____

15.

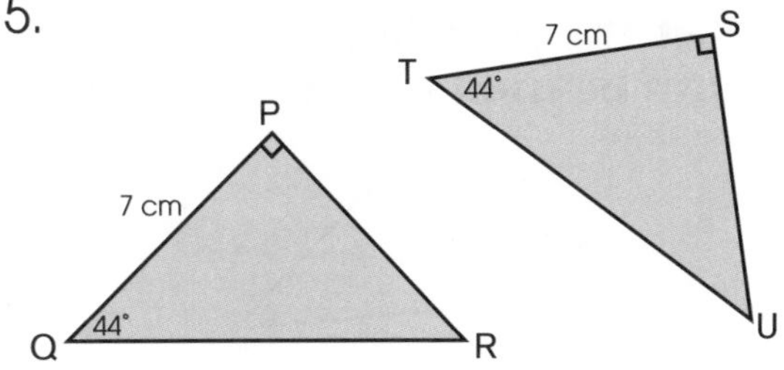

- ________________________
- ________________________
- ________________________

____

____

Circle the two congruent triangles. Then show how they are congruent.

16.

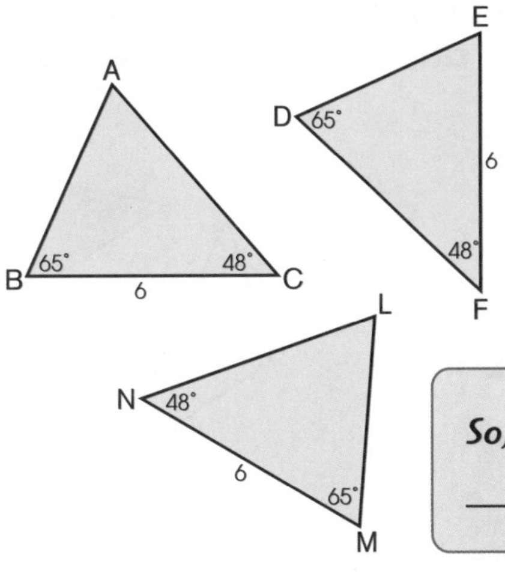

- ________________________
- ________________________
- ________________________

So, ________________________ by ________________________

Similar Figures – a similar figure can be made by shrinking or enlarging another figure

You may use grid systems to draw similar figures.

A, B, and C are similar figures.

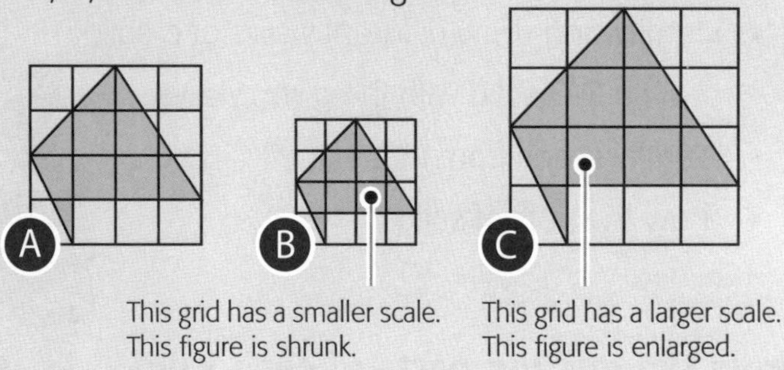
A
B
C
This grid has a smaller scale. This figure is shrunk.
This grid has a larger scale. This figure is enlarged.

Draw a similar figure on each grid.

17.

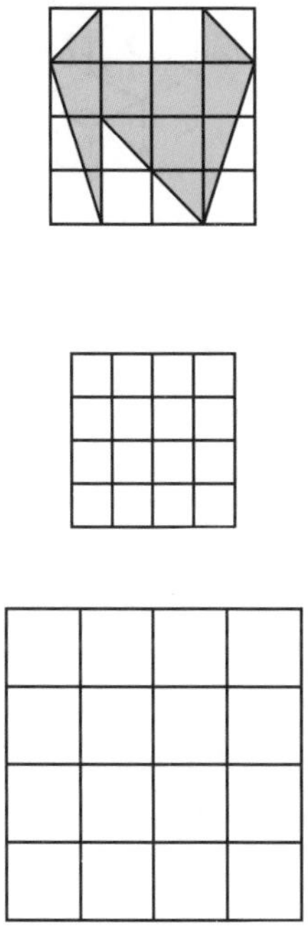

18.

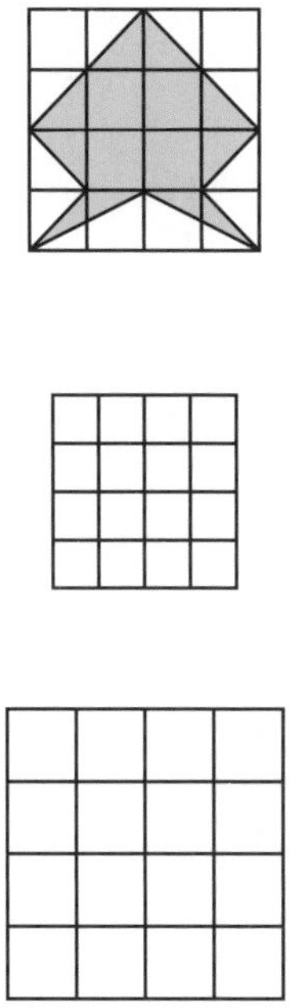

19.

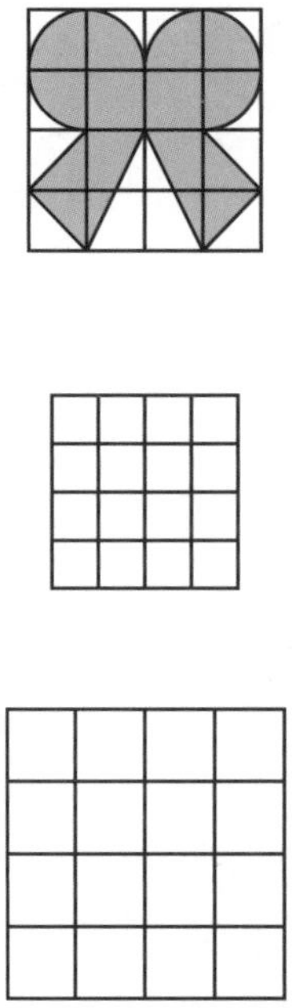

Give an example to support what Joanne says.

20.

All equilateral triangles are similar.

Solids

- draw 3-D solids on a grid
- identify and draw different views of a solid
- draw a 3-D solid with the given views
- identify solids from nets
- draw the nets of solids

Draw the missing parts of each solid.

1.

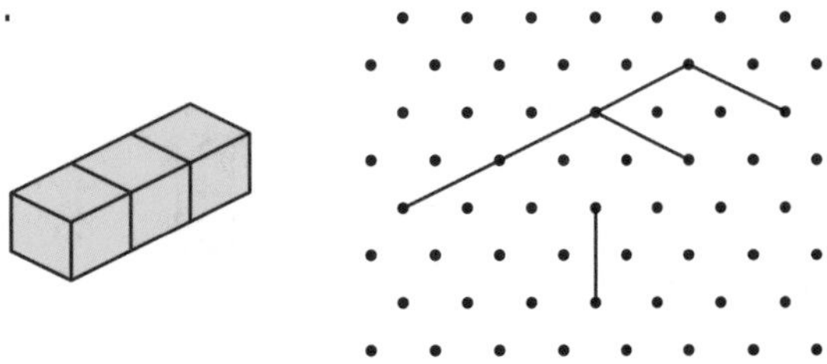

2.

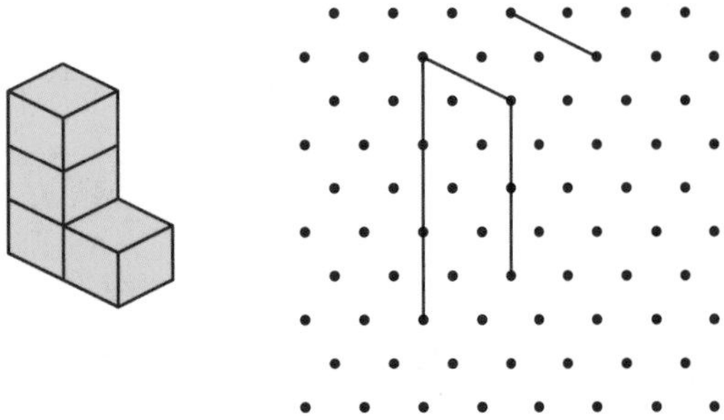

3.

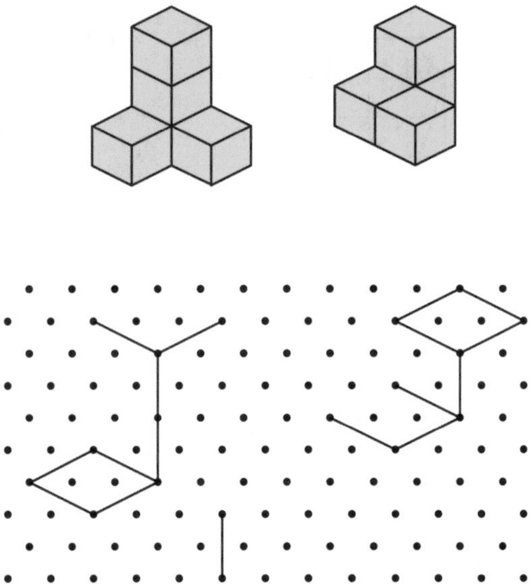

Look at the different views of the solid. Write the letters in the circles.

4.

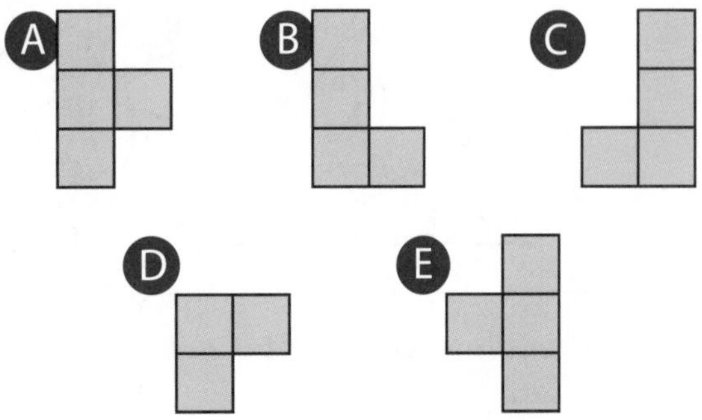

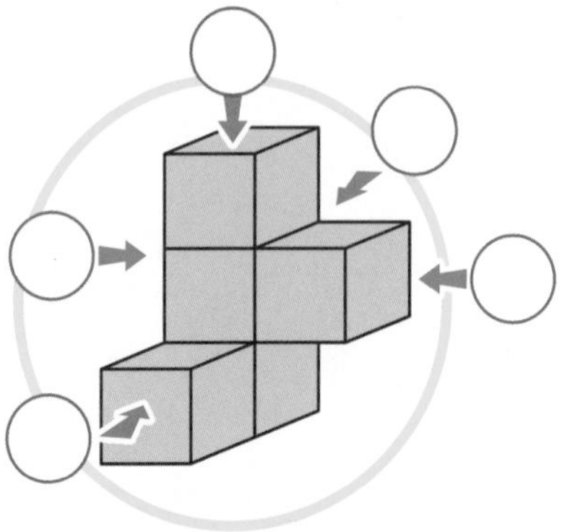

Check the solid that has the given views. Then draw the top view.

5.

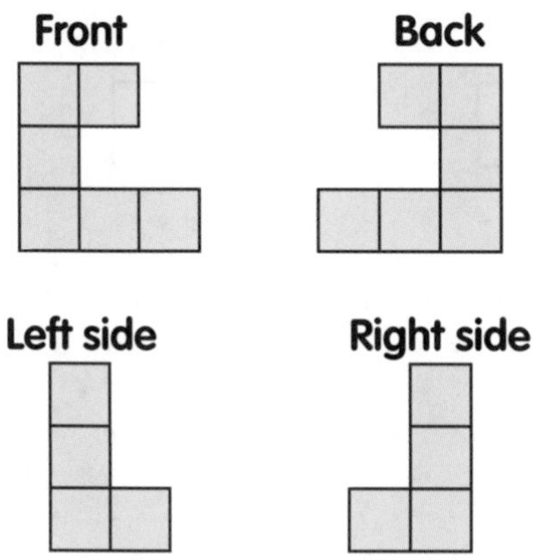

Top

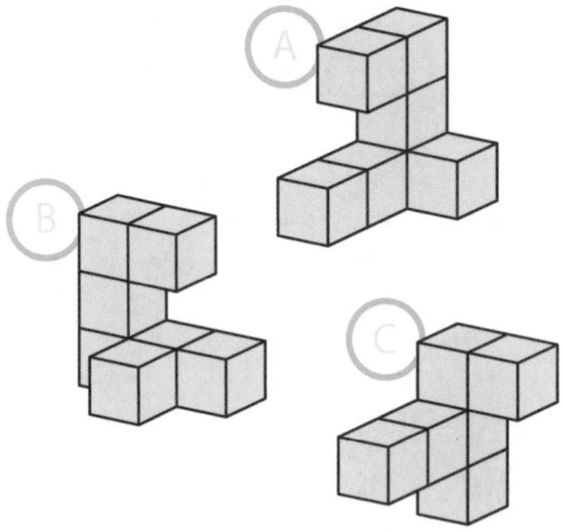

Draw the five views of each solid.

6.

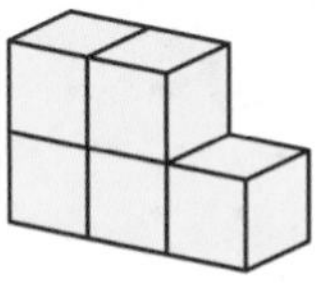

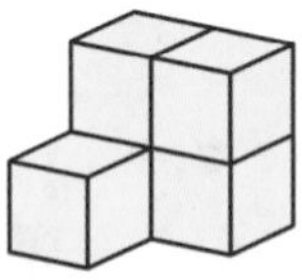

Front

Back

Top

Left side

Right side

Draw the solids with the given views.

7.

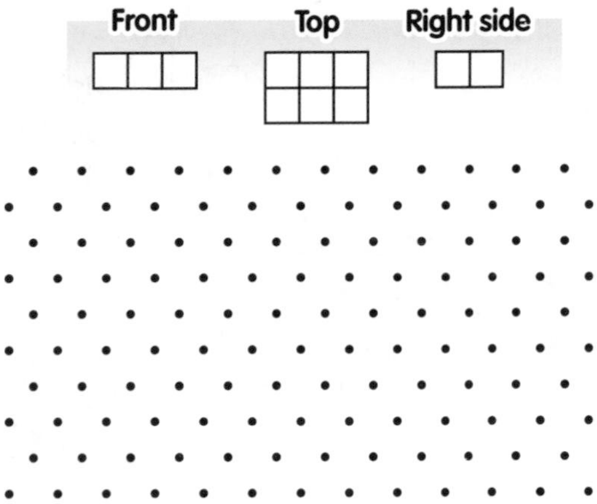

8.

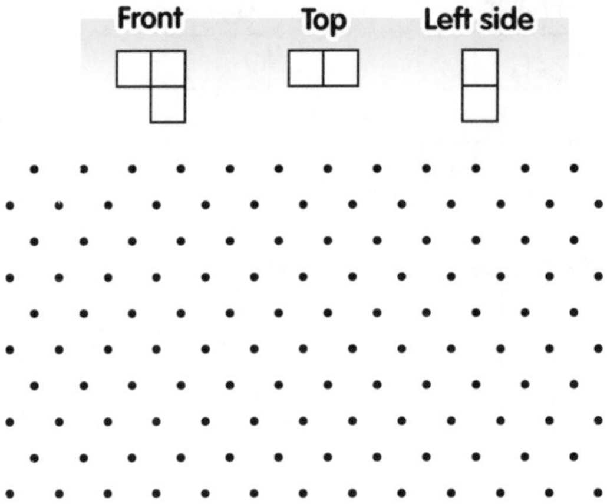

9.

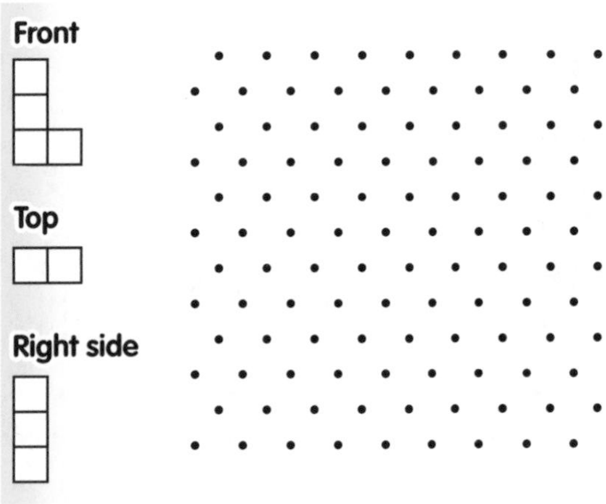

10.

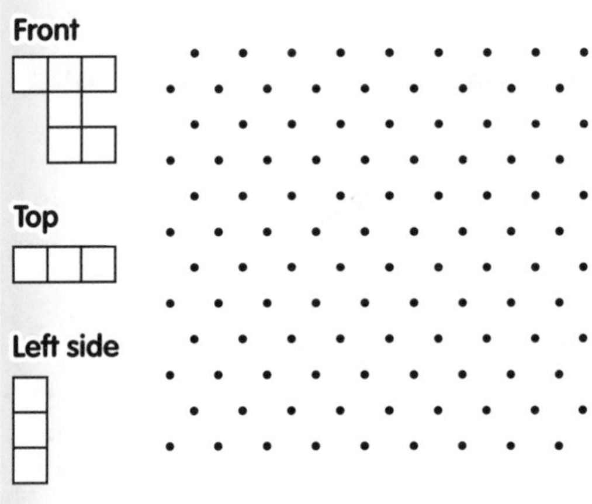

Identify the net of each solid. Name the solid.

11.

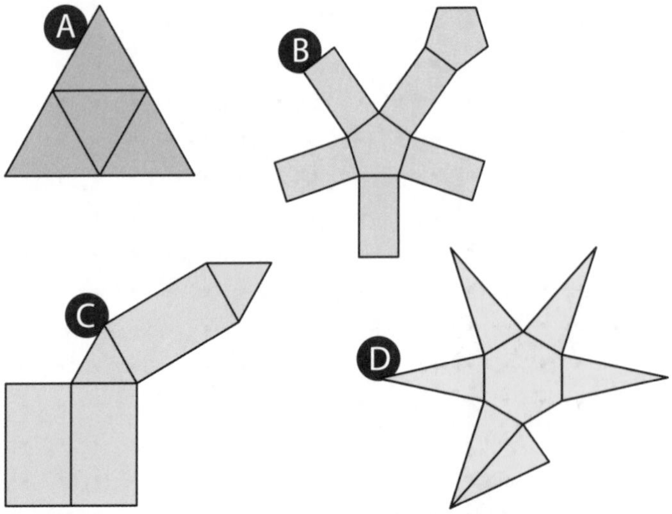

Name

A ____________________

B ____________________

C ____________________

D ____________________

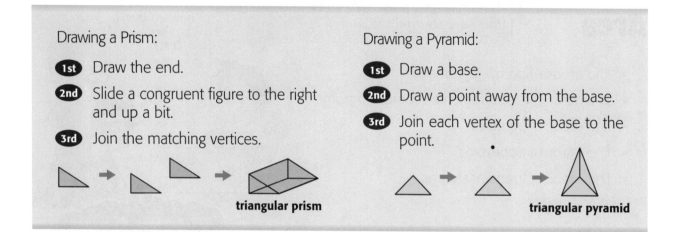

Drawing a Prism:

1st Draw the end.

2nd Slide a congruent figure to the right and up a bit.

3rd Join the matching vertices.

Drawing a Pyramid:

1st Draw a base.

2nd Draw a point away from the base.

3rd Join each vertex of the base to the point.

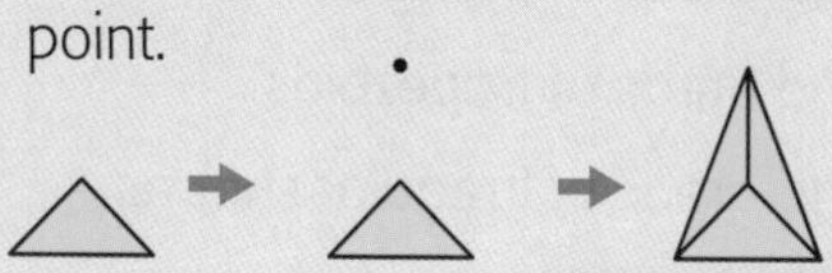

Count and write the numbers. Then sketch the polyhedron that is made by folding each net. Name the polyhedron.

12. ______ faces

______ edges

______ vertices

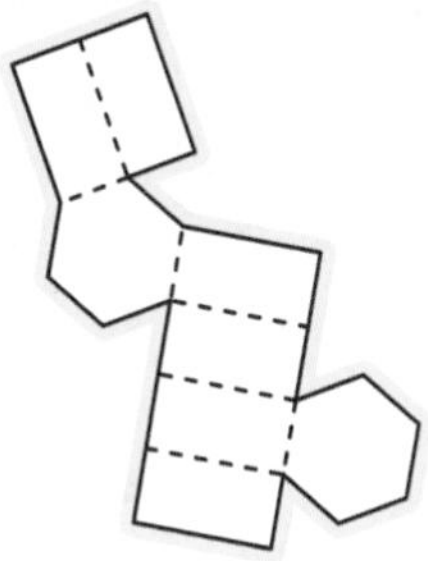

Congruent faces:

______ hexagon(s) and

______ rectangle(s)

Name: ____________________

13. ______ faces

______ edges

______ vertices

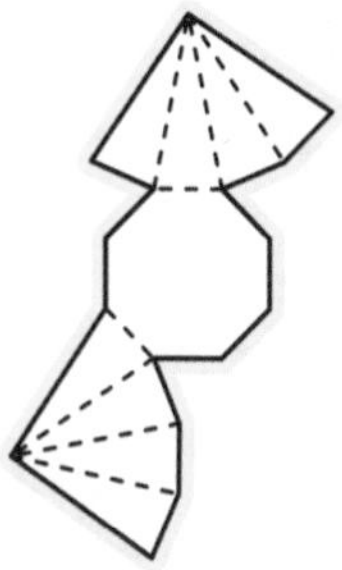

Congruent faces:

______ octagon(s) and

______ triangle(s)

Name: ____________________

Sketch the polyhedron as described. Then draw two different nets for that polyhedron.

14.

The polyhedron has 1 pentagonal face and 5 congruent triangular faces.

14

Area

I can change a parallelogram to a rectangle, but keep its area the same.
h
b
This is a fact. Everyone can do this.

Area of a ▱
= Area of a ▭ (b, h)
= **b x h**

- find areas of parallelograms
- find missing measurements in parallelograms
- find areas of triangles
- find areas of trapezoids
- find areas of irregular shapes

Trace the base and height of each parallelogram. Then find the area.

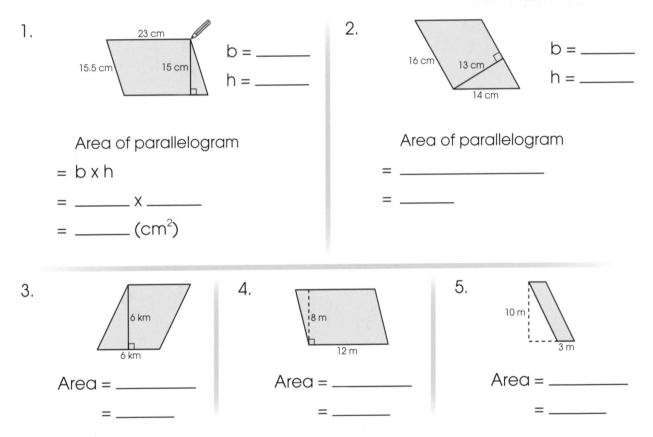

1.

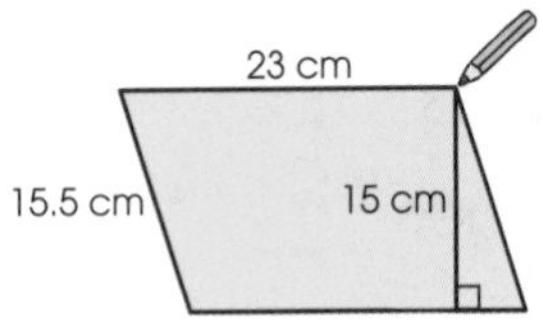

b = ______

h = ______

Area of parallelogram

= b x h

= ______ x ______

= ______ (cm^2)

2.

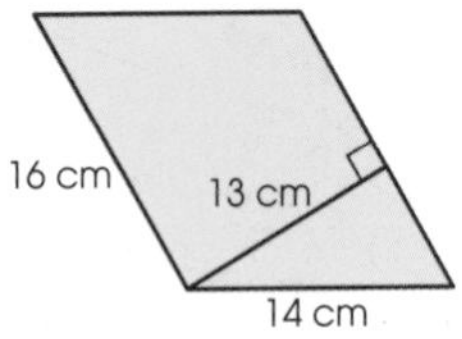

b = ______

h = ______

Area of parallelogram

= ______________

= ______

3.

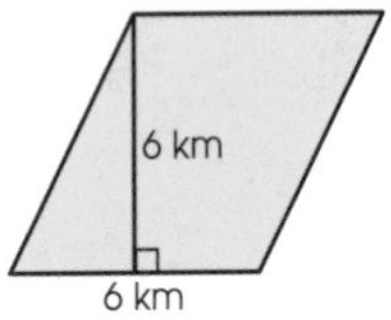

Area = __________

= ______

4.

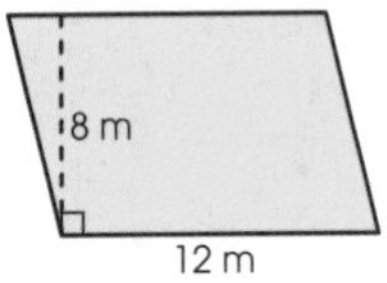

Area = __________

= ______

5.

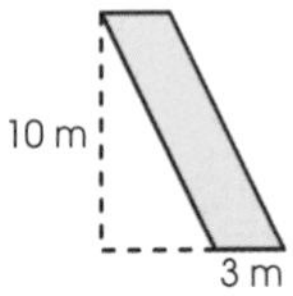

Area = __________

= ______

Find the missing measurement for each parallelogram.

6.

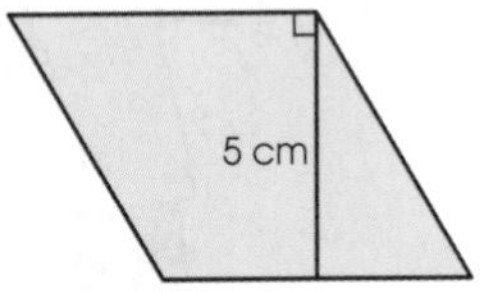

Area = 30 cm^2

Base = ______

7.

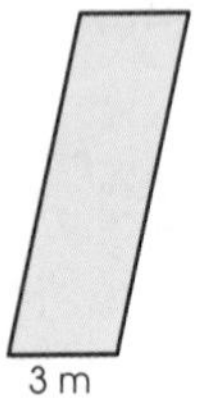

Area = 27 m^2

Height = ______

A parallelogram is formed by 2 identical triangles.

Area of a △ = Area of a ▱ ÷ 2

= **b** x **h** ÷ **2**

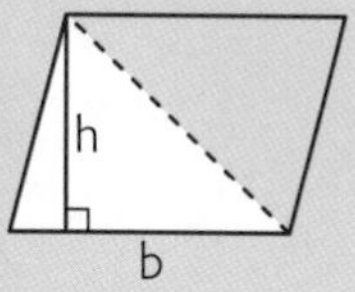

e.g. Area of △

= (b x h) ÷ 2

= (13 x 8) ÷ 2

= 52 (cm^2)

Trace the base and height of each triangle. Then find the area.

8.

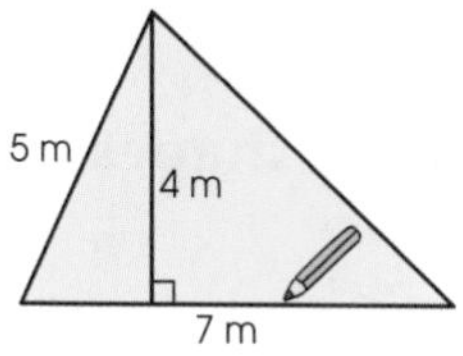

b = ______

h = ______

Area = (b x h) ÷ 2

= (______ x ______) ÷ 2

= ______ (m^2)

9.

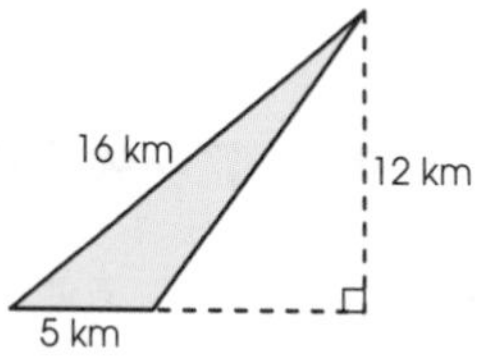

b = ______

h = ______

Area =

10.

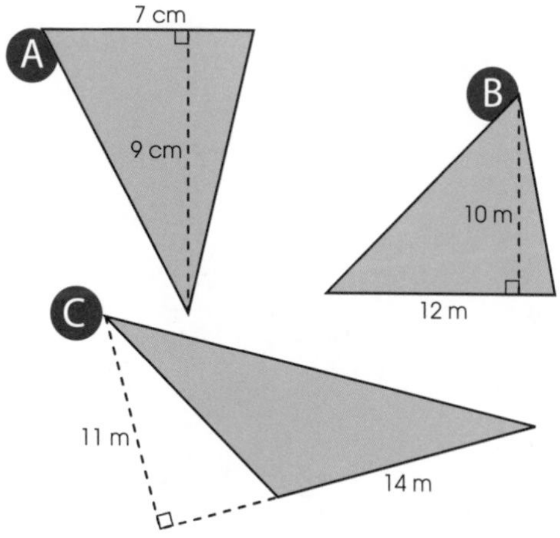

A Area =

B Area =

C Area =

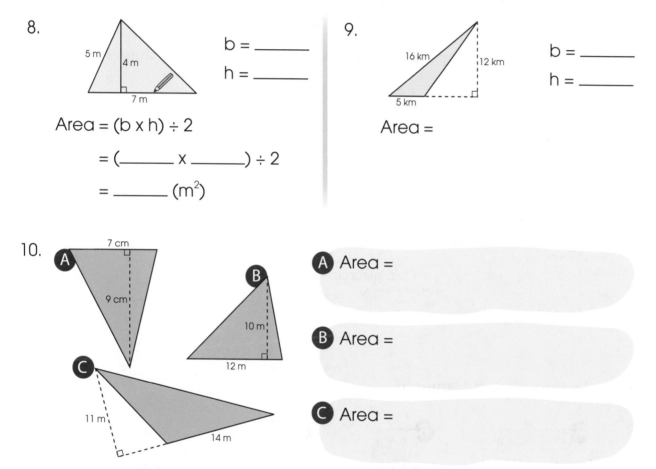

Find the missing measurement for each triangle.

11.

Area	Base	Height
35 cm^2	7 cm	
42 cm^2	6 cm	
24 m^2	8 m	

12.

Area	Base	Height
20 cm^2		5 cm
19.5 m^2		10 m
42 m^2		3 m

Find the area of a trapezoid by cutting it into 2 triangles or 1 triangle and 1 parallelogram.

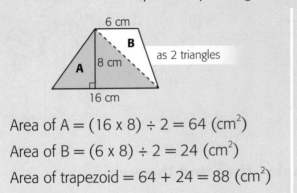

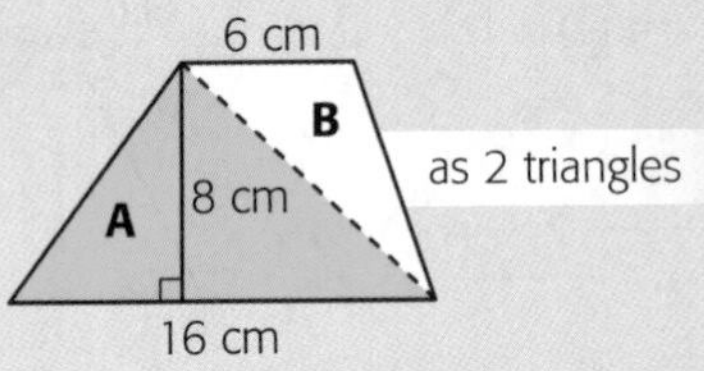

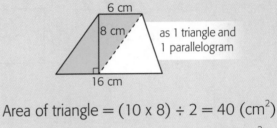

Area of A = (16 x 8) ÷ 2 = 64 (cm^2)

Area of B = (6 x 8) ÷ 2 = 24 (cm^2)

Area of trapezoid = 64 + 24 = 88 (cm^2)

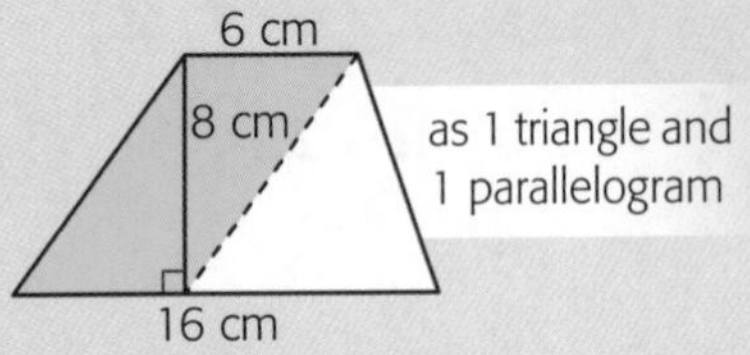

Area of triangle = (10 x 8) ÷ 2 = 40 (cm^2)

Area of parallelogram = 6 x 8 = 48 (cm^2)

Area of trapezoid = 40 + 48 = 88 (cm^2)

Find the area of each trapezoid by cutting it into the specified shapes.

13.

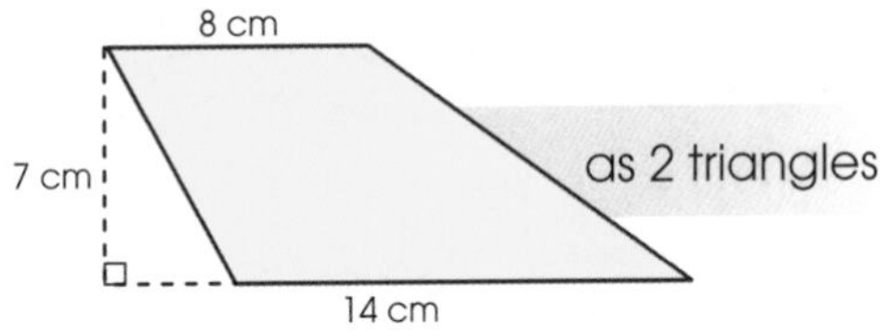

14.

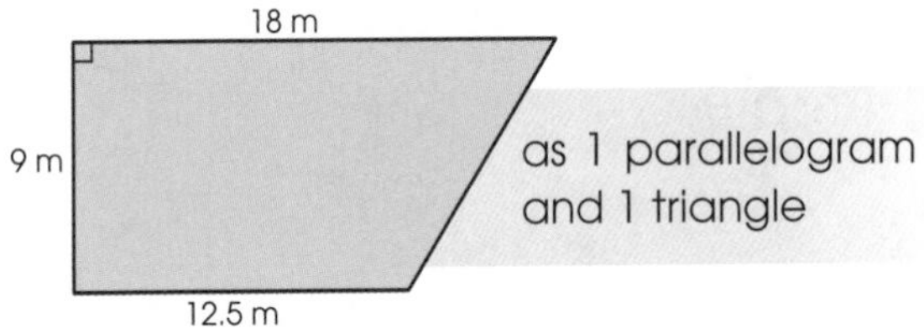

Find the area of each trapezoid.

15.

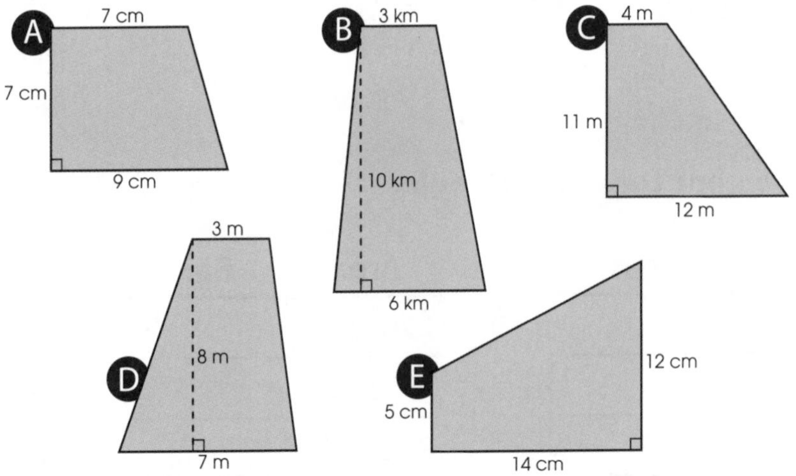

Area

A ________

B ________

C ________

D ________

E ________

Trace the dotted lines to divide each irregular figure into several shapes. Find the area of each shape. Then add to find the area of the irregular figure.

16.

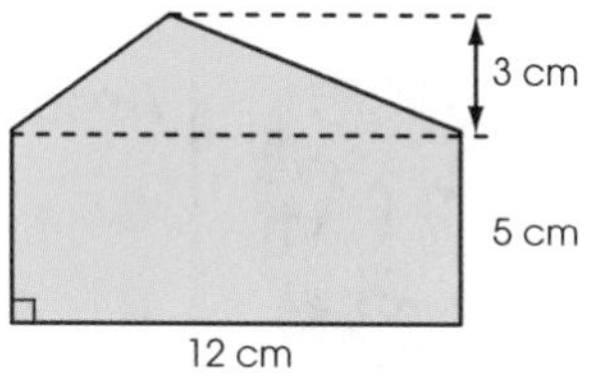

17.

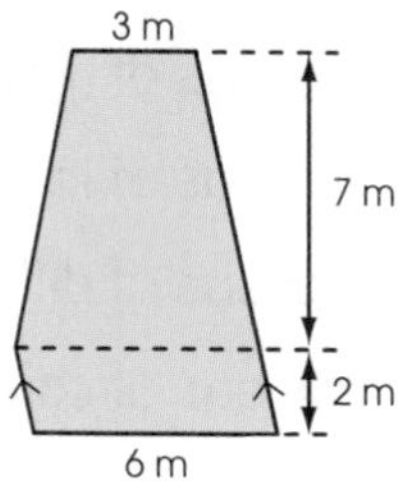

Find the area of each irregular figure.

18.

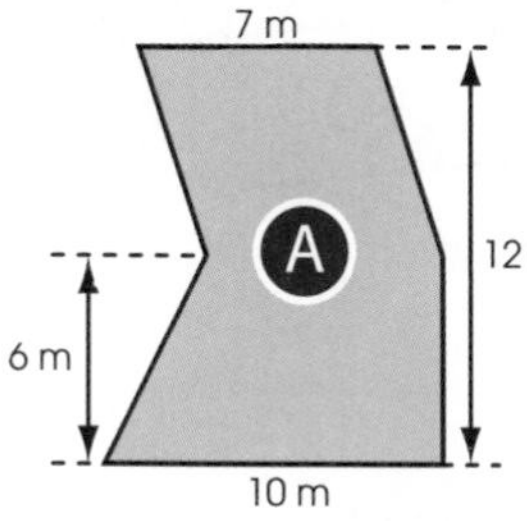

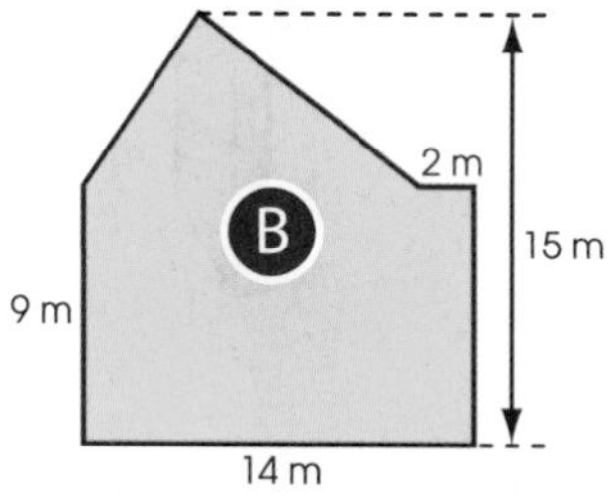

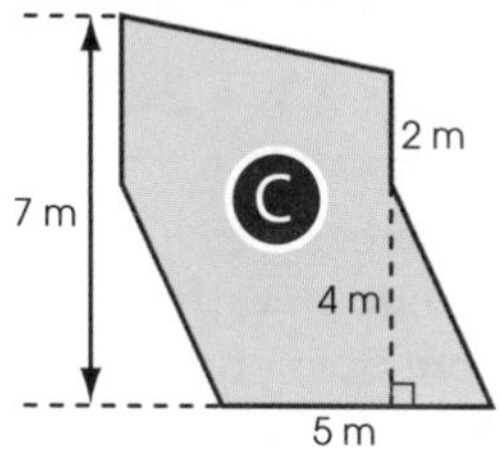

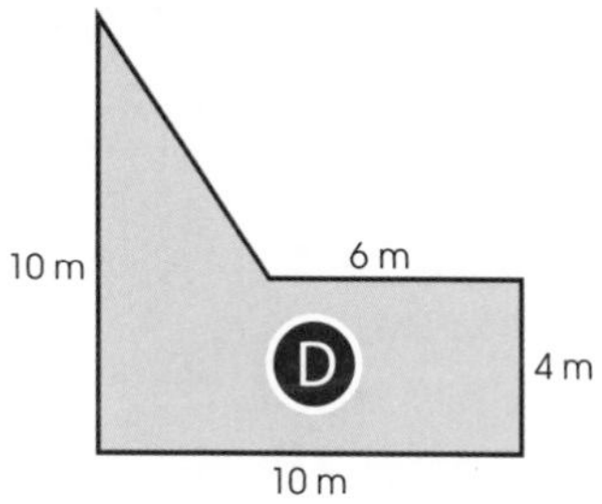

Area

A ________

B ________

C ________

D ________

Read what Harry says. Find the area of the trapezoid.

19.

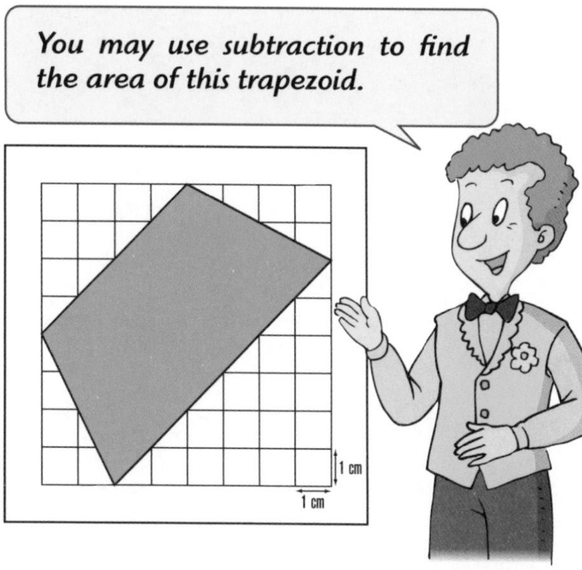

Surface Area

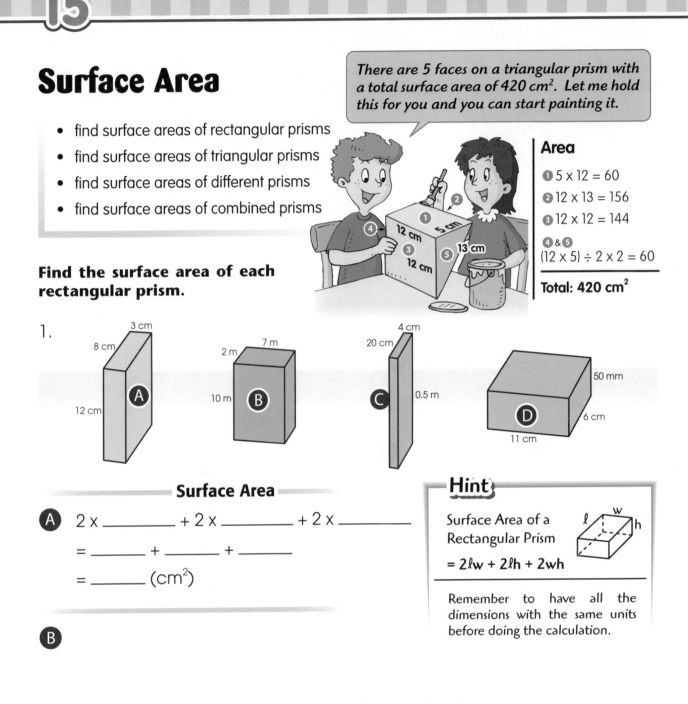

- find surface areas of rectangular prisms
- find surface areas of triangular prisms
- find surface areas of different prisms
- find surface areas of combined prisms

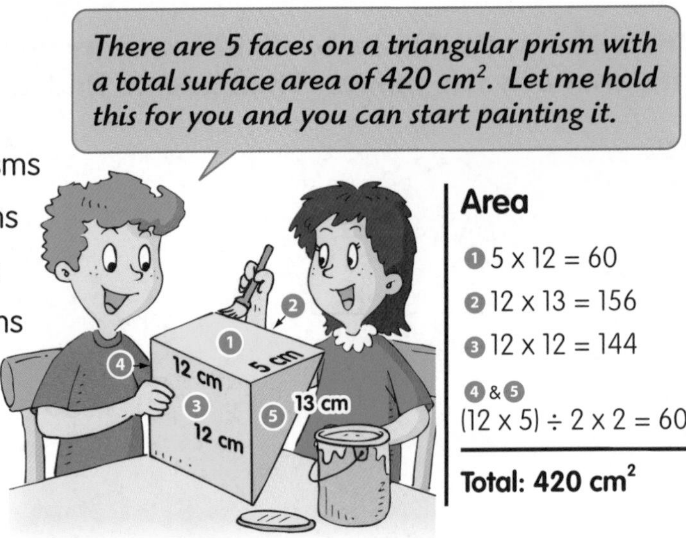

Area

❶ $5 \times 12 = 60$

❷ $12 \times 13 = 156$

❸ $12 \times 12 = 144$

❹ & ❺ $(12 \times 5) \div 2 \times 2 = 60$

Total: 420 cm²

Find the surface area of each rectangular prism.

1.

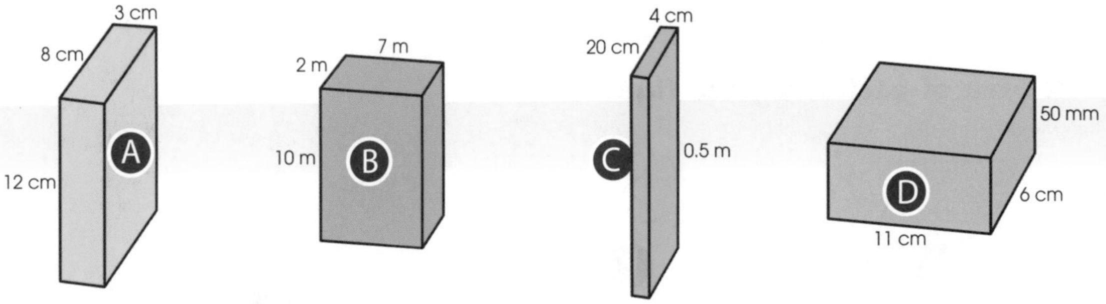

Surface Area

Ⓐ 2 x ________ + 2 x ________ + 2 x ________

= ______ + ______ + ______

= ______ (cm²)

Ⓑ

Ⓒ

Ⓓ

Hint

Surface Area of a Rectangular Prism

= 2ℓw + 2ℓh + 2wh

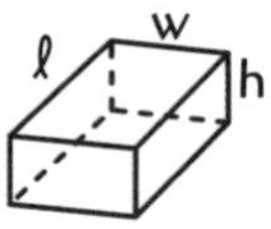

Remember to have all the dimensions with the same units before doing the calculation.

Label the measurements on the net. Find the area of each face. Then find the total surface area of each triangular prism.

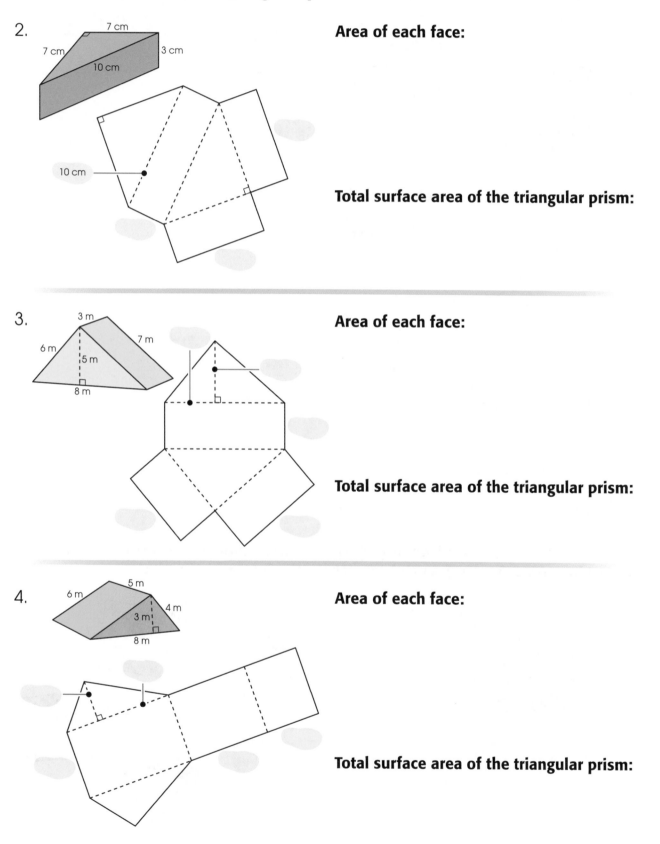

2.

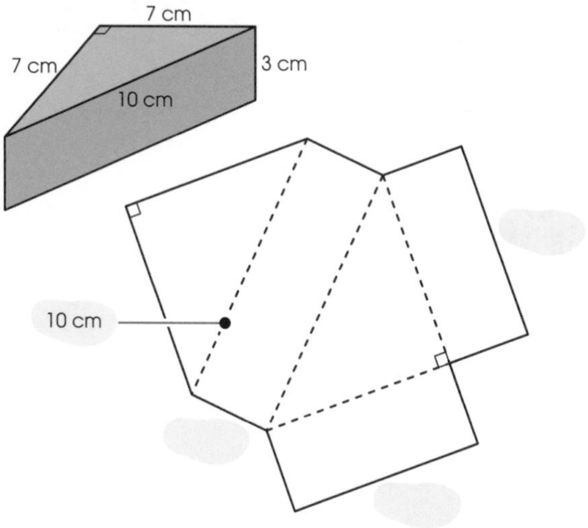

Area of each face:

Total surface area of the triangular prism:

3.

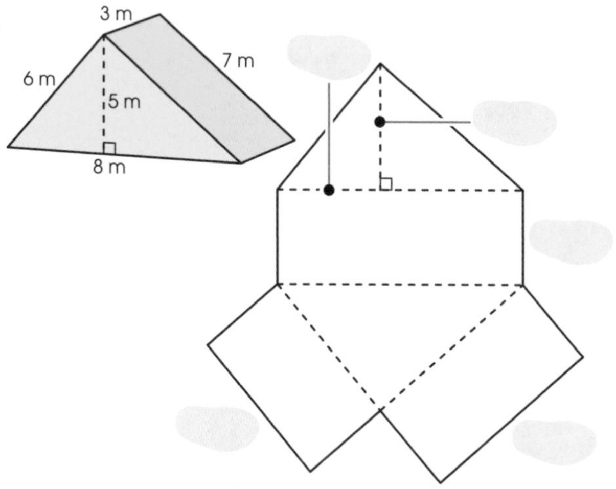

Area of each face:

Total surface area of the triangular prism:

4.

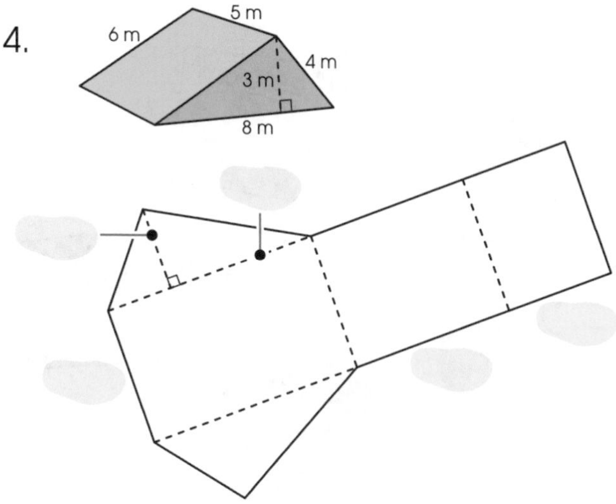

Area of each face:

Total surface area of the triangular prism:

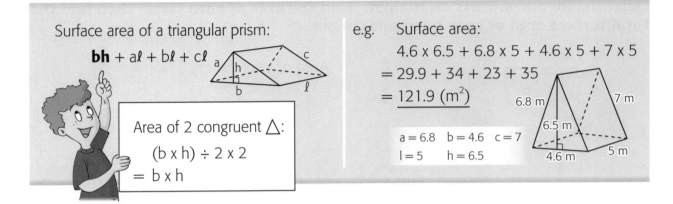

Surface area of a triangular prism:

$\mathbf{bh} + a\ell + b\ell + c\ell$

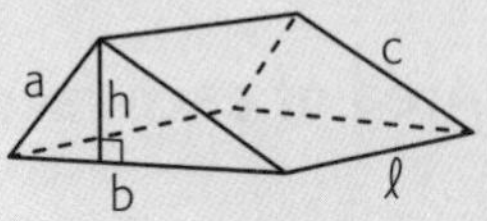

Area of 2 congruent △:

(b x h) ÷ 2 x 2

= b x h

e.g. Surface area:

4.6 x 6.5 + 6.8 x 5 + 4.6 x 5 + 7 x 5

= 29.9 + 34 + 23 + 35

= 121.9 (m^2)

a = 6.8 b = 4.6 c = 7

l = 5 h = 6.5

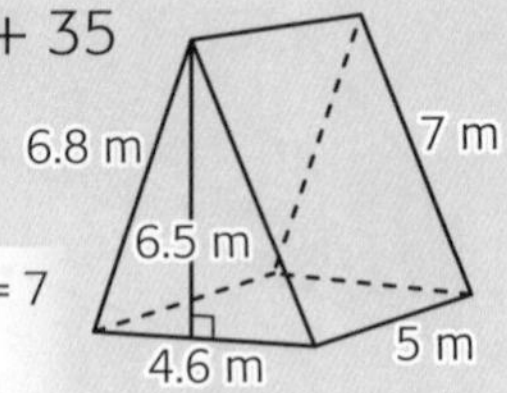

Find the surface area of each triangular prism by using the formula above.

5.

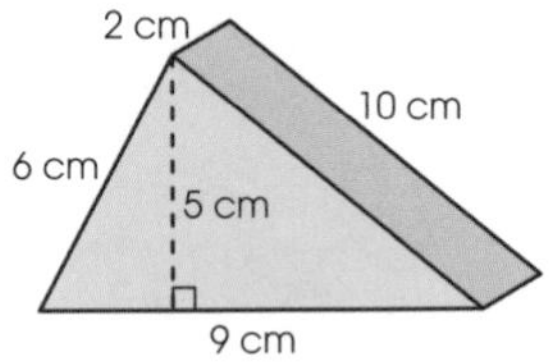

Surface area:

6.

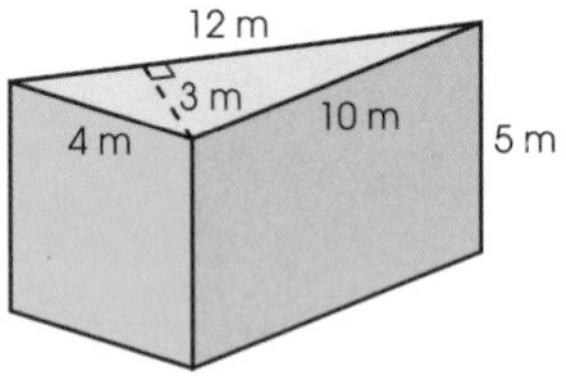

Surface area:

Find the surface area of each gift box. Then choose the most appropriate wrapping paper to wrap each box. Write the letter in the circle.

7.

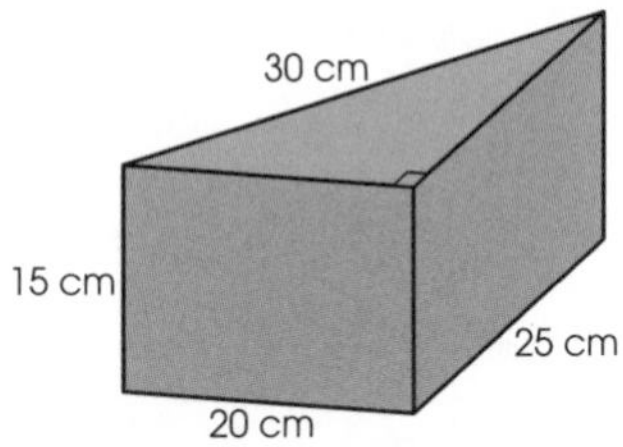

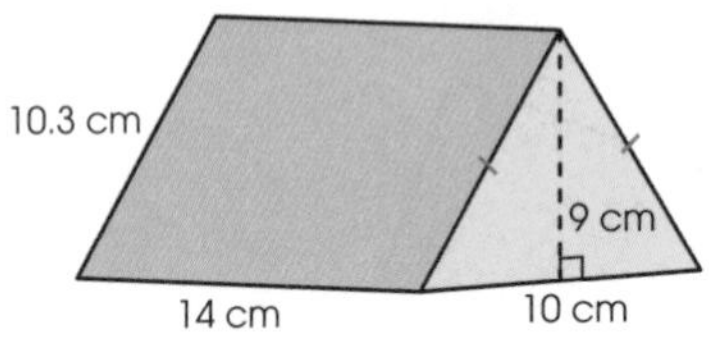

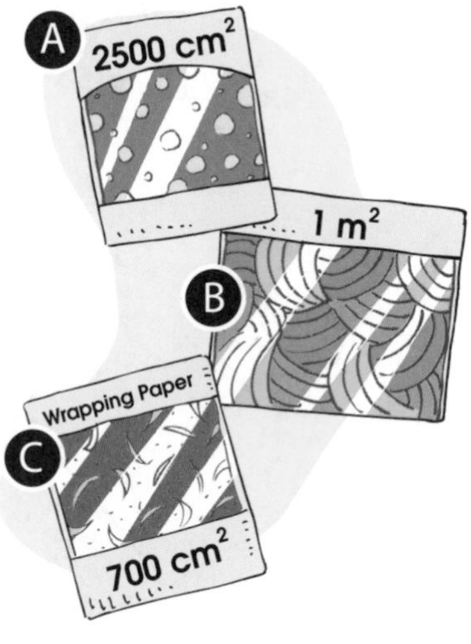

a.

b.

Complete the net of the solid and write the measurements. Then find the total surface area of the solid.

8.

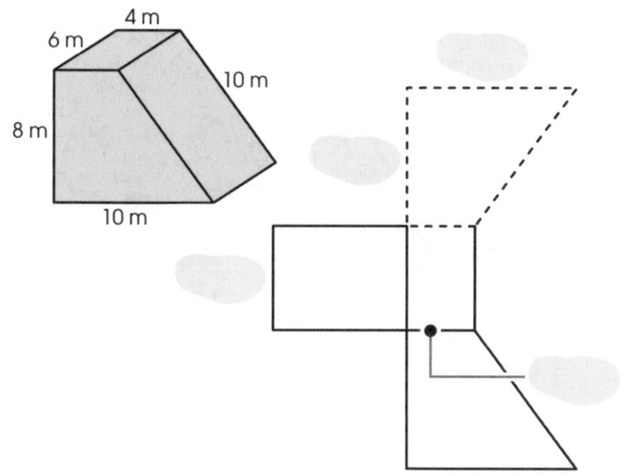

Surface Area

9.

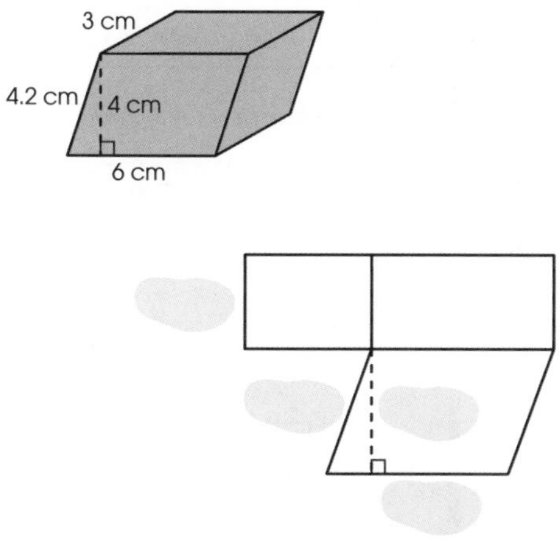

Surface Area

Joe has built two different towers with his two blocks. Find the surface area of each tower, and find which tower has a smaller surface area.

10.

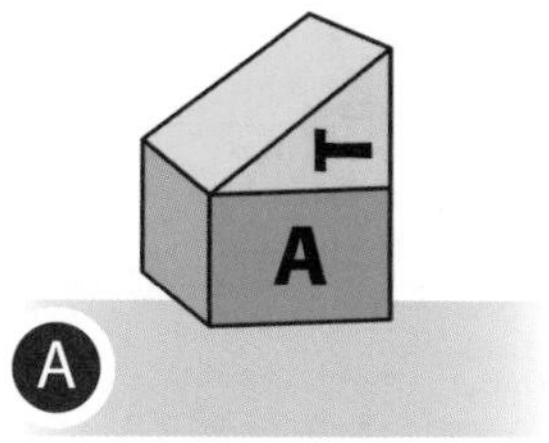

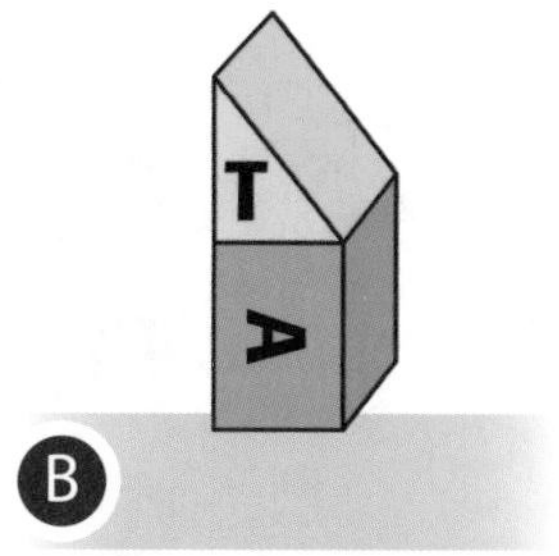

Tower ______ has a smaller surface area.

Volume

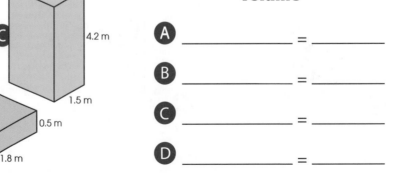

- find the volume of rectangular prisms
- find the volume of prisms that have different shapes in the base
- find the unknown measurements of prisms
- relate cm^3 to mL
- solve problems involving volume and capacity

Volume:	Volume:
$(10 \times 15 \div 2) \times 7$	$(10 \times 6) \times 8$
$= 525\ (cm^3)$	$= 480\ (cm^3)$

Find the volume (V) of each prism.

1.

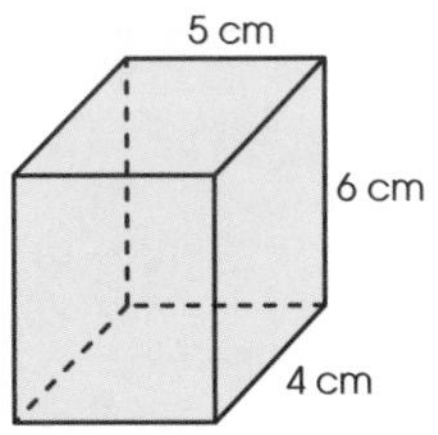

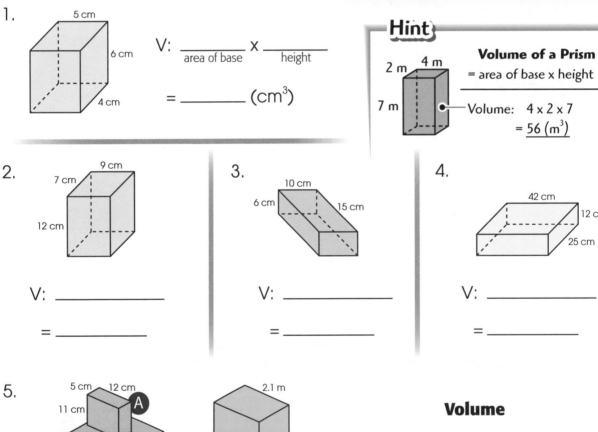

V: ________ x ________
(area of base) (height)

= ________ (cm^3)

Hint

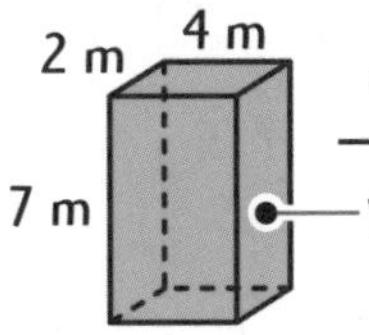

Volume of a Prism
= area of base x height

Volume: $4 \times 2 \times 7$
$= \underline{56\ (m^3)}$

2.

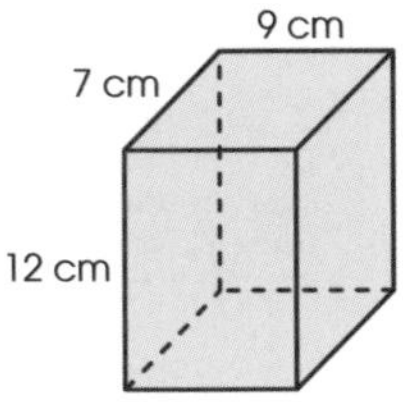

V: ____________

= ____________

3.

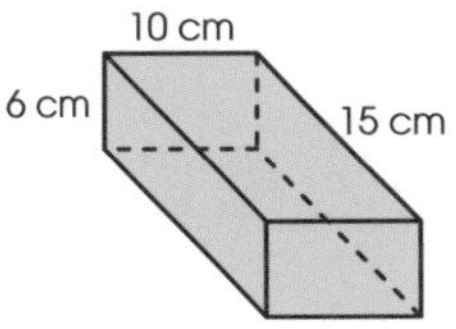

V: ____________

= ____________

4.

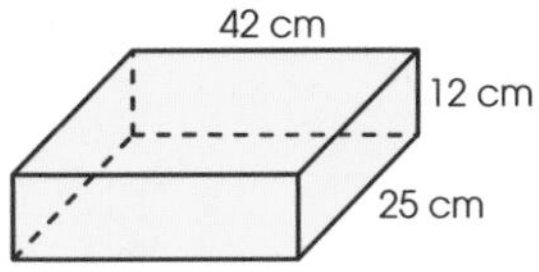

V: ____________

= ____________

5.

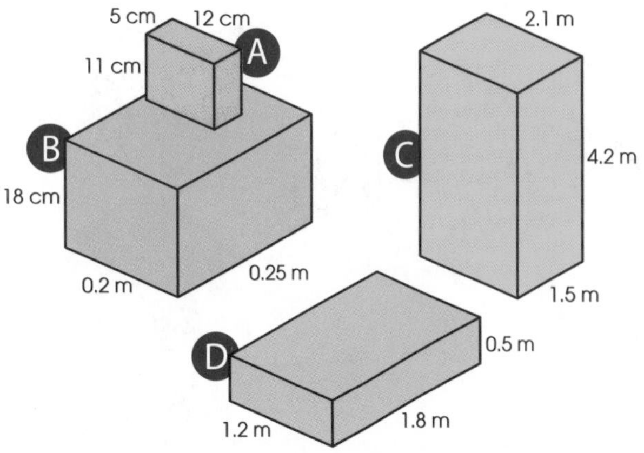

Volume

A ____________ = ________

B ____________ = ________

C ____________ = ________

D ____________ = ________

Finding the unknown side of a rectangular prism with the given volume:

1st Multiply to find the area of the base.

2nd Divide the volume by the area of the base.

e.g.

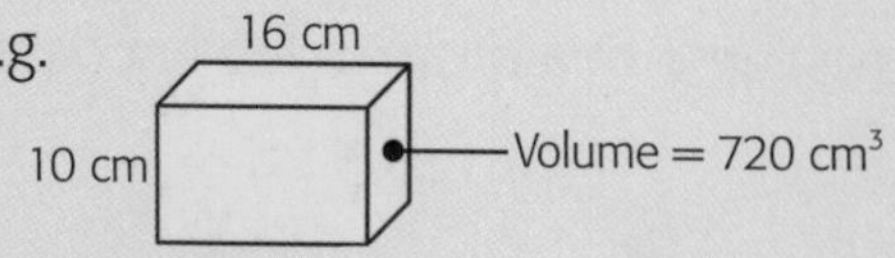

Area of base: 16 x 10 = 160

Width: 720 ÷ 160 = 4.5 (cm)

Find the unknown side of each rectangular prism.

6. volume: $13.2\ m^3$
   length: 2 m
   width: 1.8 m
   height: ________

7. volume: $118.69\ cm^3$
   length: ________
   width: 3 cm
   height: 11 cm

8. volume: $13.2\ m^3$
   length: 1.24 m
   width: ________
   height: 4.5 m

Find the length of the unknown side of each container. Then answer the question.

9.

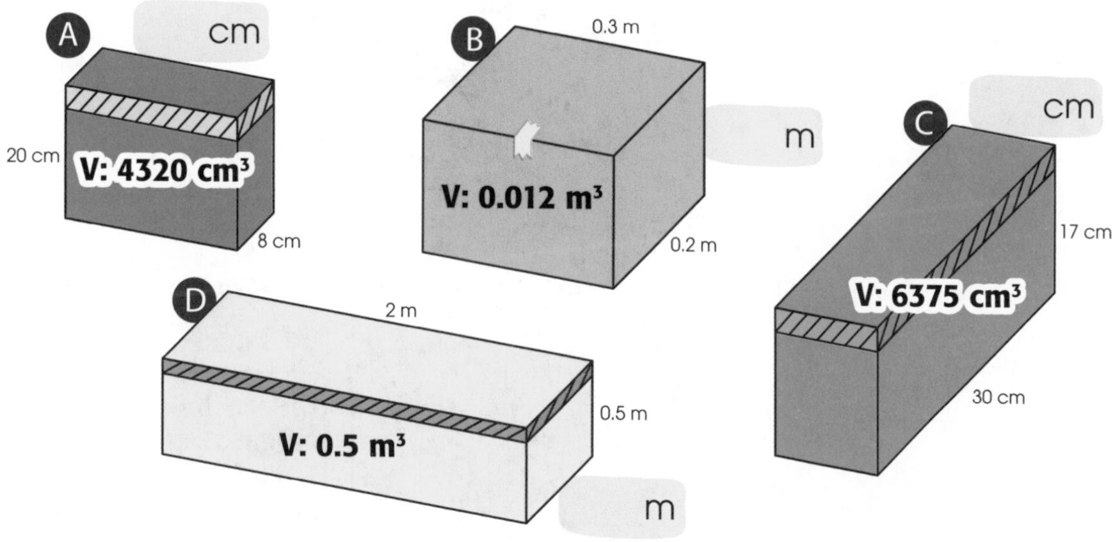

10.

How many cubes with sides of 3 cm are needed to fill up each container?

____

____

Volume of a prism = Area of base x Height

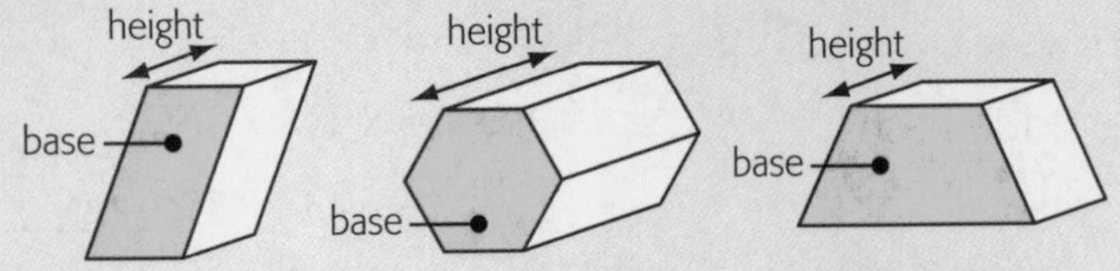

In some cases, you can use the word "thickness" to describe the "height" of a prism.

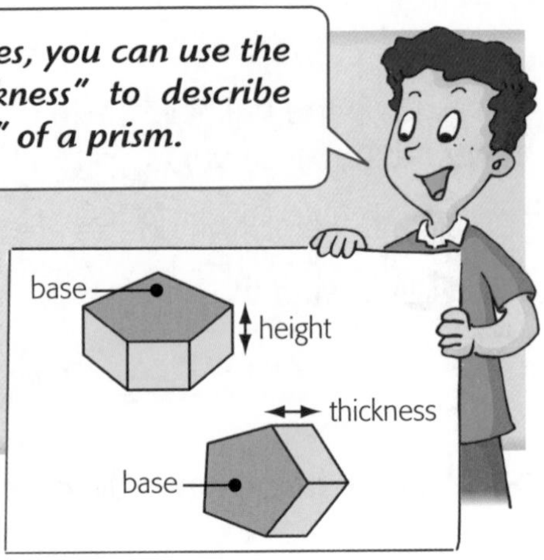

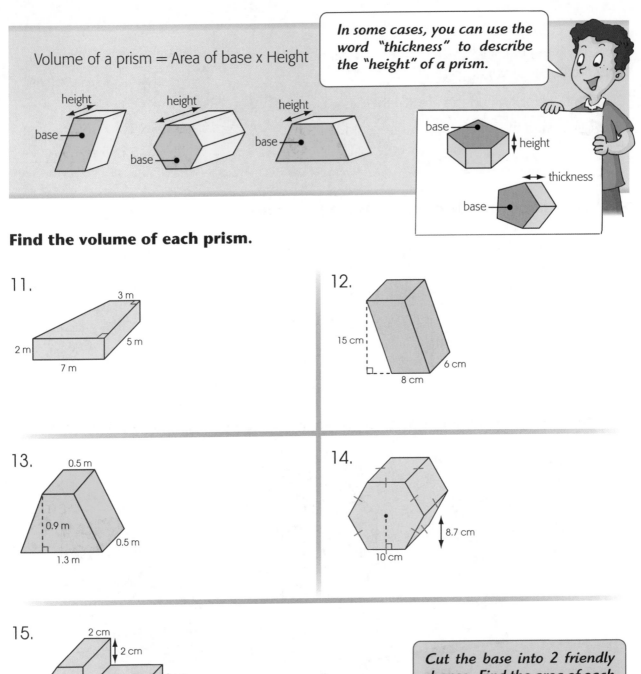

Find the volume of each prism.

11.

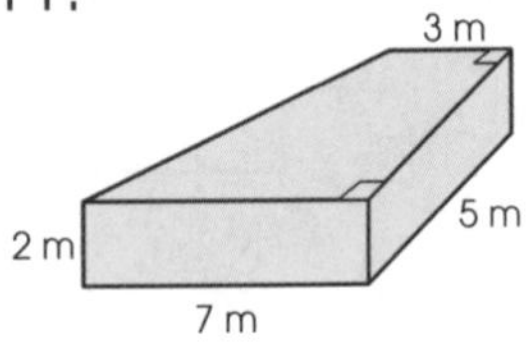

12.

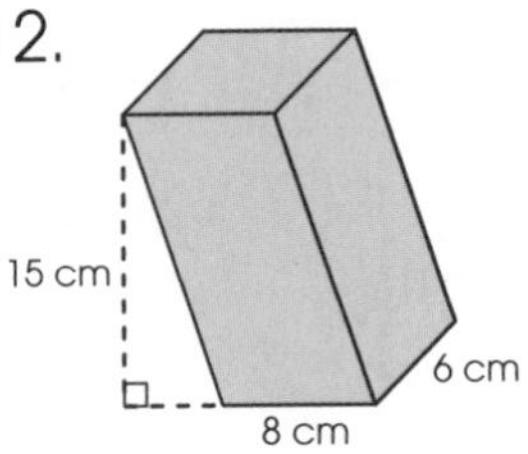

13.

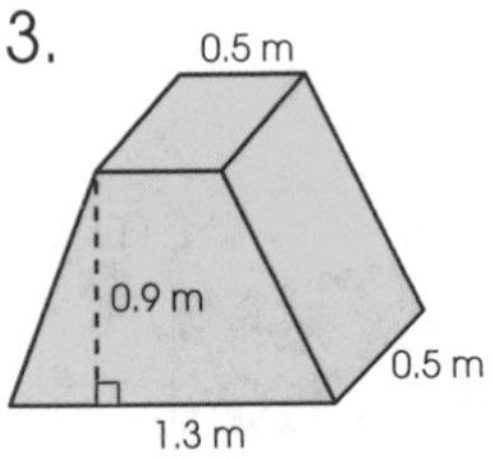

14.

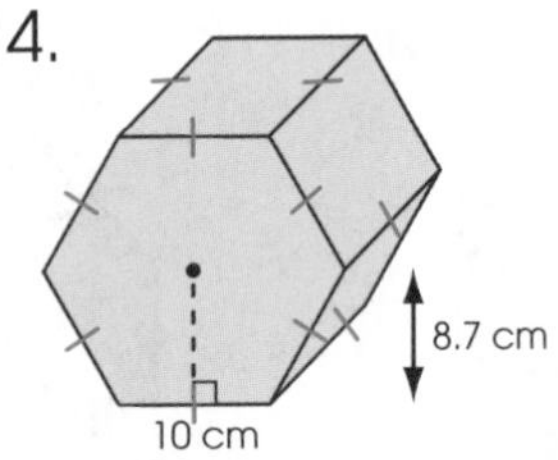

15.

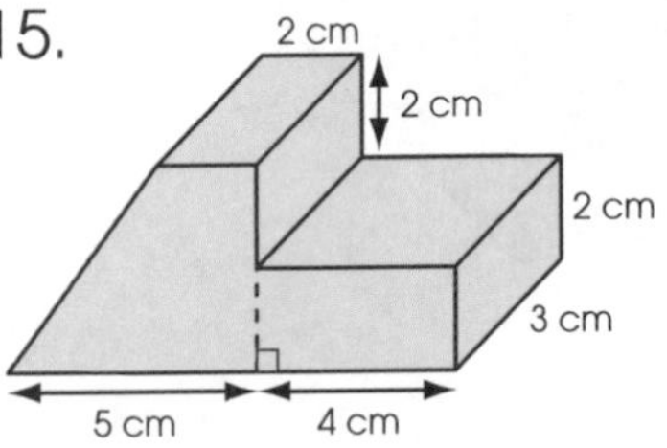

16.

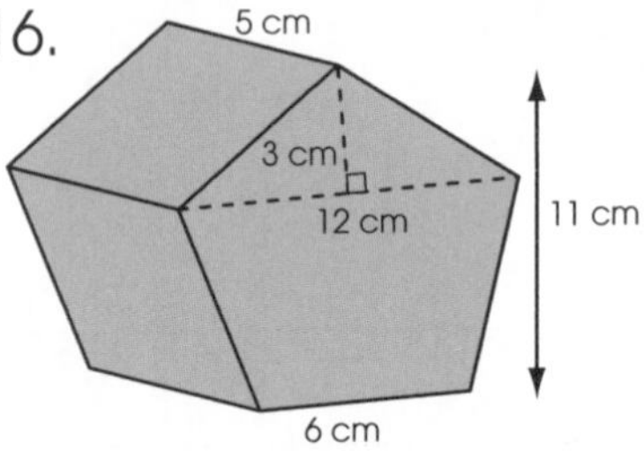

Cut the base into 2 friendly shapes. Find the area of each shape. Then add to find the base area.

Find the capacity of each vase. Then answer the questions.

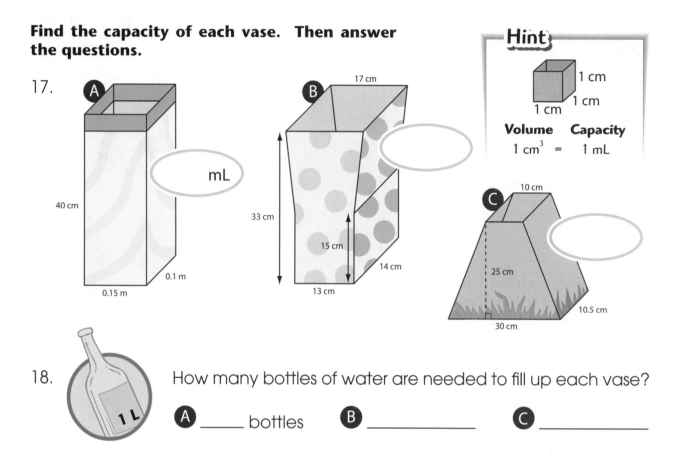

Hint

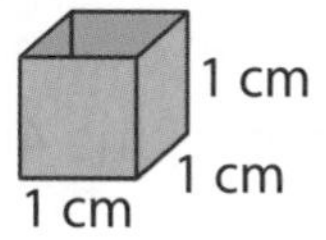

Volume **Capacity**

1 cm^3 = 1 mL

17.

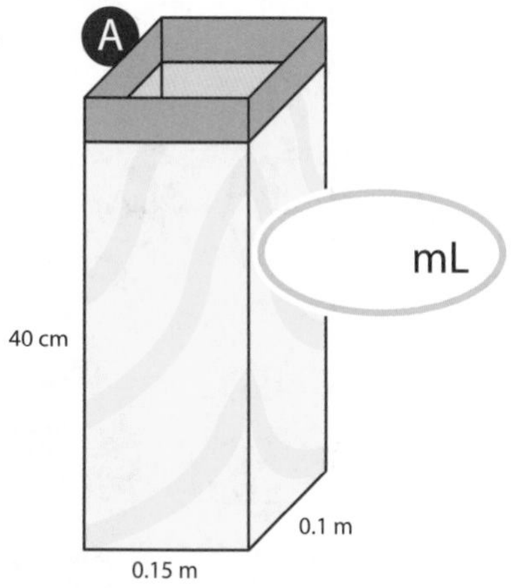

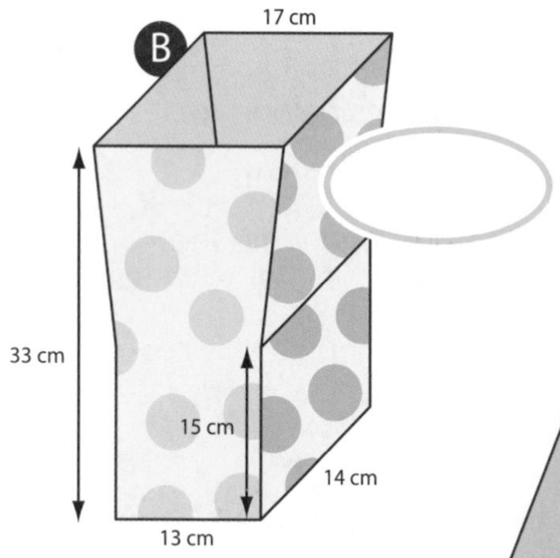

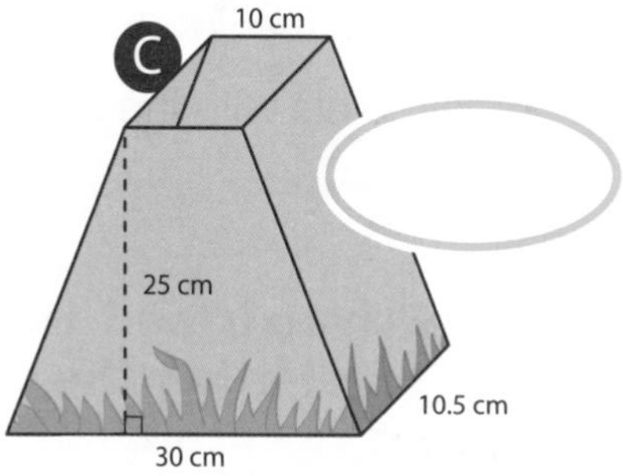

18.

How many bottles of water are needed to fill up each vase?

Ⓐ _____ bottles Ⓑ ____________ Ⓒ ____________

19. The volume of each pebble is 3.6 cm^3. If Jack puts 40 pebbles into A, how much water can A hold now?

____

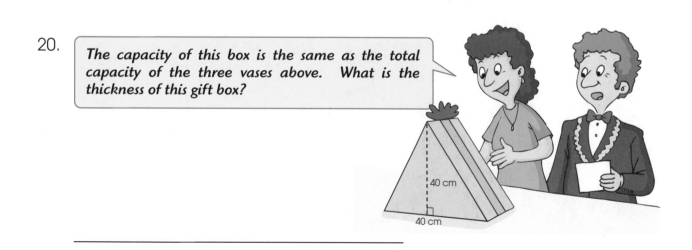

20. *The capacity of this box is the same as the total capacity of the three vases above. What is the thickness of this gift box?*

____

Coordinates

- identify the 4 quadrants
- identify which quadrants the points belong to
- plot and write the coordinates of the points
- make similar figures on the grid and write the vertices of the figures
- draw points with the given movements

Label the xy-axis and the four quadrants. Then write whether the values are positive or negative in each quadrant.

1.

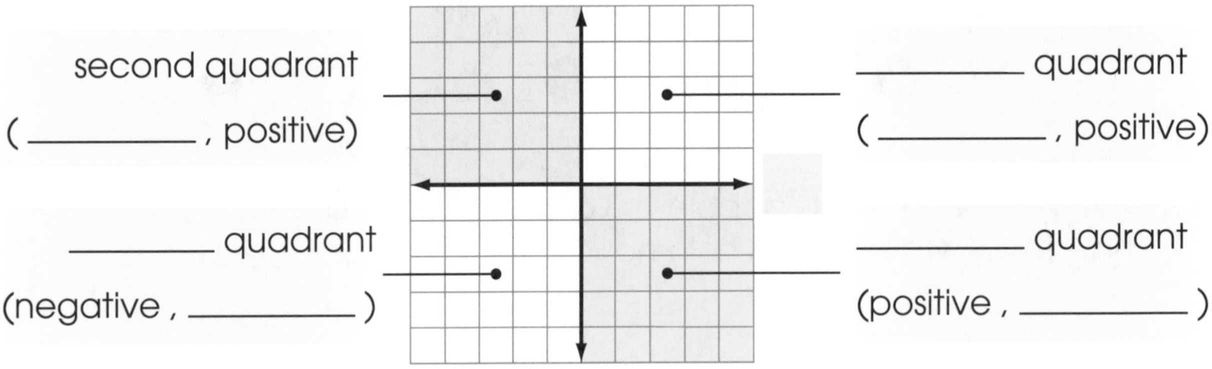

Look at the coordinates of each point. Write the point in the correct quadrant.

2. (8,-2) (6,4) (5,-3)
(10,-11) (-8,7) (19,2)
(14,5) (-2,13) (-7,-9)
(-20,28) (-15,-1) (16,4)
($\frac{1}{2}$,-1) (-6,-3.5) (-2.7,-4)
(-0.8,$\frac{1}{3}$)

Second	First
Third	Fourth

Complete the grid. Then plot the points on the grid.

3. A(3,-7)
B(-5,4)
C(-1,2)
D(0,-6)
E(-2,-5)
F(-6,3)
G(7,0)
H(2,-1)
I(-3,4)
J(1,8)

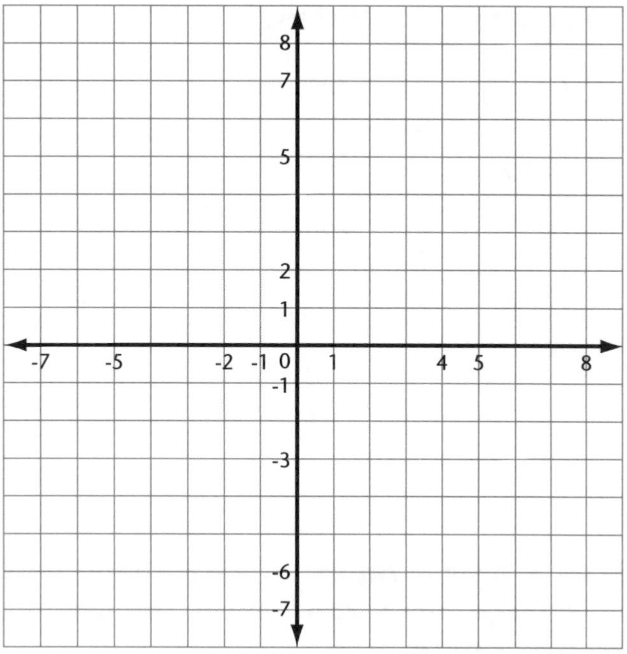

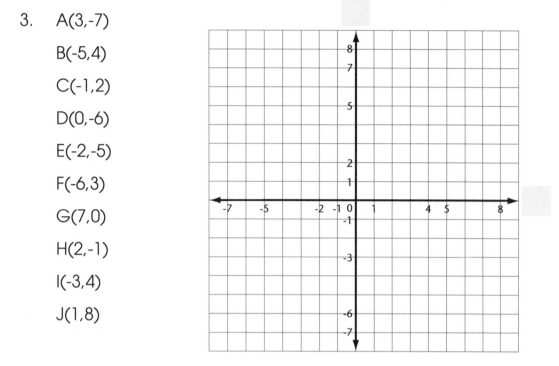

Write the coordinates of the points. Then answer the questions.

4.

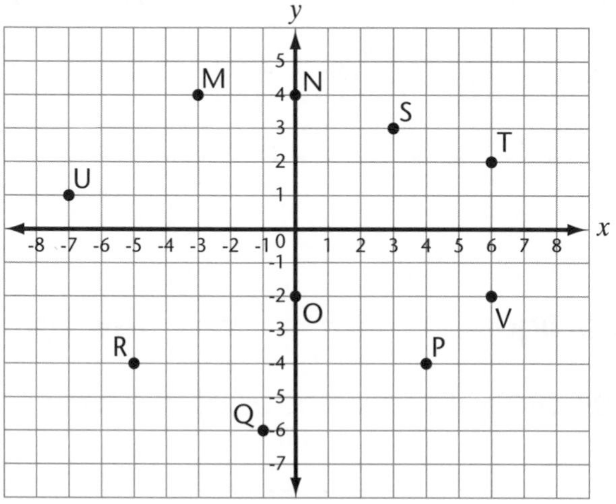

M ______ N ______
O ______ P ______
Q ______ R ______
S ______ T ______
U ______ V ______

5.

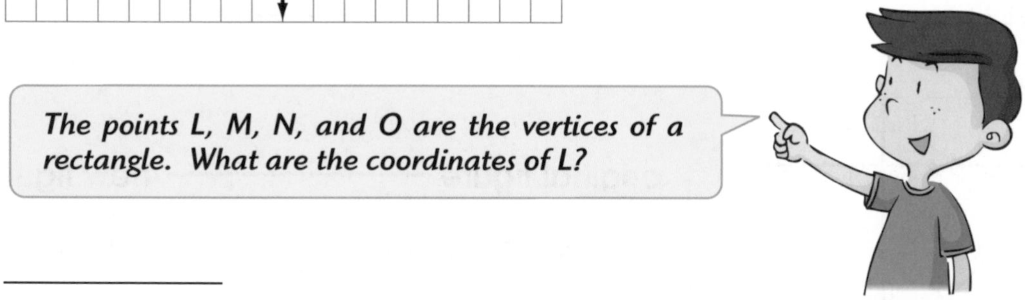

______

6. Name the polygon formed by OPQR: ______

Plot the points. Draw lines to complete each symmetrical polygon and write the coordinates of the missing vertices.

7.

Square	**Pentagon**	**Rectangle**
(-1,2)	(-1,-1)	(-2,-6)
(-5,1)	(2,1)	(-2,1)
(-4,-3)	(5,-1)	(3,1)
	(4,-4)	

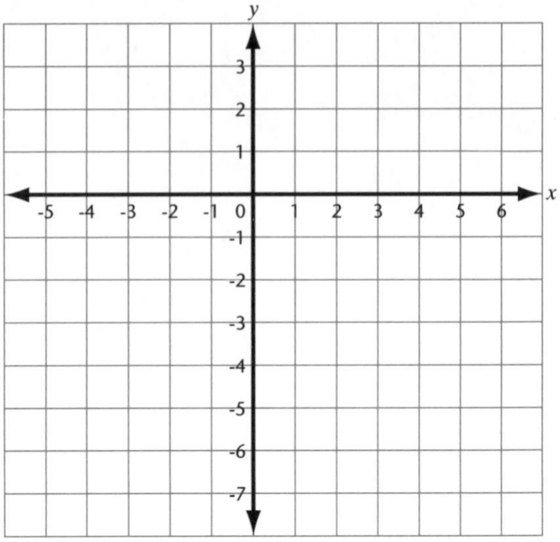

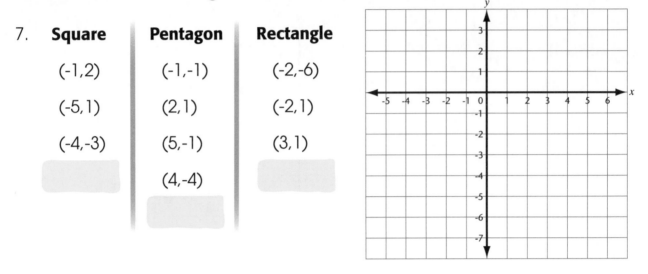

Complete and draw a similar figure of each shape with the help of the dotted lines. Then write "enlarge" or "shrink" in the coloured box and the coordinates of the vertices of the new figure.

8.

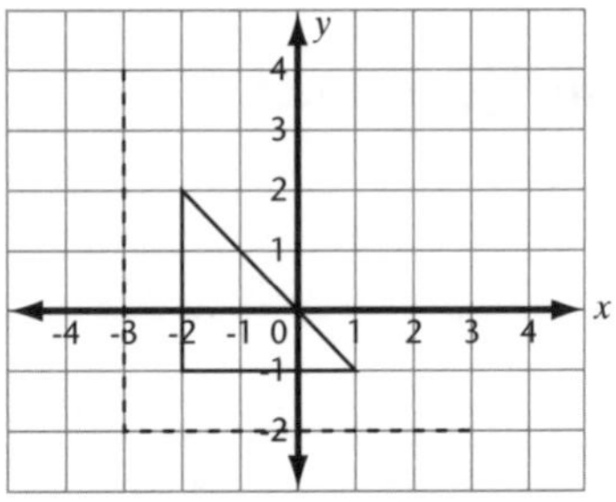

original figure ⟶ **new figure**

coordinates of the vertices of the new figure:

____

9.

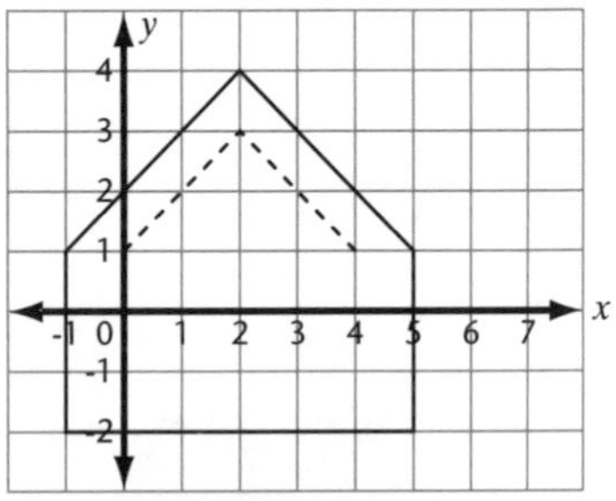

original figure ⟶ **new figure**

coordinates of the vertices of the new figure:

____

10.

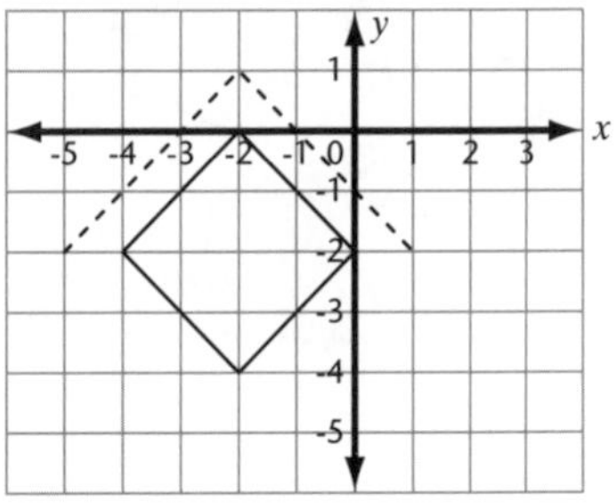

original figure ⟶ **new figure**

coordinates of the vertices of the new figure:

____

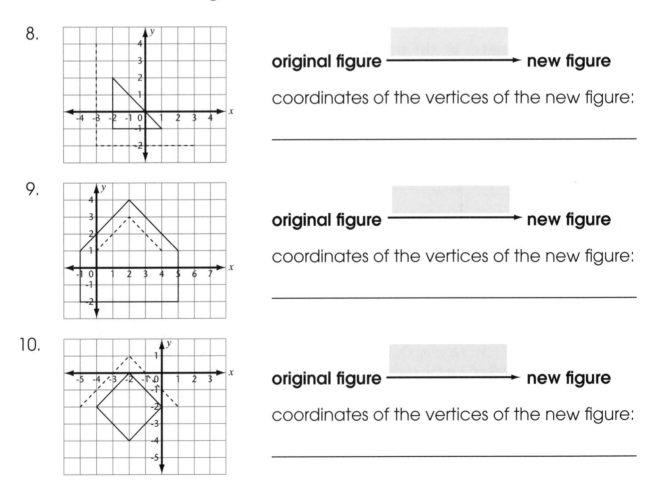

Plot the points on the grid and find the coordinates. Then answer the questions.

11.

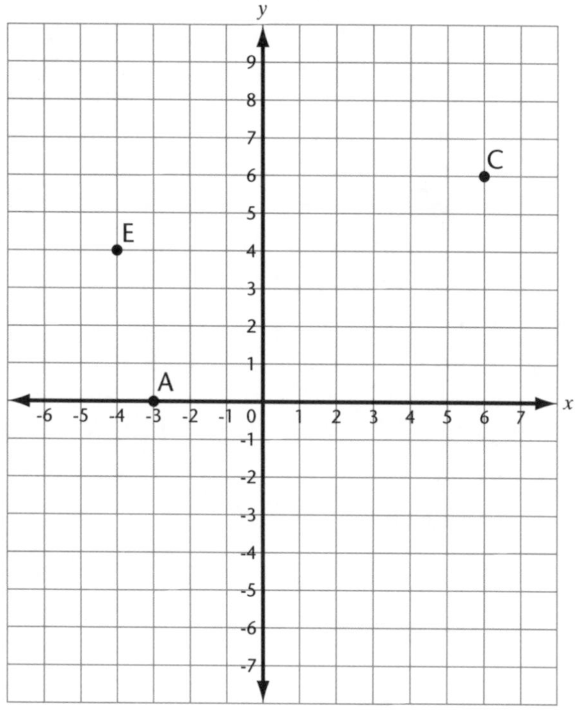

B________

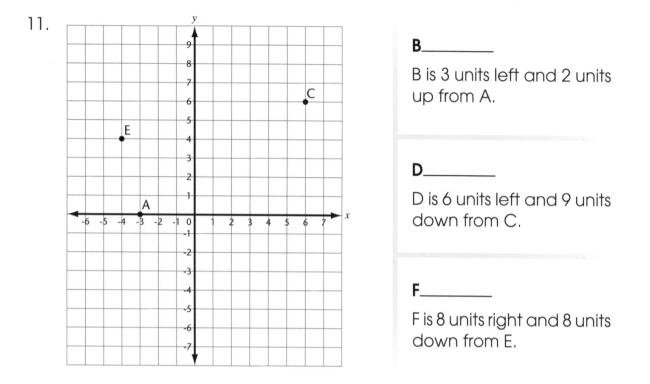

B is 3 units left and 2 units up from A.

D________

D is 6 units left and 9 units down from C.

F________

F is 8 units right and 8 units down from E.

12. Draw a line to join A and B, C and D, and E and F.

13. Is the point (-4,1) on line AB? ________

14. Is the point (3,-3) on line EF? ________

15. Write the coordinates of any three points that are on line CD.

____

16. ***Write the coordinates of any three points that are on line EF. Then describe the pattern the points follow.***

____

____

____

Transformations

- identify each of the three transformations
- transform figures and draw images
- describe simple transformations
- follow steps to draw images
- describe combined transformations
- complete and describe tiling design

Rotate a $\frac{1}{4}$ turn clockwise
STOP
STOP
This stop sign was damaged by the gusty winds yesterday. It's now showing a $\frac{1}{4}$ turn clockwise.

Identify each transformation. Write "translation", "reflection", or "rotation" on the line.

1. 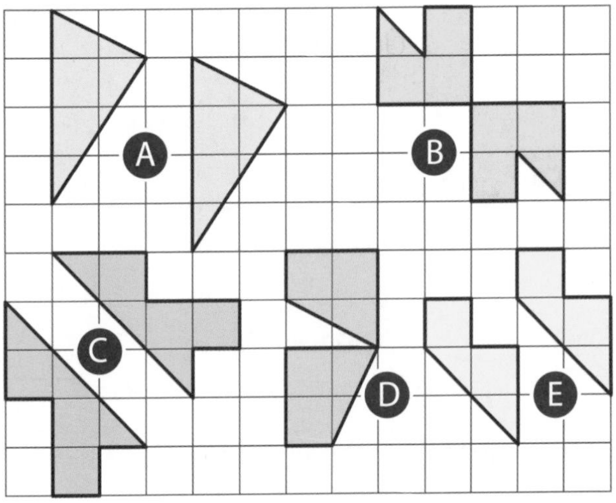

A ______________

B ______________

C ______________

D ______________

E ______________

Each labelled figure is the image of the figure in the centre. Identify each transformed image. Write the letter.

2. 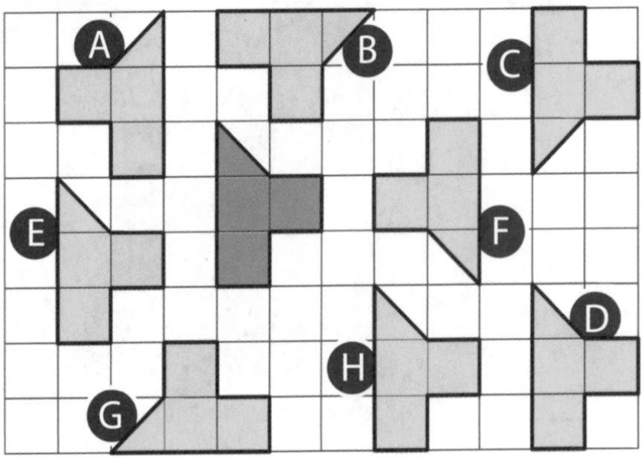

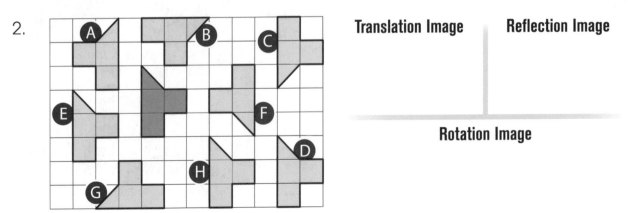

Translation Image	Reflection Image

Rotation Image

Draw the missing sides to complete the images. Then draw images for the other figures.

3. Translate each figure 2 units right and 3 units up.

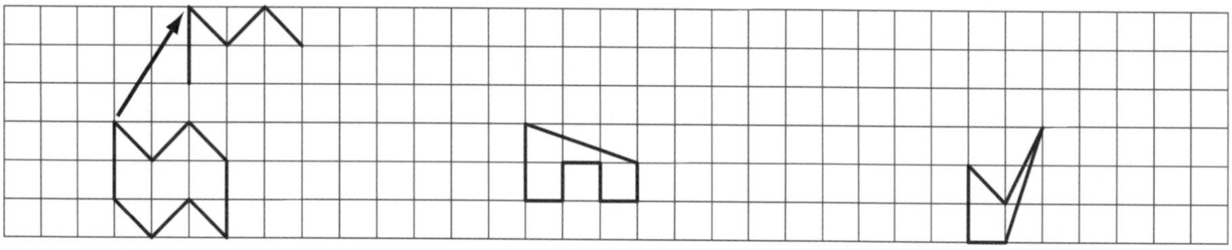

4. Rotate the first, second, and last figure a $\frac{1}{4}$ turn clockwise, $\frac{1}{2}$ turn, and $\frac{3}{4}$ turn clockwise at points P, Q, and R respectively.

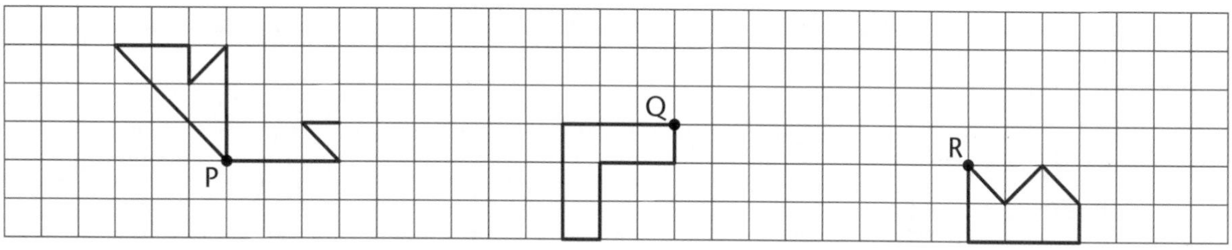

5. Flip the figures over the lines.

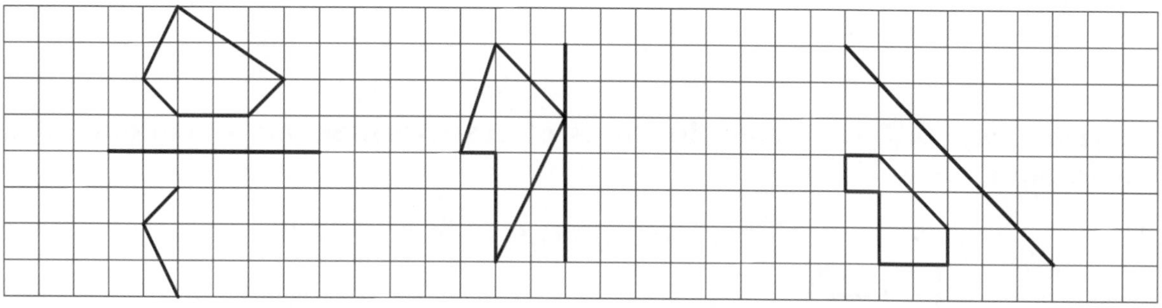

Identify and describe each transformation. Draw points, lines, or arrows in the diagram if needed.

6.

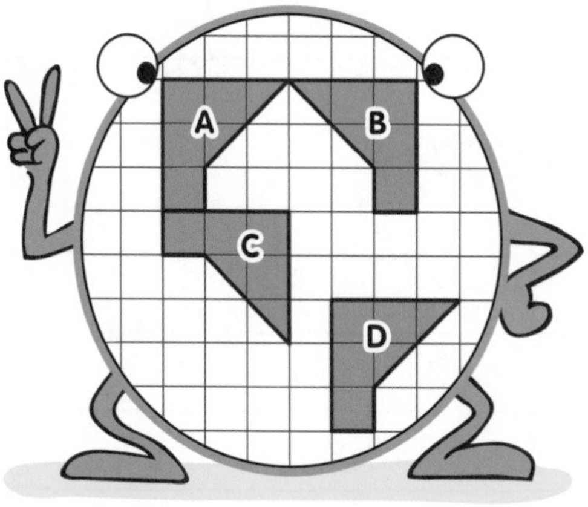

A → B: ______________________

____

A → C: ______________________

____

A → D: ______________________

____

Follow the steps to draw images.

7.
- Reflect A in line K. Label the image B.
- Translate B 3 units left and 6 units up. Label the image C.
- Rotate C a $\frac{1}{4}$ counterclockwise turn about point M. Label the image D.

8.
- Rotate P a $\frac{1}{4}$ clockwise turn about point O. Label the image W.
- Translate W 3 units up and 5 units right. Label the image X.
- Reflect image over line L. Label the image Y.

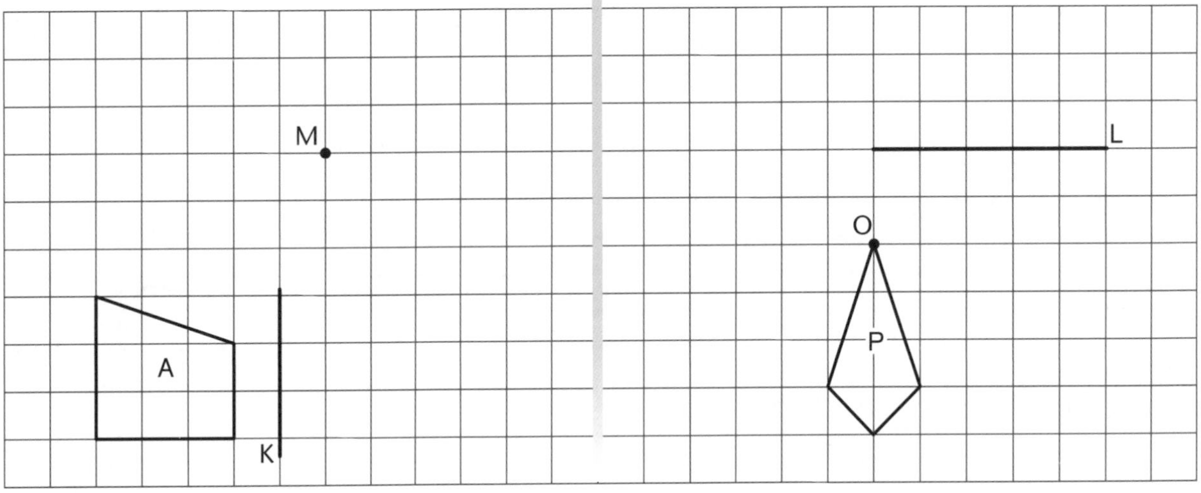

Describe two different combinations of transformations that could result in the images.

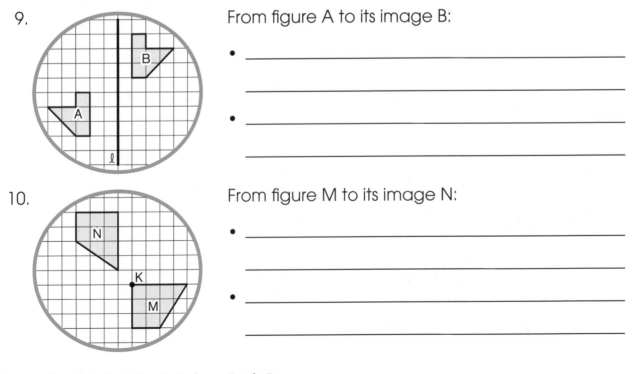

9.

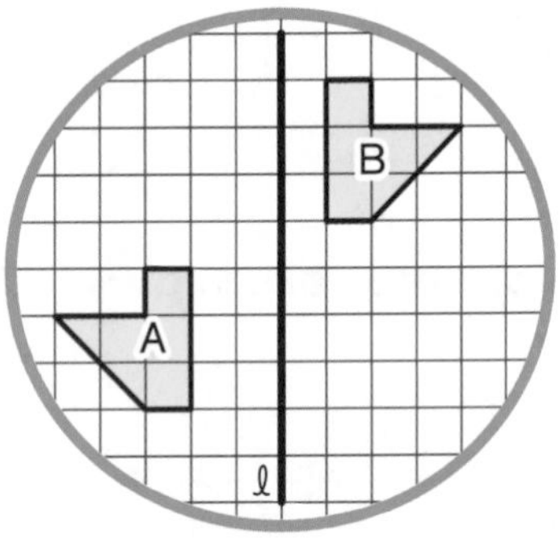

From figure A to its image B:

- ______________________________
  ____
- ______________________________
  ____

10.

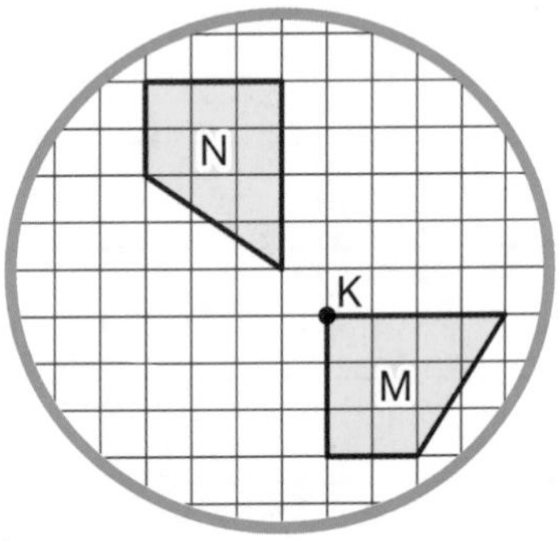

From figure M to its image N:

- ______________________________
  ____
- ______________________________
  ____

Can each coloured figure tile the plane by itself? If it can, put a check mark in the circle; otherwise, put a cross. Then complete the tile pattern on the grid.

11.

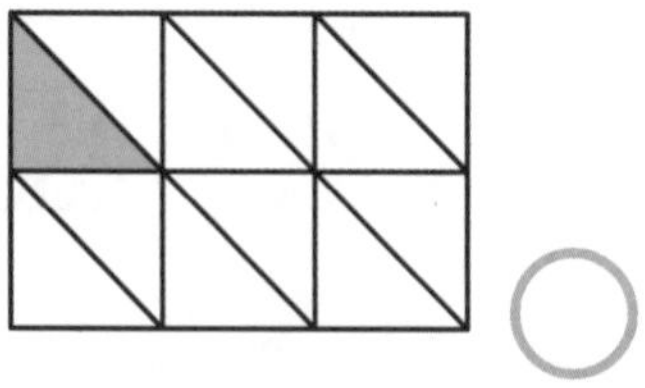

12.

13.

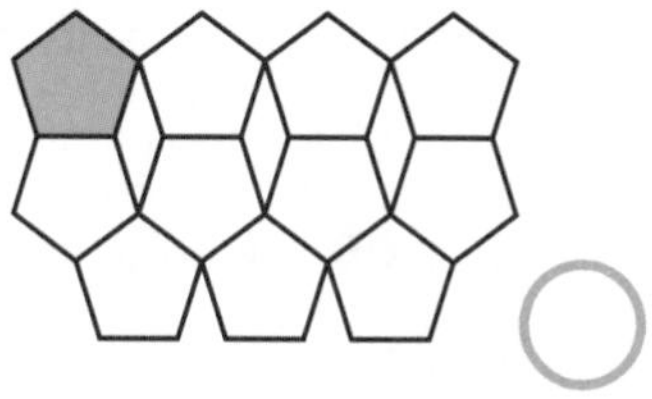

14.

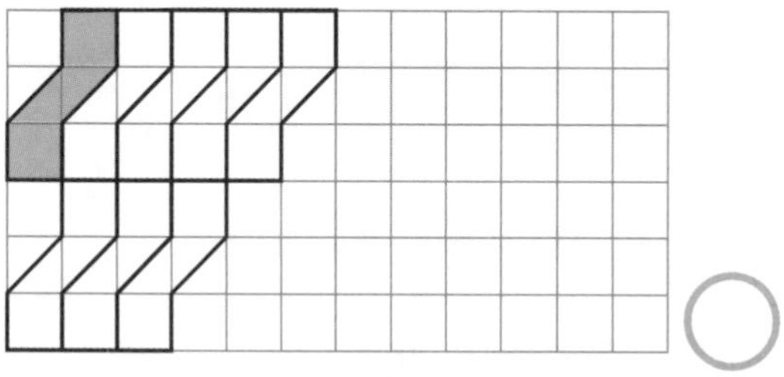

15.

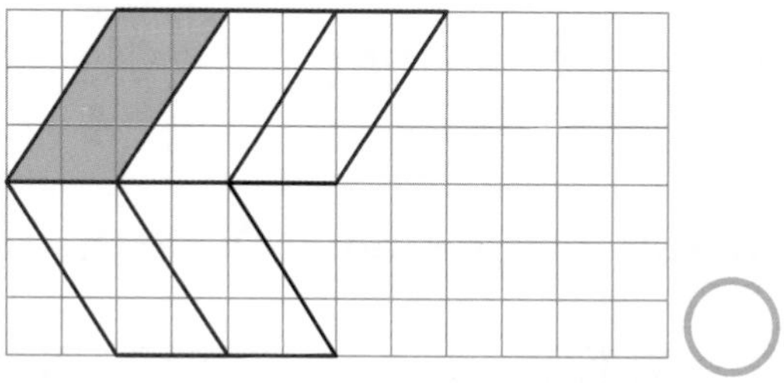

Complete the design and describe the transformations. Then complete the description of the design.

16.

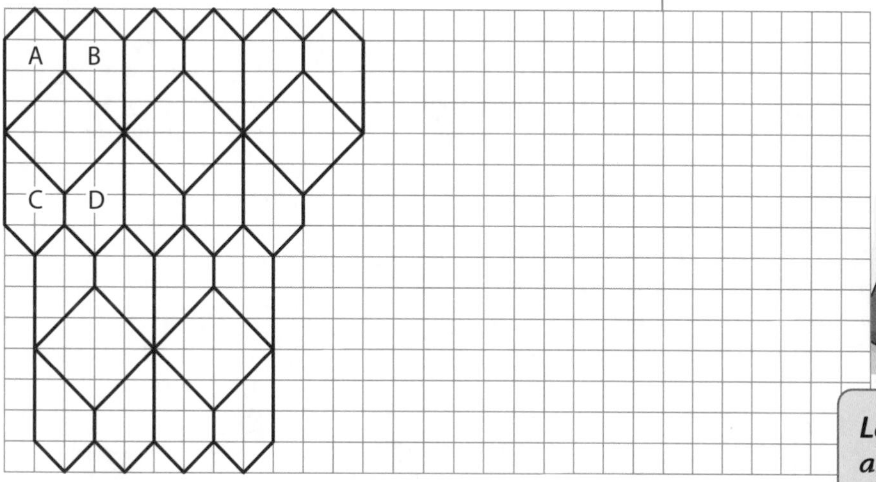

A → B: A is reflected in a vertical line along its ________ side to make B.

A & B → C & D: ____

Description of the design:

____

____

____

19

Patterning

- identify the core in a pattern
- find terms in a pattern
- find and write pattern rules
- relate term numbers to their terms
- make a graph to show the pattern

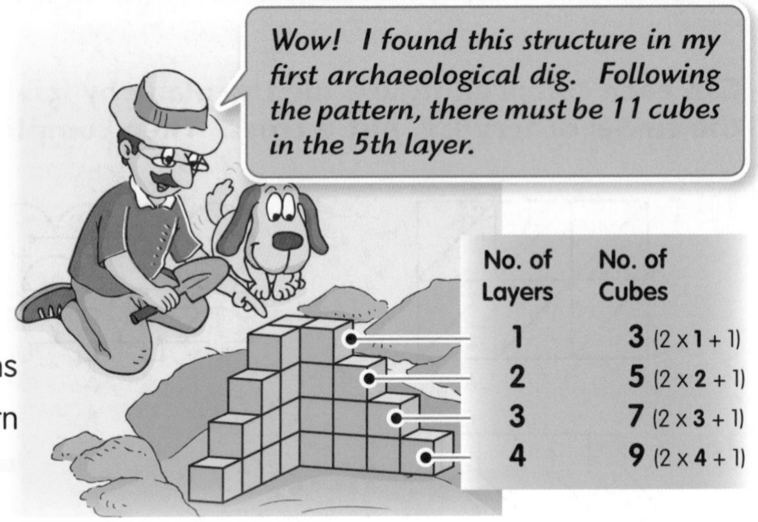

Wow! I found this structure in my first archaeological dig. Following the pattern, there must be 11 cubes in the 5th layer.

No. of Layers	No. of Cubes
1	3 (2 x 1 + 1)
2	5 (2 x 2 + 1)
3	7 (2 x 3 + 1)
4	9 (2 x 4 + 1)

Look at each pattern. Circle the core. Then answer the questions.

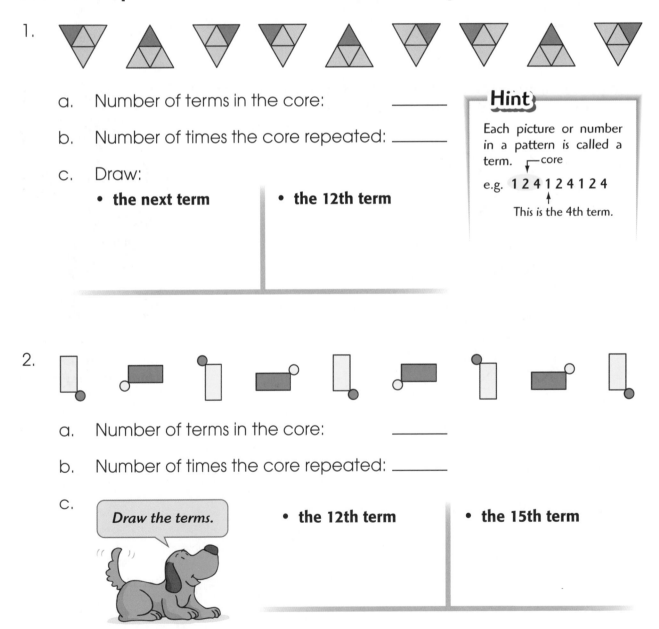

1. 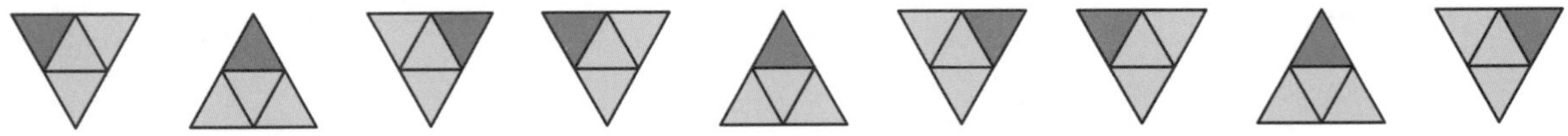

   a. Number of terms in the core: ______

   b. Number of times the core repeated: ______

   c. Draw:

   - **the next term**
   - **the 12th term**

Hint

Each picture or number in a pattern is called a term.

e.g. 1 2 4 1 2 4 1 2 4 (core: 1 2 4)

This is the 4th term.

2. 

   a. Number of terms in the core: ______

   b. Number of times the core repeated: ______

   c. 

Draw the terms.

   - **the 12th term**
   - **the 15th term**

Finding terms in a pattern:

ADKADKADK...

There are 3 terms in the core.

Steps:

1. The last term in each repeated core is K. (AD**K**AD**K**AD**K**...)
2. Compare the term number, 19, with the multiples of 3.

   Multiples of 3: 3, 6, 9, 12, 15, 18, 21...

   Since the 18th term is the last term in the core, the 19th term must be the first term in the core.

So, the 19th term is "A".

Look at each pattern. Describe the pattern and find the terms.

3. **4 A K M 4 A K M 4 A K M...**

The core of the pattern: ____________

No. of terms in a core: ______

Multiples of 4: ____________

Pattern: Every ______ terms is M.

- the 20th term: ______
- the 31st term: ______
- the 40th term: ______
- the 53rd term: ______

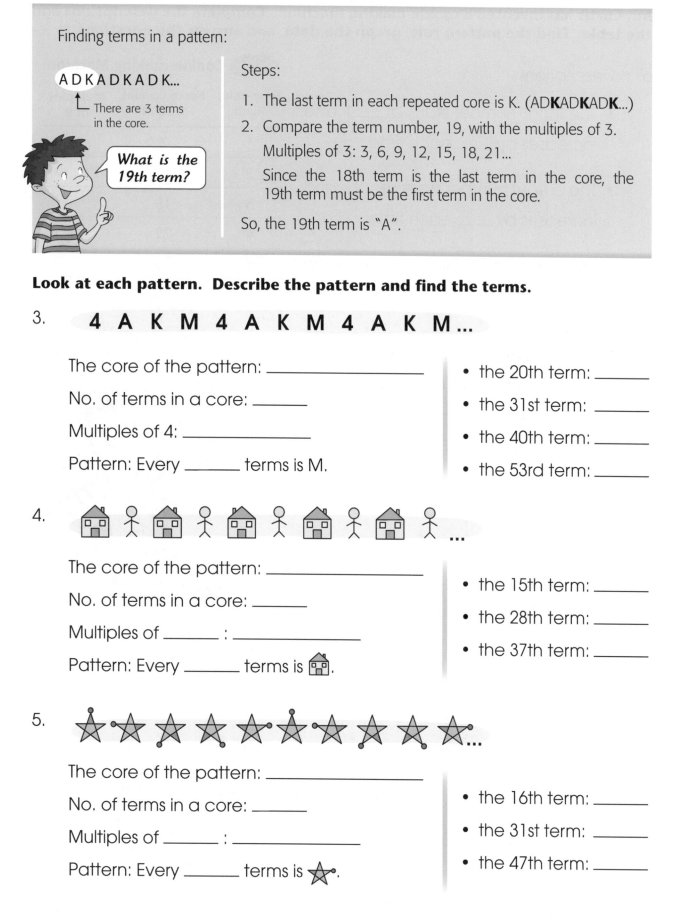

4. 

The core of the pattern: ____________

No. of terms in a core: ______

Multiples of ______ : ____________

Pattern: Every ______ terms is .

- the 15th term: ______
- the 28th term: ______
- the 37th term: ______

5. 

The core of the pattern: ____________

No. of terms in a core: ______

Multiples of ______ : ____________

Pattern: Every ______ terms is .

- the 16th term: ______
- the 31st term: ______
- the 47th term: ______

Mr. Curtis has invented a cookie-making machine. Complete the descriptions and the table. Find the pattern rule, graph the data, and answer the questions.

6. Descriptions:

- The input number starts at ____ and increases by ____ each time.
- The output number starts at ____ and increases by ____ each time.
- Each output number is ____ less than ____ times the input number.

Cookie-making Machine

Time (min) Input	No. of Cookies Output	Multiples of 8
1	3	8
2	11	
3	19	
4	27	
5	35	
6	43	

Compare the output number with multiples of 8.

So, the pattern rules for this pattern is "Multiply the input number by ____ , then minus ____ ."

Output number = Input number x ____ – ____

7.

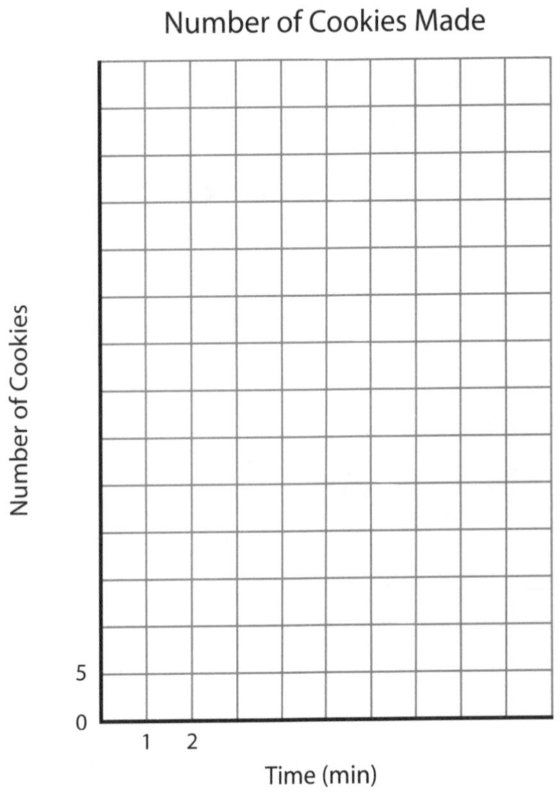

8. No. of cookies made in

- 8 minutes: ________
- 10 minutes: ________
- 15 minutes: ________

9. Time taken to make

- 67 cookies: ________
- 83 cookies: ________

Look at each pattern. Write descriptions and find the pattern rule. Then complete the table and find the terms.

10. a.

Input	Output
1	4
2	7
3	10
4	13
5	
6	

Descriptions:

- Each output number ______ (increases/decreases) by ____ each time.
- Compare the output number with multiples of ____ . Each output number is ____ more than ____ times the input number.

Pattern rule:

Output number = ____ x Input number + ____

b. Input: 15 Output: ______ | Input: 19 Output: ______ | Input: 24 Output: ______ | Input: 35 Output: ______

11. a.

Input	Output
1	3
2	7
3	11
4	15
5	
6	

Descriptions:

Pattern rule:

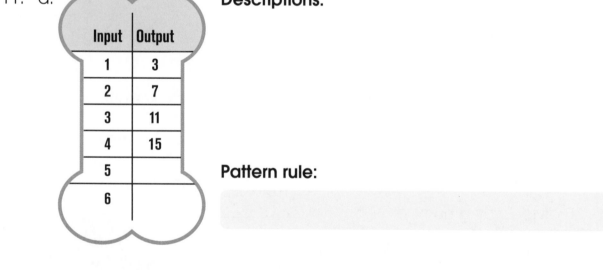

b. *The input number is the number of digs, and the output number is the number of bones found. How many bones will be found in the 20th dig?*

____

Algebraic Expressions (1)

- match algebraic expressions with statements
- identify and write algebraic expressions for different situations
- evaluate expressions
- solve problems by evaluating expressions

Match each algebraic expression with the correct statement.

1.	A number increased by 7	$6x$
	6 times a number	$8 - z$
	A number subtracted from 8	$y + 7$
	A number divided by 5	$n - 9$
	A number multiplied by $\frac{1}{2}$	$m \div 5$
	9 less than a number	$u \times \frac{1}{2}$

Write an algebraic expression for each statement. Use the variable n.

2. Triple a number ____________
3. 4 less than a number ____________
4. 50 divided by a number ____________
5. A number increased by 9 ____________
6. A number divided by 2 ____________
7. 11 more than a number ____________
8. The difference between 5 and a number

____

Check Jenny's algebraic expressions. Put a check mark in the space provided if it is correct; otherwise, write the correct expression.

	 's expressions	Check
9. 6 times a number, then add 7.	$7x + 6$	
10. Take away 2 from the sum of 5 and a number.	$2 + x - 5$	
11. 15 less than 3 times a number.	$3x - 15$	
12. Divide 10 by a number and double it.	$x \div 10 \times 2$	
13. Subtract 4 from twice a number.	$4 - 2x$	
14. Add 8 to half a number.	$\frac{x}{2} + 8$	
15. Divide a number by 3 and add 5.	$5 + \frac{x}{3}$	

Circle the correct algebraic expression for each situation.

16. m slices of pizzas cost: $\$3m$ $\$\frac{m}{3}$

17. Cost of a slice of pizza and a bowl of soup:

    $\$(3n)$ $\$(3 + n)$

18. The cost of a plate of pasta is k times the cost of a slice of pizza. How much is a plate of pasta?

    $\$(3 + k)$ $\$(3k)$

19. Jane and her sister buy a plate of pasta and share the cost. How much does each girl pay?

    $\$(\frac{3k}{2})$ $\$(3k) \times 2$

Write an algebraic expression for each situation.

20. The temperature rises at a rate of y°C per hour. What will the temperature be

  a. at 2:00 p.m.? ________

  b. at 3:00 p.m.? ________

21. What was the temperature an hour ago?

____

22. Joe has applied sunblock twice. Each time he uses p mL. How much sunblock does he have left?

____

23. Amy applies 5 mL more than twice the amount of sunblock that Joe applies each time. How much sunblock does Amy use each time?

____

Evaluate each expression by replacing the variable with the given value.

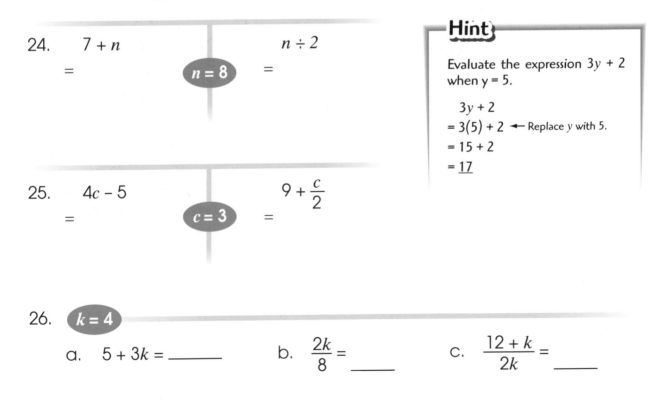

24. $n = 8$

$7 + n$
$=$

$n \div 2$
$=$

25. $c = 3$

$4c - 5$
$=$

$9 + \frac{c}{2}$
$=$

Hint

Evaluate the expression $3y + 2$ when $y = 5$.

$3y + 2$
$= 3(5) + 2$ ← Replace y with 5.
$= 15 + 2$
$= \underline{17}$

26. $k = 4$

  a. $5 + 3k =$ ______

  b. $\frac{2k}{8} =$ ______

  c. $\frac{12 + k}{2k} =$ ______

Evaluate each expression by substituting the numbers 0 to 4 for n.

27. $8n + 2$

Input n		Output $8n + 2$
0	8(0) + 2	

28. $n - n \div 2$

Input n		Output $n - n \div 2$

Each girl has written an algebraic expression for the money that she put into her piggy bank each week. Evaluate each expression by substituting the numbers 1 to 4 for n. Then answer the questions.

29. Jenny: $\$(4 + 7n)$

n	$\$(4 + 7n)$
1	
2	
3	
4	

Erica: $\$(6n - 4)$

n	$\$(6n - 4)$

Stella: $\$(12 - 2n)$

n	$\$(12 - 2n)$

30. Describe the savings pattern of each girl.

Jenny: ______________________

Erica: ______________________

Stella: ______________________

31. *This piggy bank has the money you saved in weeks 6 and 7. Do you know how much you have saved?*

____

Algebraic Expressions (2)

- evaluate algebraic expressions to complete charts
- make graphs with algebraic expressions
- model real-life problems with algebraic expressions
- solve problems with algebraic expressions

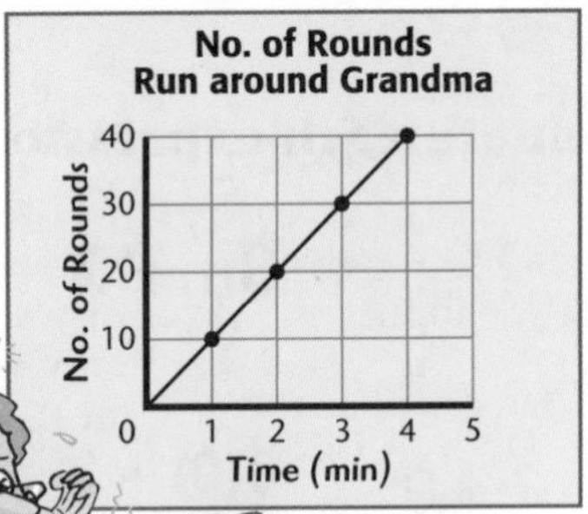

Grandma, I can run at a constant rate. My rate is 10 rounds per minute.

Complete the tables and graph the data. Then answer the questions.

1. 

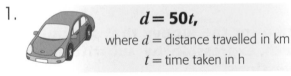

$d = 50t$,
where d = distance travelled in km
t = time taken in h

Time t	Distance Travelled $d = 50t$
1	
2	
3	
4	

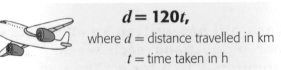

$d = 120t$,
where d = distance travelled in km
t = time taken in h

Time t	Distance Travelled $d = 120t$
1	
2	
3	
4	

2. **The Journey of Different Means of Transport**

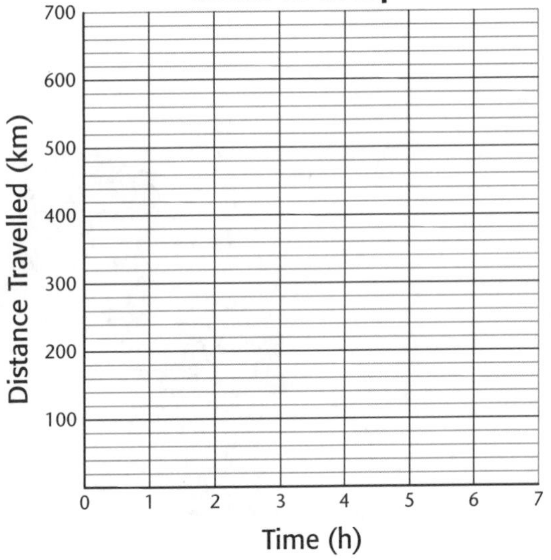

3. How far will the car travel in 6 h?

____

4. How long will it take the airplane to travel 660 km?

____

5. Describe the constant rate of the airplane.

____

____

The children participate in the regional newspaper distribution program. Find their earnings and graph the data. Then answer the questions.

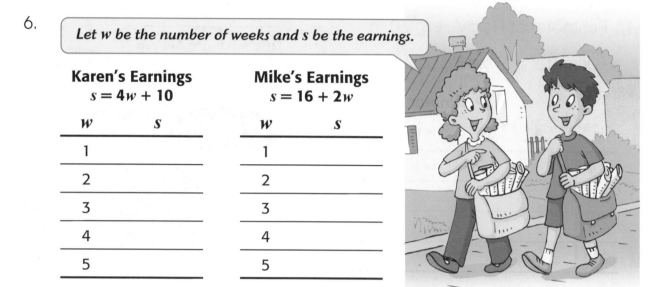

6. *Let w be the number of weeks and s be the earnings.*

Karen's Earnings
$s = 4w + 10$

w	s
1	
2	
3	
4	
5	

Mike's Earnings
$s = 16 + 2w$

w	s
1	
2	
3	
4	
5	

7. **Children's Earnings**

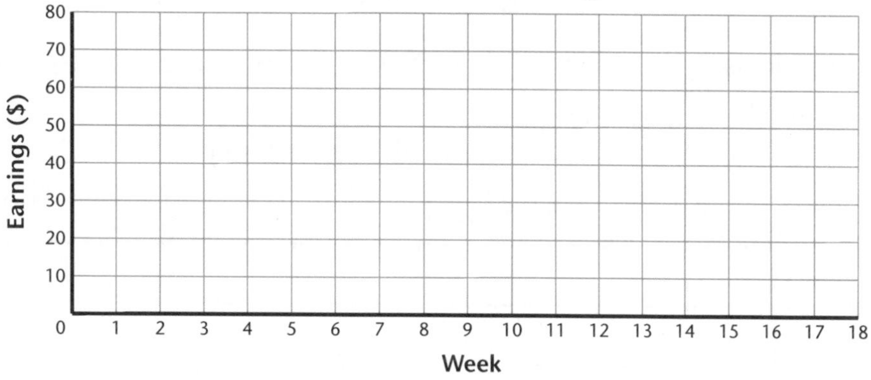

8. How much does each child earn in week 11?

Karen: ________ Mike: ________

9. Is there an intersection point on the graph? If so, what does it represent?

____

____

10. Whose pattern of earnings would you prefer if you could participate in the regional newspaper distribution program? Why?

____

____

Write an algebraic expression for each situation. Complete the tables and answer the questions.

11. Perimeter of Field A: (s) m

Perimeter of Field B: ______________

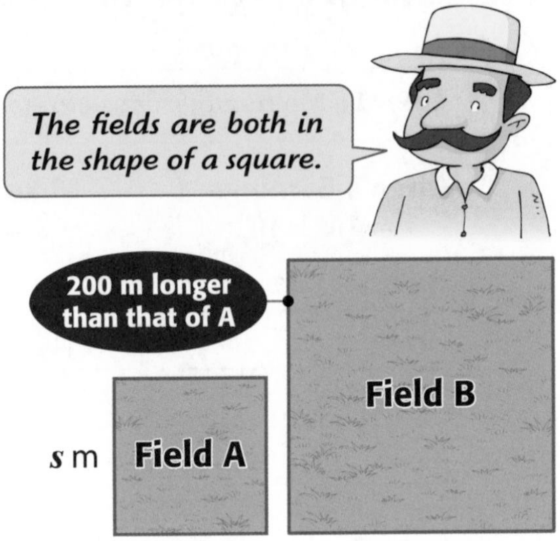

Perimeter (m)

s	A (s)	B ( )
400		
500		
600		
700		

12. Each metre of fencing costs \$$y$ and the labour fee per field is \$480.

a. If the side length of Field A is 600 m, how much is needed to fence each field?

Cost of Fencing (\$)

y	A (+)	B ( )
3		
4		
5		
6		

b. If the side length of Field B is 700 m, how much is needed to fence each field?

Cost of Fencing (\$)

y	A ( )	B ( )
3		
4		
5		
6		

Write expressions and complete the table. Then make a graph to show the total cost of admission and answer the question.

13. Write an expression for the total cost of m visits for each kind of membership.

    General: $ (________________)

    Silver: ________________

    Gold: ________________

14. Find the total costs of the first four visits for general admission and membership admission.

Total Cost

Number of Visits	General $ ( )	Silver	Gold
1			
2			
3			
4			

15.

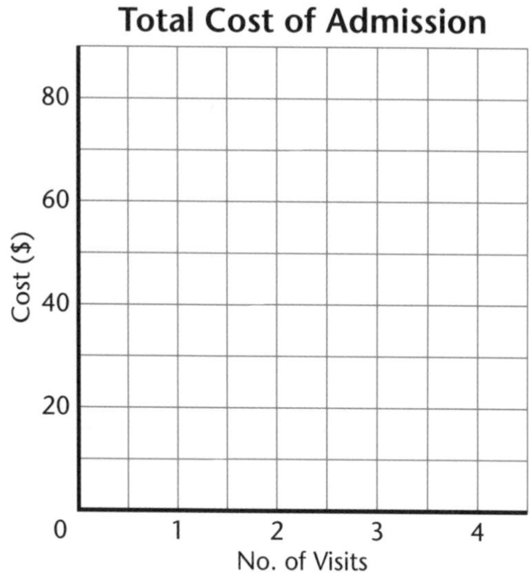

16. *Which type of admission should Jane choose if she plans to visit the waterpark 4 times this year? Explain.*

____

____

____

____

22

Equations

- match equations with statements
- write equations
- solve equations and check answers for different situations
- write appropriate situations to match equations

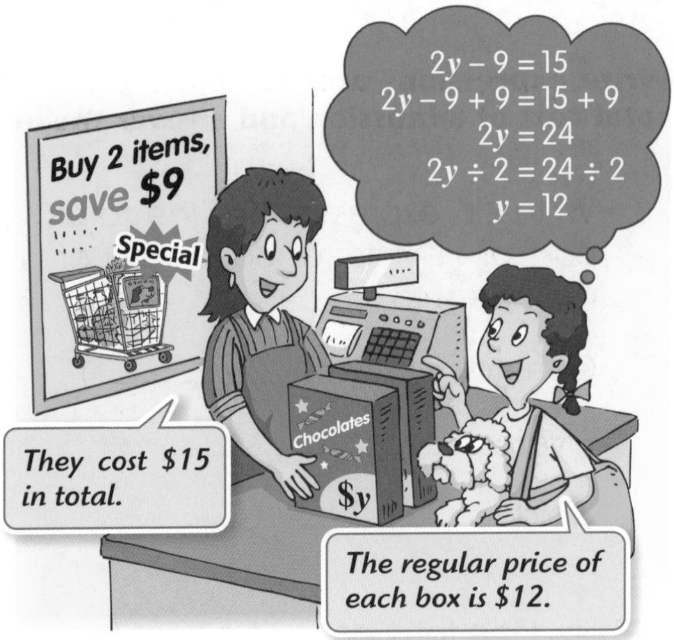

Match the equations with the correct statements.

1. $5x - 7 = 60$ •
   - 7 less than a number multiplied by 5 is 60.
   - 7 times a number decreased by 5 is 60.

2. $x \div 12 = 7$ •
   - A number divided by 12 equals 7.
   - 12 divided by a number equals 7.

3. $2 + 3x = 16$ •
   - 3 more than double a number is 16.
   - The sum of 2 and triple a number is 16.

Complete or write the equations for the sentences.

4. 18 divided by a number is 3. 18 ▢ ____ = ____
5. 21 less than a number is 20. y ▢ ____ = ____
6. A number increased by 5 is 34. ____ ▢ 5 = ____
7. Triple a number is 18. ________
8. One sixth of a number is 9. ________

Solve the equations by inspection.

9. $a + 8 = 12$ $a =$ ______
10. $s - 14 = 22$ $s =$ ______
11. $7x = 49$ $x =$ ______
12. $t \div 5 = 8$ $t =$ ______
13. $\frac{28}{k} = 14$ $k =$ ______
14. $\frac{n}{7} = 5$ $n =$ ______

Solve the equations. Show your work and check the answers.

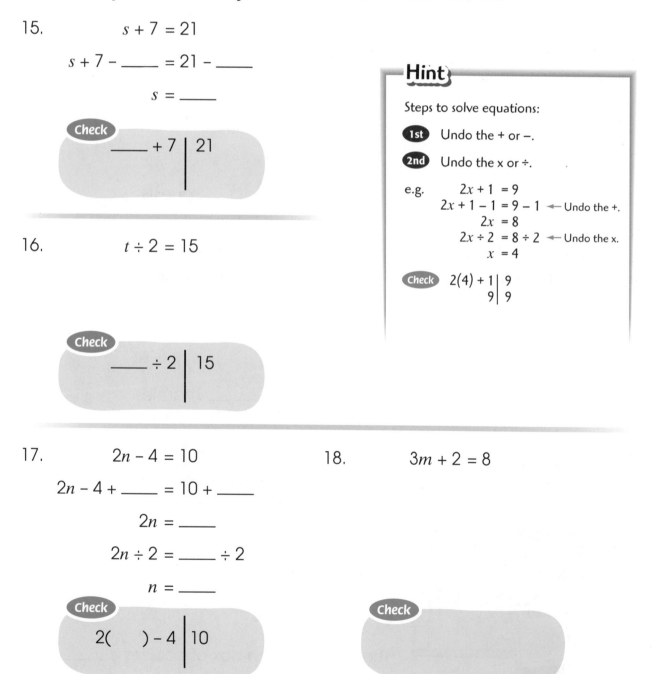

15. $s + 7 = 21$

$s + 7 -$ ____ $= 21 -$ ____

$s =$ ____

Check

____ $+ 7$ | 21

16. $t \div 2 = 15$

Check

____ $\div 2$ | 15

17. $2n - 4 = 10$

$2n - 4 +$ ____ $= 10 +$ ____

$2n =$ ____

$2n \div 2 =$ ____ $\div 2$

$n =$ ____

Check

$2(\quad) - 4$ | 10

18. $3m + 2 = 8$

Check

Hint

Steps to solve equations:

1st Undo the + or –.

2nd Undo the x or ÷.

e.g.

$$2x + 1 = 9$$
$$2x + 1 - 1 = 9 - 1 \leftarrow \text{Undo the +.}$$
$$2x = 8$$
$$2x \div 2 = 8 \div 2 \leftarrow \text{Undo the x.}$$
$$x = 4$$

Check

$2(4) + 1$	9
9	9

Check the correct equation to match each situation. Then solve it.

19. Build 7 identical towers with a box of 546 blocks. How many blocks are there in each tower?

(A) $546 + 7x = 0$

(B) $7x = 546$

(C) $x + 7 = 546$

There are ______ blocks in each tower.

20. The cost of renting a party room is \$20 and \$4 per guest. How many guests are there if the total cost is \$68?

(A) $4x - 68 = 20$

(B) $4 + 20x = 68$

(C) $4x + 20 = 68$

There are ______ guests.

21. The number of marbles that Irene has is 2 times the number of Tony's plus 17. If Irene has 89 marbles, how many marbles does Tony have?

(A) $2x + 17 = 89$

(B) $17 - 2x = 89$

(C) $2x - 89 = 17$

Tony has ______ marbles.

22. *I have paid \$54 for 6 boxes of cookies each with a \$1 off coupon. What is the price of each box of cookies before the coupon?*

(A) $6(y - 1) = 54$

(B) $6(y + 1) = 54$

(C) $54 = (1 - y)6$

The price of each box of cookies is ______ .

Write an appropriate statement to match each equation and picture.

23.

$6x = 24$

____

____

24.

$\frac{8 + n}{5} = 11$

____

____

Write an equation to describe each situation. Then solve it and check the answer.

25. The cost of a big tub of dog treats is 2 times that of a small one plus $3. If a big tub of treats costs $25, how much does a small tub of treats cost?

Let ____ be the cost of a small tub of treats.

2 ____ + ____ = ____

Check

A small tub of treats costs ________ .

26. *If Joey and I share a small tub and a big tub of treats, each of us will get 92 treats. How many treats are there in a small tub?*

Check

____

Data Management (1)

- identify discrete and continuous data
- classify primary and secondary data
- identify unbiased and biased questions
- determine whether sampling or census should be used
- record data in stem-and-leaf plot
- solve problems using given data

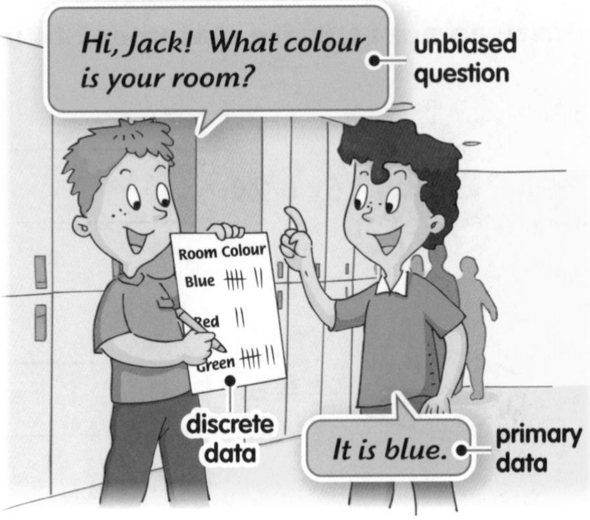

Tell whether the data collected in each situation is discrete or continuous.

1. the number of correct answers on a student's quiz __________

2. the height of a tree at a nursery __________

3. the weight of Josie's cat __________

4. the amount of air leaking from a balloon __________

5. the ages of a family's members __________

Describe what kind of data is collected by each child. Write "primary data" or "secondary data" on the lines.

I surveyed my classmates to find out the number of fruits they ate yesterday.
6. __________
I collected some data from the Internet and found that India has the fastest growing population.
7. __________
I found out that it took an average of 8 years for the doctors that I interviewed to get their medical degrees.
8. __________

Decide whether the survey questions are "biased" or "unbiased".

9.

I survey my friends on whether they prefer indoor or outdoor activities.

- Do you enjoy indoor activities more than outdoor activities? ____________
- Are you interested in indoor or outdoor activities? ____________
- Do you think it is more fun to play outdoors? ____________

10.

Let me ask my friends to see what subject they like the most.

- What is your favourite subject? ____________
- Is Science your favourite subject? ____________
- Which subject do you like the most: Science, English, or Social Studies? ____________

Decide whether you would study each situation below by "sampling" or "census".

11. the top five bestselling novels

____

12. the average height of a female

____

13. the amount of calories in a lemon

____

Hint

Sampling
a part of the population that we collect data from

Census
the data obtained from the entire population

e.g. Length of battery life - sampling
No. of people in the world - census

14. the lifespan of butterflies ____________

15. the illness related to most employees' sick leave at a company ____________

16. the average running speed of the 10 fastest runners in Canada ____________

Jason recorded the daily highest temperatures in June. Help him complete the tally chart and the bar graph. Then answer the questions.

17.

Temperature (°C)	Tally	Frequency
11 – 15		
16 – 20		

Daily Highest Temperatures (°C) in June

22	34	20	11	17	30
21	29	31	30	27	33
28	30	29	16	21	24
31	32	14	19	24	28
31	30	18	25	24	35

18. **Daily Highest Temperatures (°C) in June**

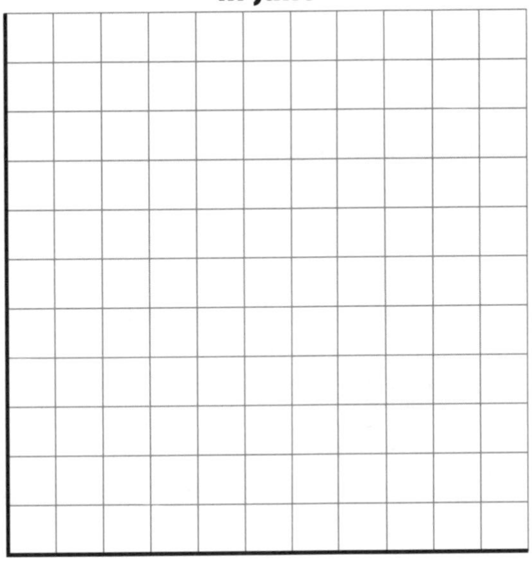

19. Describe the collected data with the help of the given terms.

____

20. What is the range of temperatures of most of the days in June?

____

21. If Jason puts the thermometer in a shed to collect data, do you think he will get the same result? Explain.

____

Read the stem-and-leaf plot. Answer the questions.

22. **Ages of the Drivers**

Stem	Leaf
1	8 8 9
2	0 1 4 7 7 8
3	1 2 4 6 6 6 9
4	2 2 5 5 5 8 8 8
5	0 1 3 3 7
6	2 3 3 5

a. ________ drivers were surveyed.

b. ________ drivers were between 16 and 25 years old.

c. The range of the drivers' ages is ________ years old.

Daven chose 35 data randomly from a record of the heights of 100 13-year-old children. Help him complete the stem-and-leaf plot and answer the questions.

23. **Heights (cm) of the Children**

Stem	Leaf
13	
14	
15	
16	
17	

Heights (cm) of the Children

139	142	161	136
157	157	164	135
161	150	164	159
152	170	158	154
158	162	155	167
159	164	153	130
	142	164	160
		155	147
		139	162
		158	172
		148	149

24. What is the range of the children's heights?

____

25. How many children are taller than 1.6 m?

____

26. *Is this a set of primary or secondary data? Explain.*

____

____

24

Data Management (2)

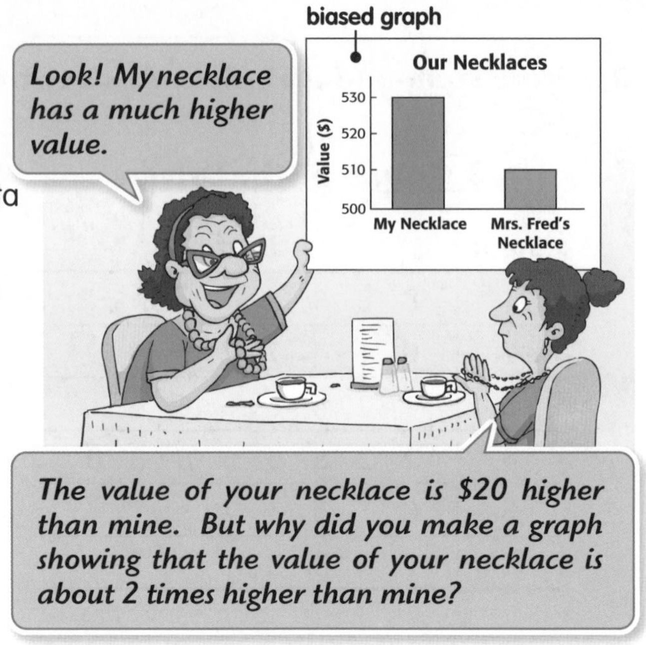
biased graph
Our Necklaces
Value ($)
530
520
510
500
My Necklace
Mrs. Fred's Necklace
Look! My necklace has a much higher value.
The value of your necklace is $20 higher than mine. But why did you make a graph showing that the value of your necklace is about 2 times higher than mine?

- plot and make a line graph with given data
- make a circle graph
- determine the most appropriate kind of graph to show different sets of data
- answer questions using information presented in graphs

Plot the points and draw lines to complete the line graph. Then answer the questions.

1. **Water Leaks from a Water Dispenser**

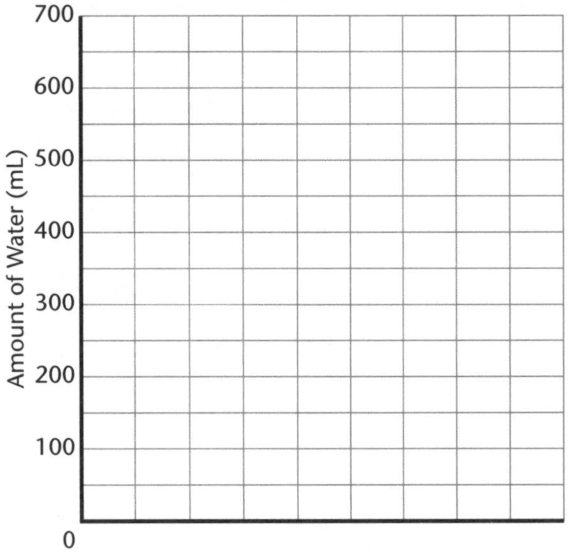
Amount of Water (mL)
700
600
500
400
300
200
100
0

Time (a.m.)	Amount of Water Collected (mL)
7:01	0
7:02	105
7:03	205
7:04	300
7:05	390
7:06	475
7:07	555
7:08	630

DOG

2. During which period of time was the most water collected? ____________

3. Was the water leaking at a constant rate? If not, describe the change in the rate.

____

____

4. Describe the trend. Predict the amount of water collected at 7:09 a.m.

____

Making Circle Graphs:

1st Find the size of the angle for each group.

2nd Graph each group in a circle graph using a protractor.

e.g.

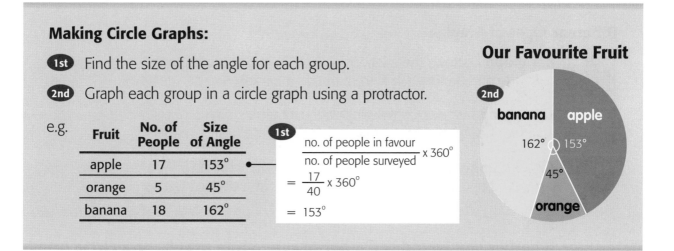

Fruit	No. of People	Size of Angle
apple	17	153°
orange	5	45°
banana	18	162°

1st

$\frac{\text{no. of people in favour}}{\text{no. of people surveyed}} \times 360°$

$= \frac{17}{40} \times 360°$

$= 153°$

Our Favourite Fruit

2nd

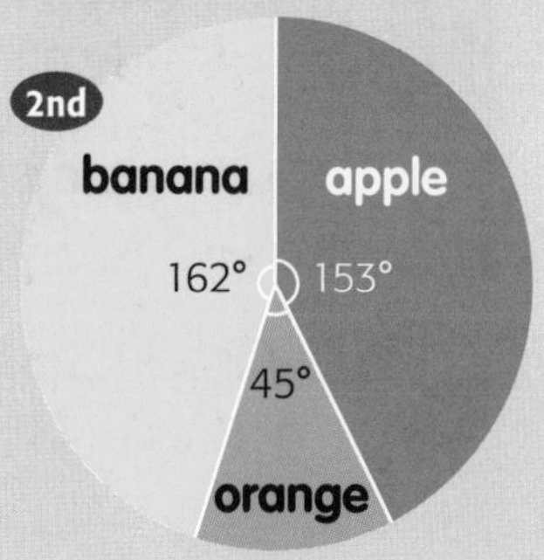

Joyce surveyed 30 students to see how they come to school. Help her complete the table and the circle graph. Then answer the questions.

5. **Ways to Come to School**

Means of Transport	No. of Students	Size of Angle
by bus	11	$\frac{11}{30} \times 360° =$ ____
by car	5	
by subway	1	
by bike	2	
on foot	9	
others	2	

6. *About what percent of the students go to school by bus or car?*

____

7. Write two sentences to describe the circle graph.

____

____

Different Types of Graphs:

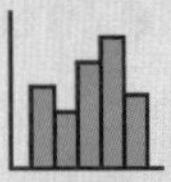

Bar graph – shows the relationship between 2 or more groups
e.g. the number of each kind of fruit in a basket

Line graph – shows continuous data over time
e.g. the height of a tree measured yearly in the past 5 years

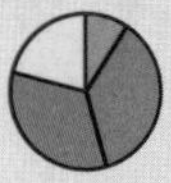

Circle graph – shows how a part relates to the whole
e.g. the population of different nationalities in a city

Determine whether you would use a bar graph, a line graph, or a circle graph to show the data in each situation. Then give an example to go with each type of graph.

8. ______
- the temperatures at different times in a day
- ______

9. ______
- the price of popsicles at different stores
- ______

10. ______
- the percent of different kinds of plants in a forest
- ______

Look at the graphs showing the height of a fertilized plant. Check the biased one and answer the questions.

11. (A)

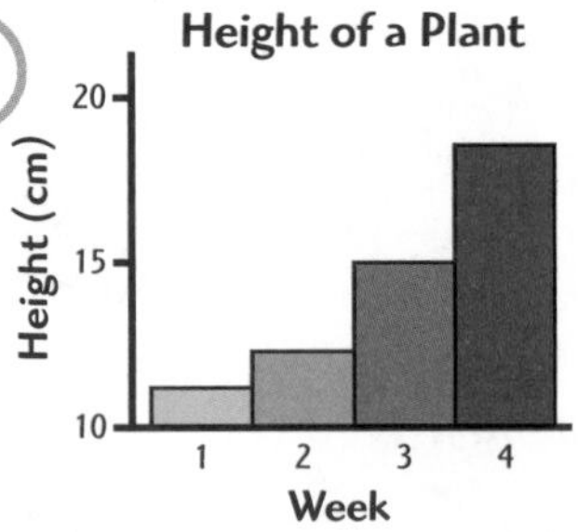

(B)

Hint

Biased graphs are misleading and usually do not start at 0 on the vertical axis.

12. *I'm the sales manager of fertilizers. Which graph do you think I should present to my customers? Why?*

______

______

Jackson is inflating a balloon. Follow the pattern to complete the table that shows the amount of air in the balloon at different times. Then answer the questions.

13.

Time Elapsed (s)	1	2	3	4	5	6	7
Amount of Air in the Balloon (cm^3)	70	220	370	520			

14. How long does it take Jackson to blow up the balloon?

I can hold 4570 cm^3 of air when I am fully inflated.

____

15. Which type of graph is the most appropriate to show the data? Explain your choice and make the graph to show the data.

____

____

You may use these words.
increase
decrease
upward
downward

16. Describe the trend of the graph.

____

____

25

Mean, Median, Mode

- define each central tendency
- identify the central tendency used
- determine which central tendency should be used in different situations
- find the mean, median, and mode
- record data in stem-and-leaf plots
- solve problems involving mean, median, and mode

You did a good job, Tim. Each of the mean, median, and mode of the times taken is around 12 s.

Sum of the data

Mean: 61 ÷ 5 = 12.2 (s)

In order:

11.8 s, 11.8 s, 12.3 s, 12.5 s, 12.6 s

Median: 12.3 s

Mode: 11.8 s

Write the meaning of each central tendency.

1. Central Tendency

Mean: ____________________

Median: ____________________

Mode: ____________________

Name which central tendency the children are talking about. Then find the value.

2.

Scores	
74	83
62	57

I added all the scores and divided the sum by 4.

__________ ; ____

3.

I told my mom the score that I got most of the time.

__________ ; ____

Scores	
81	64
53	80
72	64

My middle score is the same as that of the whole class.

__________ ; ____

Hint

If there are 2 middle values, find the average of these 2 values to get the median.

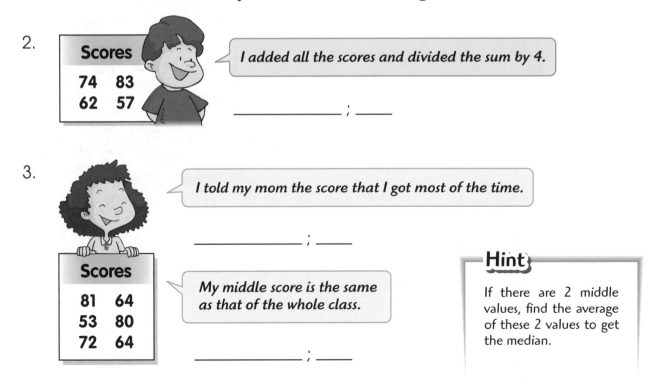

Write and explain which central tendency should be used in each situation.

4.

Amount of Funds Raised in 5 Events

mean: $567
median: $623
mode: $300

I want to let the community know that I am a successful fundraiser.

____

____

5.

Members' Ages

mean: 22 years old
median: 18 years old
mode: 20 years old

My club wants to attract new members who are around 20 years old.

____

____

Find the mean, median, and mode for the number of electronic devices sold at different stores. Solve the problems.

6.

Number of Computers Sold at 10 Stores

11	20	4	6	12
6	9	11	13	18

mean: ____________

median: ____________

mode: ____________

7.

I've collected data from 3 more stores. The new mean, median, and mode are shown. I've put all the data in order. What are the missing data?

NEW

mean: **11** tablets
median: **10** tablets
mode: **6** tablets

Number of Tablets Sold at 13 Stores

4 6 6 ____ 9 10 ____ 11 11 13 18 ____ 20

The children had a skipping contest. The tables below show the number of times the children skipped in one minute. Find the mean, median, and mode for each set of data. Then answer the questions.

8.

The Skipping Record of the Children in Mrs. Jenkin's Class

Stem	Leaf
11	0 1 3 3 4 5 7
12	2 3 4 4 4 8
13	1 1 5 9

_____ mean _____ median _____ mode

9.

The Skipping Record of the Children in Mrs. Winter's Class

Stem	Leaf
10	1 2 5 5
11	2 4 5 5 6 7
12	0 3 9
13	7 7 7 8

_____ mean _____ median _____ mode

10. The class with the higher mean wins. Which class won the contest?

_____

11. *If I want to reset the rule for winning this game, which central tendency should I refer to?*

_____

Record the data in the stem-and-leaf plot. Find the mean, median, and mode of the data.

12.

Children's Heights (cm)

Stem	Leaf

Children's Heights (cm)

154	162	140	147
152	170	154	163
159	154	162	145
143	163	169	152
158	146	175	150

13. Mean: _____ Median: _____ Mode: _____

See how many bags of marbles the children have. Help them find the mean, median, and mode. Then answer the questions.

14. *1 bag – 15 marbles each*
2 bags – 16 marbles each
4 bags – 18 marbles each

mean: ____ marbles

median: __________

mode: __________

15. *1 bag – 25 marbles each*
2 bags – 10 marbles each
3 bags – 15 marbles each
4 bags – 20 marbles each

mean: __________

median: __________

mode: __________

16. Jay has 8 bags of marbles with a mean of 18 marbles in each bag after Ann gave a bag of her marbles to him. How many marbles does Jay have now?

Jay now has ______ marbles.

Hint

Multiply the mean by the total number of groups to find the total.

mean x total no. of groups = the total

Solve the problems.

17. How many seconds did Tom take to run 5 laps if the mean time taken for each lap is 15.1 s?

Tom ran ______ seconds.

18. How many seconds did Tom run in the 5th lap if the mean time taken for the first 4 laps is 14.7 s?

Tom ran ______ seconds in the 5th lap.

Tom's Record

Lap	Time Taken (s)
1	12.9
2	13.1
3	15.8

26

Experimental Probability

- find relative frequency
- write relative frequency as fractions, decimals, and percents
- solve problems that involve relative frequency
- make circle graphs using relative frequency

They spin the spinner 100 times. It lands on "Bone" 15 times and "Fish" 85 times.

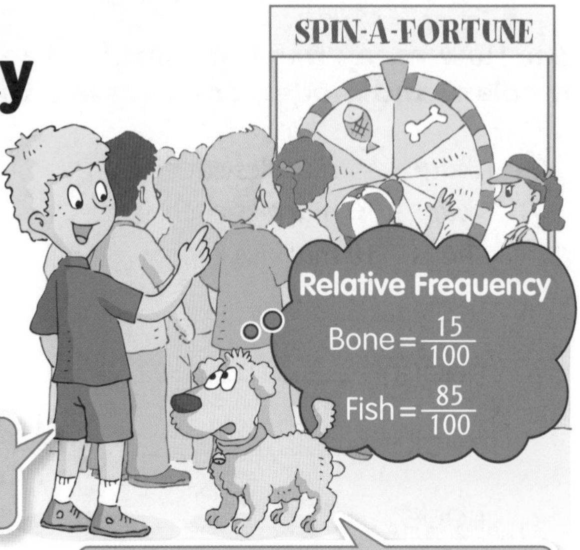

Well, the relative frequency of landing on "bone" is so low.

Joe tosses a coin. Find the relative frequency for each case.

1. **Toss 10 times** – heads: 7 and tails: 3

   Relative frequency of heads: ______

   Relative frequency of tails: ______

2. **Toss 50 times** – heads: 22 and tails: 28

   Relative frequency of heads: ______

   Relative frequency of tails: ______

Hint

Relative frequency is a ratio as described below:

$$\frac{\text{no. of successful outcomes}}{\text{total no. of trials}}$$

Look at the records. See how many times the children picked a ball from each box. Fill in the blanks and find the relative frequency for each kind of ball.

3. Mary's Record

Ball	No. of Times	Relative Frequency
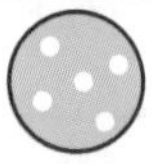	5	
	9	
	6	

Total: ______

4. Kevin's Record

Ball	No. of Times	Relative Frequency
red	6	
blue	9	
green		

Total: 30

Find the relative frequency for each case. Write the answers as fractions, decimals, and percents.

5. In a fair, some children are asked whether they like French fries, cotton candy, or corn on the cob.

	No. of Children
French fries	135
cotton candy	64
corn on the cob	81

Relative Frequency

a. French fries = ____________________

b. cotton candy = ____________________

c. French fries and cotton candy = ____________________

6. Lucy draws a ball from a bag and records the result.

	No. of Times
red	15
green	4
blue	1
yellow	45
white	20

Relative Frequency

a. red = ____________________

b. blue or yellow = ____________________

c. white or green = ____________________

d. not yellow = ____________________

Help Katie complete the table that shows the relative frequency for each number tossed. Then answer the question.

7. *The relative frequency for getting odd numbers is $\frac{12}{25}$.*

a dice labelled from 1 to 6

a.

Number Tossed	Relative Frequency
1	$\frac{3}{25}$
2	$\frac{5}{25}$
3	$\frac{4}{25}$
4	$\frac{2}{25}$
5	
6	

b. How many times did the dice land on each number?

1: ____ 2: ____ 3: ____

4: ____ 5: ____ 6: ____

c. What is the relative frequency for getting even numbers?

____

Find the passing rate for each subject. Write the answers in percents. Then answer the questions.

8.

	Number of Children		
	taking a test	passing the test	**Passing Rate**
Mathematics	31	27	
English	29	23	
Science	15	10	
History	28	23	
Geography	34	32	

Hint

You may use division to find the passing rate.

Passing rate

$= \frac{\text{No. of children passing the test}}{\text{No. of children taking the test}}$

9. Which subject has the highest passing rate? ____________

10. If Mr. Winston, the school principal, wants to offer an after school enrichment program to help the children, which subject should the program focus on? ____________

Look at the record. Find the relative frequency in decimals. Then answer the questions.

11.

Team / Result	Maple		St. Jacob	
	No. of Times	Relative Frequency	No. of Times	Relative Frequency
Win	18		15	
Loss	20		10	
Tie	5		9	

12. Which team has a better result? ____________

13. *If the Maples play 5 more games, how many games do they need to win to have a better result than the St. Jacobs? Show me your work.*

____

Identify and label the circle graphs that show the sales records of the salespersons. Then fill in the boxes with the relative frequencies in decimals.

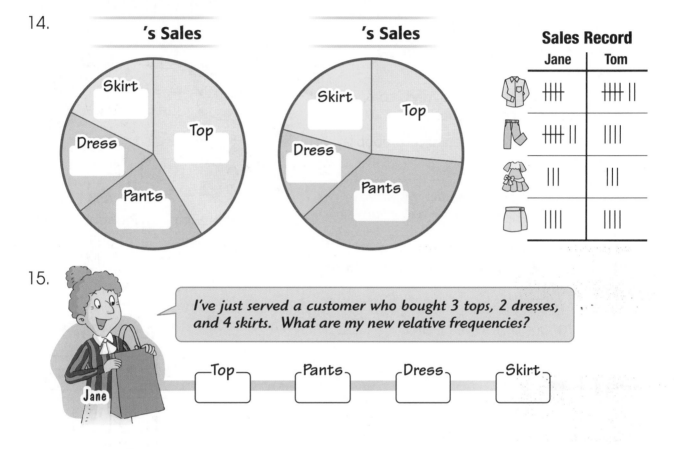

14.

's Sales

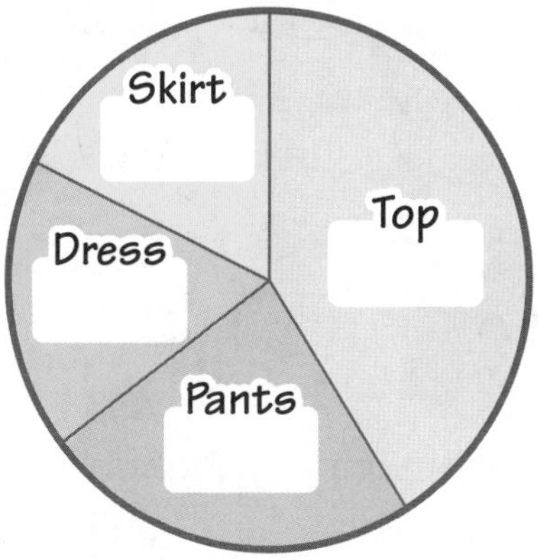

's Sales

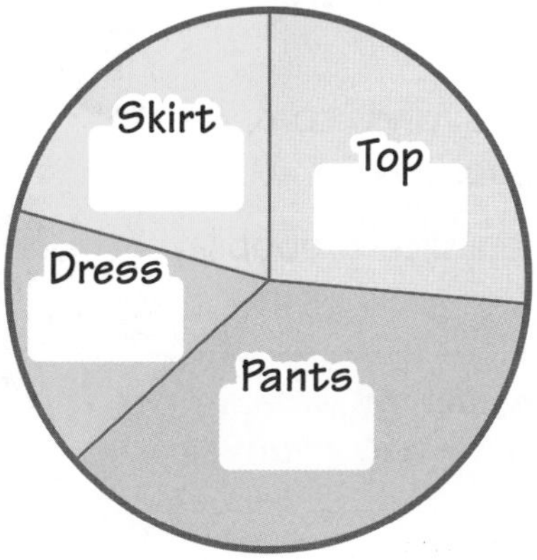

Sales Record

	Jane	Tom
	卌	卌 ||
	卌 ||	||||
	|||	|||
	||||	||||

15.

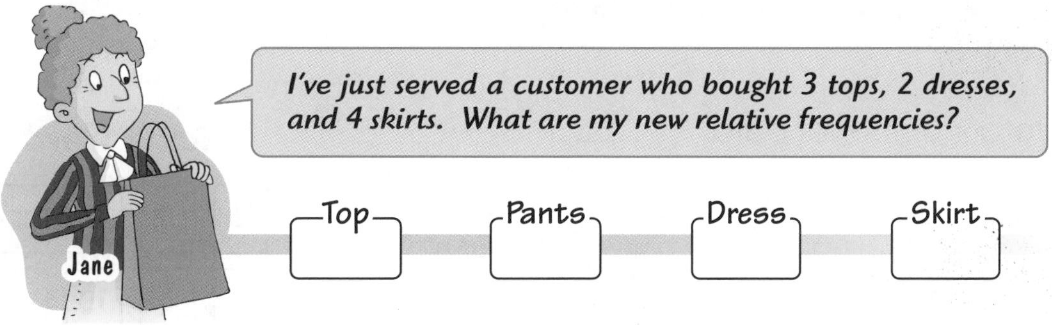

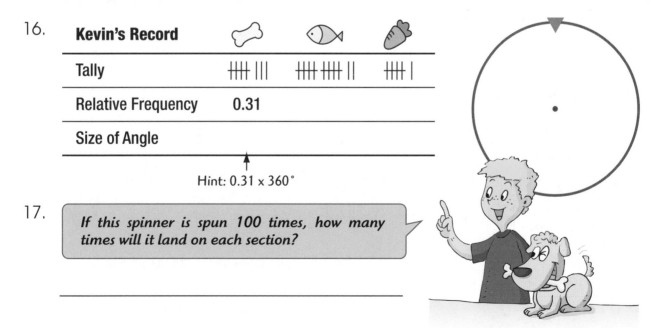

The table below records the results of spinning Kevin's spinner. Help Kevin complete the table and make a spinner that matches the result. Then answer the question.

16.

Kevin's Record	(bone)	(fish)	(carrot)
Tally	卌 |||	卌 卌 ||	卌 |
Relative Frequency	0.31		
Size of Angle			

Hint: 0.31 x 360°

17. *If this spinner is spun 100 times, how many times will it land on each section?*

____

Theoretical Probability

- find the probabilities of different events
- predict the number of times an event will occur
- find relative frequencies and compare them to theoretical probabilities
- solve problems using theoretical probability and prediction

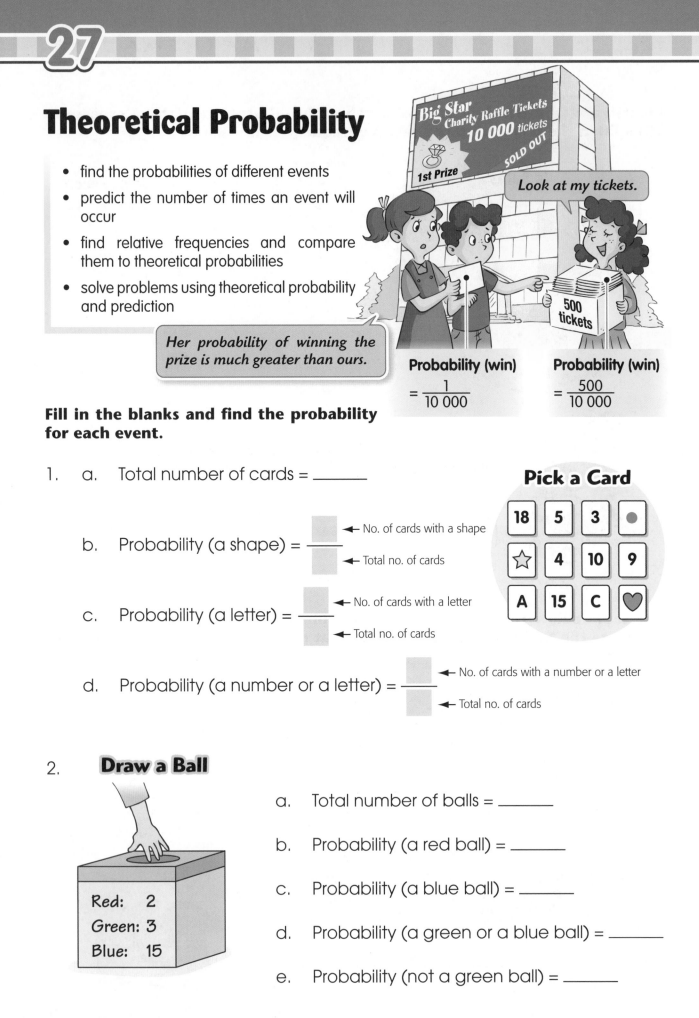

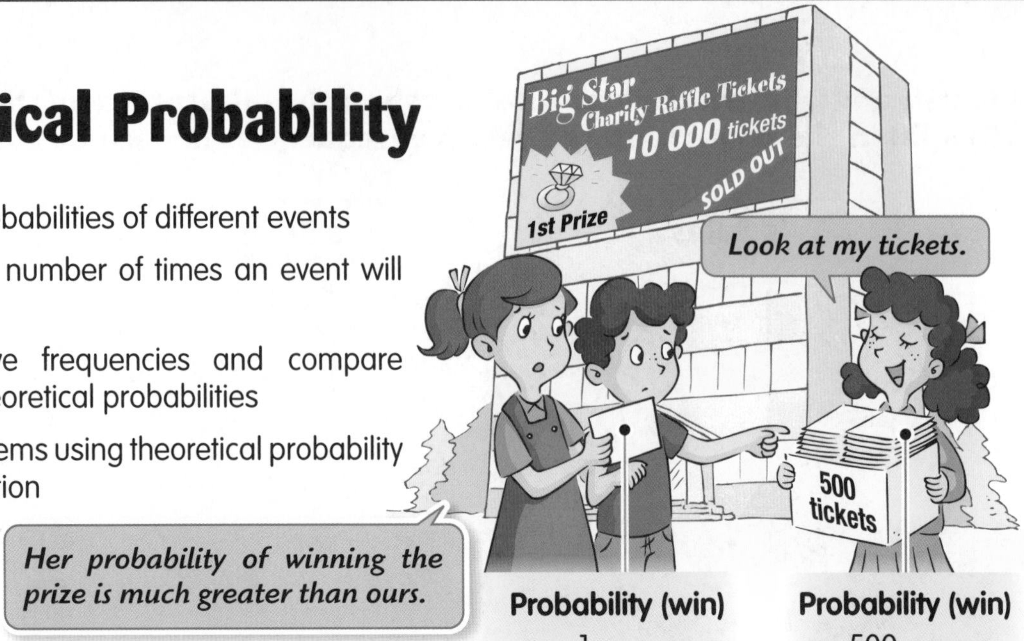

Probability (win) $= \frac{1}{10\ 000}$

Probability (win) $= \frac{500}{10\ 000}$

Fill in the blanks and find the probability for each event.

1. a. Total number of cards = ______

b. Probability (a shape) = $\frac{\square}{\square}$ ← No. of cards with a shape / ← Total no. of cards

c. Probability (a letter) = $\frac{\square}{\square}$ ← No. of cards with a letter / ← Total no. of cards

d. Probability (a number or a letter) = $\frac{\square}{\square}$ ← No. of cards with a number or a letter / ← Total no. of cards

2. **Draw a Ball**

a. Total number of balls = ______

b. Probability (a red ball) = ______

c. Probability (a blue ball) = ______

d. Probability (a green or a blue ball) = ______

e. Probability (not a green ball) = ______

Read what the children say. Find each probability.

3. Find the probability of picking out

I like milk chocolates and almond chocolates the most.
Elaine
Chocolates

Milk chocolates:	9 pieces
Dark chocolates:	8 pieces
Mint chocolates:	11 pieces
Almond chocolates:	2 pieces

a. a milk chocolate: ______

b. a dark chocolate: ______

c. a mint chocolate: ______

d. an almond chocolate: ______

e. a chocolate that Elaine likes the most: ______

f. a chocolate without nuts: ______

g. a milk or a mint chocolate: ______

4. Pick a dice and toss it.

Each dice is labelled from 1 to 6.
red
yellow
blue

Find the probability of

a. picking a red dice: ______

b. not picking a yellow dice: ______

c. tossing a "2": ______

d. tossing an odd number: ______

e. tossing a prime number: ______

5. Spin the spinner labelled with 26 letters.

I've got W, L, and L already. Let me spin it one more time.

Find the probability that he will form the word

a. WILL: ______

b. WALK: ______

c. WALL or WILL: ______

d. WALK or WELL: ______

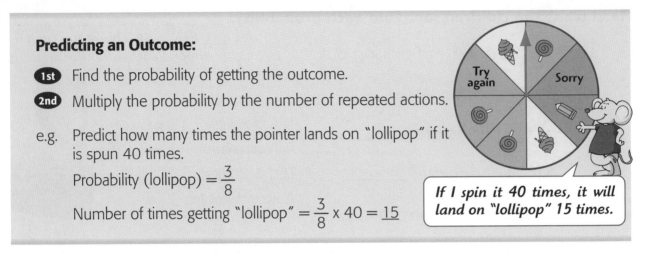

Predicting an Outcome:

1st Find the probability of getting the outcome.

2nd Multiply the probability by the number of repeated actions.

e.g. Predict how many times the pointer lands on "lollipop" if it is spun 40 times.

Probability (lollipop) = $\frac{3}{8}$

Number of times getting "lollipop" = $\frac{3}{8}$ x 40 = <u>15</u>

Try again
Sorry
If I spin it 40 times, it will land on "lollipop" 15 times.

Find the probabilities and answer the questions.

6. Lily shuffles a deck of cards and picks one without looking.

There are 3 kinds of cards in the deck. I'll pick out a card and put the card back. I'll repeat this 100 times.

Hint

The sum of the probabilities of all outcomes of an experiment is 1.

	Probability	Prediction (No. of Times)
draw a 	0.1	0.1 x 100 = ______
draw a 	0.54	
draw a 		

7. Ken draws a red ball from either one of the boxes to win a prize.

a. If Ken wants to win a prize, from which box should he draw a ball?

____

b. How many red balls should there be in box B so that it has the same winning probability as box A?

____

A
500 balls
with 3 red balls
B
1000 balls
with 5 red balls

Follow the instructions to do the activity 50 times. Record each outcome and complete the table. Then answer the questions.

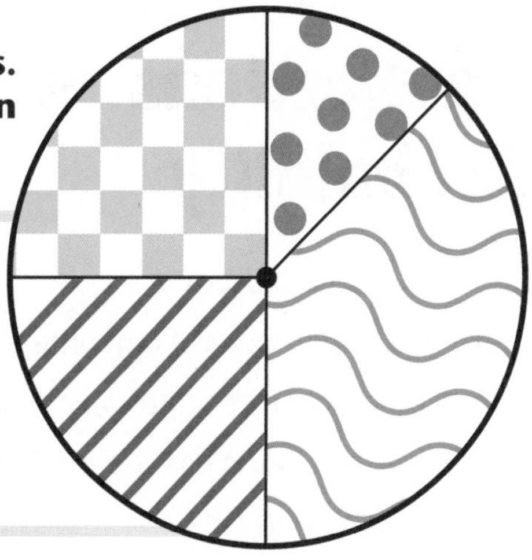

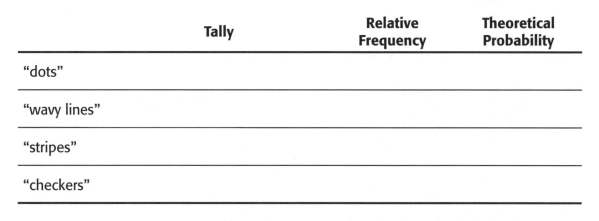

8. **Instructions**

   1. Secure a paper clip in the centre of the spinner with a pencil.
   2. Spin the paper clip and record the pattern that it lands on.

	Tally	Relative Frequency	Theoretical Probability
"dots"			
"wavy lines"			
"stripes"			
"checkers"			

9. 

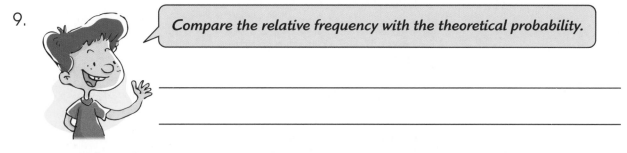

Compare the relative frequency with the theoretical probability.

10. *If I swing the paper clip 800 times, how many times will the paper clip land on each sector?*

11. *About how many times do I need to swing the paper clip to get "wavy lines" 150 times?*

Applications of Probability

- draw tree diagrams
- find the number of outcomes
- find probabilities from tree diagrams
- solve problems using tree diagrams

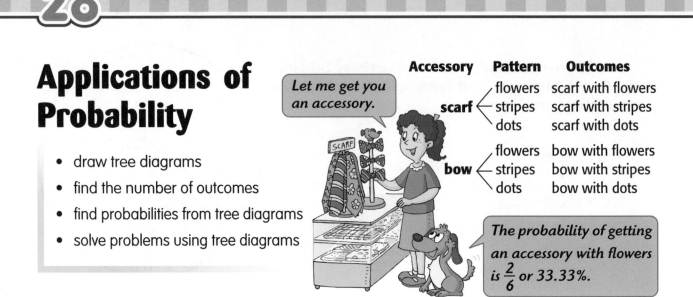

Let me get you an accessory.
SCARF
The probability of getting an accessory with flowers is $\frac{2}{6}$ or 33.33%.

Accessory	Pattern	Outcomes
scarf	flowers	scarf with flowers
	stripes	scarf with stripes
	dots	scarf with dots
bow	flowers	bow with flowers
	stripes	bow with stripes
	dots	bow with dots

Complete the tree diagram. Then answer the questions.

1.

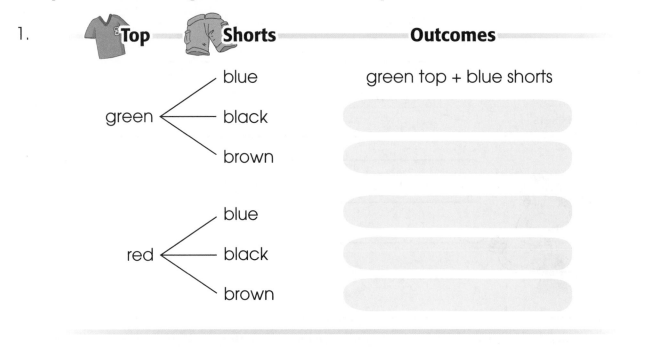

Top	Shorts	Outcomes
green	blue	green top + blue shorts
	black	
	brown	
red	blue	
	black	
	brown	

2. How many possible outcomes are there? ________

3. How many outcomes are there with blue shorts? ________

4. How many outcomes are there with a red top? ________

5. A customer is going to buy a top and a pair of shorts. What is the probability of choosing

   a. a green top and a pair of black shorts? ________

   b. a red top and a pair of brown shorts? ________

James is drawing a letter ball from each of the three boxes. Complete the tree diagram. Then answer the questions.

6. **Box 1** **Box 2** **Box 3** **Formed Words**

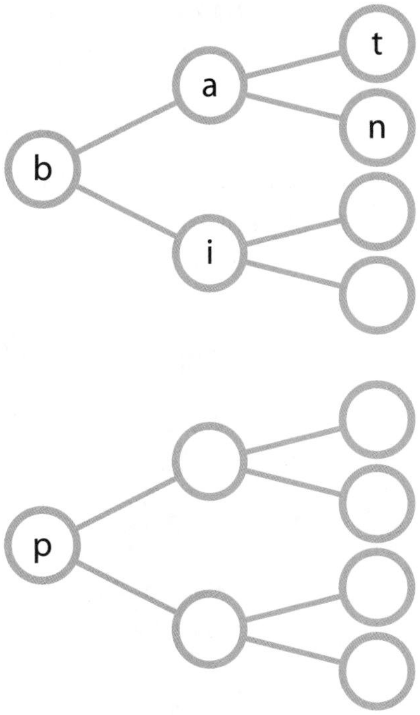

7. How many possible words are there? ________

8. What is the probability of getting "bin"? ________

9. What is the probability of getting "pan"? ________

10. What is the probability of getting a word with the letter "a"? ________

11. If James puts a ball with the letter "g" into Box 3 and draws a ball from each of the three boxes again,

    a. how many possible words are there? ________

    b. what is the probability of getting "bag"? ________

    c. what is the probability of getting a word with the letter "g"? ________

Draw a tree diagram to show the possible outcomes for ice cream cones with different toppings. Then answer the questions.

12. **Flavour** **Topping** **Outcomes**

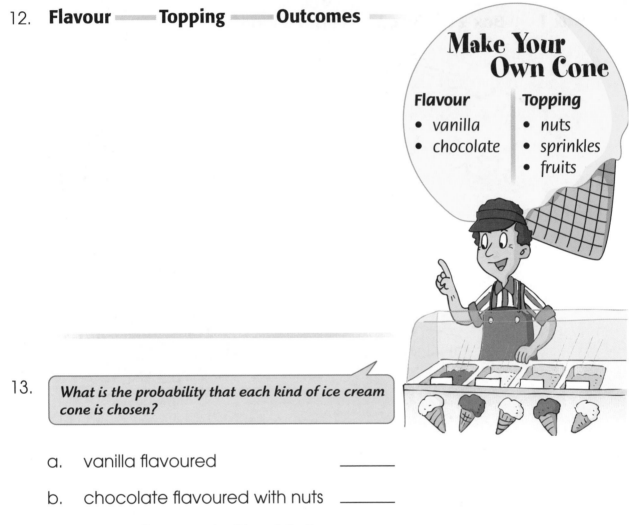

13. ***What is the probability that each kind of ice cream cone is chosen?***

a. vanilla flavoured ______

b. chocolate flavoured with nuts ______

c. vanilla flavoured without fruits ______

14. If the "fruit" topping is sold out, what will be the probability that each kind of ice cream that remains is chosen? Will the probability of choosing vanilla with sprinkles be greater than before? Show your work.

Jason is designing a treasure hunt game. Help him draw a tree diagram to show the ways to the treasure. Then answer the questions.

15. 

Character

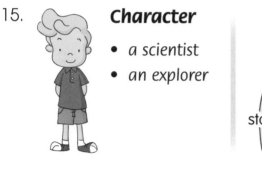

- *a scientist*
- *an explorer*

Path

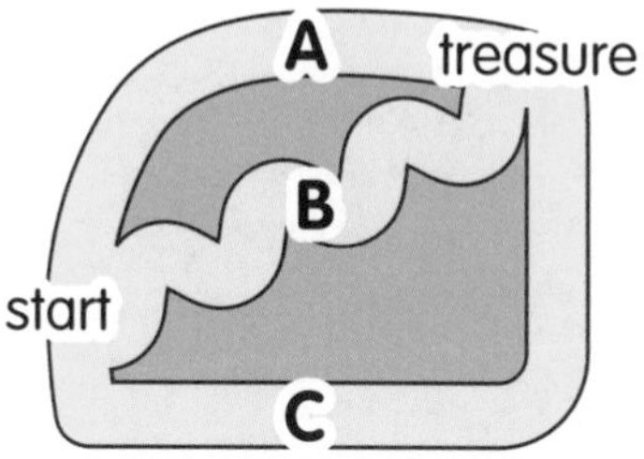

Treasure Chest Item

- *jewellery*
- *snakes*

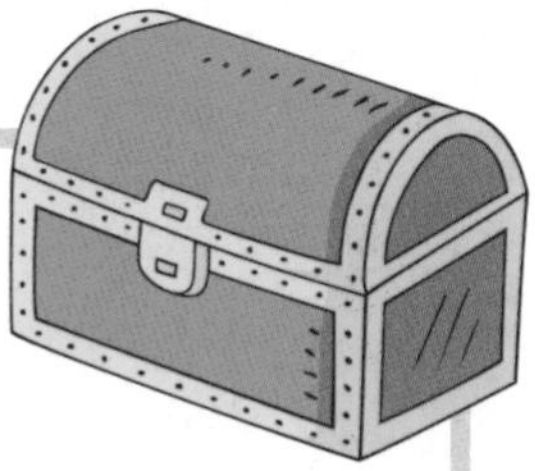

16. What is the probability that a player gets jewellery? ________

17. What is the probability that a player is a scientist and gets snakes? ________

18. *Paths B and C are very muddy. Find the probability that a player is*

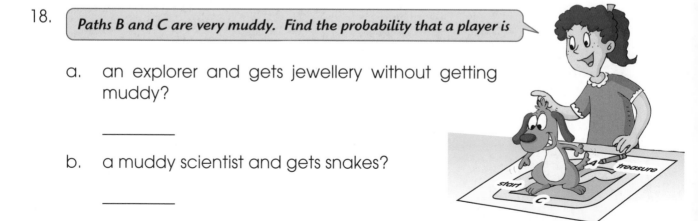

a. an explorer and gets jewellery without getting muddy?

____

b. a muddy scientist and gets snakes?

____

ENGLISH

New Year's Resolutions

Everyone, including you and me, has made New Year's resolutions, but how well did you follow through with them? It seems that very few people can let the new year roll in without giving a thought to how they can improve their lives, and make the coming year better than the last. Actually, the making of New Year's resolutions is a tradition dating back to the early Babylonians. One of their most popular resolutions was a promise to return borrowed farm equipment!

A New Year's resolution is a promise one makes to do something to better oneself. Resolutions usually involve a commitment to a lifestyle change or to ending a bad habit. Of course, resolutions need not be made with the New Year, but the fact that everyone is doing away with the old and welcoming the new often provides the motivation needed to consider such ideas. Some resolutions are very personal, such as getting fit, keeping a healthful diet, and becoming more assertive. Others are more community-minded, such as giving to charity more often and becoming more environmentally responsible.

Although the making of New Year's resolutions is a very secular activity, there are some parallels in religion. For example, many Christians give up things such as favourite sweets and junk food during the Christian fasting period of Lent, though the motive is more one of making sacrifices rather than trying to consciously improve oneself. Yom Kippur, Judaism's holiest holiday, is a time to reflect upon one's wrongdoings in the previous year and to seek and offer forgiveness.

Losing weight, as well as getting a better job, is among the most popular New Year's resolutions for adults. But resolutions are not just for adults! The American Academy of Pediatrics has lists of resolutions for children ranging from preschool age to the teen years. Their list for youth aged 13 years old and up includes:

1. I will eat at least two servings of fruits and vegetables every day, and I will limit the amount of pop I drink.
2. I will take care of my body through physical activity and nutrition.
3. I will choose non-violent television shows and video games, and I will spend only one to two hours each day on these activities.

4. I will help out in my community by volunteering, working with community groups, or joining a group that helps people in need.

5. I will wipe negative "self talk" (e.g. "I can't do it" or "I'm so dumb") out of my vocabulary.

6. When I feel angry or stressed out, I will take a break and find constructive ways to deal with the stress, such as exercising, reading, writing in a journal, and discussing my problem with a parent or friend.

7. When faced with a difficult decision, I will talk with an adult about my choices.

8. I will resist peer pressure to try drugs and alcohol.

A. Fill in the blanks with words from the passage.

1. Many people make resolutions to impove their lives in the coming year.
2. Very often, a resolution involves a person to give up a bad habit.
3. Making New Year's resolutions is a socular activity for many. However, some people make resolutions for religious reasons.
4. We make resolutions to improve ourselves concicousy.
5. Some teenagers resolve to find ______ ways to deal with stress.

B. Suppose it is the beginning of a new year. Write two New Year's resolutions for yourself.

1. work out more
2. get better marks

Subject-Verb Agreement

The verb in a sentence must **agree** with its subject in both person and number. A singular subject takes a singular verb and a plural subject takes a plural verb.

Example: One of their most popular resolutions was a promise to return borrowed farm equipment.

Note that the noun or pronoun right before the verb may not be the "real" subject of the sentence. Make sure to identify the subject and use the correct form of the verb.

With indefinite pronouns like "everybody", "someone", and "nothing", singular verbs are used.

Example: Everyone is doing away with the old and welcoming the new.

C. Circle the correct form of the verb for each sentence.

1. Everybody in class has / have to make a list of New Year's resolutions.
2. Each of the lists represents / represent the commitments made by each student.
3. The list of resolutions was / were handed in to the teacher by the end of the lesson.
4. Someone has / have left the list on the teacher's desk.
5. Nothing is / are impossible if you is / are set on it.
6. Some of the students' resolutions includes / include going to bed earlier, eating less chocolate, and saving more money.
7. All of us wants / want to get better grades in the coming year.
8. Has / Have anybody thought of eating less fast food?
9. Whoever makes / make a resolution will have to follow it through.

Other Vexing Agreement

When "either" and "neither" are used as subjects, singular verbs are required. When they are used as correlative conjunctions, the subject closer to the verb determines whether the singular or plural form of the verb should be used.

Examples: Neither of the two boys has thought about any resolutions.

Neither Issac nor his friends need to lose weight.

Words and phrases like "including" and "as well as" do not join the nouns or pronouns they introduce to the subjects, so they do not affect the forms of verbs used.

Examples: Everyone, including you and me, has made New Year's resolutions before.

Losing weight, as well as getting a better job, is among the most popular New Year's resolutions for adults.

D. The subject-verb agreements in the following sentences are incorrect. Rewrite the sentences to make them correct.

1. Either of the two resolutions are made by me.

2. Neither the girls nor Bosco think that making resolutions are useless.

3. Working out, as well as reading, are some ways to release stress.

4. Mrs. Bauer, together with her students, volunteer to help out after school.

5. Either Angie or Carl are going to be the first to tell us the resolutions.

6. Everybody, including all the teachers, are going to the New Year Camp.

The Three Roses: *a Czech Folktale*

Once upon a time, there was a mother who had three daughters. As she was preparing to go to the market, she asked her daughters what she should bring back for them. Two of them began to list many things, and demanded that she buy them all. When the mother had heard enough, she asked her third daughter, "And you, don't you want anything?"

"No, but, if you like, you can bring me three roses, please," she replied. Once the mother knew what the girls wanted, she set off for the market. She bought everything she could afford, piled it high on her back, and started for home. But soon nightfall overtook her. The poor woman got lost and could go no further. She wandered aimlessly through the woods until she grew tired. Then, she came upon a palace, which was quite strange as she had never before heard of any palace in the woods. A large rose garden surrounded the palace, and it seemed to the woman that all the roses were smiling at her. She remembered her youngest daughter, who had asked sweetly for just such beautiful roses. She thought, "There are so many lovely roses here. No one will mind if I take just three."

She tiptoed into the garden and picked the roses. Suddenly, an old wizard came down and demanded the woman's daughter in exchange for the roses. The woman was petrified and tried to throw the flowers away, but the wizard laughed and threatened to send her into the dark woods forever. The woman promised him her daughter, and then sadly made her way home, roses in hand. She gave the three roses to her daughter and said, "Here are the roses you asked for, but I had to pay dearly for them. You must now go to the palace in the woods in return for the roses. I don't know if you will ever come back."

But the youngest daughter seemed not to mind at all, and her mother led her to the palace. The wizard reappeared and told the girl that she had to feed him three fine meals a day.

For a long time, the girl worked hard to prepare fine meals for the old wizard. Then one day, the wizard asked her to cut his head off! She protested, but the wizard raged, and so she did it. The wizard's head rolled onto the ground, and from out of his body came a terrible hissing snake! Again, the snake asked her to cut his head off. This time, the girl did not hesitate and cut his head off at once. The evil serpent immediately changed into a handsome young man, and said to the girl in a pleasant and grateful voice, "This castle is mine and, now, because you have saved me, I wish to marry you."

There was a great wedding, and the young man and the girl lived happily ever after.

A. Answer these questions.

1. Why was it strange for the woman to have found a palace in the woods?

   ____

2. If you were the woman, would you promise the old wizard your daughter?

   ____

3. Why did the wizard ask the girl to cut off his head?

   ____

4. Think of a different ending to the story.

   ____

   ____

   ____

5. Can you think of a fairy tale similar to this? Explain how they are similar.

   ____

   ____

   ____

Past Perfect Tense

The **past perfect tense** is formed with "had + past participle" and is used:

- to indicate that something had happened before another past action
- to show that an action had been completed before a specific past time
- for an action that began before, and was still continuing at, a past time
- in indirect speech introduced by a past verb of saying or thinking to talk about something that had happened before the speech took place

Examples: Then she remembered her youngest daughter, who <u>had asked</u> sweetly for just such beautiful roses.

The young man said he wished to marry the girl because she <u>had saved</u> him.

B. Check if the sentences contain the past perfect tense. If not, put a cross.

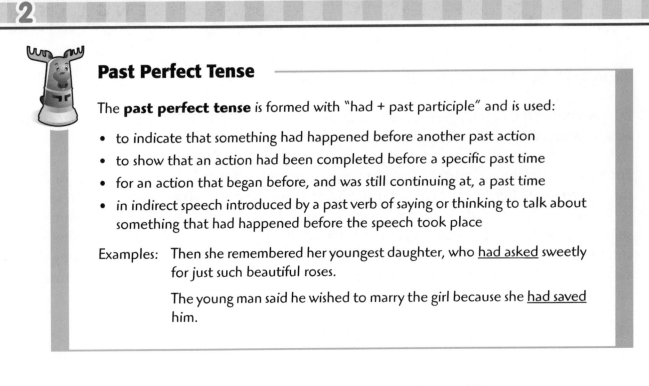

1. The old woman had three daughters. ☐
2. She had bought all the things her daughters needed before she headed home. ☐
3. The woman had not heard of a palace in the woods before. ☐
4. She has not seen such beautiful roses before. ☐
5. She picked three roses for her youngest daughter. ☐
6. The woman had never before been so scared. ☐
7. The young girl had to stay in the palace because her mother had picked roses from the garden. ☐
8. The girl had to feed the wizard three meals a day. ☐
9. The wizard asked the girl if she had prepared lunch. ☐

C. Fill in the blanks with the correct form of the verbs.

1. After she (hear) ________________ enough from her first two daughters, the old woman (ask) ________________ her youngest daughter what she (want) ________________ .

2. The woman (not be) ________________ able to get out of the woods before night (fall) ________________ .

3. An old wizard (appear) ________________ after the woman (pick) ________________ the roses.

4. The woman (give) ________________ the roses to her daughter before she (take) ________________ her to the palace.

5. After the girl (cut) ________________ the head off the serpent, it (change) ________________ into a handsome young man.

D. Complete the following.

1. Write about something you had done before you went home from school yesterday.

____

____

____

2. Write about a special event that had happened before you were in Grade 7.

____

____

____

Mythical Creatures from the World of Fantasy

Do you remember the old fairy tales you were told as a child? Your favourite stories no doubt included some of the more well-known fantasy creatures, such as mermaids, dragons, and unicorns. If you have read ancient Greek myths, then you may also be familiar with creatures like the *centaur* (half human, half horse), the *satyr* (a human with goat-like features), and perhaps the *griffin* which is often depicted as an eagle with the body of a lion. In addition to reading about them in books and seeing them in movies, we can find these mythical creatures on vases and in old paintings and ancient mosaics. They also appear as gargoyles in historical and modern architecture, such as in the churches and cathedrals of Paris, and the skyscrapers of New York and Chicago.

In fact, there are hundreds of these kinds of mythical creatures from the world of fantasy, myth, and legend. Not only have these mythical creatures been with us through the ages, but they appear throughout the cultures of the world. For example, the South Pacific nation of the Solomon Islands has mermaid-like creatures in their mythology. These "merpeople" (*mer* is the French word for "ocean") are called *Adaro*. They are part man and part fish, but that is where their similarities with the better-known merpeople end; an Adaro has a swordfish spear growing out of his head, lives in the sun, comes to earth by sliding along rainbows, and is not very nice to humans!

Dragon-like sea creatures appear in many different cultures as well. For example, the *Tarasque*, the French version of a dragon, has a lion's head, a turtle's shell, a scorpion's sting, and legs like a bear's! This particular dragon not only spews fire, but likes to swim, and is said to inhabit the waters of Ha Long Bay, off the coast of northern Vietnam, which used to be a French colony. It joins the pantheon of other mysterious sea creatures throughout the world, which includes *Amemasu*, the lake monster of Ainu mythology in Japan; *Jormungandr*, the sea spirit of

Norse mythology; and the fearsome water demons of Slavic lore, the *Bagiennik*. There are more recent examples of mysterious sea creatures, which people claim to see today. There are the Canadian sea monsters, such as *Ogopogo*, which inhabits Lake Okanagan in British Columbia, and *Manipogo*, which has been sighted in Manitoba's Lake Winnipeg. And, of course, there is the world-famous *Loch Ness Monster* in Scotland. But it seems these more modern sea monsters are friendly and good for tourism!

In many cases, it is not difficult to understand the folklore roots of these mythical creatures. There often seems to be a grounding in the nature of the area. For example, in Inuit lore, the *Akhlut* is part wolf and part whale. And in Irish lore, there is the *Dobhar-chu*, half dog and half fish, and the *Kelpie*, a water-horse. It is not surprising to discover that the folklore of many of the world's desert-dwelling people focuses more on ants and bats and birds, rather than fish and whales.

There will never be a list that includes all of the mythical creatures from around the world, since our collective imaginations will forever be creating new ones!

A. Give a brief description of the physical features of each creature below.

1. centaur

____

2. satyr

____

3. griffin

____

4. Adaro

____

5. Tarasque

____

6. Akhlut

____

Active and Passive Voices

A sentence in the **active voice** focuses on the doer of the action while one in the **passive voice** puts the emphasis on the thing or person being acted upon.

Examples: Painters depict the griffin as an eagle with the body of a lion. (active)

The griffin is depicted as an eagle with the body of a lion. (passive)

Note that in using the passive voice, we sometimes leave out the doer so that the reader's attention is further directed to the person or thing being acted upon.

If it is necessary to mention the doer of the action in a passive voice sentence, the word "by" is used.

Example: The griffin is depicted as an eagle with the body of a lion <u>by</u> the famous painter Tobias Malone.

B. Write "active" if the sentences are in the active voice and "passive" if they are in the passive voice.

1. Grandma told me lots of fairy tales when I was young. ________________
2. The mythological "merpeople" of the South Pacific nation of the Solomon Islands are called Adaro. ________________
3. The Tarasque is said to inhabit the waters of Ha Long Bay. ________________
4. Some mythical creatures appear as gargoyles in modern architecture. ________________
5. The Manipogo has been sighted in Lake Winnipeg in Manitoba. ________________
6. Nessie, the Loch Ness Monster, has attracted many tourists to Scotland. ________________
7. Mythical creatures have appeared in different cultures' myths around the world for ages. ________________

C. Rewrite each sentence below using the active voice.

1. A lecture on mythical creatures was delivered by Professor Rayner.

2. *Exploring the World of Fantasy* was written by Nina Kirwan.

3. That picture of a unicorn flying in the sky was drawn by me.

4. The Inuit legend was staged by Mr. Reid's class.

5. All the costumes and props for the play were made by the students themselves.

D. Rewrite each sentence below using the passive voice. Leave out the doer if it does not affect the clarity of the sentence.

1. Our teacher told us to do a project on Greek mythology.

2. A thief stole the famous painting *The Rebirth of the Phoenix*.

3. They built a statue of the Ogopogo in a park in Kelowna.

4. Elves and fairies inhabit the island nation of Iceland.

5. Someone has sent a picture of Nessie to the press.

Most young people know what Facebook is: a free-access Internet social networking website popular among teenagers, and adults, too. It was founded by a Harvard University student named Mark Zuckerberg and launched on February 4, 2004. Initially, it was intended only as a networking site for Harvard's campus community, providing a handy tool to help everyone on campus – students, faculty, and other staff – get to know one another. Almost immediately, it expanded to include Stanford, Columbia, and Yale Universities, and then several more Ivy League schools, including MIT and Northeastern. Now, Facebook has evolved into a vast social network for anyone over the age of 13, with more than 1.35 billion active users.

Facebook – Are You Revealing Too Much?

As the name suggests, faces are an integral part of the website – and of social networking, too, one could say. Facebook.com is the top Internet site for uploading photos, with about 350 million photos uploaded every day! People continued to expand their personal profiles with photos, though a feature that allows blogging was later added to the site. There was even a way to send friends virtual "gifts" – such as happy face balloons, heart-shaped boxes of virtual chocolates, and dog bones – from Facebook's virtual gift shop! Some of the additional features included a Marketplace site which allowed users to post free classified ads. Similarly, under other network headings, people can let others know about events and post videos. In this way, Facebook has increased in popularity and broadened the demographic of its usership, and it has increased its value for the owner. So far, Zuckerberg has declined to sell his site (rival networking site MySpace.com was sold to News Corp) even though it is estimated to be worth around $200 billion!

But sometimes success can lead to a downfall of sorts; Facebook is not without controversy. Ironically, at least one university has blocked access to the site saying that logging onto Facebook violates its acceptable use policy. The government of Ontario blocked access to the site for its public employees in 2007. Privacy is also a major concern. In some cases, the identities of people, such as those involved in crimes as victims or perpetrators, are released to the general public through posts on such sites, even before permission is granted by the families or by the police. When this happens, it seems that website administrators cannot keep up with users who are determined to keep the information posted, no matter how many times it is taken down. There are instances of unflattering, embarrassing, or even unlawful materials being posted about third parties, resulting in significant damage to people's reputations, sometimes with tragic results.

Moreover, as some people have become more and more interested in chatting with their new online friends, their real-life relationships have suffered. Psychologists are seeing an increase in problems among people who are addicted to these types of sites. Backlash against the use of these social networking sites is now occurring, and once-devoted fans of sites like Facebook are committing "Facebook Suicide" – saying a virtual goodbye to their virtual friends and returning to their "real" lives, developing friendships with people in real life, and enjoying the real warmth and rewards that only face-to-face friendships can offer.

A. Write "T" for the true sentences and "F" for the false ones.

1. Facebook is a free social networking website for students only. ______
2. Facebook was intended to be a website to help those at Harvard University get to know one another. ______
3. There is a total of 350 million photos currently on Facebook. ______
4. Classified ads for virtual gifts can be posted on Facebook's Marketplace. ______
5. The founder of Facebook sold his site for $200 billion dollars. ______
6. Ontario government employees cannot access Facebook at work. ______

B. In your own words, state the pros and cons of Facebook.

Pros

____

____

Cons

____

____

Verbals

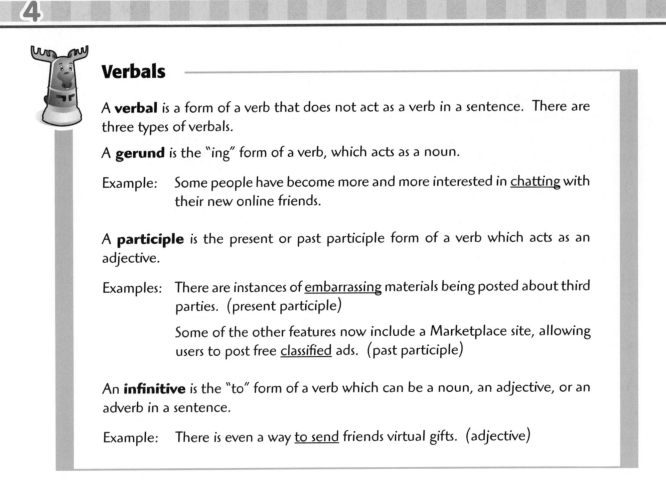

A **verbal** is a form of a verb that does not act as a verb in a sentence. There are three types of verbals.

A **gerund** is the "ing" form of a verb, which acts as a noun.

Example: Some people have become more and more interested in chatting with their new online friends.

A **participle** is the present or past participle form of a verb which acts as an adjective.

Examples: There are instances of embarrassing materials being posted about third parties. (present participle)

Some of the other features now include a Marketplace site, allowing users to post free classified ads. (past participle)

An **infinitive** is the "to" form of a verb which can be a noun, an adjective, or an adverb in a sentence.

Example: There is even a way to send friends virtual gifts. (adjective)

C. Identify the types of verbals underlined in the sentences below. Write "G" for gerunds, "PSP" for present participles, "PTP" for past participles, and "I" for infinitives.

1. My friend sent me a dancing happy face on Facebook. ______
2. Chatting with friends online can be time-consuming. ______
3. You need to be 13 years old or above to join Facebook. ______
4. The Lintons like putting their family photos on Facebook. ______
5. They can share the posted albums with their friends. ______
6. This website has a large group of devoted fans. ______
7. Visiting the site has become his daily routine. ______
8. It's easy to post videos on Facebook. ______
9. The many interesting features and functions of Facebook have attracted many people to use this website. ______

D. Underline the infinitive in each sentence. State whether it functions as a noun, an adjective, or an adverb.

1. Kate promised her parents not to spend more than an hour on Facebook every day. ____________

2. Benny has chosen some photos to be put on Facebook. ____________

3. Remember to read the site's privacy agreement before signing up. ____________

4. You may be able to find some of your old friends on Facebook. ____________

5. The site continues to develop as more and more people join it. ____________

6. To have real-life interactions with others is essential. ____________

E. Change the verbs below to verbals and use them in sentences of your own.

1. visit (gerund)

____

2. participate (present participle)

____

3. write (past participle)

____

4. create (infinitive as noun)

____

5. help (infinitive as adverb)

____

"My Olympic Hero" *Speech Competition*

Good morning Principal Smith, teachers, and fellow students. Even though Sang Lan has never competed in the Olympic games, I think of her as my Olympic hero. You might think my choice is strange, or perhaps not a proper topic for this speech, which should be about "My Olympic Hero". Allow me to explain.

More than 15 years ago, Sang Lan was one of China's top gymnasts. While competing at the Goodwill Games in New York in 1998, she fell during a practice vault and broke her neck. She thought that her dream of becoming an Olympic athlete was lost forever.

But soon Sang Lan realized she didn't want to live a life of despair, sorrow, and bitterness. After months of difficult rehabilitation in the United States, Sang Lan returned to China and created a life for herself as a friendly personality and an inspiration to other disabled people in China. She continued with daily physical therapy, gaining back the use of her arms and shoulders to a significant degree. She wanted to get on with her life and live it the best way she could. She went back to school to work on a journalism degree, impressing her classmates with her "courage and exceptional spirit".

Sang Lan also began to realize that she could achieve her Olympic dream in other ways. For example, she was part of the Beijing Olympic Games Bid Committee. In 2004, she carried the Olympic torch during the Athens Olympic Games torch relay. She also carried the torch through Beijing during the torch relay leading up to the 2008 games. In addition, she hosted a TV talk show in China about the games, called "Sang Lan Olympics 2008". Sang Lan dreamed of representing China in the 2008 Paralympic Games as a ping-pong player, but this dream was not realized as her hands cannot grasp properly. Though Sang Lan cannot participate in any Olympic Games as an athlete, she plans to continue to be involved in future Olympics.

The story of Sang Lan shows me that tragedy does not have to remain forever, and even a catastrophic injury does not have to define you. We must remember that when things don't always go the way we want them to, we can find other ways to achieve our dreams, and help other people achieve their dreams, too. Sometimes it may require us to tweak our dreams, but the end result is that we simply achieve new goals, and feel just as good about it.

So, next time I am watching the Olympic events on television, I will also be thinking about Sang Lan, wondering if she is in the stadium, watching – and dreaming – along with me.

A. Read the clues and complete the crossword puzzle with words from the passage.

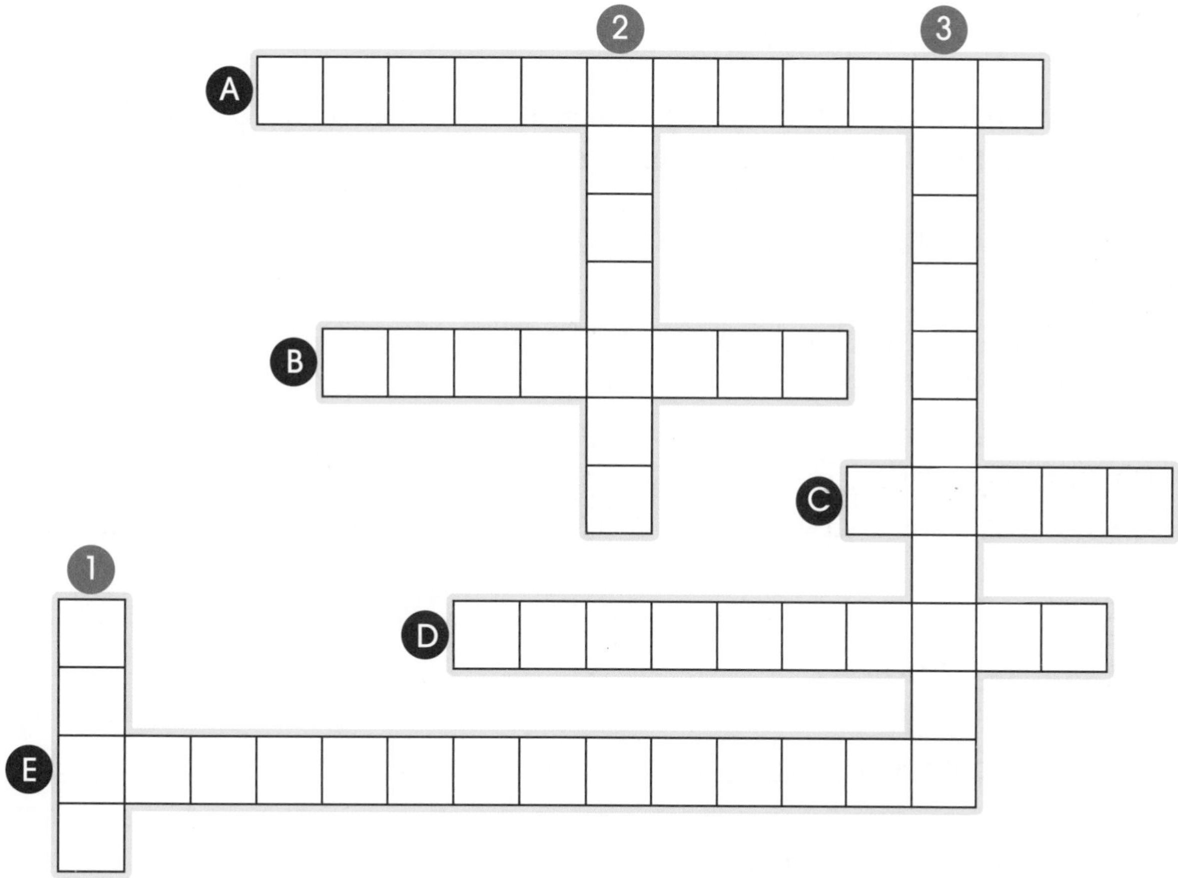

Across

A. Sang Lan's ____ injury did not cause her to live a life of despair and sorrow.

B. Sang Lan was among China's top ____ before the accident.

C. Sang Lan broke her neck during a practice ____ .

D. She wanted to get a degree in ____ .

E. Sang Lan's ____ in the United States was a hard experience.

Down

1. Sang Lan is the writer's Olympic ____ .
2. With daily physical ____ , Sang Lan regained the ability to use her arms.
3. Sang Lan is an ____ to other disabled people.

Noun Phrases

A **noun phrase** is a group of words that includes a noun as head and all its modifiers. It functions like a single noun in a sentence, and may be the subject, object, or complement of the sentence.

Examples: The story of Sang Lan shows me that even tragedy does not have to remain forever. (subject)

Sang Lan fell in a practice vault and broke her neck. (object)

More than 15 years ago, Sang Lan was one of China's top gymnasts. (complement)

B. Identify the underlined noun phrases as the subject (SUB), object (OBJ), or complement (COM) of the sentences.

1. Sang Lan is the writer's Olympic hero. ________

2. Her tragic accident took place in 1998 at the Goodwill Games in New York. ________

3. Daily physical therapy helped Sang Lan gain back the use of her arms and shoulders to a significant degree. ________

4. Sang Lan has become an advocate for disabled people in China. ________

5. She took journalism degree courses at Peking University. ________

6. "Sang Lan Olympics 2008" was a TV talk show hosted by Sang Lan. ________

7. Sang Lan's tough training to be a gymnast played an important role in shaping her strong character. ________

8. Competing in the 2008 Paralympic Games as a ping-pong player was a dream that Sang Lan could not realize. ________

C. Read the following paragraph from the passage. Underline all the noun phrases.

Sang Lan also began to realize that she could achieve her Olympic dream in other ways. For example, she was part of the Beijing Olympic Games Bid Committee. In 2004, she carried the Olympic torch during the Athens Olympic Games torch relay. She also carried the torch through Beijing during the torch relay leading up to the 2008 games. In addition, she hosted a TV talk show in China about the games, called "Sang Lan Olympics 2008". Sang Lan dreamed of representing China in the 2008 Paralympic Games as a ping-pong player, but this dream was not realized as her hands cannot grasp properly. Though Sang Lan cannot participate in any Olympic Games as an athlete, she plans to continue to be involved in future Olympics.

D. Rewrite the following sentences by changing the underlined nouns to noun phrases.

1. All the people here are <u>athletes</u>.

   ____

2. <u>Rehabilitation</u> was a hard experience for Sang Lan.

   ____

3. What we all need is <u>practice</u>.

   ____

4. Every Olympic athlete has <u>dreams</u>.

   ____

Family "Memoirs" – the Gift of a Lifetime

Scrapbooking has become a booming industry in recent years. Walk into a scrapbooking shop or browse online, and the selection of colours, papers, patterns, stickers, borders, covers, and albums – not to mention entire scrapbooking furniture sets – will make your head spin. Why do so many people put so much effort into this pastime? For many of us, it is important to remember life's lessons, good or bad, because these are the memories you want to share. It is about keeping your past alive in the present and future. The finished product is a keepsake, and the process itself also generates memories.

There are many ways to make memory books. Scrapbooking items can be bought online or in local shops. Pages can also be laminated and coil-bound, or slipped into the plastic pages of a clear book bought at any stationery store. If photography has been your preferred way to tell your family history, various websites specialize in making photo books. Doing an online search with the words "photo album making" will quickly find you a long list of online businesses that can create any family memento you can dream up. But this kind of family bookmaking does not need to be only for photos. People are starting to write their own family history books. If you give it a try, you will be amazed at how grateful your cousins and aunts and uncles will be. The project will also inspire some of them to do a similar project relating to the other side of their family. Think of the fun you can have putting your favourite family photos on the book cover. You can hire printers to make any number of copies, large or small, and even hire book packagers and print-on-demand publishers to help see your project through for a more professional-looking finished product.

But family memories need not be on paper only – clothes can also be used and turned into precious family heirlooms. Old furs, woollen coats, chenille bedspreads, and ancient tweeds are being turned into gorgeous old-fashioned teddy bears, sold in the most up-market gift shops. The old baby clothes you are reluctant to part with can be given a new and practical lease on life by being sewn into quilts that can be kept for years and passed down – and used during the coldest weeks of

Canadian winters. Making use of the clothes you feel you cannot give away is a way of bringing memories back to life, not only for yourself but for others as well. And do not forget, there are other options as well: having your old baby shoes bronzed; having plaster casts of hands and feet (and not just a baby's!) made; turning favourite photos into canvas tote bags or coffee cups – all of these make treasured mementoes that have the benefit of utility as well.

So next time you are wondering about what special gift you can give to family or friends – or to yourself – think about creating family "memoirs" in any form. There is no better gift than the wisdom of a lifetime, or the chronicle of a life whose memories might otherwise fade way.

A. Use your dictionary to find the definitions of these words.

1. scrapbook ____________________
2. album ____________________
3. memoir ____________________
4. keepsake ____________________
5. memento ____________________
6. heirloom ____________________

Look at the definition of the word "memoir" you have found above. Do you know why the word is put in quotation marks in the title and the passage?

____

____

____

____

B. Among the different ways of creating family "memoirs" in the passage, which one would you choose? Why?

____

____

____

____

Verb Phrases

A **verb phrase** is a group of words that functions as a single verb in the sentence. It has a verb as its head.

Examples: Scrapbooking items can be bought online or in local shops.
(head of verb phrase – "bought")

People are starting to write their own family history books.
(head of verb phrase – "starting")

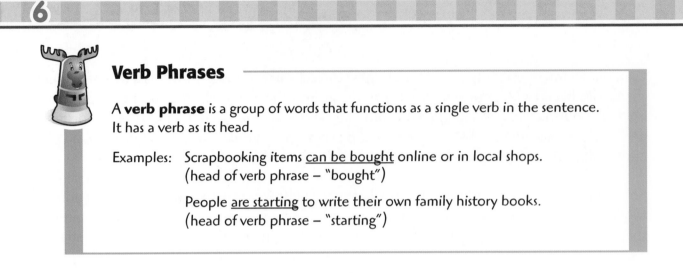

C. Underline the verb phrases and circle the head of each one in the following sentences.

1. Jenny is making a memory book.

2. She has taken a lot of photos to be put in the book.

3. She will bind the pages with a pretty ribbon.

4. Drawings of family members and friends can also be added.

5. What would be the best family "memoirs"?

6. You can buy any materials you can think of in this shop.

7. He would not have been able to think of what to make if I had not brainstormed ideas with him.

8. This quilt was made by Grandma and is treasured by everyone in the family.

9. My brother and I made a family photo DVD for our mother's birthday. She was so happy and surprised that she could not say a word.

10. This would be regarded as the best present Mom has ever received.

Verbal Phrases

A **verbal phrase** is a phrase that contains a gerund, a participle (present or past), or an infinitive. It functions as a noun, an adjective, or an adverb in the sentence.

Examples: It's about keeping your past alive with the present and future. (gerund phrase – noun)

Scrapbooking has become a booming industry in recent years. (present participle phrase – noun)

The finished product is a keepsake. (past participle phrase – noun)

For many, it is important to go through life and remember its lessons. (infinitive phrase – adverb)

D. Identify the types of verbal phrases below and make sentences of your own with them.

1. to organize the photos (phrase)

____

2. constructing a memory book ( )

____

3. the written family history ( )

____

4. getting the whole family involved ( )

____

5. to win the hearts of others ( )

____

6. the fading memories ( )

____

Superstitions around the World

Have you ever walked around a ladder that was blocking your path, or turned down a side street to avoid walking where a black cat had just crossed? Have you ever worried about something bad happening if you cracked a mirror or spilled some salt? We are all aware of superstitions, and have heard stories about how to avoid bad luck or gain good luck that actually seem silly to us. But it is amazing to learn that many superstitions exist across different cultures, telling us that there is more to these ancient beliefs than just silly sayings.

A lot of superstitions are related to the naming of children. Based on the sheer amount of "dos and don'ts" regarding this topic, it is clear that the naming of children is an important undertaking in any culture and, it could be said, an indication of just how much we value our children. In the Dominican Republic, children are given nicknames ("apodo"), which are commonly used instead of given names. A given name is regarded as an important part of a person and must be kept secret to prevent the name from being used in a spell or a curse from a witch ("brujo"). Among Ashkenazi Jews, it is considered bad luck to name a child after a living relative. It is believed that this superstition originated from a common belief in the Middle Ages: that the Angel of Death could mistakenly take the infant instead of the aged relative it was named after. In the Jewish faith, it is a popular practice to name a child after a deceased relative because doing so creates a deep bond between the soul of the child on earth and the soul of the person already in heaven, which would benefit the child.

In many places, such as India and Sri Lanka, parents are very concerned about their children being gazed upon by the "Evil Eye" (a malign spirit similar to the "brujo" of the Dominican Republic). To prevent this, parents used to give their children insulting names in the belief that it would save the child's life – after all, what spirit would want to take a child with the name of "Cowdung", "Rag", or "Rubbish"? Assigning infant children such strange names was also practised in countries such as China and Korea for the same reason.

But perhaps we can think of superstitions – at least some of them – as common sense. For example, placing a hand over your mouth when sneezing may not have anything to do with preventing your soul from escaping – but it will cut down on the spread of germs! And why not make a wish next time you see a falling star or find a four-leaf clover? It is fun to be a hopeful and optimistic person. It certainly is bad luck to open an umbrella in the house – because in doing so you may easily knock something over and break it. And, as for bad luck happening when you walk under a ladder – face it, walking under a ladder is a tight fit for most of us, running the risk of knocking over the ladder and causing injury to ourselves, if not others.

Perhaps there is more wisdom in those silly, old superstitions than we thought. Even so, it is undoubtedly a good thing that superstitions are no longer adhered to by so many people. After all, would you like to be given the nickname "Old Shoe"?

A. Read the clues and complete the crossword puzzle with words from the passage.

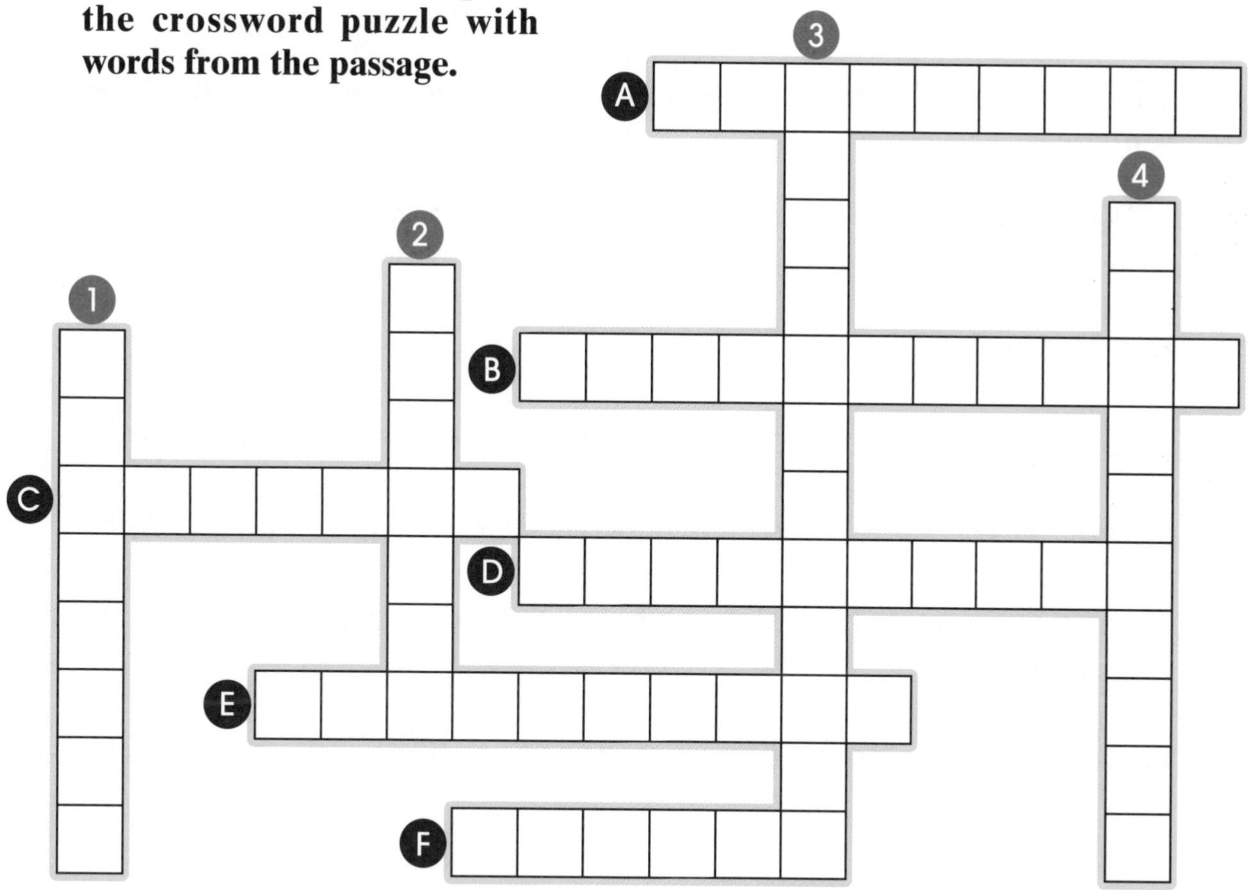

Across

A. giving
B. task or job
C. remained faithful
D. began to exist
E. hopeful about the future
F. harmful

Down

1. something that people do regularly
2. do good to
3. belief in things that cannot be explained
4. regarded as

Adjective Phrases

An **adjective phrase** is a group of words with one or more adjectives as head. It functions like a single adjective in a sentence.

Examples: In many places, parents are very concerned about their children being gazed upon by the "Evil Eye".
(head of adjective phrase – "concerned")

It is more fun to be a hopeful and optimistic person.
(heads of adjective phrase – "hopeful"; "optimistic")

B. Underline the adjective phrases and circle the head of each in the following sentences.

1. Making a wish upon seeing a shooting star is very common practice.
2. Some people give their children strange and insulting names out of superstition.
3. To convince others not to be so superstitious is somewhat difficult.
4. It is awfully silly of you to believe in the magical power of that product.
5. Mom is quite upset because, on her way home, a big black cat crossed her path.
6. Objective and scientific evidence does not affect some people's beliefs.

C. Write two sentences, each containing at least one adjective phrase.

1. ______________________________

____

2. ______________________________

____

Adjectival Phrases

An **adjectival phrase** can be any phrase that functions like an adjective. Adjectival phrases are usually hyphenated when they precede the nouns they are modifying.

Example: Make a wish next time you find a four-leaf clover.

D. Check if the underlined words form an adjectival phrase in the sentence.

1. The three-hour documentary unveils the strangest superstitions of different cultures. ☐
2. The professor is doing an in-depth study on the ancient beliefs of his country. ☐
3. The baby girl is named after her great-great-grandmother. ☐
4. She talked about the strange practice with a matter-of-fact look on her face. ☐
5. The play is a re-creation of the ancient practice on stage. ☐
6. Some people say that superstitions are by-products of people's ignorance. ☐
7. Janice is an easy-going person, so she does not care much about any superstitions. ☐

E. Write two sentences of your own using adjectival phrases.

1. ____________________

____

2. ____________________

____

Muhammad Yunus
and the Grameen Bank

> *"This is not charity. This is business: business with a social objective, which is to help people get out of poverty."*
>
> *- Muhammad Yunus*

One day in 1976, an economics professor went to a poor village in the countryside of his home country of Bangladesh. He met a woman who made bamboo stools for a living. Although she worked hard, she was very poor because she was forced to pay a very high price for the bamboo. She did not have enough money to buy the bamboo herself, and the village moneylenders charged usurious fees. All the woman needed was 25 cents! The man knew that he could not simply give her the money she needed; doing so would rob the woman of her dignity. Instead, he asked people in the village how much money they needed to get started on their own small businesses and to free themselves from their cycle of poverty. The man then lent the equivalent of about US $27.00 from his own pocket to 42 of the village women.

That man was Muhammad Yunus, and that day in the village was the start of something big! Those women then started their own small businesses, earning money to support their families (their net profit on that first loan amounted to about two cents each). Muhammad Yunus went on to found the Grameen Bank, which has helped over two million Bangladeshi women escape the chains of poverty. The world now knows about the concept of "microcredit" – the granting of "micro-loans" to the very poor, to those without collateral and who would otherwise be rejected by conventional banks as loan recipients.

In 2006, the Nobel Peace Prize was awarded jointly to Muhammad Yunus and the Grameen Bank "for their efforts to create economic and social development from below". The Nobel Prize committee made a wise choice, reminding us that the road to peace must include concerted efforts to reduce the number of people living in poverty. The idea that microcredit can be a guiding principle for successful businesses is catching on throughout the developing world and also in developed nations like Canada and the United States. Like the Grameen Bank, the new microcredit lending institutions lend mostly to women.

Muhammad Yunus is a hero around the world. At one point, he was thinking about becoming involved in politics in Bangladesh, and formed a political party called "Citizens' Power" in 2007. So far, he has not embarked on a political career, but became a member of an international think tank of leaders called The Elders, of which Nelson Mandela was a founding member. He now speaks out about his theory of the "social business enterprise", which places value on enterprises that "generate social improvements and serve a broader human development purpose" in addition to focusing on economic gains. Yunus stresses that capitalism is too narrowly defined in that it focuses solely on profit maximization. Given what industrialization has done to this planet in the name of profit maximization, it is clear that the time has come for the world to get on board with Muhammad Yunus.

A. Write "T" for the true sentences and "F" for the false ones.

1. The woman Muhammad Yunus met in Bangladesh did not have money to buy stools, so she had to make her own bamboo stools. ______
2. Muhammad Yunus did not want to rob the woman of her dignity. ______
3. Muhammad Yunus lent money to the village women so that they could free themselves from poverty. ______
4. The village women started their own businesses and earned a net profit of two cents in all on the first loan. ______
5. "Microcredit" is the granting of "micro-loans" to very poor women in Bangladesh. ______
6. According to the writer, Muhammad Yunus's act of reducing the number of people in poverty will eventually lead to peace. ______
7. Microcredit lending institutions are set up in both developed and developing countries. ______
8. The Elders is a political party formed by Muhammad Yunus in Bangladesh. ______
9. Muhammad Yunus's theory of the "social business enterprise" does not simply emphasize economic gains. ______

Adverb Phrases

An **adverb phrase** is a group of words that describes a verb, an adjective, or an adverb. It functions like an adverb in a sentence.

Example: Yunus stresses that capitalism is too narrowly defined.

A **prepositional phrase** is an adverb phrase when it functions as an adverb.

Example: Yunus asked people how much money they needed to free themselves from their cycle of poverty.

An **infinitive phrase** can also be an adverb phrase.

Example: Those women then started their own small business to earn money.

B. Identify the underlined adverb phrases in the following sentences. Write "P" for prepositional phrases and "I" for infinitive phrases.

1. Muhammad Yunus is famous for introducing the concept of "microcredit" to Bangladesh. ______

2. Yunus founded the Grameen Bank to give loans to the poor in Bangladesh. ______

3. Conventional banks were not interested in giving loans to those without collateral. ______

4. Muhammad Yunus and the Grameen Bank were jointly awarded the Nobel Peace Prize in 2006. ______

5. Yunus would use part of his award money to set up a company to produce low-cost and high-nutrition food for poor people. ______

6. Yunus wrote *Banker to the Poor* to explain how he employed the idea of "microcredit" in the Grameen Bank to help the world's poor. ______

7. Many micro-lending programs have been established around the world. ______

C. Rewrite the following sentences by changing the underlined adverbs to adverb phrases.

1. The Elders is a group of <u>widely</u> respected world leaders.

2. The Elders contribute <u>greatly</u> to solving some very tough global problems.

3. The Elders are <u>generously</u> sponsored by a group of founders.

4. Nelson Mandela worked <u>actively</u> in fighting for freedom and equality in African countries.

5. The Elders respond <u>quickly</u> to conflict situations around the world.

D. Write two sentences containing the following phrases as adverbs.

1. prepositional phrase

2. infinitive phrase

The New 7 Wonders of the World

You have heard of the Seven Wonders of the Ancient World: the Great Pyramid of Giza, the Hanging Gardens of Babylon, the Temple of Artemis at Ephesus, the Statue of Zeus at Olympia, the Mausoleum at Halicarnassus, the Colossus of Rhodes, and the Pharos of Alexandria. You have heard of the Seven Natural Wonders of the World: Mount Everest, the Great Barrier Reef, the Grand Canyon, Victoria Falls, the Harbour of Rio de Janeiro, Paricutin Volcano, and the Northern Lights. But that is not all; it seems that we love to make lists of wonders!

There are also the Seven Wonders of the Medieval Mind (including Stonehenge, the Leaning Tower of Pisa, and the Great Wall of China), the Seven Underwater Wonders of the World (including Lake Baikal, Palau, and the Galapagos Islands), and the Seven Wonders of the Modern World (including the Empire State Building, the Panama Canal, and the CN Tower). To add to the never-ending lists of seven wonders, there are the Seven Forgotten Natural Wonders (including the Bay of Fundy, Niagara Falls, and Mount Kilimanjaro), the Seven Forgotten Modern Wonders (including Mount Rushmore, the Eiffel Tower, and the Aswan High Dam), and the Seven Forgotten Wonders of the Medieval Mind (including Angkor Wat, the Parthenon, and Mont Saint-Michel).

On July 7, 2007, a New 7 Wonders of the World list was announced. With the help of the Internet, people around the world were allowed to vote, and over 100 million online votes were cast. The website of the New 7 Wonders Foundation, which was administering the competition (www.new7wonders.com), was inundated with so many "hits" that its server crashed! From a whittled-down list of 21 sites, the final tally produced the definitive list of the world's top new human-made wonders: the Great Wall of China, Petra in Jordan, Brazil's statue of Christ the Redeemer, Peru's Machu Picchu, Mexico's Chichen Itza pyramid, the Colosseum in Italy, and India's Taj Mahal. The 14 runners-up included the Eiffel Tower, Timbuktu, the Statue of Liberty, Angkor Wat, Hagia Sophia, the Kremlin/St. Basil's, Stonehenge, and the Sydney Opera House.

The "New 7 Wonders" list was the idea of a Swiss businessman Bernard Weber, who felt that the people of the world should be able to decide – "not some government, not some individuals, not some institutions" – and that modern technology had finally made that prospect possible. UNESCO, the United Nations' cultural organization, is not affiliated with this "new wonders" project and has a much longer list of wonders in its World Heritage List – over 1000 sites at the moment – and it is still expanding (check it out at http://whc.unesco.org).

Whichever list you wish to peruse, there are plenty of places to imagine, to learn about, and even to visit – enough to fill many lifetimes. What a wonderful world we live in!

A. Complete the chart with the different lists of seven wonders in the passage and give an example for each.

List of Seven Wonders	Example

Prepositional Phrases

A **prepositional phrase** is a group of words with a preposition as head. It modifies a noun like an adjective, or a verb, an adjective, or an adverb like an adverb in a sentence.

Example: With the help of the Internet, people around the world were allowed to vote.

"With the help of the Internet" and "to vote" function like adverbs and modify the verbs "vote" and "allowed" respectively. "Of the Internet" and "around the world" function like adjectives and modify the nouns "help" and "people" respectively.

B. Write "ADJ" if the underlined prepositional phrases function like adjectives and "ADV" if they function like adverbs.

1. There are various lists of wonders of the world. ________
2. Did you vote for the New 7 Wonders of the World online? ________
3. The new list was announced in Lisbon, Portugal in 2007. ________
4. You can visit the website of the New 7 Wonders Foundation to learn more about the new list. ________
5. The New 7 Wonders of Nature was officially announced in the autumn of 2011. ________
6. The New 7 Wonders list was the idea of a Swiss businessman Bernard Weber. ________
7. "If we want to save anything, we first need to truly appreciate it," said Bernard Weber. ________
8. UNESCO has a World Heritage List of over 1000 sites. ________

C. Fill in the blanks with the appropriate prepositional phrases.

with 91 steps | at the centre | at the site
of the Mayan culture | in the Mayan language
for astronomical purposes | in 2007 | of its four sides

Chichen Itza in Mexico is a UNESCO World Heritage Site and is rated as the most important archaeological site 1. ____________________ . The name means "at the mouth of the well of the Itza" 2. ____________________ . There are many outstanding ruins 3. ____________________ , among which is the Temple of Kukulkan, also known as El Castillo (the castle), situated 4. ____________________ of the city. The temple was voted one of the New 7 Wonders of the World 5. ____________________ . It is a square-based pyramid 6. ____________________ on each 7. ____________________ . It is the largest and most important ceremonial structure at Chichen Itza and was built 8. ____________________ .

D. Write two sentences, one using a prepositional phrase as an adjective and the other using one as an adverb.

1. ____

____

2. ____

____

Harmful Microorganisms

Some microorganisms are beneficial to us, while others can cause infectious diseases. Disease-producing microorganisms, such as viruses, bacteria, protists, and fungi, are called pathogens. They attach to the host tissue at the time of exposure, penetrate it, and then multiply. The host tissue becomes damaged, resulting in an infectious disease. Most pathogens invade our body through skin wounds or through the layers of cells that line the cavities and surfaces of our digestive, respiratory, urinary, or reproductive systems.

At first, the number of pathogens that enter the host is too small to cause any damage; however, under favourable environmental conditions, such as an adequate nutrient supply, suitable temperatures, and suitable pH levels, the pathogens multiply rapidly in the host tissue, causing damage and illness. For example, viruses can take over the host cells' replication mechanisms and start multiplying in the host cells. Bacterial cells can block blood vessels or heart valves, or clog the lungs' air passages. A large number of pathogens may trigger an excessive inflammatory response in the host, as in the case of pneumonia. Many pathogenic bacteria, protists, and fungi damage the host by producing toxins or enzymes. Toxins diffuse into the host cells, disturbing their normal functions; enzymes break down the host's defence barriers, causing the spread of pathogens deeper into the tissues and further throughout the body.

Some microorganisms can also trigger food-borne infection or food poisoning. Food-borne infection is caused by the growth of pathogenic viruses in our body after eating contaminated food, whereas food poisoning is caused by the ingestion of toxins produced by microorganisms. Inadequate storage or refrigeration, inadequate cooking or reheating, contaminated ingredients or utensils, inadequate hand washing, or infection by food handlers can all lead to diseases. In this case, the diseases are usually acute, meaning that symptoms (nausea, abdominal pain, vomiting, diarrhea, fever, and fatigue) arise quickly and recovery can be quick as well, although death can sometimes occur if left untreated.

The Salmonella bacterium is one of the most common causes of food-borne infection. Poultry, eggs, food made from raw eggs, and pre-cooked meat such as sausages, are commonly contaminated by Salmonella. Other causes include E. coli (found in the intestines of warm-blooded animals), which commonly contaminates undercooked beef, and noroviruses, found in fecal-contaminated water, which contaminate shellfish and vegetables washed in the water. The most common type of food poisoning is caused by the toxins produced by the Staphylococcus aureus bacterium. These bacteria exist in air, sewage, water, dust, milk, and on food equipment, humans, and animals. They are easily transferred to the skin, wounds, or nasal cavities of food handlers. When the contaminated food is left in a warm place (between 4°C and 60°C), the bacteria grow quickly and secrete a heat-stable toxin that disturbs the intestines of humans.

Since the SARS (Severe Acute Respiratory Syndrome – a serious and highly infectious form of viral-borne pneumonia) outbreak of 2003, we have become more concerned about the harmful effects of microorganisms and the occurrence of infectious diseases. It is good to know that most outbreaks can be mitigated or avoided by developing good hygiene habits and adhering to safe food preparation and handling methods.

A. Briefly describe the terms below.

1. pathogens

____

____

2. Salmonella

____

____

3. Noroviruses

____

____

4. Staphylococcus aureus

____

____

5. SARS

____

____

Clauses

A **clause** is a group of words that consists of a subject and a predicate. Every sentence consists of one or more clauses. A simple sentence is the most basic kind of sentence structure that is formed with one clause. A sentence with more than one clause has one or more conjunctions that link the clauses together.

Examples: Disease-producing microorganisms are called pathogens.
(a simple sentence with one clause)

Some microorganisms are beneficial to us, while others can cause infectious diseases.
(a sentence consisting of two clauses linked by "while")

B. Underline the clauses in the following sentences.

1. Pathogenic microorganisms are harmful because the diseases they cause may be fatal.

2. When meat is left at room temperature for many hours, the bacteria in it may multiply and contaminate the meat.

3. Illness caused by noroviruses is characterized by nausea, vomiting, and diarrhea.

4. Pathogens can evolve rapidly to avoid being detected by our immune system.

5. Most bacteria are harmless and a few are even beneficial, but some can cause infectious diseases.

6. Although influenza is often confused with the common cold, it is a more severe disease caused by a different kind of virus.

7. At human body temperature, flu viruses can remain infectious for a week but at 0°C, they can last for more than 30 days.

8. When we cough, we have to cover our mouth to avoid the spread of flu viruses.

Coordinate Clauses and Subordinate Clauses

Coordinate clauses are clauses linked by coordinating conjunctions such as "and", "or", and "but".

Example: The symptoms arise quickly and recovery can be quick too.

A **subordinate clause** is a clause that depends on another clause to complete its meaning. It is linked to the clause it depends on, known as the **main clause**, by a subordinating conjunction like "when", "if", or "since".

Example: When the contaminated food is left in a warm place,
(subordinate clause)
the bacteria grow quickly.
(main clause)

C. Find an example for each type of clause from the paragraph below.

We have to be very careful with what we eat, for food poisoning can be fatal. Even eating at home does not mean that we are safe from this infection. If we do not handle food properly, food poisoning can still occur. In fact, what we need to do is simple. Just remember the following: always wash your hands before and after preparing food. Never put raw meat close to cooked food or raw fruits and vegetables, and cook food thoroughly to destroy harmful germs. If you suspect that you have food poisoning, seek medical assistance immediately.

1. **Coordinate Clause**

____

____

2. **Subordinate Clause**

____

____

3. **Main Clause**

____

____

The Science of Dreams

It used to be that if someone called you a dreamer, it was an insult. But these days, people are beginning to appreciate the importance of being a dreamer – both during the day and at night! During the day, a form of "dreaming" is welcomed by innovative, creative businesses. For example, the company 3M (makers of Scotch Tape) allows employees to spend as much as 15% of their work time on their own "pet projects" and interests. This freedom to dream did provide a very good payoff to the company. Because of this policy, 3M employees Arthur Fry and Spencer Silver invented the Post-it note.

As for nighttime dreaming, it is now clear to us that we dream when we sleep, whether we remember it or not. We dream during the REM (rapid eye movement) stage of sleep, as well as at non-REM times. Some believe that dreams are a sort of re-creation of certain psychologically important events, and others ascribe meanings of dreams to long lists of all the things you see in your dreams, but the truth is that there are still many unanswered questions regarding the science of dreams.

Did you know?

- The word "dream" comes from the Middle English word "dreme" meaning *joy* and *music.*
- A third of your life is spent sleeping, and over a lifetime you will have spent six years dreaming.
- We dream about two hours per night.
- We can have, on average, four to seven dreams per night.
- Dreams not only are visual images, but can also include sounds, smell, and tactility.
- Most dreams are forgotten within ten minutes of waking up.
- Most people around the world dream about similar things, characters, social interactions, and emotions.
- Anxiety is the most common emotion associated with dreams.
- While people usually dream something once, many people experience recurring dreams. More females than males experience recurring dreams.

- People who cannot dream, due to sleep disorders, can suffer from personality disorders due to lack of dreaming, in addition to sleep-related illnesses.
- Blind people dream, but only those that once had sight say they dream with visual images.
- Scientific tests have shown us that our brains are more active when we are dreaming than when we are awake!
- You cannot dream when you are snoring.
- If you are awakened right after REM sleep, you may recall your dream better than if you were allowed to sleep until morning.
- Many people have reported experiencing déjà vu in their dreams. This is also more common in females than in males.
- Not everyone dreams in colour. Some people's dreams are exclusively in black and white.

Who would have thought there is so much to know about the hours when we sleep?

A. Choose and underline the correct answers.

1. "Pet projects" are ____ .

   A. projects related to the behaviours of different pets

   B. projects or goals pursued as personal favourites, rather than because they are regarded as necessary or important

2. Employees of 3M can spend ____ .

   A. no less than 15% of their work time on their own interests

   B. 15% of their work time at most on their own interests

3. We dream ____ .

   A. about two hours every night during both REM sleep and non-REM sleep

   B. about one third of our sleeping time during REM sleep

4. We can recall our dreams better if ____ .

   A. we sleep until morning

   B. we are awakened after REM sleep

Noun Clauses

A **noun clause** is a clause that functions as a noun in a sentence.

Example: Some people believe that dreams are a sort of re-creation of certain psychologically important events.

In this sentence, "that dreams are a sort of re-creation of certain psychologically important events" functions as the object of the verb "believe".

B. Check if the underlined words are noun clauses. Cross if they are not.

1. Whatever we dream of will be forgotten soon after we wake up. ____
2. A huge cockroach chased after me in my dream. ____
3. Do you remember the name of that famous dream interpreter? ____
4. I know that even animals have dreams. ____
5. Whether or not we understand the meaning of our dreams is not important. ____
6. Maggie writes down whomever she saw in her dreams. ____
7. I can tell that my baby brother is having a nightmare. ____
8. Sometimes my dreams are in black and white, but more often, they are in colour. ____
9. I am not surprised at what she dreamed of. ____
10. That he has never dreamed before is impossible. ____
11. I was so happy in the dream that I was still laughing the moment I woke up. ____

Adverb Clauses

An **adverb clause** is a clause that functions as an adverb in a sentence. It gives additional information about when, where, why, or how something happens.

Example: You cannot dream when you are snoring.

In this sentence, "when you are snoring" tells when you cannot dream.

C. Underline the adverb clauses in the text below.

Whenever you mention déjà vu to your friends, there will surely be one or two among them that tell you they have had this experience before.

Déjà vu means "already seen" in French. It refers to an uncanny feeling that you have experienced a new situation before.

When I was very young, I had this dream. I came to a temple on a beach. There was an open area built with concrete in front of it. I saw many old people sitting at big round tables. Although they were having a feast, I couldn't hear any sound. Then I saw a Chow-chow tied to a pole. I went over and played with it for a while. After I played with the dog, I turned around and found that all the old people were gone. I was all alone!

Many years later, I went on a trip with my family to an island in Southeast Asia. The tour guide took us to a beach. There I saw a temple with a concrete open area in front. It gave me the creeps the moment I saw it because it was the first time I had been to that island, but everything was exactly the same as in my dream, even the colours of the temple! The only difference was that there were no old people around. Do you know what the weirdest thing was? There was a Chow-chow tied to a pole near the temple!

It is said that "necessity is the mother of invention". This saying helps us understand why humans invented the wheel, learned to use fire for useful purposes such as cooking raw meat, and domesticated horses and dogs. Surely in this day and age there is nothing more we need, but maybe you disagree. Perhaps the need to create, or to invent, is part of our human DNA, or perhaps it is an irresistible urge, similar to the urge we have to express ourselves through the arts. There is still no shortage of strange inventions and crazy new contraptions, but it must be said that some of them may have been created to put a smile on our faces more than to serve a practical purpose.

In Japan, there seems to be quite a lot of these kinds of strange inventions. In fact, a word has been coined to describe such creations: *chindogu*. According to Kenji Kawakami, the amateur inventor and writer who coined the term in the late 1980s, chindogu is "the art of invention based on an 'unuseless' idea". In other words, chindogu inventions may seem silly, but actually serve a real purpose. One example is a pillow with sensors that are meant to measure when the user has fallen into a deep sleep, at which time an alarm in the pillow will go off. This pillow is meant for the busy "salaryman" (a Japanese term for a busy office worker) who may be having a nap at his desk during lunchtime. Other chindogu inventions include: a hay-fever hat consisting of a roll of toilet paper strapped to one's head making it convenient for the person to blow his or her nose, a noodle-eater's hair guard consisting of a 15-centimetre-wide rubber ring fitted snugly around one's face to prevent liquids from splashing onto hair or clothes as he or she slurps up ramen or udon, a portable office tie fitted with tiny pockets on the underside – perfect for stashing necessities such as scissors, a calculator, paper clips, a pen, and credit cards.

Chindogu: Strange Inventions We Can Actually Use

According to Kawakami's "Ten Tenets of Chindogu", a chindogu contraption must exist, that is, a prototype must have been made. Also, these inventions cannot be for real use, and yet, paradoxically, they are tools for everyday life. Humour must not be the only reason for creating such items. Another tenet is that chindogu inventions should have the inherent spirit of anarchy. Kawakami adds that chindogu items are not for sale, are not propaganda, are never taboo, cannot be patented, and are without prejudice.

However, since chindogu inventions are a lot of fun and actually do serve a practical purpose, many things in Japan and elsewhere that seem chindogu at first have made it into the mainstream. In Canada, for example, one can buy a certain dental hygiene product that looks like quilted-cotton finger puppets, but are in fact bristle-less "toothbrushes" for people who want to brush on the go. Such an item, albeit with bristles, is already in the chindogu catalogue. Also, at the 2006 Hong Kong Footwear Design Contest, a pair of running shoes made from computer keyboards, called "IT", won top prize in the sports category. Does this mean "IT" is something from which we can no longer run away? How chindogu!

A. Write in point form Kawakami's "Ten Tenets of Chindogu".

Ten Tenets of Chindogu

- ______________________
- ______________________
- ______________________
- ______________________
- ______________________
- ______________________
- ______________________
- ______________________
- ______________________
- ______________________

Relative Clauses

A **relative clause** is a subordinate clause that helps identify someone or something, or provides information about it. It is also called an adjective clause or adjectival clause since it describes a noun. It goes immediately after the noun it relates to. A **relative pronoun** (who, whom, whose, which, that) or a **relative adverb** (when, where, why) is used to link a relative clause to the part of the sentence it describes.

Example: The bristle-less "toothbrushes" are for people <u>who want to brush on the go</u>.

B. Underline the relative clause in each of the following sentences.

1. Necessity is the reason why there are so many inventions.
2. The pillow has sensors that measure when the user has fallen into a deep sleep.
3. This invention is meant for the busy "salaryman" who may be having a nap during lunchtime.
4. Kenji Kawakami, whose books have been translated into many different languages, is the founder of the International Chindogu Society.
5. The inventor to whom the prize was awarded has become famous worldwide.
6. That was the time when these two great inventors first met in history.
7. Have you been to the country in which the design contest is held?
8. The convention centre where the exhibition was held will be closed for renovation.
9. The little problems that we encounter in our daily lives are inspirations for many chindogu inventions.
10. This is the invention that has been voted The Strangest Invention of the Year.

Defining and Non-defining Relative Clauses

Relative clauses can be defining or non-defining.

A **defining relative clause** identifies or describes a particular person or thing.

A **non-defining relative clause** simply provides additional information about the person or thing. It is separated from the main sentence by commas.

Examples: The amateur inventor <u>who coined the term "chindogu"</u> is also a writer. (defining)

Kenji Kawakami, <u>who coined the term "chindogu"</u>, is an amateur inventor and writer. (non-defining)

The relative clause in the first example is defining because without it, one cannot tell which amateur inventor the sentence is about.

C. Add a defining or non-defining relative clause to each of the following sentences.

1. The inventor ____________________

   ____________________ has come up with a fun invention.

2. A chindogu invention should be one ____________________

   ____________________ .

3. Will you join the design competition ____________________

   ____________________ ?

4. There are a lot of chindogu inventions in Japan, ____________________

   ____________________ .

5. The running shoes "IT", ____________________

   ____________________ , won top prize in the sports category.

6. The "Ten Tenets of Chindogu", ____________________

   ____________________ , was written by Kenji Kawakami.

Totem Poles

Have you ever seen a totem pole? Even if you have not had the good fortune of seeing them in person along the Pacific Northwest, you have probably seen them on television. They are monuments carved in wood, usually from large red cedar trees, and are an important tradition in many of the aboriginal cultures along the Pacific Northwest coast of North America. It is believed that the English word "totem" comes from an Anishinaabe word *doodem*, meaning "clan".

Totem poles are a type of heraldry recording a variety of information, depending on the group involved. Some totem poles record clan lineage, while others are in fact historical records of the community. There are also some that depict the group's legends. This art form is ancient, but due to the humid climate of the region (which encourages decay of organic matter), very few totem poles built prior to the 1800s are still around today. The Royal British Columbia Museum in Victoria, B.C. has one that is dated pre-1400s! Totem pole construction declined in the early 1900s as European settlers discouraged Aboriginal groups from continuing with their traditional ways.

Ainu, the aboriginal people of the northern island of Hokkaido, Japan, are also makers of totem poles. Their totem poles are smaller because the sources of wood are much smaller trees than those found along the Pacific Northwest, and they are not painted. You can find Ainu totem poles in the Vancouver area at Burnaby Mountain Park, near Simon Fraser University. Staring up at these awesome carvings, you may wonder how it came to pass that the aboriginal culture of Japan – the Ainu – would have something so similar in their tradition to the First Nations' totem poles in Vancouver. Perhaps it is more proof of the "land bridge" that is said to have existed across today's Bering Sea, and that the aboriginal cultures of Canada and Asia are indeed related.

Totem poles can also be found in other parts of the world, although they are a little different. The Maori people of New Zealand have smaller "totem poles", as do cultures in Tahiti, India, and parts of Africa. Anthropologists tend to make a distinction between the totem poles of Canada and the wooden figures of these other places. They refer to the latter carvings as "ancestor figures", "greet figures", "talismans", or "tikis". This is because, in the latter cultures, these wooden figures were made for the purposes of ancestor worship or identifying taboos, or as depictions of their gods.

Totem poles are sacred objects and cannot be made by just anyone. In Canada, authentic totem poles can only be made by trained members of West Coast Aboriginal groups. Only in very rare cases can a non-aboriginal be sanctioned to do this work. The totem pole must also be sanctioned or "blessed" in a special ceremony undertaken by qualified elders.

The majestic and awe-inspiring totem poles we see in Aboriginal villages, and in parks lucky enough to have been gifted one or several, are not only testaments to the beauty of Aboriginal art, but also to the beauty of Aboriginal heritage.

A. Based on the information in the passage, explain the cause or effect of the following.

1. Cause: Humid climate encourages decay of organic matter.

   Effect: ______________________________

   ____

2. Cause: ______________________________

   ____

   Effect: Totem pole construction declined in the early 1900s.

3. Cause: ______________________________

   ____

   Effect: Ainu totem poles are smaller.

4. Cause: Wooden figures found in places like Tahiti and India were made for ancestor worship or identifying taboos, or as depictions of their gods, unlike the totem poles found in Canada.

   Effect: ______________________________

   ____

5. Cause: ______________________________

   ____

   Effect: Authentic totem poles can only be made by trained members of West Coast Aboriginal groups.

Types of Sentences

Simple sentence: consists of one single clause

Compound sentence: made up of two or more coordinate clauses linked by "and", "or", or "but"

Complex sentence: made up of one main clause joined to one or more subordinate clauses with subordinate conjunctions like "because" and "although"

Compound-complex sentence: made up of two or more coordinate main clauses along with one or more subordinate clauses

B. Identify the types of sentences below. Write "S" for simple sentences, "CP" for compound sentences, "CX" for complex sentences, and "CPX" for compound-complex sentences.

1. My parents had a week's holiday last month, and they took my sister Angie and me on a trip to Vancouver. ________

2. We flew there so that we could have more time in Vancouver. ________

3. Since Angie has a great fear of heights, she did not enjoy the flight. ________

4. We visited some tourist attractions, including Grouse Mountain, the Vancouver Aquarium, and the Burnaby Village Museum. ________

5. As my cousin Lucas studies at the University of British Columbia, and he resides on the campus, we went there to visit him. ________

6. He had planned to take us to the Museum of Anthropology to see the totem poles, but the museum was closed for renovations. ________

7. He took us to see the famous totem poles at Stanley Park instead. ________

C. Find an example of each below from the passage.

1. a simple sentence

2. a compound sentence

3. a complex sentence with the conjunction "while"

4. a complex sentence with the conjunction "although"

5. a complex sentence with the conjunction "even if"

6. a complex sentence with the conjunction "as"

7. a compound-complex sentence

One More Reason to Save the Rainforest

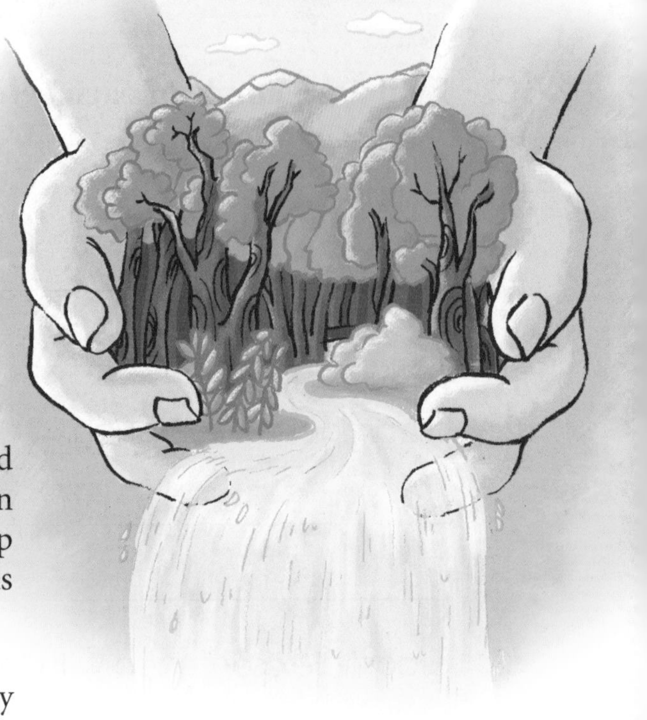

As we all know by now, the large rainforests scattered around the world, and the Amazon Rainforest in particular, are the "lungs" of our planet. They soak up much of the carbon dioxide we produce and give us life-sustaining oxygen in return.

The world's rainforests are also home to the majority of the planet's plant and wildlife species; we can thank rainforests for the *biodiversity* of our world, which has benefited the human species in many ways. For example, rainforest ecosystems have provided us with not only a variety of herbs and medicines, but also many very healthy things to eat! In fact, some of our favourite snacks contain ingredients originally sourced from the rainforest, such as the cocoa in chocolate and the kola nut from which cola drinks are derived, not to mention coconuts, cashews, macadamia nuts, ginger, vanilla, bananas, corn, and cinnamon. And what would we dip our nacho chips in if we did not have the tomatoes and avocadoes needed for salsa?

The foods listed above are all commercially grown now and are known to people around the world. We are also becoming familiar with a variety of rainforest foods that provide real health benefits. These are called "superfoods", and the indigenous peoples inhabiting the world's rainforests have long known about their healthy benefits. These days, urban dwellers and people in far-away places can also benefit from these "magical" plant items. Below are three "superfoods" that may be unknown to you.

The acai berry (pronounced as-sigh-ee) is a small purple fruit grown in bunches (like grapes) on tall palm trees. It tastes like a blend of field berries and chocolate, and is full of antioxidants, amino acids, and essential fatty acids. Antioxidants help lower the risk of heart disease, and these little berries have 30 times more antioxidants than red grapes. Fatty acids help brain function, and acai also provides loads of energy. It can be mixed into smoothies or sorbet, or drunk as a juice.

The yerba mate is a type of holly found in subtropical South American countries. A special tea can be made by steeping dried leaves and small twigs from this plant. It tastes like herbal tea – slightly grassy – but does not become bitter when steeped for a long time. It gives us minerals we need, such as potassium, magnesium, and manganese. It has a kind of caffeine-like stimulant, but is gentler on the stomach than coffee or tea.

The cupuassu is a tree found in the rainforests of Brazil. The fruit of this tree is encased in brown, fuzzy, oblong pods, up to two kilograms in weight and covered in a thick skin. The cream-coloured, pulpy fruit inside is wonderfully fragrant and contains theacrine, an alkaloid believed to boost our immune systems, lower cholesterol levels, and ward off cancer. It is often mixed into ice cream and jams or made into juice blends.

These three rainforest products – all from South America – are becoming increasingly popular among society's more health-conscious members. More and more special food items like these are being discovered every week. We need to protect our rainforests to make sure that these types of plants are not lost to us before they can even be "discovered".

A. Write in your own words the main idea of each paragraph.

Paragraph 1 ____________________

____

Paragraph 2 ____________________

____

Paragraph 3 ____________________

____

Paragraph 4 ____________________

____

Paragraph 5 ____________________

____

Paragraph 6 ____________________

____

Paragraph 7 ____________________

____

Word Roots

Many English words are derived from Greek and Latin **word roots**. Understanding these roots helps us get the meanings and spellings of the derivatives right more easily.

Example: word root – extra
meaning – outside; beyond
derivatives – extracurricular ; extraterrestrial; extraordinary

B. Find derivatives that contain the word roots below from the passage.

	Root	Meaning	Derivative
1.	maj	greater; larger	________________
2.	kilo	thousand	________________
3.	de	from	________________
4.	anti	against	________________
5.	di	two	________________
6.	bene	good	________________
7.	medic	heal; cure	________________
8.	bio	life	________________
9.	eco	home	________________
10.	pop	people	________________
11.	vari	different	________________
12.	super	beyond; more than	________________
13.	sub	below	________________
14.	con	with; together	________________

Prefixes and Suffixes

Groups of letters can be added to some base words to modify their meanings.

A **prefix** refers to a group of letters added to the beginning of a base word.

Example: perfect → imperfect (not perfect)

A **suffix** refers to a group of letters added to the end of a base word.

Example: perfect → perfectly (in a perfect manner)

C. Find words from the passage that are derived from the base words below and have the meanings in the parentheses. Make sentences of your own with the derivatives.

1. dwell (people who dwell in a place) ____________

____

2. know (not known) ____________

____

3. herb (consisting of herbs) ____________

____

4. gentle (with a higher degree of gentleness) ____________

____

5. origin (with respect to origin) ____________

____

6. cover (found something previously not known) ____________

____

The Endangered Tibetan **Antelope**

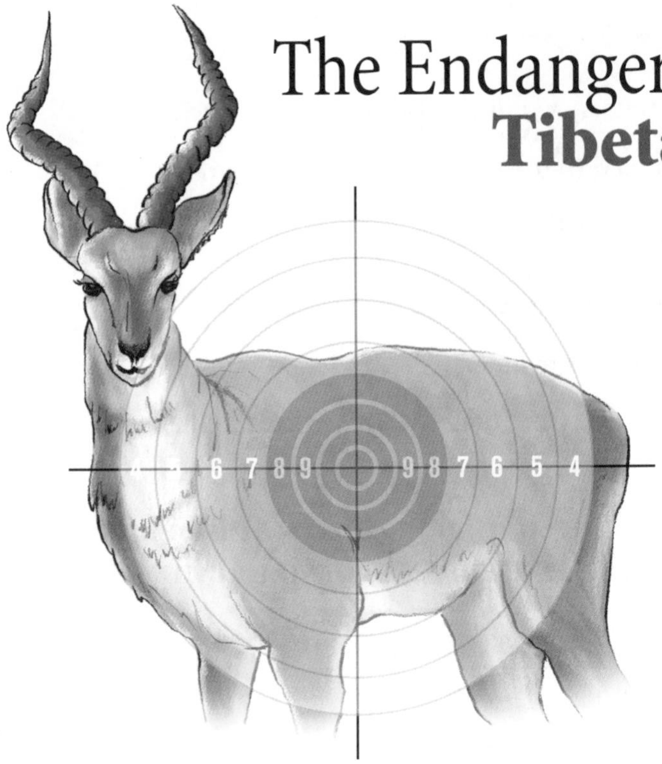

The Tibetan antelope, commonly called chiru, or "Tsod" in Tibetan and "Zanglingyang" in Chinese, is the only large mammal native to the Tibetan Plateau. It lives primarily in the Tibet Autonomous Region, Qinghai Province, and the Xinjiang Autonomous Region of China. Some Tibetan antelope have been spotted in Ladakh, an area in northwest India. These hearty creatures love the cold alpine meadows and deserts of this vast and windswept region.

The Tibetan antelope is related to wild goats and sheep. Males are 80 to 85 centimetres high at the shoulder and weigh about 35 to 40 kilograms. They have slender, curving black horns that can grow to as long as 50 to 60 cm! Females are slightly smaller and do not have horns. Their coat colouring ranges from grey to reddish-brown with a white underside. In the winter, the male Tibetan antelope develops black markings on its face and legs. The Tibetan antelope can survive in temperatures as cold as -40°C, grazing on the sturdy plants and grasses of the region. It seems like an inhospitable place for such a gorgeous animal.

A hundred years ago, it is believed that herds of a million chiru roamed the Tibetan Plateau. Today the estimated number is less than 75 000. This is because these animals have been hunted down for the fine hair beneath their thick coat of wool (the secret to how they stay so warm), called shahtoosh. Each animal must be killed in order to harvest the ultra-fine hairs at the skin; the hair cannot be shorn as in the case of sheep's wool. This shahtoosh is desired by people all over the world. It is very warm, and can be woven into shawls so fine they can pass through a wedding ring! One shahtoosh shawl is worth thousands of dollars, and is one of the most sought-after items among wealthy people.

Because of this, people illegally hunt the Tibetan antelope, despite the fact that it is protected by Chinese law. Each year, between three and five thousand Tibetan antelope are killed by poachers to supply the illegal trade in shahtoosh fibre. Some estimate that the figure could be as high as 15 or even 20 thousand! Wildlife officials in the region are outnumbered by the armed hunters who shoot the animals and then sell the shahtoosh to international smugglers.

Why is it that so many people are willing to kill endangered animals when they know it is wrong? Just as in the trade of ivory, poverty causes some people to resort to criminal activity in order to feed their families and get their daily necessities. Many think we cannot blame the impoverished poachers. Instead, to solve the problem of illegal poaching, we must target not just the suppliers, but also those who demand these luxury products. Efforts are being made to ban the sale of shahtoosh around the world as a way to protect this endangered species, but this will not be enough. Fewer people are now wearing fur, compared to a couple of decades ago, due to the efforts of those against the slaughter of animals for fur. These same people must now turn their attention to the Tibetan antelope, and tell the world that it is not fashionable or glamorous to kill such a beautiful animal simply to wear a fabric that can fit through a wedding ring.

A. Complete the chart about the Tibetan antelope below.

The Tibetan Antelope

Other Names:	1. ____________________
Species:	related to 2. ____________________
Habitat:	3. ____________________ ____________________
Population:	4. ____________________
Size (Male):	5. ____________________ ____________________
(Female):	6. ____________________
Coat Colour:	7. ____________________
Special Features:	8. ____________________ ____________________ ____________________ ____________________
Main Diet:	9. ____________________

Easily Confused Words

We often confuse words that have similar sounds or spellings, or are related in meanings. We should look up words in a dictionary when in doubt, to make sure we are using the right words.

B. Fill in the blanks with the correct words to complete the paragraphs.

The Tibetan antelope 1. ____________ (lives/leaves) in the Tibetan Plateau region, which is covered with widespread 2. ____________ (deserts/desserts) and cold alpine meadows. They 3. ____________ (grace/graze) on the sturdy plants and grasses in the region. Male Tibetan antelope have 4. ____________ (slander/slender), black horns, while females are hornless. Tibetan antelope have ultra-fine hair called shahtoosh under 5. ____________ (there/their) thick coat of wool. This is the 6. ____________ (secret/secrete) to how they stay warm in their cold habitat, where temperatures can reach as low as 40 7. ____________ (decrees/degrees) Celsius below zero.

Since shahtoosh can be woven into very warm shawls and sold at very high 8. ____________ (prices/prizes), 9. ____________ (porches/poachers) kill Tibetan antelope for these ultra-fine hairs and 10. ____________ (sale/sell) them to smugglers, 11. ____________ (despise/despite) the fact that it is against Chinese law to hunt these endangered animals.

C. Write sentences with the words below to show the difference in their meanings.

1. grace ______________________

   graze ______________________

2. slander ______________________

   slender ______________________

3. secret ______________________

   secrete ______________________

4. decree ______________________

   degree ______________________

5. sale ______________________

   sell ______________________

6. despise ______________________

   despite ______________________

As a Canadian student, you have access to a computer. Perhaps you even have one all to yourself. These days, especially for students, a computer is considered a necessity, not a luxury. You may even have spent time wondering how on earth people managed without computers, which is what was done in the years before you were born.

Canadian students are lucky; there is a high standard of living in this country, and most people can afford the cost of a computer. But in developing countries, this cost is way beyond the reach of most people. How do students in those countries manage without computers? Imagine how much more those students could learn if they had their own computer! And not only that, imagine how students around the world could communicate with one another if each one had a computer. It could help to make the world a better place.

This was the dream of Nicholas Negroponte, the founding chairman of the Massachusetts Institute of Technology's Media Lab. To make it happen, he set about developing a computer that would cost only U.S. $100. This price tag would motivate governments of poor countries to purchase computers for all their students. Negroponte met with government leaders and got assurances from several (including the leaders in Nigeria, Brazil, and Thailand) that they would buy millions. The more computers that could be produced for purchase, the cheaper the cost. And so began Nicholas Negroponte's One Laptop Per Child (OLPC) project.

One Laptop Per Child

In November 2005, at the World Summit on the Information Society in Tunisia, Negroponte and UN Secretary General Kofi Annan unveiled a working prototype of the computer, called XO. In addition to word processing capability, this green and white laptop had a built-in wireless network interface and a colour camera. It had no hard disk, but came with 1 GB of flash memory. To help save power (a major concern in developing countries), the computer had a dual-mode screen; it could switch from black-and-white to colour. By the end of 2006, the first prototypes had been shipped, and the first large-scale production line began in November 2007. The final cost of this computer turned out to be about U.S. $188 per unit, but for many, it was close enough, and people around the world were looking forward to the notion of students in developing countries being given their own personal laptop computer, a better education, and a brighter future.

But the story of the $100 laptop has not been smooth sailing. Negroponte's plan was to supply computers to children as a not-for-profit endeavour. Companies who were in the business of making and selling computers knew that this would have an adverse effect on their profits. So the larger computer manufacturers began developing their own low-cost computers, with software to go with it, not to mention brand recognition. As a result, some of the governments of countries who, at first, pledged to buy the XO, backed out of the deal and bought the laptops developed by OLPC's new competitors. Whatever the future of the OLPC organization, Nicholas Negroponte and his team at MIT must be recognized as the leaders of the global movement to provide affordable computers to children around the world.

A. Answer these questions.

1. In what ways can computers enrich our learning experience?

2. What problem did the OLPC project encounter?

3. If you were the government leader of a developing country, would you purchase computers for all the students in your country? Why or why not?

Capitalization

Follow these basic rules of capitalization:

1. at the beginning of a sentence, except for one that is put in parentheses within another sentence
2. names of particular people, things, projects, and organizations
3. titles when used before names but not after names
4. names of places and countries, and adjectives derived from names of countries
5. days of the week, months, holidays, and special events
6. main words in titles – do not capitalize articles, prepositions, and coordinating conjunctions
7. abbreviations

B. Refer to the rules above. Decide which rules of capitalization the underlined words in the sentences below follow. Write the numbers on the lines.

1. Many Canadian students have access to a computer. ______
2. Nicholas Negroponte is the founding chairman of the Massachusetts Institute of Technology's Media Lab. ______
3. He began the One Laptop Per Child project. ______
4. Negroponte and UN Secretary General Kofi Annan unveiled a working prototype of the computer in 2005. ______
5. The computer was named XO. ______
6. It came with 1 GB of flash memory. ______
7. The computer could switch from black-and-white to colour. ______
8. The mass production of the XO computer started in November 2007. ______
9. I first learned about OLPC from the article "OLPC Gives Poor Children Hope". ______

C. Rewrite the following sentences using proper capitalization.

1. xo was unveiled at the world summit on the information society held in tunisia in November 2005.

2. inspired by the olpc project, the brazilian government started to investigate the use of laptops in education.

3. i came across an article about the features of xo in the computer magazine today's technology.

4. mr. negroponte aimed to eliminate poverty in developing countries through the one laptop per child project.

5. daisy told me her family has bought a new computer, so she can do research on the internet for our english project.

6. this laptop has a maximum memory capacity of 5 gb.

Yummy International Desserts

Who does not love desserts? We all have our favourite desserts for different reasons, whether it is a fondness for certain flavours, or because they bring back memories of another time, place, event – or even a person. Many desserts are made for special occasions, but every once in a while, we know that a specific food – especially a sweet one – will give us a lift when we feel we need it (we call these foods "comfort foods").

It is always fun to try new things, but even if we tried a new dessert every day for the rest of our lives, we would never sample all the desserts the world has to offer! One thing we could do, however, is to try the desserts that are favourites in many parts of the world. These desserts show up more often than others on the menus of fine restaurants around the world.

Pies are the favourite desserts of many people. They are often made of fruit. The most popular fruit pies are peach, blueberry, raisin, rhubarb, strawberry, and of course, apple. Fruit pies can even include citrus fruits, like key lime and lemon meringue pies. There are also cream pies, such as banana cream, coconut cream, and chocolate cream pies. Some pies are made from non-fruit items, such as the pumpkin pie and the pecan pie.

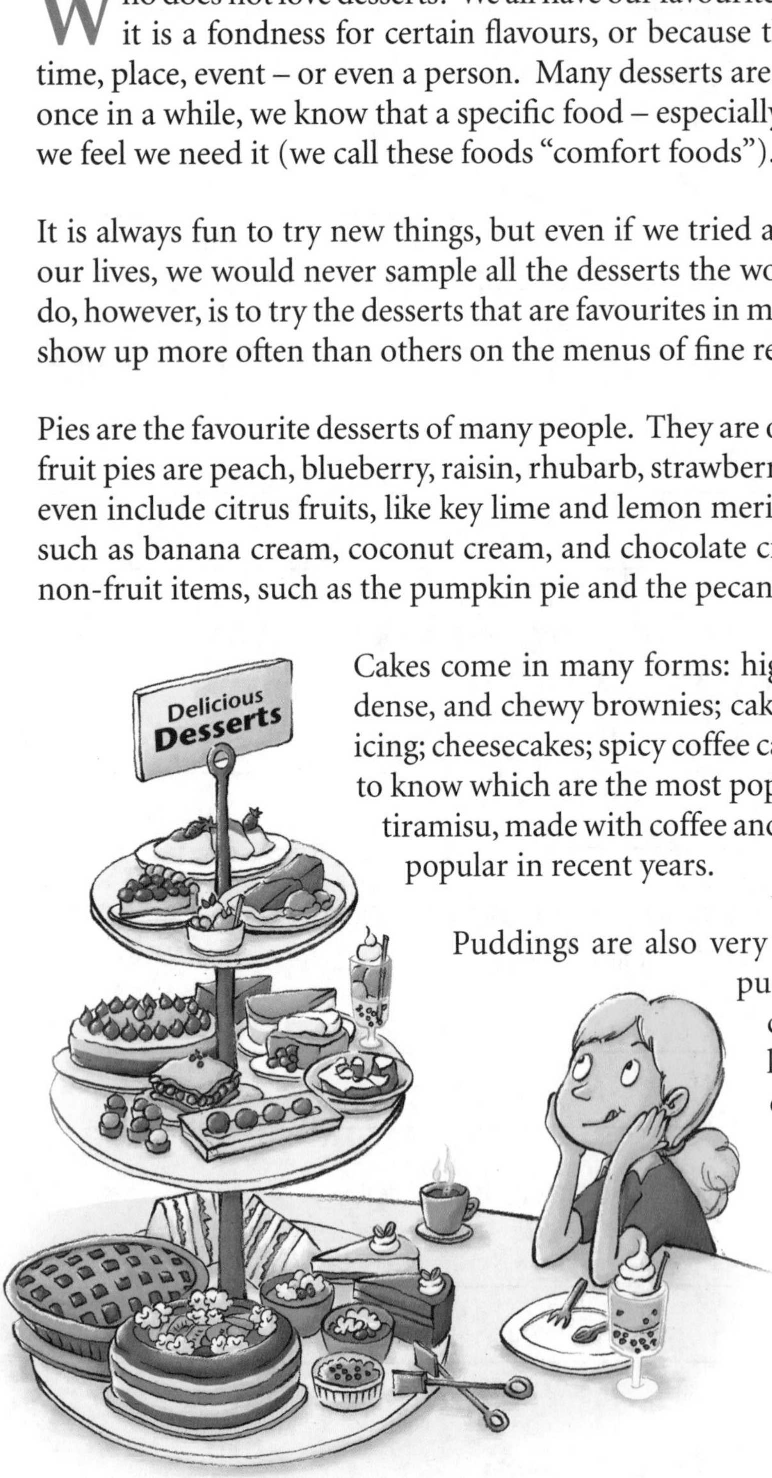

Cakes come in many forms: high and spongy angel food cakes; flat, dense, and chewy brownies; cakes in layers covered in fruit or jam or icing; cheesecakes; spicy coffee cakes... The list is endless, and it is hard to know which are the most popular. But an old Italian dessert called tiramisu, made with coffee and mascarpone cheese, has become very popular in recent years.

Puddings are also very popular desserts. Some, like bread pudding or rice pudding, are made with cheap and abundant ingredients but loved by the rich and poor alike. A list of some of the most popular puddings today includes chocolate mousse and its vanilla-flavoured equivalent, panna cotta. Custards (a kind of dessert similar to puddings) are also popular, especially in the form of almond-flavoured blancmange and egg-flavoured crème caramel, or a warm version called crème brûlée with its hard crunchy layer of burnt sugar on top.

With the rise of international travel and immigration, everyone can now know the favourite desserts of cultures in far-away places. Some of the best-loved "international" desserts would have to include the following: Baklava originating from the Middle-East and Mediterranean countries – a sweet, sticky dessert made of layers of phyllo pastry, honey, and pistachio nuts; English trifle – custard, fruit, jam, and bits of sponge cake or biscuits layered in a bowl and topped with whipped cream; Gulab Jamon from South Asian countries – delicious balls of cake soaked in a sweet rose water syrup; and Crêpes Suzette from France – thin pancakes rolled in a sauce of orange juice, sugar, and liqueur. There are too many international favourites to name! How fun life would be if we became experts on yummy desserts of the world!

A. Complete the chart below.

Dessert	Origin	Description
Baklava		
Trifle		
Gulab Jamon		
Crêpes Suzette		

B. If you were to recommend a dessert from your culture to your friends, what would your choose? Briefly describe this dessert and explain why you would recommend it.

____

____

____

____

____

____

Colons and Semicolons

We use a **colon** to set off a list, a quotation, or an explanation. It shows that what follows is closely related to the introducing clause.

We use **semicolons** to separate items in a list, especially when the items are long and contain commas within, or to separate closely related independent clauses.

Example: Cakes come in many forms**:** high and spongy angel food cakes**;** flat, dense, and chewy brownies**;** cakes in layers covered in fruit or jam or icing**;** cheesecakes**;** spicy coffee cakes...

C. Add colons and semicolons in appropriate places.

1. Rachel has a sweet tooth she likes all kinds of desserts.

2. We ordered three desserts cheesecake topped with blueberries, raspberries, and strawberries yogourt parfait with layers of yogourt, fruit, and granola crepe filled with bananas, fresh cream, and chocolate sauce.

3. The world-famous restaurant expects one thing from the new pastry chef creativity.

4. Have you heard of this saying "A world without ice cream is a world in darkness"?

5. The four-judge panel for the dessert competition includes Mrs. Emily Miller, Principal of the French Culinary Academy Mr. Ryan Cann, Executive Chef of North Windsor Hotel Ms. Hannah Evans, Chief Editor of *Fine Cuisine Magazine* Mr. Logan Ramos, former winner of the competition.

6. We need these ingredients to make waffles flour, sugar, eggs, milk, and baking powder.

7. This is the first cake I made a chocolate shortcake topped with sweetened strawberries and whipped cream.

Dashes, Parentheses, and Quotation Marks

We use **dashes** to insert or set off appositions and explanations to further the reader's understanding of the sentence.

We use **parentheses** to enclose phrases or statements as additional information that is not an essential part of the main statement and that does not normally fit into the flow of the text.

We use **quotation marks** to enclose direct quotations or fragments of quotations, words or phrases used with special meanings, and titles of short stories, articles, and poems.

Example: Once in a while, we know that a specific food – especially a sweet one – will give us a lift when we feel we need it (we call such foods "comfort foods").

D. Add dashes, parentheses, and quotation marks in appropriate places.

1. The soufflé at this restaurant I don't remember its name is excellent. You must give it a try.
2. The article How to Make Award-Winning Desserts has given us useful information.
3. Simply Delight a cozy café in downtown Toronto offers a fantastic assortment of desserts and special drinks.
4. Wow, this is the most scrumptious lemon meringue pie I've ever had! exclaimed Josh.
5. Valeria is learning to make chocolate éclair a favourite dessert of everyone in her family.
6. This Japanese chef uses *nori* dried seaweed in many of his desserts.
7. Tiramisu an Italian dessert made with coffee and masarpone cheese is loved by many.
8. Elmo gave the brownie a big bite he would have put the whole piece into his mouth if he could and was already reaching for the last piece on the plate.

"After the Boom"

Canada has its share of "boom" towns: places that began or grew rapidly in response to a certain commodity being found and developed nearby. Probably the best-known boom town is Dawson City, Yukon. When gold was discovered in 1896 in a nearby river, the Klondike Gold Rush began, and Dawson City went from being a fishing camp to a bustling town of 40 000. The gold rush ended only a few years later, and people began to leave in large numbers. Although there were "mini-booms" over the decades related to the fortunes of the mining industry, the search for gold was all but over by the 1960s. Today, Dawson City is a town of about 1300 year-round, growing to 5000 during the summer. There have been many towns like Dawson City all over Canada through the decades. Some of these towns have been able to "reinvent" themselves, primarily as "eco-tourism" destinations, but most of them are simply sad reminders of what once was.

At present, Canada's biggest and most "booming" boom town is Fort McMurray, located about 450 kilometres northeast of Edmonton. The reason it exists has mostly to do with the "oil sands" (a mixture of sand, clay, water, and heavy crude oil) located in this area in vast quantities. The First Nations peoples of the area have long known about these oil sand deposits. For example, they used the tar-like substance to waterproof their canoes. The oil sands were first described by the explorer Alexander MacKenzie in his 1790 chronicles.

Fort McMurray was established as a Hudson's Bay Company trading post in 1870 at the confluence of the Athabaska and Clearwater Rivers, but it grew because of the oil sands. The first company to exploit the resource was Abasands Oil, back in the 1930s. However, the process by which the oil could be extracted from the sand was not cost effective. As the price of oil increased, greater efforts were made to tap into the vast reserves. In 1966, the population of Fort McMurray was only 2000, but with the opening of the Suncor plant in 1967 and then the Syncrude consortium mine in 1978 (still the biggest mining operation of any kind in the world), the population grew to over 30 000 by 1980. During these years, the price of oil was relatively high due to tensions in the Middle East, the world's main oil-producing region. The growth of Fort McMurray levelled off during the late 1980s and 1990s when the price of oil fell sharply.

Now, however, the price of oil has surged again. Companies like Syncrude are no longer worried about the cost of extracting the oil from sticky oil sands. All the companies involved are stepping up production. The population of Fort McMurray is now more than 70 000. As is the case with such towns, there is a significant social and environmental impact stemming from the oil-extraction and processing industry. Pollution from the tailing ponds is said to be contaminating the land, rivers, and also the local wildlife population. Among the inhabitants of the area, there is a high rate of depression, drug abuse, illness, and social dysfunction.

What will become of Fort McMurray after the boom?

A. Write the events that took place in the following years.

1790 ______________________________

1870 ______________________________

1896 ______________________________

1930s ______________________________

1960s ______________________________

1967 ______________________________

1978 ______________________________

B. Do you think Fort McMurray will face the same fate as other boom towns like Dawson City one day? Why or why not?

____

____

____

____

____

____

Spelling Rules

1. Drop the silent "e" when the suffix begins with a vowel.
   Examples: bustling, mining, trading

2. Retain the silent "e" when the suffix begins with a consonant.
   Examples: relatively, movement, useful

3. Change the ending "y" to "i" before a suffix, except when the "y" follows a vowel or when the suffix is "ing".
   Examples: companies, played, studying

4. Double the ending consonant of a word when the suffix begins with a vowel, except when the ending consonant is preceded by two vowels.
   Examples: logging, booming, tailing

5. Do not double the ending consonant of a word with more than one syllable when the word is accented on the first syllable.
   Examples: murmuring, tutored, comforting

6. Put "i" before "e", except after "c" and for words that rhyme with the letter "a".
   Examples: yield, deceive, weight

C. Circle the correctly spelled word in each pair.

1. heating / heatting
2. steming / stemming
3. worryed / worried
4. purposeful / purposful
5. heirarchy / hierarchy
6. employed / emploied
7. referred / refered
8. visuallized / visualized
9. speculative / speculateive
10. terrifiing / terrifying
11. reciever / receiver
12. reindeer / riendeer
13. hurries / hurrys
14. development / developement

D. Read the clues and complete the following crossword puzzle.

Across

A. that can be proven right or reasonable
B. sound made by a horse
C. produce
D. attractive
E. someone who examines accounts officially
F. dishonest

Down

1. filled with deep regret
2. working something out in detail
3. moved from one place to another
4. providing food and services for a banquet
5. making something free of dirt or harmful substances
6. gave something to someone for approval

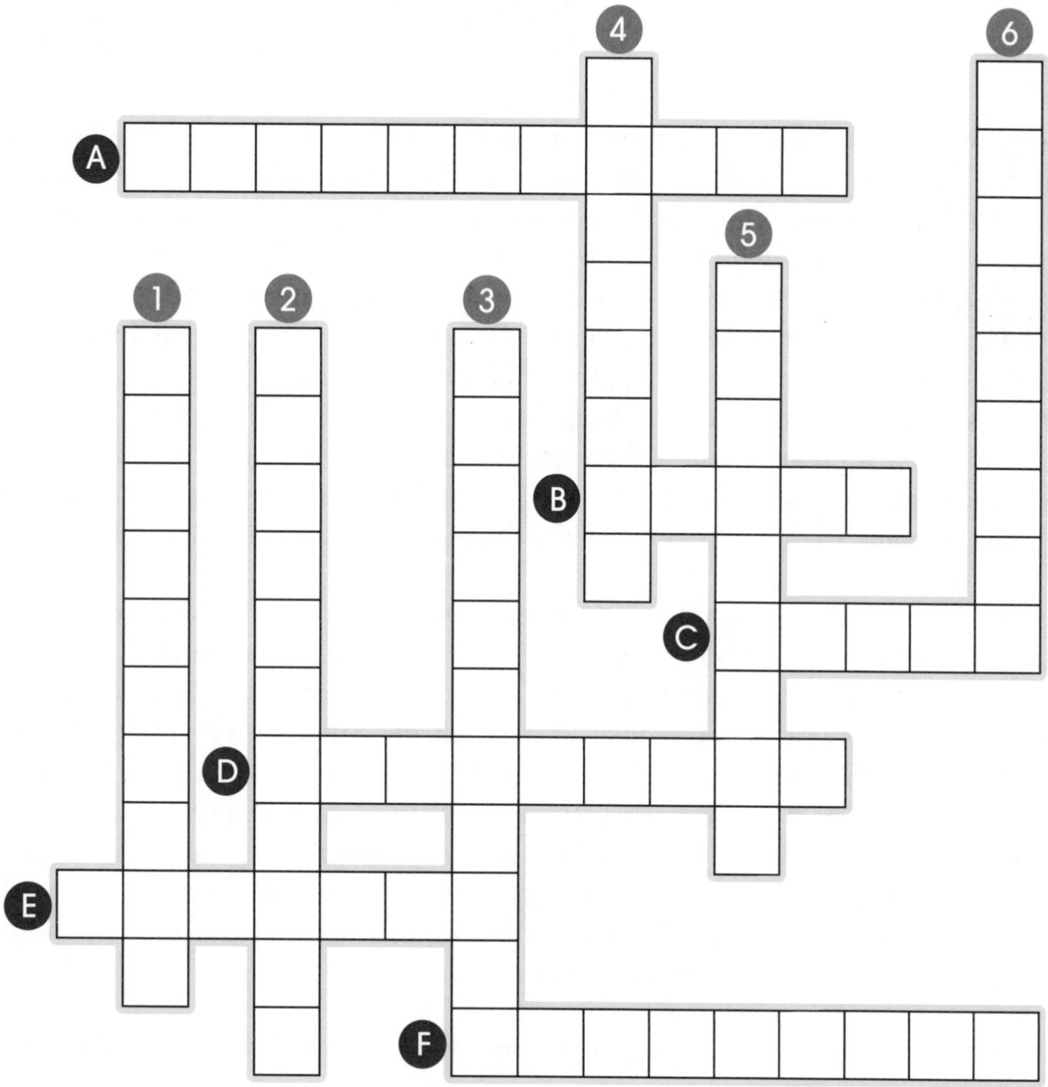

From St. Laurent to the Smithsonian

The tiny town of St. Laurent, Manitoba, is located approximately 80 kilometres north of Winnipeg, and sits at the south-east corner of Lake Manitoba. It has its share of local folklore, including the following: the lake monster Manipogo, sightings of which date back as far as 1908; a legendary white horse, brought from Mexico by a Cree Chief as a gift to the local Assiniboine Chief in return for his beautiful daughter's hand in marriage; even stories of UFO sightings by several residents! Past and current residents include a former Lieutenant Governor of the province, a former baseball player for the national baseball team of Australia, several famous fiddlers of all ages, and a renowned wildlife photographer. This is all pretty impressive for a place where there are only about 1200 residents throughout most of the year – although the population triples during July and August when cottagers from near and far come to spend their summer along the shore of peaceful Lake Manitoba.

However, St. Laurent is a special community in more ways than this: about half of the permanent population of the town is of aboriginal or Métis descent, and it is one of the few places in the world where the Métis culture is still very active, as shown in the way people earn their livelihoods, and in their festivals and music. The language of the Métis people (called Mitchif), which is a mixture of Cree or Salteaux, French, and English, is spoken here too. For this reason, the town received a visit from two representatives of the famed Smithsonian Institution in Washington, D.C., United States. Founded in 1846, the Smithsonian Institution is a research and education centre and the largest museum in the world. The Institution had been planning to build a new museum, called the National Museum of the American Indian, and curators wanted St. Laurent to be included in an exhibit.

Some of the items provided by the townspeople to the National Museum of the American Indian include: several historical photos, an ice chisel and ice augur, nylon fishing nets and hooks, a muskrat trap hook, a chair made of willow branches, and even an old Bombardier snowmobile! These items reflect the fact that hunting, trapping, and fishing had been the mainstay of the community for generations, and are an important part of Métis history and culture. The museum also took a CD of songs written by a popular local band called Coulee which, according to lead vocalist Serge Carriere, "reflect the great spirit of Lake Manitoba that weaves us together as a community... [and] celebrate the Métis language, and other aspects of Métis culture such as our relationships to nature and to each other, and how we fit in the world." The exhibit opened in the fall of 2004, thereby enshrining a part of Métis culture for all to see in one of the most visited, and most revered, places of learning.

So, if you cannot make it to Washington, D.C. to learn more about a culture that has so much to do with Canada's history, then why not come to Manitoba, to the little town nestled in the south-east corner of peaceful Lake Manitoba? See for yourself what the unique, and very Canadian, Métis culture has to offer!

A. Complete the following information about St. Laurent.

1. Location:

 ____

 ____

2. Local folklore:

 ____

 ____

 ____

3. Average population:

 ____

4. Language of the Métis people:

 ____________________ (a mixture of ____________________

 ____)

5. Name of a popular local band:

 ____

Avoiding Repetition

To make our writing more interesting to read, we have to avoid repeating the same words. We can do so by using synonyms or words with similar meanings. A thesaurus would be helpful.

Examples: several famous fiddlers

a renowned wildlife photographer

the famed Smithsonian Institution

B. Complete the crossword puzzle with synonyms of the clue words.

Across

A. placid
B. abandon
C. homesick
D. apparent
E. endure

Down

1. hygienic
2. scarce
3. moan
4. concede
5. frightening

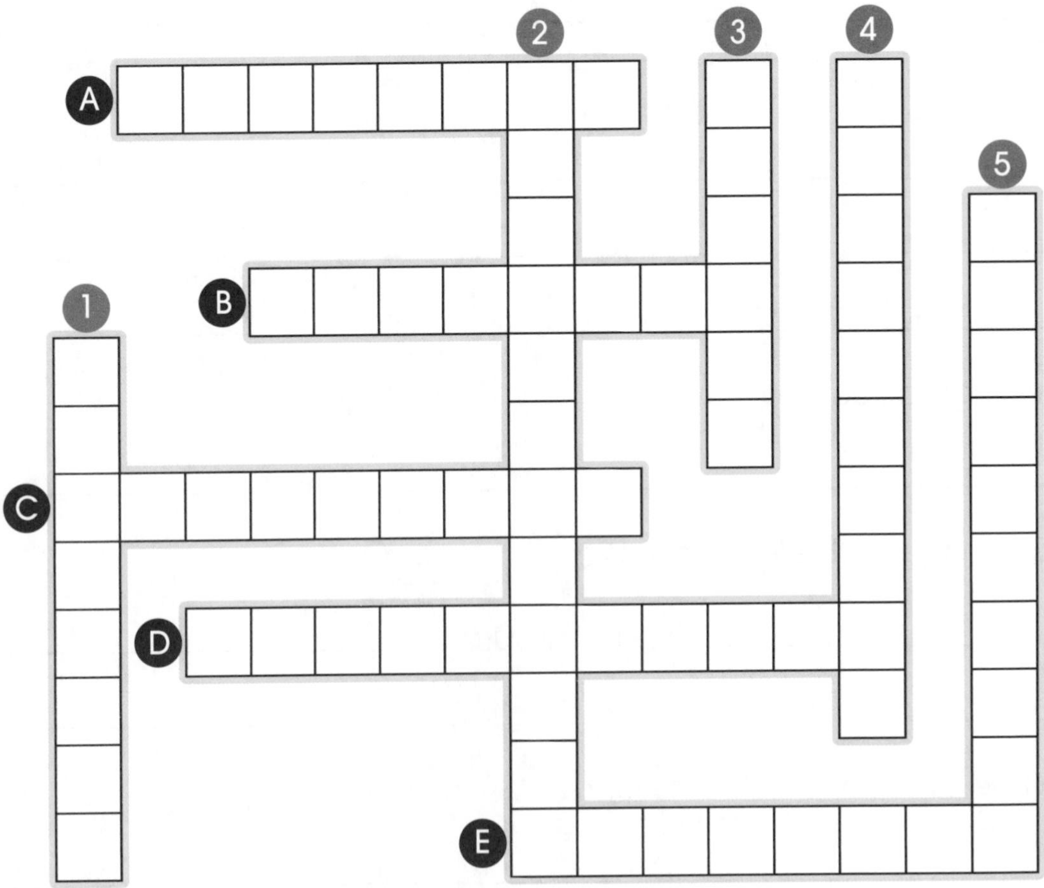

C. For each of the following words, write three words that have similar meanings.

1. brave ______ ______ ______
2. restrict ______ ______ ______
3. ring (noun) ______ ______ ______
4. shiver ______ ______ ______
5. amazing ______ ______ ______
6. cease ______ ______ ______

D. Rewrite the following paragraph by replacing the underlined words with words that have similar meanings to avoid repetition.

Manipogo is a legendary creature that lives in Lake Manitoba. Those who claimed to have seen it described it as a huge snake-like creature that swam fast. Some people believe it to be a living dinosaur that <u>lives</u> in the lake. Every year, tourists flock to Lake Manitoba hoping to have a chance to <u>see</u> this <u>huge</u>, <u>legendary</u> creature with a body that resembles a <u>snake</u>.

____

____

____

____

____

____

____

____

____

The Making of a *Sea-faring* Legend

The world of sea-faring has been rich with legend and superstition for centuries. Deep-sea fishing and ocean explorations through the ages have meant that the brave souls lucky enough to return to shore have spoken of their adventures – and who could dispute what they have said? These stories have inspired great literary works. For example, famed poet Samuel Taylor Coleridge's *The Rime of the Ancient Mariner*, which mentions frightening sea creatures, was said to be inspired by the exploratory South Pacific voyage of Captain James Cook. Herman Melville's classic novel *Moby Dick*, published in 1851, is about an encounter with a long and "pulpy" sea creature. Another poet, Alfred Lord Tennyson, also wrote about a sea monster in his poem, *The Kraken*.

The Kraken - *Alfred Lord Tennyson*

Below the thunders of the upper deep;
Far, far beneath in the abysmal sea,
His ancient, dreamless, uninvaded sleep
The Kraken sleepeth: faintest sunlights flee
About his shadowy sides; above him swell
Huge sponges of millennial growth and height;
And far away into the sickly light,
From many a wondrous grot and secret cell
Unnumber'd and enormous polypi
Winnow with giant arms the slumbering green.
There hath he lain for ages, and will lie
Battening upon huge seaworms in his sleep,
Until the latter fire shall heat the deep;
Then once by man and angels to be seen,
In roaring he shall rise and on the surface die.

This poem later influenced novelist Jules Verne's classic, *Twenty Thousand Leagues Under the Sea*, published in 1870. In fact, stories of such sea monsters have appeared as far back as the Norse Sagas and as recently as C.S. Lewis's "Narnia" series and J.R.R. Tolkien's *The Lord of the Rings*. Scandinavian children have long heard legends of the Kraken – told by parents who wish to keep them wary of wading too far into the water. The word "Kraken" is derived from their word *krake*, meaning "something that is twisted", or otherwise "an unhealthy animal". In the German language, the word for "sick" is *krank*, and the word *krake* means "octopus" – and herein lies the answer to what exactly was scaring sailors in far-off waters all those years!

Recent marine explorations, which incorporate the use of deep-sea roaming cameras, as well as rare catches by fishing boats much better-equipped than the wooden sailing ships long ago, have resulted in the discovery of the real-life inspiration for all these myths and legends about sea monsters. While the general consensus had been for ages that these stories were based on encounters with large octopuses, it is now believed that the Kraken is actually the elusive giant squid, with its torpedo-shaped mantle, eight enormous arms, and two even longer tentacles!

A. Answer these questions.

1. People who returned from ocean explorations have told of their adventures, and the writer of "The Making of a Sea-Faring Legend" says "...and who could dispute what they have said?" Why do you think the writer says so?

___

___

___

2. What do literary works such as *The Rime of the Ancient Mariner*, *The Kraken*, and *Twenty Thousand Leagues Under the Sea* have in common?

___

___

___

3. Find an example of a sea-faring superstition from the library or the Internet. Do you believe in it? Why or why not?

___

___

___

Creating Images with Precise Words

In writing, we **create images** to arouse the reader's interest and imagination. This can be achieved by using precise words instead of more common and general words to create vivid images in the reader's mind.

Example: The giant squid has a triangular mantle, eight big arms, and two even longer tentacles. (general)

The giant squid has a torpedo-shaped mantle, eight enormous arms, and two even longer tentacles. (more precise)

B. Rewrite the sentences by replacing the underlined words with more precise ones.

1. For many years, the sea creature Kraken has appeared in stories told by sailors.

___

2. The Kraken was believed to have strong arms that could break a large ship.

___

3. Returning from the trip, the man wrote a book about his story.

___

4. Last night, I had a dream. I was chased by an ugly monster.

___

5. The animal we saw was small but it was fierce.

___

6. Do you see a weak light moving in the thick fog?

___

7. You can find more information about what this creature is from the book.

___

Creating Images with Literary Devices

Literary devices like personification, similes, and metaphors are also employed to create vivid images in writing.

Personification is the attribution of human qualities to inanimate objects.

A **simile** is a descriptive comparison of two things that have some characteristics in common using "as" or "like".

A **metaphor** is a comparison of two things without using "as" or "like". We describe something as though it were something else.

C. Identify the literary devices used in the sentences below. Write "P" for personification, "S" for similes, and "M" for metaphors.

1. According to some stories, the Kraken was the king of the ocean. ______
2. The creature swam past the cruiser as fast as a speedboat. ______
3. Deep under the sea, it is dark like a black hole. ______
4. The giant ray dances gracefully in the water. ______
5. The sea monster was as tall as the mast of a large ship. ______

D. Imagine you saw a sea monster on a voyage. Describe the sea monster using the three literary devices you have learned in this unit.

Who is Oscar? And why do people always talk about him on the night of the Academy Awards? Oscar is the nickname of the gold-plated statuette, officially called the Academy Award of Merit, that winners receive on this special night when the Academy of Motion Picture Arts and Sciences rewards its top achievers of the year.

Outside the Dolby Theatre in Los Angeles, where the Academy Awards ceremony is held, and before the ceremony starts, another very important show is going on. People who registered months in advance to sit on bleachers outside the theatre watch the stars exit their limousines and walk the red carpet to the theatre's entrance. Here, the stars chat with celebrity interviewers and have their pictures taken.

These interviewers will ask, "Who are you wearing?" No, their grammar is not wrong. They are asking the stars who designed their clothes because fashion is a very important part of being a star. Maybe the interviewers will ask, "Who do you think has a shot at the (Best Picture) Oscar?" The stars are happy to talk about who designed the clothes they are wearing, but most will only smile when asked for their Oscar predictions.

The Academy Awards: Oscar's Big Night

The opening ceremony usually includes a big musical number. Then we may hear, "Ladies and gentlemen, your host for the evening is..." The host, the Master of Ceremonies, is usually a famous comedian. Soon it is time for the first Oscar to be awarded, and the first pair in a long line of celebrity presenters will come on stage. They will joke with each other, talk about the Oscar category, and then say, "And the nominees are..." After the nominees are shown, we hear, "And the Oscar goes to..." It's all very exciting! The winners come on stage and give a short speech, usually starting with, "I'd like to thank..." They will want to thank everyone they can think of!

Oscars are given in a variety of categories, such as screenwriting, costume design, makeup, cinematography, film editing, animation, documentary filmmaking, sound editing and mixing, as well as special visual effects. But perhaps the presentations that viewers are most eager to

see are the ones for best foreign language film, best song, best supporting actor/actress, best actor/actress, best director, and best picture. Of course, the Oscar for best picture of the year is always given at the very end.

By now, if you are watching an evening telecast of the show, it may be quite late, especially if the winners have taken more than the two minutes given for their "thank-you" speeches. For us, when the show is over, we go to bed. But once the show is over in Los Angeles, it is time for everyone, winners and losers, to celebrate at an after party. They will party until dawn and enjoy the greatest night in show business: the Oscars.

A. Answer these questions.

1. "Fashion is a very important part of being a star." Do you agree with what the writer thinks? Why or why not?

____

____

____

2. Why will the stars only smile when interviewers ask about their predictions of Oscar winners? Give your opinion.

____

____

____

3. Why do you think the host of the Academy Awards is usually a famous comedian?

____

____

____

4. Name three presentations of Oscars that you are most eager to see. Give reasons for your choices.

____

____

____

Using Phrases to Begin Sentences

To make our writing more interesting to read, we can vary the construction of sentences. One way to do so is to start a sentence with a phrase instead of the subject.

Examples: Outside the Dolby Theatre, another very important show is going on. (prepositional phrase)

To watch the entire show, we have to stay up late. (infinitive phrase)

Not knowing who will win, the nominees wait anxiously. (gerund phrase)

Surprised with the result, the winner forgot whom to thank. (participle phrase)

B. Rewrite each of the following sentences by starting it with a phrase.

1. The winner held the Oscar in his hands, and he was too excited to say a word.

2. The people got excited when they saw the celebrity exiting the limousine.

3. The presenter paused before announcing the winner to create suspense.

4. People registered for the bleacher seats outside the theatre months in advance.

Using Appositives

Combining simple sentences can make our writing more concise and stylish. One way to do so is to use appositives. An **appositive** is the renaming of a word that immediately precedes it. It is set off from the rest of the sentence with commas.

Example: The host is the Master of Ceremonies. The host is usually a famous comedian.

The host, the Master of Ceremonies, is usually a famous comedian.

C. Use an appositive to combine each pair of sentences below.

1. The Academy Awards ceremony is the greatest event in show business. It is held annually.

2. The Oscar is a gold-plated statuette. It is presented to every Academy Award winner.

3. James Cameron is a Canadian-American director and screenwriter. He won the Best Director Award for *Titanic*, released in 1997.

4. The Oscar is one of the most recognized awards in the world. It is a symbol of achievement in the film industry.

A Story of
What Kids Can Do

Have you ever heard of the global organization, Free The Children? Ontario native Craig Kielburger founded the organization in 1995, when he was just 12 years old. It is now the world's largest network of children helping children. And it all began one day when Craig was reading the local newspaper.

The article Craig read was about another 12-year-old boy named Iqbal Masih who lived in Pakistan. The boy had been murdered after speaking out about the terrible conditions he and other child-labourers had to endure while working in the carpet-making industry. Craig was determined to do something. He convinced his parents to let him accompany Alam Rahman, a Canadian human rights worker, to various South Asian countries. He wrote about the terrible injustices against children he saw on that trip in his first book *Free the Children*.

Craig had only just begun. He founded Free The Children with his 12-year-old friends. The group started petitioning governments, demanding that they stop child labour. Craig would meet with world leaders and tell them in person, sometimes when he was not even invited to do so! Even though Craig's cause was a good one, some adults felt that he, as a child and also as a person from North America, had no right to tell adults and politicians what they should or should not do. But this did not stop Craig.

Since those early years, Craig, along with his elder brother Marc, has founded a youth leadership training organization called "Leaders Today" and has written several books. In 2007, Craig was awarded the Order of Canada medal by the Governor General, Canada's top civilian honour. Craig has also won a variety of distinctions from around the world, including: The Reebok Human Rights Award, The Roosevelt Freedom Medal, The 2005 Kiwanis World Service Medal, The Nelson Mandela Human Rights Award, The Community of Christ International Peace Award, and The World Economic Forum GLT Award. He has been awarded an honorary degree in law from the University of Guelph, and a Doctorate in Education from

Nipissing University. He has appeared on *CNN* and *60 Minutes*.

Of course, Craig Kielburger is deserving of all these accolades, but do you think they are what motivate him to do what he does? Do you think Craig works toward the goal of freeing children around the world from enslavement so he can meet celebrities and world leaders? Surely not. Craig Kielburger's commitment to children is clearly stated in one of his founding mottos: "If we are to achieve true peace in this world, it shall have to begin with the children."

We would be lucky if all world leaders felt this way and followed Craig's example of positive action. Check out www.freethechildren.com to learn more about what this great organization is doing and how you can be a part of it!

A. Check the true statements. Rewrite the false ones to make them true.

1. Free the Children is a global organization founded by Craig Kielburger. ☐

   ____

2. In his first book, Craig Kielburger wrote about the injustices against children in Pakistan. ☐

   ____

3. Craig founded "Leaders Today" with his elder brother Marc and his 12-year-old friends. ☐

   ____

4. "Leaders Today" runs leadership training programs for young people. ☐

   ____

5. Craig received an honorary degree in education from Nipissing University. ☐

   ____

6. Craig Kielburger believes that world peace has to begin with world leaders. ☐

   ____

Omitting Superfluous Words and Phrases

Clear and concise writing makes it easier for the reader to follow your ideas. To write concisely, we have to avoid using superfluous words or phrases. Replace these words or phrases with fewer words that mean the same or simply delete them without affecting the meaning.

Example: Free The Children is <u>at this point in time</u> the world's largest network of children helping children. (✘)

Free The Children is <u>now</u> the world's largest network of children helping children. (✔)

B. Replace each of the superfluous phrases below with a word.

1. in the absence of ____________
2. in light of ____________
3. in order to ____________
4. on account of the fact that ____________
5. despite the fact that ____________
6. prior to the time of ____________
7. subsequent to ____________
8. in conjunction with ____________
9. am in the opinion that ____________
10. with the exception of ____________
11. in the event that ____________
12. in spite of the fact that ____________
13. owing to the fact that ____________

C. Cross out the superfluous words and phrases in the following sentences.

1. Craig Kielburger is the kind of person who always thinks of freeing children around the world from enslavement.
2. Craig Kielburger's successful achievements in fighting for child rights can be proven by the various distinctions he has received.
3. "Leaders Today" organizes programs that are intended to train young people as leaders.
4. You do not need to have any past volunteer experiences to join the group.
5. All new volunteers will have to attend the orientation tomorrow at 12 o'clock noon.

D. Rewrite the following sentences by deleting the superfluous phrases or replacing them with fewer words.

1. Child labour has existed in some countries for a very long period of time.

   ____

2. Despite the fact that he was not invited, Craig would meet with world leaders and demand that they stop child labour.

   ____

3. In order to achieve world peace, it is absolutely essential to ensure children's rights.

   ____

4. In my opinion, I think that young people have the power to change the world into a better one.

   ____

5. Free The Children has built more than 500 schools in China, Kenya, Sri Lanka, and etc.

   ____

23

The Truth about CARBS

Carbohydrates – nicknamed "carbs" – have become an increasingly popular topic of discussion. Usually this discussion is about obesity and the increasing levels of it, especially among young people. This fact has given rise to all sorts of diets and books about diets, which some people get wealthy writing and publishing. Some of the most popular weight-loss regimes, such as the Atkin's Diet and the Paleo Diet, are "low-carb" or even "no-carb" diets. In these regimes, one cuts out all carbohydrates – pasta, bread, rice – and eats very few fruits and vegetables. However, dieters can eat all the fats and proteins, such as meat, butter, and cheese, they wish. Although weight will come off quickly this way, it never stays off once a dieter stops dieting. Moreover, most people who adhere to a diet made up mostly of proteins and fats will eventually suffer from ill health. The truth is, we need carbohydrates in our diet.

Carbohydrates are, in fact, our most important and readily available energy source. The energy is formed through a complex chemical process in our bodies. Broken down into simple sugars, all carbohydrates are absorbed into our bloodstream. As our blood sugar level rises, a hormone called insulin is released by the pancreas, which moves the sugar into the cells. The cells then use that sugar as their energy source. This energy gives us the "get-up-and-go" feeling we need to work and play all day long. When we are more energetic, we use up more of this energy source, which we measure in calories.

It is important to know that there are different kinds of carbohydrates. First of all, there are two main forms: simple carbs and complex carbs. Simple carbs are also referred to as simple sugars, such as the lactose we find in dairy products, the fructose we find in nutritious fruits, and the glucose we find in natural sweets such as maple sugar and honey. Complex carbs are starches found in vegetables such as potatoes, as well as in grains, rice, bread, and cereals.

These simple and complex carbohydrates are all good, but modern food manufacturing has also created "bad" carbs – those found in "refined" foods such as candy, soft drinks, white sugar, white flour in pastas and white bread, and many things we love to eat like doughnuts, cakes, and pastries. Because of the widespread availability and marketing of these types of products, they are being consumed in larger quantities than ever before. This, and more affordable and common home entertainment systems and computers which lead to more sedentary lifestyles, has helped create the high levels of obesity and obesity-related illnesses, such as diabetes, among young people.

Doctors recommend that up to 60% of the diet of young people should be comprised of carbohydrates. Make sure that your 60% comes in the form of the "good" carbs, found in food items such as whole-grain cereals, brown rice, whole-grain breads, fruits, vegetables, and low-fat dairy products, which are available everywhere. And along with a healthy diet, stay active!

A. Based on the information in the passage, explain the cause or effect of the following.

1. Cause: A person cuts out all carbohydrates and adheres to a diet rich in proteins and fats.

   Effect: ______________________________

   ____

2. Cause: ______________________________

   ____

   Effect: The pancreas releases a hormone called insulin, which moves the sugar into the cells.

3. Cause: Sugar is moved into the cells.

   Effect: ______________________________

   ____

4. Cause: ______________________________

   ____

   Effect: Bad carbs are being consumed in large quantities.

5. Cause: ______________________________

   ____

   Effect: Young people are leading more sedentary lifestyles.

Faulty Parallels

Coordinate elements in a sentence must be parallel in structure. A **faulty parallel** occurs when these elements do not have a consistent grammatical construction.

Example: Some people cut out all carbohydrates and very few fruits and vegetables are eaten. (✘)
Some people cut out all carbohydrates and eat very few fruits and vegetables. (✔)

Remember not to omit necessary words in the parallels.

Example: Starches found and extracted from potatoes are complex carbs. (✘)
Starches found <u>in</u> and extracted from potatoes are complex carbs. (✔)

B. Rewrite the following sentences to correct the faulty parallels.

1. To live healthy lives, we must choose our food wisely and working out regularly.

____

____

2. Carbohydrates provide the energy we need to work and for playing in our everyday lives.

____

____

3. This book focuses and gives detailed explanations of the benefits of low-carb diets.

____

____

4. Dietitians promote proper eating habits and participation in research.

____

____

Dangling Modifiers

A **dangling modifier** refers to a modifier that modifies something that it should not be modifying. When constructing a sentence, we need to keep the modifier close to the words it modifies to avoid confusion in meaning.

Example: Broken down into simple sugars, our bloodstream absorbs all carbohydrates. (✘)

Broken down into simple sugars, all carbohydrates are absorbed into our bloodstream. (✔)

(It should be "all carbohydrates", not "our bloodstream", that are broken down into simple sugars.)

C. Rewrite the following sentences so that they do not have dangling modifiers.

1. Classified as a simple carb, we find lactose mainly in dairy products.

____

____

2. Although easily digested, dietitians do not recommend the carbs from refined foods.

____

____

3. As a carbohydrate found in plants, our bodies do not digest fibre.

____

____

4. Like a sponge, water is absorbed by insoluble fibre to help move solid waste out of our bodies.

____

____

24

Your Carbon Footprint

A new, somewhat funny-sounding term has been coined in recent years to help us understand how we are damaging our planet: the "carbon footprint". According to carbonfootprint.com, a carbon footprint is "a measure of the impact human activities have on the environment in terms of the amount of greenhouse gases produced, measured in units of carbon dioxide".

Why must we be aware of how our activities factor into the creation of greenhouse gases, which include, in order of abundance, water vapour, carbon dioxide, methane, nitrous oxide, and ozone? The answer is clear, and is also contained in two other relatively new terms: global warming and global climate change. We need these "greenhouse gases" to help keep our Earth warm, but too much of them, in particular carbon dioxide, causes the planet's atmosphere to heat up, with catastrophic effects ranging from melting glaciers to poleward spreading of tropical diseases to extreme weather.

There are two types of carbon footprint. The primary footprint is a measure of direct carbon dioxide emissions created by the burning of fossil fuels such as oil, coal, and natural gas. Domestic energy consumption, automobile, and air transportation account for a great percentage of this "footprint". The secondary footprint measures indirect carbon dioxide emissions based on the manufacturing and eventual disposal and breakdown of the products we use. In fact, the breakdown of the average person's carbon footprint shows us the following: electricity consumption – 12%, private transport – 10%, public transport – 3%, holiday flights – 6%, food and drink – 5%, clothes and personal effects – 4%, carbon in car manufacturing – 7%, household – 9%, recreation and leisure – 14%, financial services – 3%, gas, oil, and coal – 15%, and a person's share of public services – 12%.

So, how can we reduce our carbon footprint? According to carbonfootprint.com, the five best ways to reduce our primary footprint are: (1) avoid air travel for the holidays; (2) sign up for a renewable energy source of electricity; (3) use solar heating instead of gas for heating water; (4) use public transportation; (5) participate in carpools.

Then what can we do to reduce our secondary footprint? We should avoid drinking bottled water, reduce our meat consumption, avoid buying food, drinks, and clothes from far-off countries, and avoid buying goods with a lot of unnecessary packaging. But there are so many other things we can do! We can become more energy efficient in many ways: take shorter showers, bike to school, switch to LED light bulbs, and buy foods and clothing with fair-trade labels.

There are even carbon "offset" schemes that allow people to "cancel out" the carbon dioxide creating effects in their everyday lives. For example, if you are taking a long-haul flight for your next holiday, you can go to the website of a carbon-offsetting organization and use their carbon calculator to find out the amount of emissions the flight would create. This will be worked out to a fee. In turn, the organization uses the money you pay to fund projects such as reforestation or the distribution of energy-efficient light bulbs. A flight from Toronto to London, UK, might cost you about $25 to "neutralize". The purchase of carbon offsets is becoming increasingly popular with both individuals and corporations who are eager to live – another new term – "carbon neutral" lives.

A. Write the main idea of each paragraph.

Paragraph 1: ______________________________

____

Paragraph 2: ______________________________

____

Paragraph 3: ______________________________

____

Paragraph 4: ______________________________

____

Paragraph 5: ______________________________

____

Paragraph 6: ______________________________

____

Developing Paragraphs

A **paragraph** consists of a group of sentences with a common topic. It is made up of a topic sentence and supporting sentences. The topic sentence states the main idea of the paragraph. It is usually the first sentence of a paragraph. The supporting sentences explain the main idea further or add details to it. A paragraph may end with a closing sentence that restates the main idea, gives a conclusion, or leads on to the paragraph that follows.

B. Write a topic sentence for each of the following groups of sentences.

1. ____________________

____

One of them is the more frequent occurrence of heat waves. The excessive heat, usually accompanied by high humidity, leads to heat-related illnesses such as heat stroke and heat rash, and even death. Heat waves that occur in dry areas or during droughts may cause wildfires, which may burn down massive areas of forests and agricultural lands. Scientists warn that global warming will continue to have disastrous effects on our planet.

2. ____________________

____

Take a shower instead of a bath. Never leave the light on when nobody is in the room. Think carefully of what you want to get before you open the fridge door. Walk or bike to school if possible. These are just a few among the many easy ways to save energy in our everyday lives.

3. ____________________

____

First, we can put a composter in our backyard. Through composting, organic material is converted into a soil-like material called humus, which can be used to nourish the plants in the garden. Another way is to separate organic waste like fruit and vegetable scraps, coffee grinds, and egg shells from garbage and recyclable material, and put it in the green bin. With these two ways, the amount of household waste that goes to landfills will be greatly reduced.

C. Develop a paragraph with each of the topic sentences below.

1. Yesterday was Plant a Tree Day at my school.

2. I read an interesting story about how an alien helped a little girl save some endangered animal species on Earth.

The Biofuel Controversy

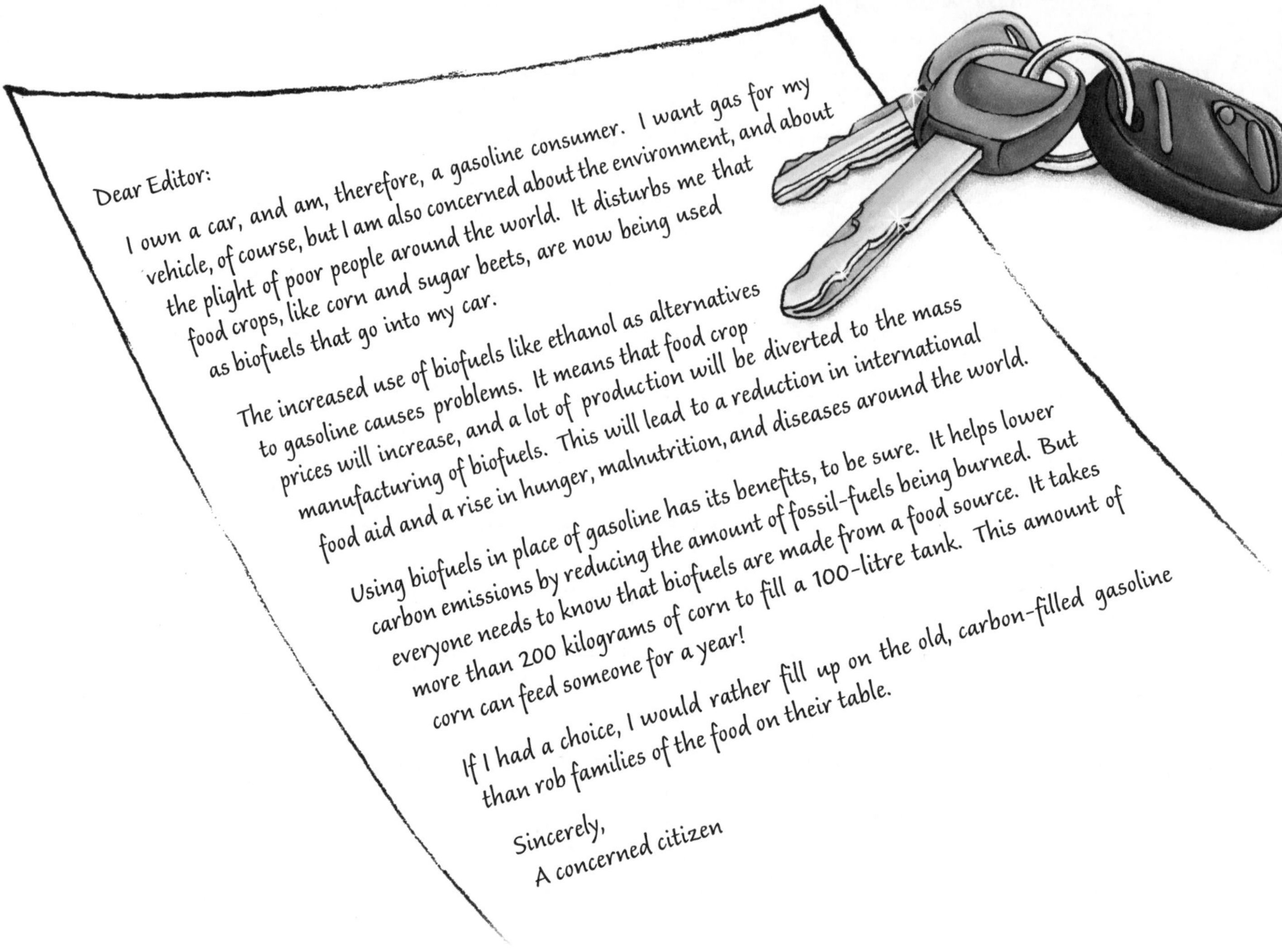

Dear Editor:

I own a car, and am, therefore, a gasoline consumer. I want gas for my vehicle, of course, but I am also concerned about the environment, and about the plight of poor people around the world. It disturbs me that food crops, like corn and sugar beets, are now being used as biofuels that go into my car.

The increased use of biofuels like ethanol as alternatives to gasoline causes problems. It means that food crop prices will increase, and a lot of production will be diverted to the mass manufacturing of biofuels. This will lead to a reduction in international food aid and a rise in hunger, malnutrition, and diseases around the world.

Using biofuels in place of gasoline has its benefits, to be sure. It helps lower carbon emissions by reducing the amount of fossil-fuels being burned. But everyone needs to know that biofuels are made from a food source. It takes more than 200 kilograms of corn to fill a 100-litre tank. This amount of corn can feed someone for a year!

If I had a choice, I would rather fill up on the old, carbon-filled gasoline than rob families of the food on their table.

Sincerely,
A concerned citizen

What do you think of this letter to the editor? Do you agree or disagree with the writer? The growing use of food for fuel is becoming a serious controversy. While it seems that biofuels are part of an answer to the huge issue of global warming, the reasons for the biofuel controversy are as much environmental as they are economic and political.

People will not stop buying cars. In fact, Tata Motors in India unveiled a new car there in 2008, the Tata Nano, which can be purchased for the same price as a fancy laptop computer. This car is not a hybrid vehicle, nor one powered purely by non-carbon fuels. The existence of such an inexpensive car has come at precisely the time when governments need to be improving public transit systems and encouraging people to give up their "love of the open road" to a more collective mentality for the common good.

Moreover, if global mass motorization becomes that much more common, it means that the production of biofuels is going to increase. We already know that this will lead to increased commodity prices, such as the prices of corn, sugar beets, sugar cane, soybeans, palm-oil, and rapeseed, making it more difficult for people to buy those products to eat. It will also mean that forests will be cut down even more in order to provide the land needed to increase the production of these plants for biofuels. We have already seen this happen in the case of removing forests for raising cattle to supply the fast food restaurants of the world.

There are groups in society, such as agro-industrial corporations, that say biofuels are the way to move forward. What do you think?

A. Rewrite the false statements below to make them true.

1. Gasoline is used in place of biofuels to reduce carbon emissions.

____

____

2. Mass production of biofuels will result in a decrease in food crop prices.

____

____

3. 200 kilograms of corn can feed a family for a year.

____

____

4. The Tata Nano is powered by non-carbon fuels.

____

____

5. Forests will be cut down for the construction of biofuel production plants.

____

____

Formal Writing – a Letter to the Editor

A letter to the editor serves the purpose of expressing one's opinion with the public as audience. It usually contains the following:

- **Introduction**: states clearly the issue that you are concerned about
- **Body**: gives details about the issue; builds up evidence to support your opinion
- **Conclusion**: restates your opinion or offers a solution

As a letter to the editor is a type of formal writing, complete sentences should be used throughout, and contractions and informal language should be avoided.

Pay attention to the following when writing a letter to the editor:

- stick to only one topic
- keep your letter brief
- use facts and figures to support your arguments

B. Read the letter to the editor on page 216 again. Name the different parts with the given words. You may use the words more than once.

body　closing　introduction　salutation　conclusion

Dear Editor: ____________

Paragraph 1 ____________

Paragraph 2 ____________

Paragraph 3 ____________

Paragraph 4 ____________

Sincerely, ____________

C. Suppose you read the letter to the editor on page 216 in a newspaper. Write your response to that letter to the editor, expressing your view on the biofuel controversy.

When you are writing a response to a letter to the editor, be specific by stating the date that letter was published.

A Letter from Sammy in Mali

Hi Kiyoka,

I hope you're doing well. I still think a lot about my visit to your home in Japan a few years ago. I'll never forget it. In fact, I'll always remember Japan as the place that made me realize that I wanted to see the world! See the postmark on this letter? I'm on another big adventure right now, as a member of a Canada World Youth delegation. I'm so excited!

When I returned to Canada from Japan, I started to look in my school's guidance office and browse online to find ways to achieve my goal of seeing the world. My guidance counsellor at school told me that the Canadian government has programs for young people that might interest me. Since I was going to graduate soon from high school, I decided to apply to Canada World Youth. They've been organizing educational exchanges for over 40 years.

After talking with my parents and grandparents, I sent in my application, and was selected to attend a day-long seminar in which other candidates and I learned about the program. We were told that it wouldn't be easy to go to a foreign country for three months, and then live with our "counterpart" in another part of Canada for an additional three months. We would need to handle things like culture shock and would have to do things like eat strange foods so as not to be disrespectful to our host families. Several weeks after the seminar, I got the call – they wanted to send me to Mali in West Africa!

So, Kiyoka, I'm writing to you from a place called Gao, not too far from the famed city of Timbuktu. We live and work as a group here, helping build heat-efficient ovens from clay. We also help out with AIDS awareness programs. My Malian counterpart is a nice girl my age named Worokia. She speaks both French and her local language. I'm glad that my own French is going to get much better by the time this exchange is over. That's because when Worokia and I and the rest of the team head back to Canada, we'll be living in rural Quebec! Worokia and I will be living with a farming family, so we'll probably be helping out with the harvest.

I'm so thrilled about this experience, and thrilled with myself. If you asked me if I ever thought I would live and work in Africa, I would have said "No". But here I am, and even though there are challenges (like scorpions, sometimes), I'm proud to stick them out, and grateful for this opportunity. Can't wait to show Worokia my own country!

Enclosed is a photo of me and Worokia in Gao. Take care, Kiyoka. Will write again soon.

Love,

Sammy

A. Read the clues and complete the crossword puzzle with words from the letter.

Across

A. chance

B. adviser

C. having knowledge of

D. group of representatives

E. well-known

F. very excited

Down

1. gain or reach
2. people who are considered for something
3. appreciative of something received
4. of the countryside
5. meeting to discuss a particular topic

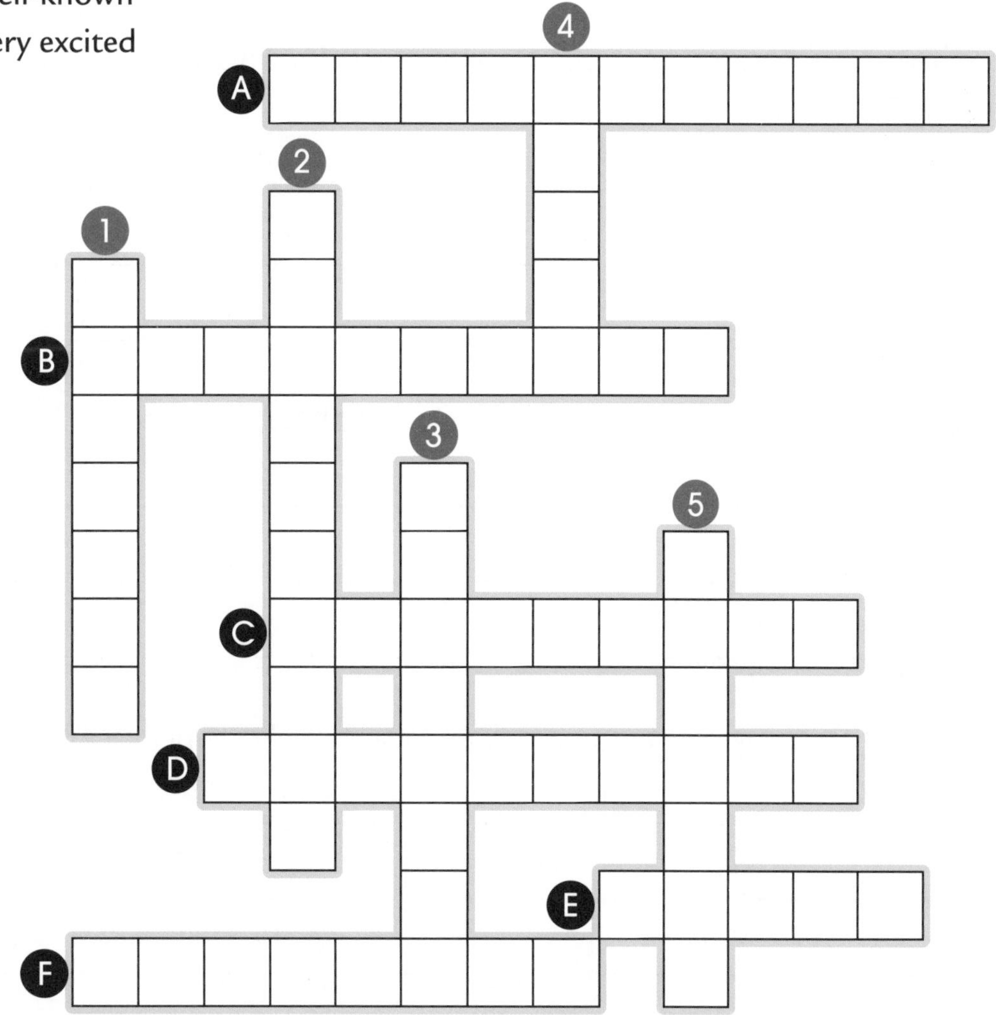

Informal Writing

Informal writing is a casual way of communicating with our family and friends. It does not have to follow precise rules of grammar, and the sentence structure can be casual, which often includes contractions, utterances, or brief sentences. Friendly letters or e-mails, notes, postcards, and greeting cards are examples of informal writing.

B. Read "A Letter from Sammy in Mali" again and complete the following activity.

1. What is the informal salutation in this letter?

   ____

2. What is the casual closing?

   ____

3. Find three sentences that contain contractions from the letter. Circle the contractions.

   a. ______________________________

   b. ______________________________

   c. ______________________________

4. Find three sentences that are not grammatically correct in the letter.

   a. ______________________________

   b. ______________________________

   c. ______________________________

5. Why are the sentences you gave above not grammatical?

   a. ______________________________

   b. ______________________________

   c. ______________________________

C. Imagine you volunteered to help at a summer camp and have just returned home. Write an e-mail to your friend telling him/her about the summer camp.

Everyone can and does write! But if you want to write captivating stories, and deliver them with prose that shines, and in a style that is uniquely yours, there are things you must consider. Below are the main concepts integral to writing good fiction.

Plot is the story you wish to tell, and it should answer the question, "What's happening?" Novels usually include subplots, which are inner "stories" connected to the main plot and are less important than the main plot. Short stories usually do not have subplots. In terms of plot structure, a story usually starts with a situation and a problem, or conflict. What follows is a rising action, followed by a climax and the resulting dénouement, or resolution, and a conclusion. Another, less common form of story is in the picaresque style, where the plot is simply a series of adventures without a clear "resolution", since one is not called for. Most stories are structured in chronological order, although many have been written out of order, or even backwards! Flashbacks, time-lapse, and flashforwards are literary devices of structure that you can use to create a story that is unique.

The Elements of Fiction

Conflict is the struggle between two people or between a person and something. Conflict is essential in a story. It would be a boring story indeed if the characters encountered no problems. Conflict can come in different forms, such as a person against another person, against nature, against himself/herself, against fate, and against society.

Characters are the people who act out the plot. The central character is the protagonist, and the antagonist is the force providing conflict for the central character. Some stories include a character foil, which is someone whose traits are meant to highlight the traits of the protagonist. Minor characters may be employed to help further the story quickly if necessary. Main characters need to be fully developed, with good and bad qualities. They must also be dynamic, that is, they must change over the course of the story.

Setting refers to the place and the time in which the plot takes place. The setting may be an important part of the plot or conflict, or it can simply act as a backdrop to the story, with no effect on outcomes.

Theme refers to the underlying meaning of the story: the reason for writing the story and what the writer expects the reader to learn. The theme can be explicit (stated openly in the story) or implicit (implied by the plot, the characters' actions, etc.).

Point-of-view refers to the way a story is narrated. A "first-person" point of view means that the main character is telling the story, so we read about "I". A story can be narrated in the "third person", in which case we read about "he" or "she". The narrator may be "omniscient" (meaning that he/she knows everything about the story and the characters), "limited-omniscient", or "objective" (in which case he/she knows nothing more than the reader).

Style refers to the language the author uses to deliver the story. The style can be conversational, unusual, and can include the use of dialect. Related to style is tone, which reflects the author's (or character's) attitude towards the story as well.

Give these things the consideration they deserve, and you, too, can be a great writer!

A. Briefly explain what each of the following terms means.

1. Plot ____________________

2. Conflict ____________________

3. Characters ____________________

4. Setting ____________________

5. Theme ____________________

6. Point-of-view ____________________

7. Style ____________________

Descriptive Writing

When writing fiction, we can draw the reader into the world of our story by using descriptive language. Many plain and common words can be replaced with more descriptive words to create vivid images and enhance the reader's visual experience. Descriptive adjectives, adverbs, and phrases that appeal to the five senses add details to our descriptions, making our story more interesting to read.

B. Think of the setting and characters for the story below. Write as many descriptive words and phrases as you can for each of them.

A Day with Rudolph the Reindeer

Setting: ______________________________

Descriptive words and phrases for the setting:

____

____

____

Character 1: ______________________________

Descriptive words and phrases for this character:

____

____

____

Character 2: ______________________________

Descriptive words and phrases for this character:

____

____

____

C. Based on the setting and characters you have created in (B), develop the descriptive story "A Day with Rudolph the Reindeer".

A Day with Rudolph the Reindeer

Who Will Be Next on the Moon?

When the former USSR (now primarily Russia) sent cosmonaut Yuri Gagarin into orbit around the Earth on April 12, 1961 aboard Vostok 1, that country became the first to send a man into space. Only weeks later, on May 5, Alan Shepard became the first American in space. It took more than seven years for the United States to win the race to the moon, though: on July 20, 1969, astronauts Neil Armstrong and Buzz Aldrin stepped out of the Apollo 11 vehicle and took those famous "giant steps for mankind".

Despite the significance of this achievement, no other country can claim to have sent a space traveller to the moon in the 40 years since. The American and Russian Shuttle programs have resulted in astronauts from other countries (such as Canada and Japan) orbiting the Earth and spending time at the International Space Station, and many countries have sent un-manned spacecraft and satellites into space for decades (Canada sent Anik 1, the world's first domestic communications satellite, into space way back in 1972). However, no countries other than the U.S.A. and Russia have been able to send their own personnel into orbit, and only the U.S.A. has sent anyone to the moon. It may surprise you then that the next person to land on the moon may be neither American nor Russian – but Chinese!

On October 15, 2003, China launched its Long March rocket in the Gobi Desert, carrying Chinese astronaut Yang Liwei on board the Shenzhou 5 spacecraft, becoming the third country to send a manned vehicle into space. He orbited Earth 14 times during his 21-hour flight. In 2005, the country completed its second manned mission. As awesome as the achievement seems – to be the third country to send a human into space – it is only the beginning of China's ambitious space program, which is geared towards placing a human on the moon once again.

The Chinese Lunar Exploration Program is being carried out by the China National Space Administration (CNSA), China's space agency, and includes explorations by unmanned robotic vehicles as well as human missions. CNSA has launched three unmanned lunar explorations since 2007. The first lunar orbiter, Chang'e 1, was the first phase of this project and was launched on October 24, 2007 at the Xichang Satellite Launch Centre in the Sichuan province. It stayed in orbit around the moon for a year, at about

200 kilometres above the moon's surface, undertaking analyses of the moon's geology and chemistry. Chang'e 2 was launched on October 1, 2010, armed with improved instruments and higher-resolution optical devices that helped pave the way for Chang'e 3, which soft-landed on the moon's surface on December 14, 2013 and deployed China's first rover. The CNSA has three more unmanned Chang'e lunar missions planned by 2020 and manned landings are expected to start around 2025. This seems like a long time to a young student, but now there are millions of young students in China who share the dream of becoming an astronaut, and of walking on the moon.

A. Write 1 to 6 to put the events in order.

☐ The first domestic communications satellite was sent into space.

☐ Neil Armstrong and Buzz Aldrin stepped on the moon.

☐ Yuri Gagarin was sent into orbit around the Earth.

☐ Yang Liwei orbited the Earth on Shenzou 5.

☐ Alan Shepard was sent into space.

☐ Chang'e 1 orbited the moon.

B. Answer these questions.

1. What do you think "giant steps for mankind" means?

____

____

2. Why do you think the writer describes China's space program as an "ambitious" one?

____

____

3. Describe briefly the Chinese Lunar Exploration Program.

____

____

Expository Writing

Expository writing is frequently used by students, especially when we write for school projects. The purpose of expository writing is to inform, describe, explain, define, or instruct. We have to assume that the reader has no prior knowledge of the topic. A good piece of expository writing should remain focused on its topic, be clear and logical, and have strong organization. To achieve this, we can organize facts according to their common topics, list events in chronological order, analyze cause and effect relationships, and compare objects to show their similarities and differences.

C. Organize the facts about Chinese astronaut Yang Liwei below and compose an expository composition about him.

- dreamed of flying at a young age
- an astronaut of the China National Space Administration (CNSA)
- selected as an astronaut candidate in 1998
- born in Liaoning, China
- promoted to colonel after his first mission
- joined the Chinese People's Liberation Army (PLA) in September 1983
- born on June 21, 1965
- was a lieutenant colonel at the time of his first mission in space
- excelled in sciences when studied at school
- first Chinese citizen in space on board China's first manned spacecraft Shenzhou 5
- promoted to major general on July 2, 2008
- graduated from the No. 8 Aviation College of the PLA Air Force in 1987 and became a fighter pilot
- underwent five years of training at the Astronaut Training Base in Beijing with 13 other candidates since 1998
- launched into space aboard the Shenzhou 5 spacecraft on October 15, 2003
- received the title of "Space Hero" from the chairman of the Central Military Commission of China on November 7, 2007
- participated in the screening process for astronauts in 1996

Title

Opening Paragraph (state the subject of your composition, make it interesting to read)

Body Paragraphs (organize the facts and put them into paragraphs, each with a common topic)

Concluding Paragraph (summarize your writing or lead the reader to think further about the topic)

HISTORY

Daily Life in Early Canada

The people in New France lived by the Seigneurial system, where the habitants and seigneurs had different responsibilities.

A. Read the paragraph. Label the pictures with the words in bold. Then fill in the blanks.

Seigneurial Life

It had been over a hundred years since the French first arrived in Canada. Territories of Indigenous Peoples, including the Haudenosaunee, Wendat, Abenaki, and many more, were gradually occupied by European settlers who established a system of land ownership and distribution. Most settlers in New France were farmers. They lived by a system of land distribution called the Seigneurial system. Under this system, the ***king*** *of France owned all of the land and allocated large areas to* ***seigneurs****. Seigneurs then divided their land into strips among tenant farmers called* ***habitants****. Each strip had a section of riverfront so that the farmers had access to water. The strips of land extended to uncleared forests.*

King

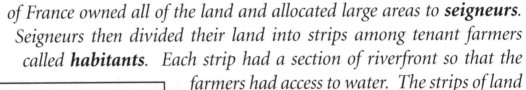

Responsibilities: **grain, church, disputes**

Segeniurs

- building a 1. ____________ and a flour mill where habitants can grind their 2. ____________
- settling 3. ____________ among their tenants

Responsibilities: **labour, taxes, harvest**

Habitants

- paying 4. ____________
- performing unpaid 5. ____________ for the seigneur a few days a year
- giving their seigneur a portion of their 6. ____________ annually

B. Look at the comparison chart about the lives of the habitants (European settlers) and the Haudenosaunee (a First Peoples group). Answer the questions.

	The Habitants	The Haudenosaunee
Gender Roles	• all members of the family worked in the fields • men cleared land, built homes, hunted, and fished • women did household chores	• men and women shared the responsibility in taking care of the children • men took greater responsibility in clearing land, hunting, and fighting in battles • women took greater responsibility in planting and harvesting crops, and making clothing
Shelter	• lived in loghouses on a seigneury	• lived in a village of longhouses
Food	• main food was bread	• main food was corn, beans, and squash
Education	• priests and nuns taught children in schools	• the Elders, parents, and grandparents taught the children about their traditions and history
Religion/ Beliefs	• most were Roman Catholic; the Church played an important role in the colony	• believed in the Great Spirit, the creator of everything, including people, animals, and plants

Write two similarities and two differences between the habitants and the Haudenosaunee.

Similarities

Shelter,

Differences

food, gender roles, beliefs, education

2

The Expulsion of the Acadians

Acadia was caught in the middle of the rivalry between France and Britain. The entire community, including the descendants of the French settlers and the Indigenous Peoples, was eventually deported south to the Thirteen Colonies and to Europe.

Fill in the blanks to complete the timeline. Then answer the questions.

History of Acadia

France Charles Lawrence Britain Treaty
Thirteen Colonies Acadia deported allegiance

Acadia was a colony in New France. It was made up of eastern Quebec and the Maritime provinces.

1604 French settlers settled in an area called 1.______________ that consisted of eastern Quebec, New Brunswick, Nova Scotia, and Prince Edward Island.

1713 The 2.______________ of Utrecht was signed. It was an agreement to end hostilities between Britain and 3.______________ . France ceded Acadia to Britain.

1730 The majority of Acadians signed an oath of 4.______________ to the British Crown but stated that they would not take up arms against France.

1755 Tensions rose between Britain and France once again. Fearing that the Acadians would side with France if war ensued, British Governor 5.______________ issued an ultimatum: swear unconditional loyalty or be 6.______________ .

The Acadians agreed but Lawrence was not convinced. The Acadians were deported to 7. ____________________ , France, and the British colonies in the south called the 8. ____________________ . Located on the east coast of North America, the Thirteen Colonies was an area of land that had been seized from the First Peoples during British colonization. This deportation is known as the Great Expulsion. Many people died aboard the ships carrying them to exile.

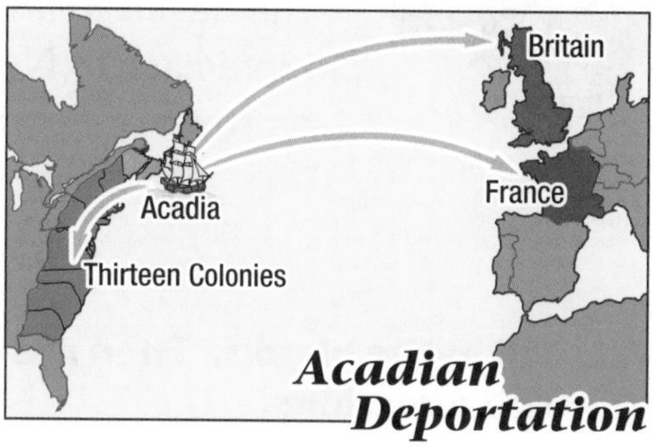

Acadian Deportation

1764 The British government allowed the Acadians to return home but when they did, the Acadians found that their land and homes were occupied by British settlers. They had to look for a new place to settle.

1765 Some deported Acadians moved to Louisiana where there was already a French population. They became known as the Cajuns. Today, the Cajun population is large and has a strong cultural presence in the United States.

9. Why did the Acadians refuse to fight against France?

____

10. Why did Governor Charles Lawrence pressure the Acadians to swear unconditional loyalty?

____

____

11. How did the Acadians affect the cultural landscape of Louisiana?

____

____

Seven Years' War

The Seven Years' War was fought between France and Britain over supremacy in North America. The outcome had a significant impact on the First Peoples and the future of Canada.

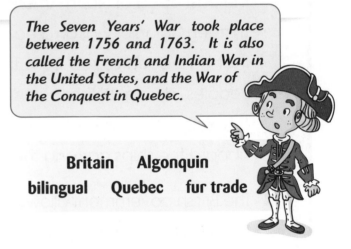

The Seven Years' War took place between 1756 and 1763. It is also called the French and Indian War in the United States, and the War of the Conquest in Quebec.

Britain **Algonquin**
bilingual **Quebec** **fur trade**

A. Fill in the blanks. Then answer the questions.

1. The war was driven by the rivalry between France and __________ as both tried to expand their empires across North America.

2. In 1754, there was a battle over the Ohio River Valley, which both countries claimed to further their __________ business. This battle escalated into the Seven Years' War.

3. The war worsened the relations between certain First Peoples groups that had already been conflicted. Their conflicts grew when the Iroquois allied with Britain, and the __________ and the Huron allied with France.

4. In 1759, the war turned in favour of Britain when the British captured __________, an important French colony; in 1760, they captured Montreal.

5. In 1763, the Treaty of Paris was signed, officially ending the Seven Years' War. France gave Canada to Britain. Having endured both French and British occupations, Canada became a __________ country.

6. What are other names for the Seven Years' War?

 ____

7. What was the purpose behind the Seven Years' War?

 ____

B. Read the article. Identify the people and answer the questions.

In 1759, the Battle of the Plains of Abraham took place. General James Wolfe led the British army in an invasion of Quebec against the Marquis de Montcalm and his French and Indigenous troops. Quebec was an important colony to the French because it was along the St. Lawrence River, which was used to send supplies and reinforcements to French colonies. This battle was a turning point as the odds turned against the French and their Indigenous allies. Britain experienced more victories and at the end of the Seven Years' War, France ceded Canada to Britain.

I led my troops of French soldiers, Canadian militia, and First Peoples warriors. Unfortunately, we lost the battle and surrendered Quebec.
I led an army of over 40 000 British soldiers and captured Quebec. This helped Britain later in taking control of New France.

1. Why was it important for Britain to capture Quebec?

____

____

2. Why was the Battle of the Plains of Abraham a turning point?

____

____

3. Canada was colonized by both Britain and France. How did this affect Canada?

____

____

The Royal Proclamation and the Quebec Act

After its victory in the Seven Years' War, Britain made important political changes to its newly-acquired territories in North America. These changes had significant impacts on various groups of people.

Read the Royal Proclamation and the Quebec Act. Fill in the blanks and answer the questions.

The Royal Proclamation

All lands not purchased by Britain are First Peoples' lands.

All lands west of the Thirteen Colonies are reserved for the First Peoples; British colonists are prohibited from expanding into these areas.

Quebec Act

Practising the Catholic faith is allowed.

Practising Catholics can now serve in public office.

French civil law is reinstated.

Boundary of Quebec is expanded.

The Royal Proclamation

France settlement First Peoples rights

During European settlement and colonization, treaties were negotiated between the British Crown and the First Peoples. When Britain became the dominant European power in North America, one of the main concerns the British faced was an uprising from the ______________, if they did not address Indigenous Peoples' rights to their ancestral lands and territories. Some First Peoples had a strong relationship with ______________ and they did not want to ally with Britain. To avoid hostilities and to reconcile them to British rule, King George III issued the Royal Proclamation on October 7, 1763 to ensure a peaceful understanding between Britain and the First Peoples. This document was significant because it recognized First Peoples' ______________ to ownership and occupation of their ancestral lands, as well as their rights to the lands' resources. Not everyone agreed, however, as the Proclamation outlawed ______________ to the west of the Thirteen Colonies, which angered the British colonists in the Thirteen Colonies.

Quebec Act

Catholics revolution Quebec colonists

The Quebec Act of 1774 was an act of the Parliament of Great Britain that set new provisions for the governance of ____________ . When Britain gained France's lands in North America, it also gained their French subjects and the Indigenous Peoples in Quebec. Quebec's population was almost entirely French ____________ and the Quebec Act was an attempt to accommodate them. Also, the ____________ in the Thirteen Colonies were beginning to rebel and Britain did not want the French to support them. Unfortunately, the act only angered the colonists even more and ultimately caused the colonists to wage a ____________ .

1. Complete the table.

	The Royal Proclamation	Quebec Act
Date		
Who benefited?		
Whom did it anger?		

2. How did the Royal Proclamation recognize First Peoples' rights?

____

____

3. In what way did the Quebec Act give the French inhabitants cultural and religious freedom?

____

____

4. How did the Royal Proclamation and the Quebec Act contribute to the colonists' growing anger toward Britain?

____

____

5

Displacement: the Loyalists

During and after the American Revolutionary War, the Loyalists, who stayed loyal to Britain, left the Thirteen Colonies and settled in Canada.

A. Read the paragraphs. Answer the questions.

America's Independence

The American Revolutionary War (1775-1783) occurred between Britain and its North American colonies. The war arose from the colonists' increasing dissatisfaction with Britain. They did not like Britain forcing taxes on them and preventing them from occupying lands in the west. The Thirteen Colonies wanted national independence. But when war ensued, not everyone supported the cause. The colonists were divided between the Patriots, who fought for America's independence, and the Loyalists, who remained loyal to Britain.

The Loyalists supported British rule for various reasons. Some were loyal to Britain because they had relatives and businesses there. Others supported Britain because they thought Britain had a right to impose taxes in return for protection during the Seven Years' War. Many African-American slaves were Loyalists because they were promised freedom if they supported Britain. Similarly, many Indigenous Peoples supported the British because they had signed agreements with them that addressed their rights. Supporting Britain and fighting alongside the British militia, the Loyalists were branded as traitors. They faced harassment, torture, imprisonment, exile, and even death. Many Loyalists fled to escape persecution. Roughly 50 000 people came to Canada and settled in Quebec, Cape Breton, Nova Scotia, New Brunswick, and Prince Edward Island.

We were displaced by the revolutionary war. Hostilities from the Patriots forced us to leave our homes and properties. Years later, some of us went back, but most never returned.

1. ____________________ : America's war for independence

____________________ : people who fought for the revolution; also called "revolutionaries"

____________________ : people who fought for Britain; branded as traitors

a Loyalist

2. What factors led to the American Revolutionary War?

3. How were the Loyalists considered displaced people?

4. How did the war affect the lives of the Loyalists?

B. Put the letters in the correct circles. Then answer the question.

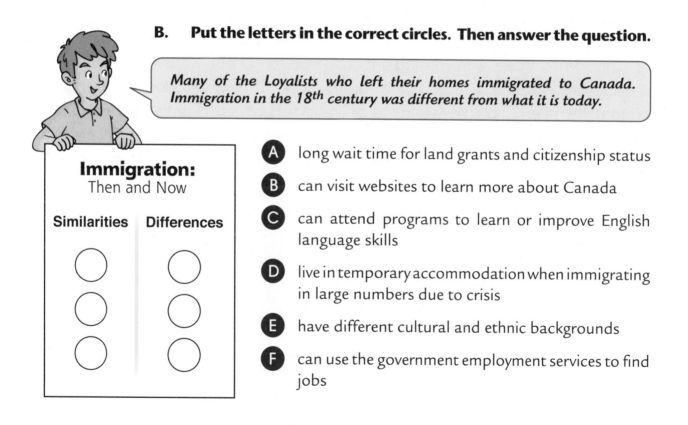

Many of the Loyalists who left their homes immigrated to Canada. Immigration in the 18th century was different from what it is today.

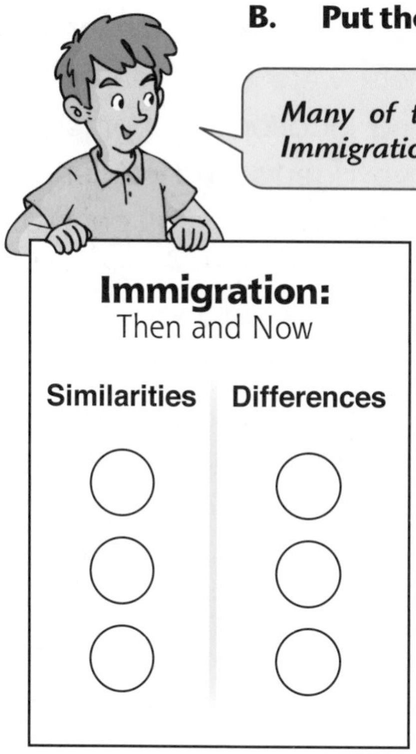

- **A** long wait time for land grants and citizenship status
- **B** can visit websites to learn more about Canada
- **C** can attend programs to learn or improve English language skills
- **D** live in temporary accommodation when immigrating in large numbers due to crisis
- **E** have different cultural and ethnic backgrounds
- **F** can use the government employment services to find jobs

What programs and services would you set up to make starting a life in Canada easier?

Interactions

During the fur trade, the French inhabitants in New France and the Indigenous Peoples, particularly the Métis, interacted and developed different types of relationships with one another.

A. Fill in the blanks. Then complete the diagram and answer the question.

unlicensed fur skills needed populations compete trading transported

New France was a 1. ______________ colony and fur was its most lucrative commodity. The Indigenous Peoples, particularly the Métis, traded with French fur traders: the former traded 2. ______________ and the latter traded metal items such as pots, kettles, and knives. Men called coureur des bois were 3. ______________ fur traders, meaning they were not hired by a company. They travelled deep into the interior of Canada to trade with the Indigenous Peoples. There were also men called voyageurs who 4. ______________ the fur from one trading location to another by canoe. The interactions between the coureur des bois, voyageurs, and Indigenous Peoples resulted in marriages between Indigenous women and French-Canadian men. The children of these unions are called the Métis and many of them played a vital role in the success and prosperity of the fur trade. They were skilled navigators, traders, hunters, and interpreters. This interaction proved beneficial to both groups. From the First Peoples, the fur traders learned important 5. ______________ needed to survive in the Canadian wilderness and learned how to navigate the land, while the European tools the First Peoples acquired made daily tasks easier to accomplish. However, there were also negative effects. The fur trade made the First Peoples 6. ______________ against one another for hunting grounds. This competition occurred because the First Peoples were cut off from some of their lands, water sources, and food supply due to European settlement. Participating in the fur trade was a means of survival as well as a way to utilize their strengths and survival strategies as hunters, traders, and merchants. Diseases from the Europeans found their way into Indigenous communities and wiped out large 7. ______________ . The fur trade became the priority for the First Peoples out of necessity. Eventually, they hunted for trade purposes, not subsistence. Even their relationship with nature changed. Before the fur trade, they only hunted for what they 8. ______________ , but because of the fur trade, they hunted excessively as a means of survival.

9.

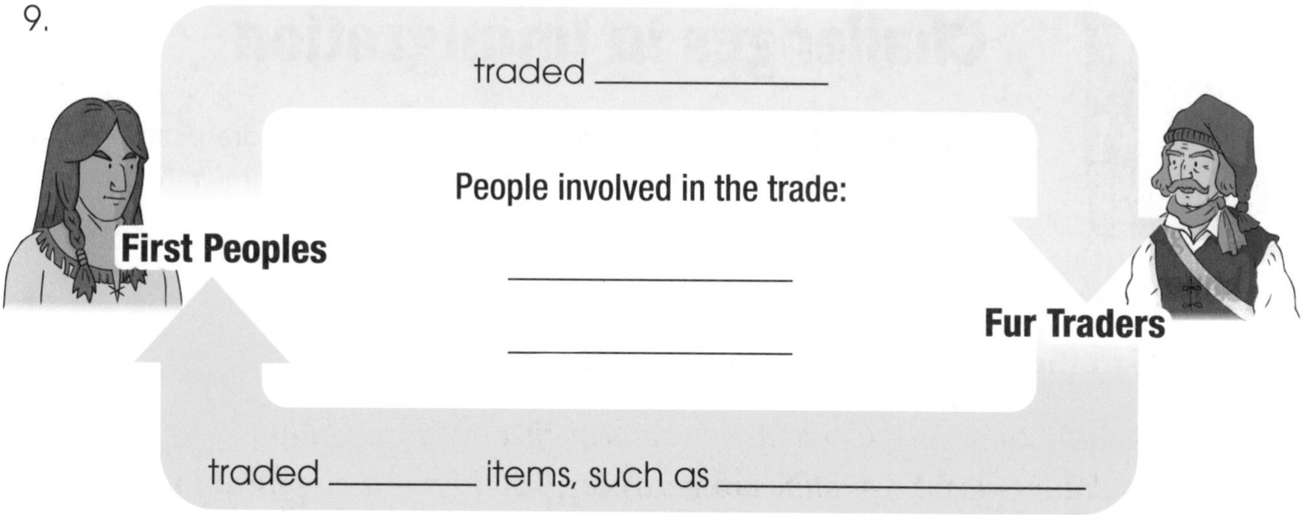

10. Write about how the close interaction with the First Peoples affected the fur traders, and vice versa, in the following areas.

- *daily tasks*
- *beliefs*
- *population*
- *food*
- *relations with other groups*

____

____

____

____

____

B. Read the paragraph. Answer the question.

The close interaction between the two groups resulted in marriages. Indigenous women often married European fur traders. These women played a vital role in the fur trade by helping their husbands with tasks they could not perform. Their skills and knowledge of the land, as well as their ability to translate between languages, make and repair clothing, cook food, and heal wounds, helped their husbands survive. The women made snowshoes and moccasins, tended the garden for food, and translated between the two cultures. They even accompanied the men in their travels. These marriages were beneficial to both the First Peoples and the European fur traders because they were both eager to establish strong relationships with their allies and trading partners.

What benefits were there for the fur traders when their Indigenous wives accompanied them in their travels?

____

Challenges in Immigration

In the early 19th century, Canada's population grew drastically. People were coming to Canada for a better future but mass immigration brought with it some deadly repercussions.

A. Read the paragraphs. Answer the questions.

The British came to Canada in consequence of the Industrial Revolution. The Revolution meant economic prosperity for Britain but it also meant that manual labour was being replaced with machinery, which resulted in severe job loss.

In the 1840s, there was an influx of Irish immigrants when Ireland was struck by the Great Famine (also known as the Potato Famine), which caused mass starvation, disease outbreaks, and emigration.

The journey to North America was strenuous and people often died from illness and malnutrition aboard ships, but immigrants were attracted to the promise of new land and opportunities. However, people suffered further upon arrival. Immigrants were not accustomed to the Canadian climate and they had a hard time adapting to the harsh winters. These immigration periods ultimately shaped Canadian identity. These cultures, the British and the Irish, integrated and became a part of today's Canadian culture.

1. Write about the two events that caused people to immigrate to Canada.

2. What challenges did the immigrants face?

3. How have the British and Irish cultures become a part of the Canadian culture we know today? Give one example for each.

____

____

____

____

B. Fill in the blanks. Then answer the question.

Cholera Epidemic	blamed treat quarantine organizations disease healthy

One of the main dangers of mass immigration was 1. ______________ . When people immigrated, they brought diseases with them. In 1832, the cholera epidemic occurred. It was a particularly deadly disease because no one knew how it spread or how to 2. ______________ it.

In an effort to control the epidemic, a 3. ______________ station was set up in Grosse Île, Quebec. All immigrant ships stopped there for inspection and only the 4. ______________ immigrants were allowed to continue on. The epidemic resulted in the establishment of public health 5. ______________ ; poverty and sickness were now being properly addressed. However, the immigrants were discriminated against and 6. ______________ for the disease.

What were the positive and negative effects of the cholera epidemic?

Positive ____

Negative ____

1800 – 1850

The Timber Trade

The timber trade was a major industry in the 19th century in Upper and Lower Canada. It provided employment, encouraged immigration, and helped boost the colonies' economy.

A. Fill in the blanks. Then answer the questions.

Ottawa River pine timber economic export

The decline of the fur trade was followed by the rise of the 1. ____________ trade. In the 1800s, the most important trade in Upper and Lower Canada was the 2. ____________ timber trade. It was an industry that fostered the colonies' population and 3. ____________ growth. It began when France imposed a blockade that prevented Britain from accessing wood from the Baltic region. Needing wood to build ships during the Napoleonic Wars, Britain turned to the Ottawa River Valley which provided an abundance of white 4. ____________ forests. Britain became a major client, which boosted the timber industry, as timber became a major 5. ____________ product. The timber trade lasted until the early 20th century but the demand for wood is still high, even today.

6. How was the timber trade beneficial to Upper and Lower Canada?

____

7. What caused Britain to become a major client of the Ottawa River timber trade?

____

8. Wood is still a highly valuable product today. Why? Give examples.

____

____

B. Identify each person in the timber trade.

merchant raftsmen lumberman

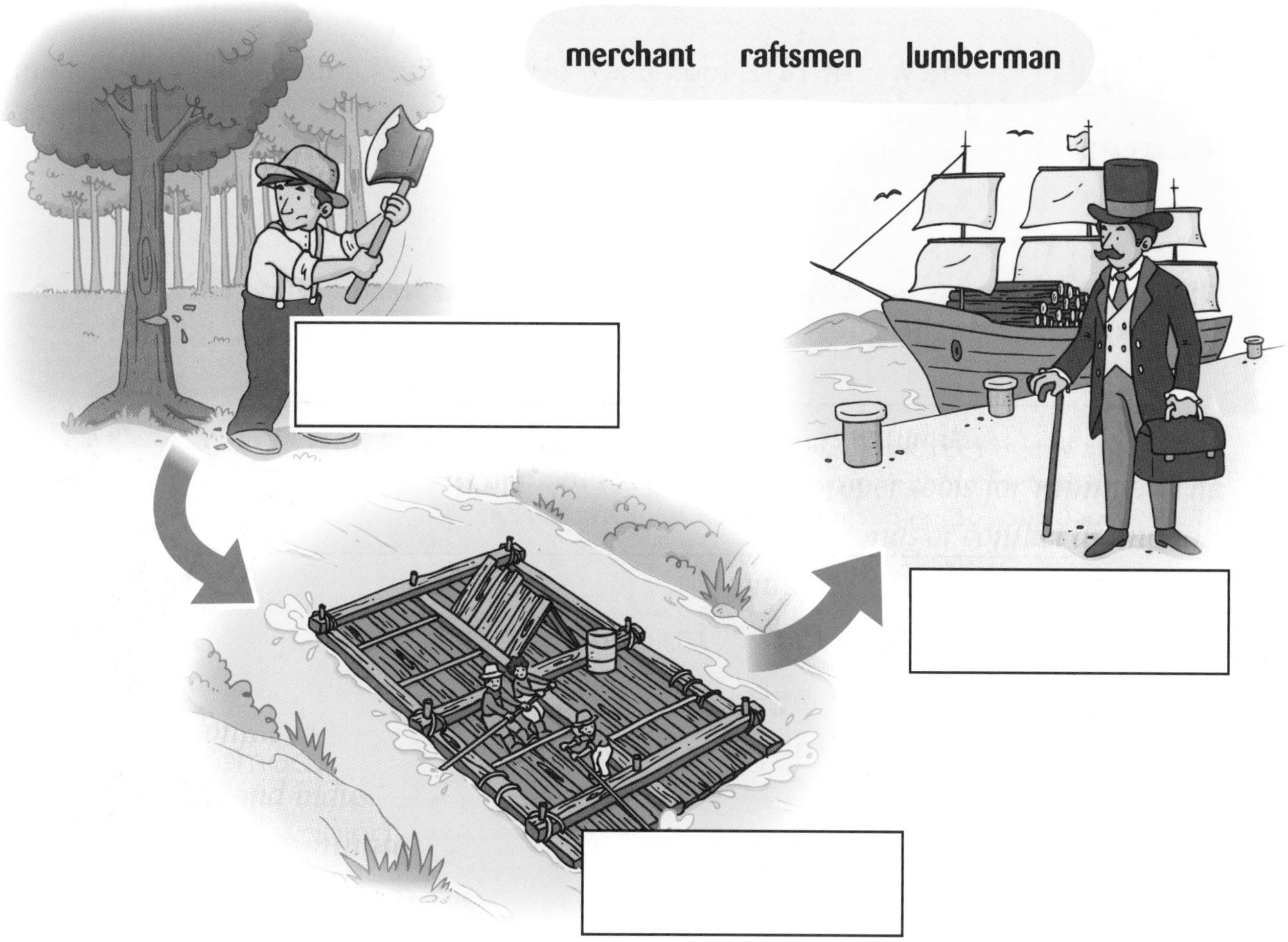

C. Read the passage. Then describe how the timber trade affected the population and employment of Upper and Lower Canada in the 19th century.

When ships returned to Quebec after delivering timber to Britain, they brought with them British immigrants. The ships offered cheap transportation and the immigrants looked to Canada for a better future.

9

War of 1812

The War of 1812 took place between the United States and Britain. The conflict ended with the Treaty of Ghent, which returned everything to status quo.

Fill in the blanks to see which groups were involved in the war. Then fill in the chart and answer the questions.

The War of 1812 was fought between the United States and Britain but also included the colonies in Canada and the First Peoples. The United States declared war on June 18, 1812.

War of 1812 – Parties Involved

Lower Canada **Britain** **The First Peoples**
The United States **Upper Canada**

1. ____________________

declared war because Britain was seizing their trade vessels to prevent them from trading in Europe

2. ____________________

tried to cripple the economy of their main rival, France, by stopping American trading vessels from trading with the French

3. ____________________

fought alongside Britain because they shared the common goal of resisting American expansion to the west; strengthened local troops and were exceptional fighters

4. ____________________

the large population of American Loyalists in Ontario supported Britain as it was the Americans who forced them to leave during the American Revolutionary War

5. ____________________

the French inhabitants of Quebec sided with the British, believing that the Americans would not grant them the same cultural freedom as Britain had

The war ended in a stalemate on the battlefield. The Treaty of Ghent was signed on December 24, 1814 to end the conflict between the United States and Britain. The treaty offered a status quo, the status that had existed before the war.

For Canada, the treaty established a clearer boundary of the future country and set the course to national independence.

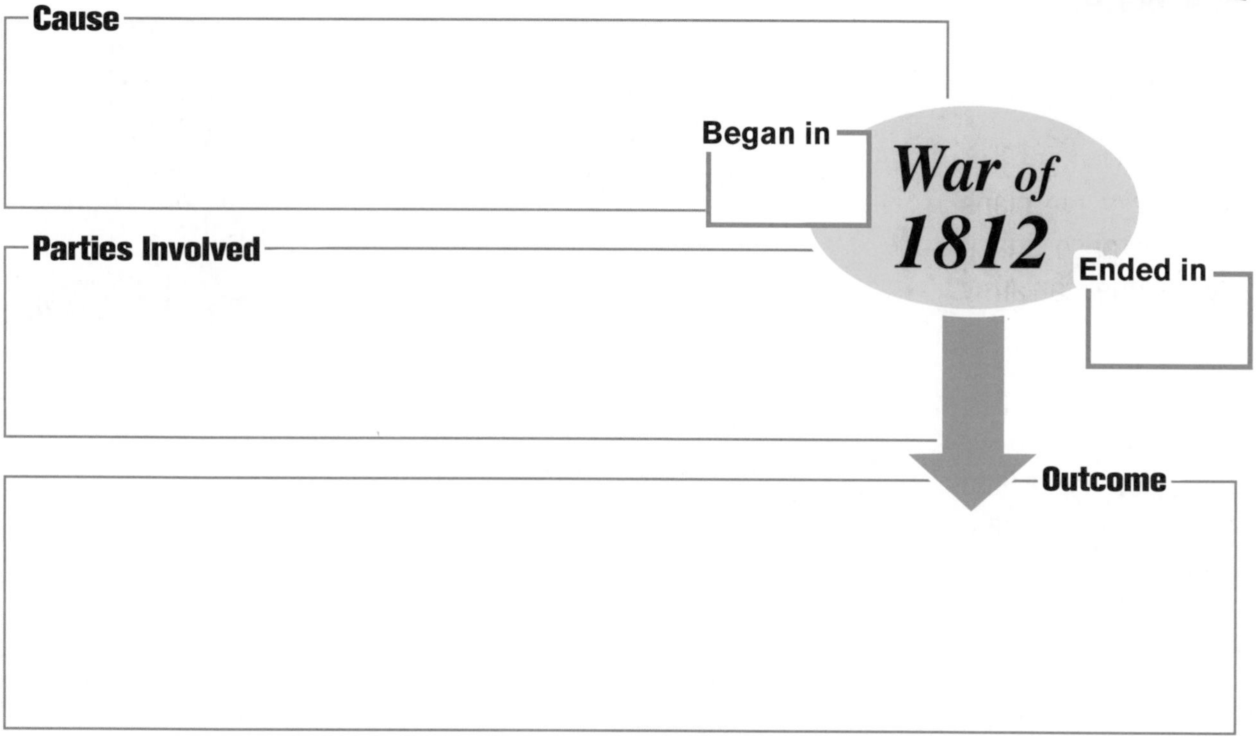

6. What does "the treaty offered a status quo" mean?

____

____

7. Canada was able to resist the American occupation. How do you think this shaped Canada's future?

____

____

____

10

1800 – 1850

Important Personalities

Many people have been recognized for their contributions to Canada's history. Richard Pierpoint and Laura Secord were two unlikely figures that played important roles in the War of 1812.

A. Write the facts about Richard Pierpoint and Laura Secord in the correct places.

Facts

learned of the plans for a surprise attack by the American army

rewarded with a land grant in the Niagara Region

became a celebrated war heroine after her death

was offered the chance of freedom in return for fighting for Britain in the American Revolutionary War

Name: Richard Pierpoint
Born: 1744 (in Senegal)
Died: 1837 (in Ontario)

- captured into slavery, brought to North America and sold to a British officer
- ______________________________
  ____
- ______________________________
  ____
- signed the Petition of Free Negroes, which demanded their land grants be next to each other; petition was an attempt to form a black community
- at the beginning of the War of 1812, offered to form an all-black regiment
- his offer was accepted on the condition that the regiment was headed by a white officer
- fought for Captain Runchey's Company of Coloured Men; fought in the Battle of Queenston Heights
- after the war, petitioned the government to send him back to Senegal; petition was denied

Name: Laura Secord
Born: 1775 (in Massachusetts)
Died: 1868 (in Ontario)

- husband served under Isaac Brock in the Battle of Queenston Heights
- lodged American soldiers in her home in June 1813
- ______________________________
- walked 20 miles to warn the British army of a surprise attack that would give the Americans more control of the Niagara Peninsula
- British forces attacked American militia near Beaver Dams; ended in British victory
- spent years petitioning the government to give her recognition for her contribution
- ______________________________

B. Write "T" if the statement is true and "F" if it is false.

1. African-Americans were discriminated against during the War of 1812. ______
2. Laura Secord was recognized for her efforts immediately after the war ended. ______
3. Richard Pierpoint was an advocate for the African-American community. ______
4. The British army did not heed Laura Secord's warning. ______

C. Describe how Richard Pierpoint and Laura Secord helped pave the way for our Canadian identity today.

Richard Pierpoint

____

____

Laura Secord

____

____

11

1800 – 1850

The Rebellions

The Rebellions of 1837 and 1838 were uprisings that happened in Upper and Lower Canada. The discontented populations rebelled against their governments and fought for political reform.

A. Fill in the blanks. Then answer the questions.

Rebellion in Lower Canada

suppressed British ethnic Patriotes

The rebellion was fuelled by 1.____________ division between French Canadians and 2.____________ inhabitants. In the government, the French made up an elected assembly but was overruled by an appointed Legislative Council dominated by wealthy British merchants called the Chateau Clique. This group 3.____________ French culture and rights. Louis Joseph Papineau and his group, called the 4.____________ , sent the 92 Resolutions, which was a list of demands for political change to London. The list pleaded for responsible government. When the demands were denied, the Patriotes reacted with violence against British forces in November of 1837 and 1838. The rebellion to overthrow British rule was defeated and Papineau fled in exile.

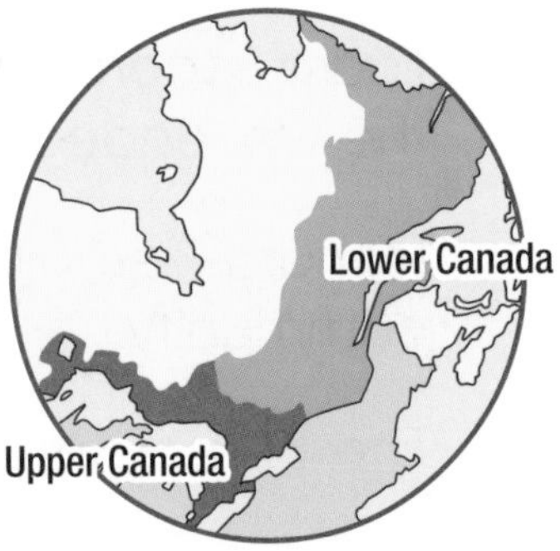

Rebellion in Upper Canada

gain refuge debt oligarchic

The rebellion in Upper Canada was less violent and smaller in scale. The people were dissatisfied with the 5.____________ government, which was run by a small elite group called the Family Compact. This group used their position for personal 6.____________ , taking advantage of the power they held over the colony's economy. Local farmers suffered under this rule and many were in 7.____________ . A leader named William Lyon Mackenzie, encouraged by the events in Lower Canada, gathered a group of rebels in December 1837 and attempted to overthrow the government. The battle was short-lived. The rebels were quickly defeated. Mackenzie sought 8. ____________ in the United States and did not return to Canada for ten years.

9. Describe each of the following.

(A) Chateau Clique (B) the 92 Resolutions (C) Family Compact

(A) ____________

(B) ____________

(C) ____________

10. How was power divided between the French and British inhabitants in Lower Canada?

____

____

11. Why were the people in Upper Canada discontent?

____

____

B. Answer the question.

A Proposal

The rebellions led to the appointment of Lord Durham, who was sent to evaluate the situation in the two colonies. He wrote the Durham Report that proposed the union of Upper Canada and Lower Canada, to be governed by responsible government. This meant that the government would be accountable to an elected assembly.

What proposal did Lord Durham make to solve the problems in Upper and Lower Canada?

____

The Province of Canada

The Durham Report and the Act of Union were two political changes that ultimately led to the development of Canada as an individual nation.

A. Read about Lord Durham. Then complete his report.

In 1838, Lord Durham was sent to Upper Canada and Lower Canada to investigate the causes of the two rebellions. He wrote the Durham Report that gave recommendations on how to better govern the two conflicting colonies. His report received mixed reactions. Britain did not like his ideas of giving the colonies a representative government and the French Canadians disliked his degrading view of their culture. Nonetheless, the Durham Report is considered to have played a vital role in the development of Canadian democracy.

The Durham Report

- internal affairs
- united into one political entity
- based on ethnic division
- elected by the public

- Upper and Lower Canada should be 1. ____________________ .
- In order to assimilate the French Canadians into British culture, British citizens should immigrate to British North America.
- Responsible government should be granted, in which the Legislative Assembly would be 2. ____________________ .
- The colonial governments should have control over 3. ____________________ .
- Durham declared that the French Canadians had "no literature, and no history".
- In Lower Canada, Durham concluded that the conflict was 4. ____________________ .

B. Read about the Province of Canada. Then complete the chart and answer the questions.

Lord Durham's proposal of a unified province was accepted and in 1840, the Act of Union was passed. The Act united Upper and Lower Canada into one colony called the Province of Canada. Each side had equal parliamentary representation. The new government was headed by the governor general, who was assisted by an Executive Council and a Legislative Council. A Legislative Assembly represented the public as members were elected, not appointed.

Lower Canada did not like this union. One of the provisions of the Act required Lower Canada to help pay Upper Canada's mounting debt even though it had little debt of its own. They were also angry that they did not have more representation in the government, considering that they were a much larger population. The Act was also an attempt to assimilate the French Canadians. The French became a minority after joining the predominantly English-speaking Upper Canada. In the end, however, the French were able to preserve their culture.

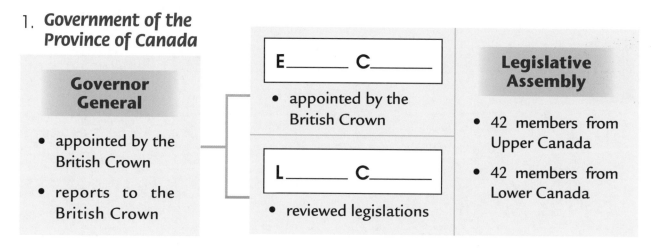

1. **Government of the Province of Canada**

Governor General

- appointed by the British Crown
- reports to the British Crown

E________ C________

- appointed by the British Crown

L________ C________

- reviewed legislations

Legislative Assembly

- 42 members from Upper Canada
- 42 members from Lower Canada

2. Why was the Act of Union unfair to Lower Canada?

____

____

3. How did the Act impact the French Canadians?

____

____

____

GEOGRAPHY

Natural Processes and Landforms

The Earth's constantly changing natural processes physically affect the land, creating new landforms and changing existing ones.

A. Identify the natural processes of "Deposition" and "Plate Tectonics". Then fill in the blanks to complete the descriptions.

Natural Processes

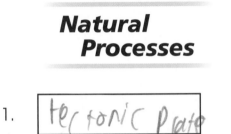

~~collide~~	~~Grand Canyon~~
~~tectonic~~	~~sediments~~ rock
~~Himalayas~~	~~pressure~~ ~~delta~~
~~mountain ranges~~	~~shallow~~ ~~water~~

1. tectonic plate

The Earth's crust is made up of many different tectonic plates which are constantly moving because of activities below the Earth's surface. When these giant plates colide, they crumple, lifting huge pieces of surface rock upward and forming mountain ranges. The world's major mountain ranges, like the Himilayas and the Andes, were formed where tectonic plates collided.

2. deposition

This natural process adds to existing landforms or builds new ones by depositing sejiments from rocks carried by water, ice, or wind. An example is a river delta, which is formed when a river loses energy upon entering a shallow area near the river mouth. Here, the force of water can no longer carry the grand canyon particles in it, thereby depositing them in the shallow area.

The process of deposition repeats, forming new layers on top of old ones. Over many years, with other natural processes like weathering and erosion at work, deposition can result in distinct landforms. An example is the pressure in the United States, where layers of rock deposits, pressed down by rocks over long periods of time, are visible.

B. Read the passage. Then fill in the blanks and answer the question.

Weathering and Erosion

Weathering is a process in which large pieces of rocks are broken down into smaller pieces. Weathering can be mechanical, chemical, or organic. Mechanical weathering takes place when rocks are physically broken up. For example, when water gets into the cracks of a rock and freezes, it expands and widens the cracks. Repetition of this process splits the rock into smaller pieces. Chemical weathering happens when rocks and minerals fall apart into pieces due to chemical reactions that break down the bonds that hold them together. For example, water dissolves limestone and breaks it apart. Organic weathering is the breaking up of rocks by plants and animals. Plant roots penetrating rocks and breaking them up is an example of organic weathering.

Erosion is the process in which soil and rock particles are removed from one place and transported elsewhere. The particles are carried away by the force of wind, the movement of water or ice, or the pull of gravity, and deposited in other places.

1. **Three Types of Weathering**

   Mechanical: Rocks are physically broken up

   chemical : Chemical reactions break down the bonds that hold rocks and minerals together.

   orgaic : rocks are broken up by plants

2. How do weathering and erosion work together to change or build landforms?

   it breks down rocks and lanforms

Land and Water

Different landforms affect the flow of water and shape the various bodies of water. Similarly, the flow of water also continues to shape and reshape existing landforms.

A. Fill in the blanks and label the diagram.

aquatic boundary mouth saturated stream land

A drainage basin is an area within which water from rain, snow, or melted snow flows downhill into a single body of water. It includes a river system, consisting of a main river and all its tributaries, as well as many other features.

Drainage Basin

Ⓐ A tributary is a small ____________ that joins a larger river or the main river.

Ⓑ A drainage divide is the ____________ of a drainage basin, which separates it from adjacent basins. It runs along a ridge of highland, on either side of which water flows into different basins.

Ⓒ A wetland is an area permanently or seasonally ____________ by surface water or groundwater, which supports the growth of ____________ plants. Swamps, marshes, bogs, and fens are some examples of wetlands.

Ⓓ A lake is a large area filled with water and surrounded by ____________.

Ⓔ A river delta is a landform at the ____________ of a river where sediments are deposited before the river enters the sea.

B. Circle the correct words to complete the passage. Then answer the question.

The Indus River System

The Indus River System consists of the Indus River and its tributaries. It covers parts of China, India, and Pakistan and is one of the largest river systems in the world. The area, the flow of water, its **depth / height** , and velocity all depend on the physical features of the land around it. Similarly, the physical environment is also shaped by the patterns of the river system.

The Indus River's source is Lake Mansarovar, which is fed by the melted glacial ice of the Himalayan mountains. The river is formed as the water runs **uphill / downhill** . Although the river is not very wide at this stage, it runs **fast / slow** due to the steepness of the mountainous terrain. The force of the water in this area has formed unique physical features, including one of the deepest gorges in the world in Kohistan. As the river reaches the plains of Punjab and is joined by numerous tributaries, it becomes **narrower / wider** and **loses / gains** speed. Its depth **increases / decreases** and sedimentation occurs. The land around the river becomes extremely **fertile / barren** due to the rich deposits from river water. Landforms such as alluvial terraces and a delta are formed at this stage as the river widens at its **source / mouth** and flows into the Arabian Sea.

Give an example from the passage of each of the following.

1. how a landform affects the flow of water

   ____

   ____

2. how water shapes or reshapes a landform

   ____

   ____

3

Climate Patterns

A climate pattern, which is the recurring characteristics of a climate, is affected by a complex combination of factors. By analyzing climate patterns, the climate of different regions across the globe can be predicted.

A. Look at the pictures. Identify the factors affecting climate patterns. Then fill in the blanks to complete the descriptions.

Factors Affecting Climate Patterns

Elevation

Ocean Currents

Latitude

Closeness to Water

cool

higher

temperatures

sea level

cooler

raise

Equator

longer

→ : sun's rays

1. [ ]

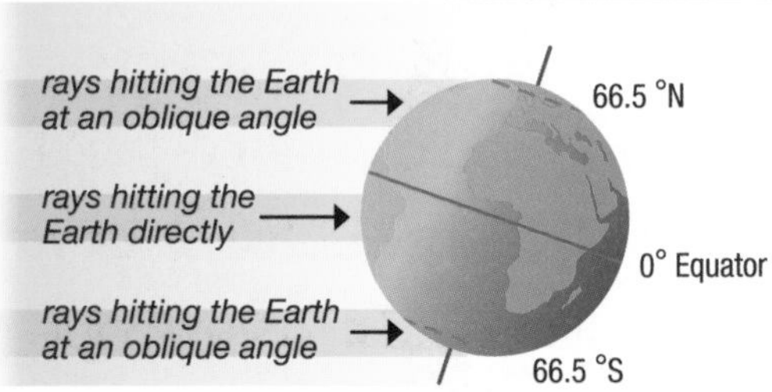

This is the distance of a place from the __________. It is measured in degrees north or south of the Equator. Areas close to the Equator have __________ temperatures because they receive the most direct rays from the sun.

2. [ ]

This is the height of a place above a reference point, particularly above __________. Places at higher elevations have lower __________.

3. [ ]

Areas close to bodies of water are much __________ in summer and warmer in winter than other areas at the same latitude and elevation because it takes __________ for large bodies of water to heat up and cool down than land masses.

4. [ ]

Warm ocean currents from the Equator ________________ the temperatures of coastal land along their route toward the poles. Similarly, ________________ ocean currents from the poles lower temperatures along their way back to the Equator.

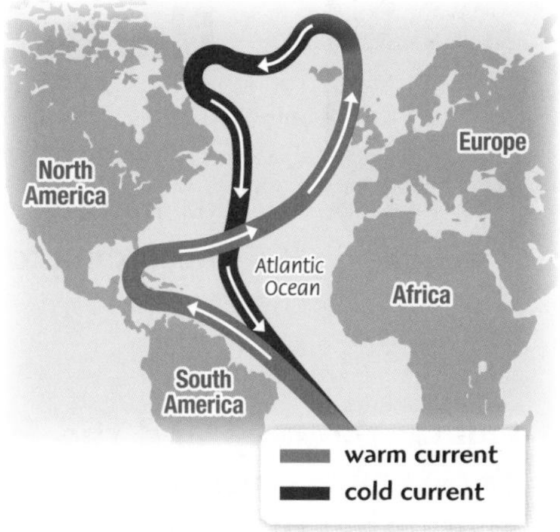

B. Look at (A) again and the climate graph below. Answer the questions.

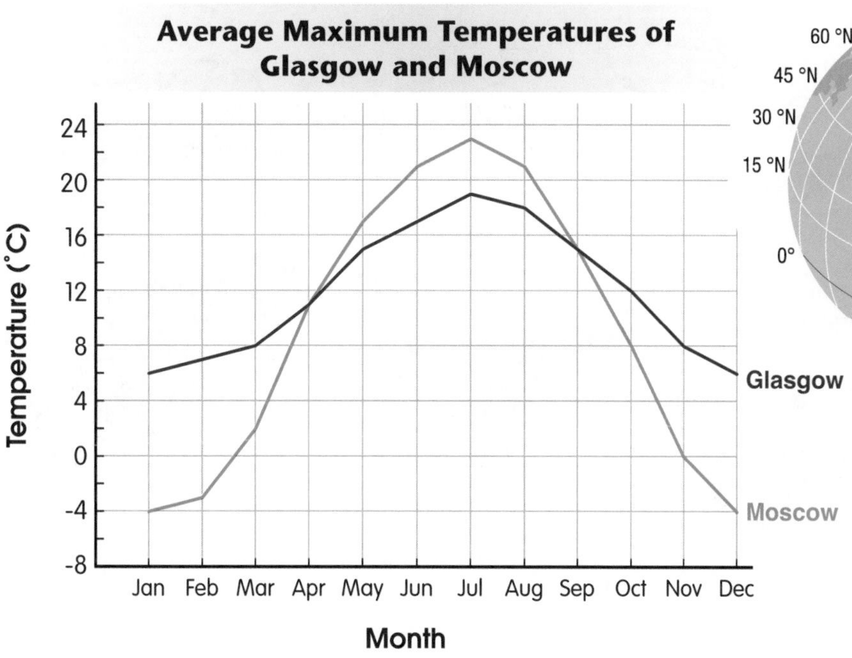

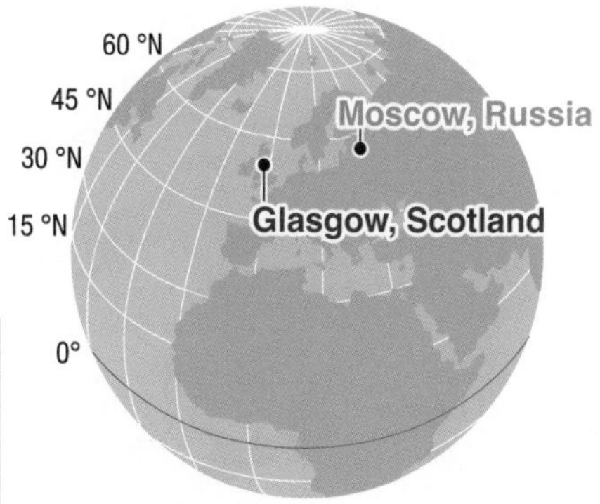

1. The city with lower temperatures in winter months: ________________

2. The latitude of: Glasgow – ________________
   (Do some research.)
   Moscow – ________________

3. Which factors account for the difference in temperatures between the two cities in winter? Explain.

____

____

____

4

Natural Vegetation

The location, climate, and physical characteristics of a place determine its natural vegetation. Regions around the world can be mapped according to their local natural vegetation.

Follow the map and the legend to label each type of natural vegetation and circle the correct words to complete the information. Then identify the natural vegetation shown in each picture and name a country where it is found.

World's Natural Vegetation

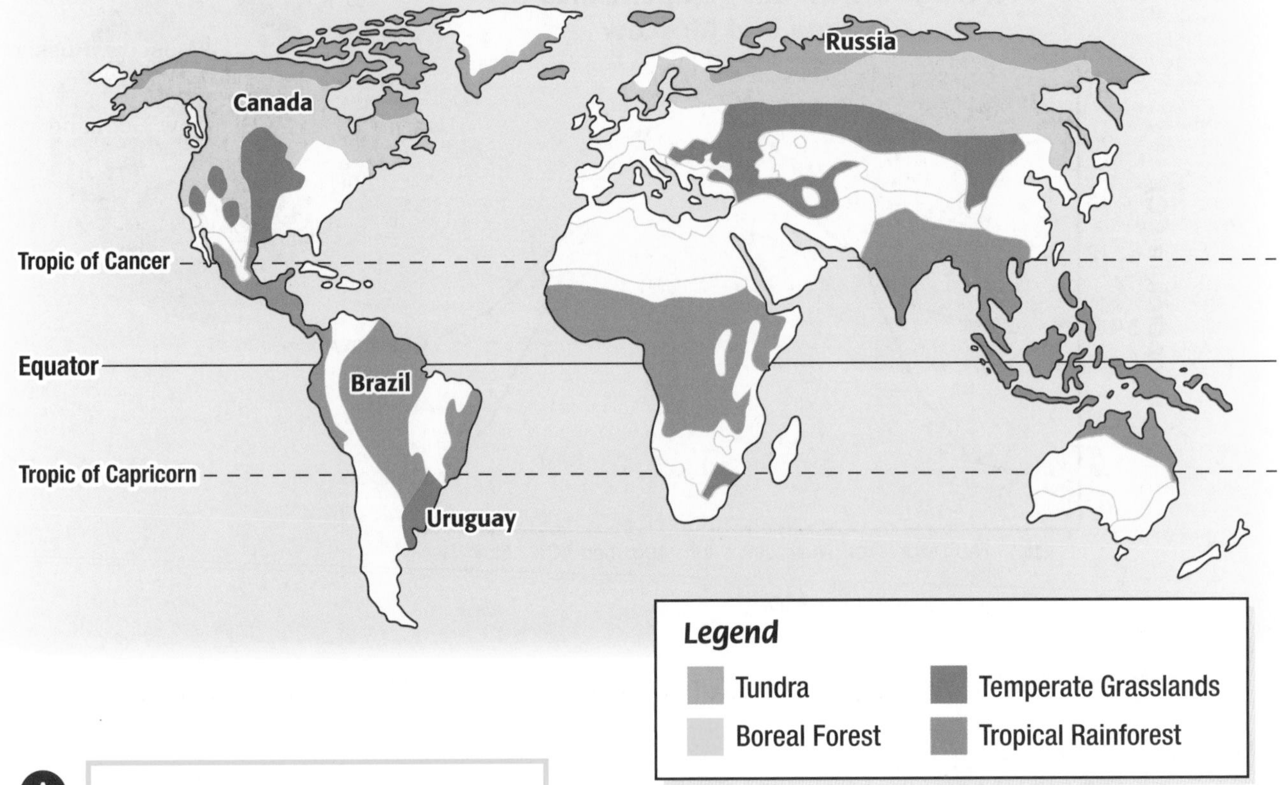

A ______________________

- located throughout the **Northern / Southern** Hemisphere, just bordering the tundra
- has a **long / short** growing season
- characterized by a tree layer and a ground layer
- contains evergreen, needleleaf, **deciduous / coniferous** trees, such as pines, spruces, and firs

B [ ]

- located mostly in the **Arctic / equatorial** regions
- has a long growing season due to **scarce / abundant** rainfall
- divided into four main layers: forest floor, understorey, canopy, and emergent layer
- has a diverse variety of plants with broad leaves

C [ ]

- located **north / south** of the Tropic of Cancer and south of the Tropic of Capricorn
- has low precipitation and seasonal **flooding / drought** which prevents the growth of trees and shrubs
- characterized by fertile soil and treeless natural vegetation
- largely covered with various types of **rocks / grasses**

D [ ]

- located throughout the Arctic regions
- has extremely low average temperatures with brief growing seasons, presence of permafrost, and limited precipitation in the form of **rain / snow**
- characterized by shallow-rooted plants that are low to the ground
- examples of plants include **trees / shrubs**, mosses, and lichens

Country:

Country:

Country:

Country:

5

Impact of Human Activities

People have been using nature to their advantage for many centuries. Human activities can lead to environmental changes, very often negative ones. An example is the construction of dams, like the Kariba Dam between Zambia and Zimbabwe.

A. Fill in the blanks to describe the human activities. Then match the impacts with the human activities.

Human Activities

wood   factories   irrigate   electricity

1. Humans build dams to generate ________________ and to control the flow of water.

2. A large number of trees are cut down in the mountains to provide ________________ for us.

3. Water is pumped from rivers to ________________ farmland along river banks.

4. ________________ are built near rivers for easy access to water for daily operations and for easy transportation of goods.

Impacts

(A) Fertilizers used on farmland pollute the water, making it saline and full of harmful chemicals.

(B) Smoke emissions from the factories pollute the air and the waste water produced threatens the wildlife in wetland habitats.

(C) This alters the natural flow of water and can result in sedimentation.

(D) This results in the loss of forest habitat and can also lead to landslides.

B. Read the passage. Then answer the question.

The Kariba Dam in Southern Africa

The Kariba Dam sits between Zambia and Zimbabwe in Southern Africa, capturing water from the Zambezi River below the Kariba Gorge. The idea was conceived by the colonial Rhodesian government. Construction of the dam began in 1956 to service the electricity needs of nearby communities of both countries, and the dam remains an important part of the region's overall energy strategy.

However useful the dam is, it has created significant environmental problems since its construction. Water levels of the Zambezi began rising rapidly. By 1959, they had skyrocketed – and the results were disastrous. More than 50 000 of the indigenous Tonga people were forced to relocate from their homes around the Gorge due to flooding. They later resettled in a number of areas, many of them suffering from routine droughts and lacking soil-rich environment to produce crops. The move was a severe disruption of their way of life and the compensation was minimal.

Wildlife suffered in similar ways. Flooding disrupted or outright destroyed many habitats, leading to the deaths of an uncountable number of animals. Eventually, Operation Noah emerged. The campaign became a six-year government-led mission to rescue animals suffered from flooding and habitat loss. From 1958 to 1964, around 6000 animals were successfully evacuated from the area. Most animals were relocated to the Matusadona National Park and around Lake Kariba.

Write what different groups might have thought about the construction of the Kariba Dam.

Rhodesian government: ______________________________

____

Residents of Zambia and Zimbabwe: ______________________________

____

Indigenous Tonga people: ______________________________

____

The rescue team in Operation Noah: ______________________________

____

Impact of Natural Disasters

Natural disasters of any magnitude are responsible for changing the socio-economic, political, and physical environment of an area.

A. Read about the natural disasters. Then answer the questions.

2013 Pakistan Earthquake

A 7.7-magnitude earthquake struck the province of Balochistan, Pakistan in 2013. The mud-brick houses, built due to the lack of economic resources, collapsed easily. This caused a large number of casualties and injuries. In the hours following the earthquake, people witnessed the formation of a small island that appeared off the coast of a nearby port as a result of the tremors.

2011 Japan Tsunami

A powerful tsunami hit the North Pacific coast of Japan in 2011. The death toll was estimated at 18 000, and about 452 000 people were displaced. The World Bank estimated that Japan suffered around $235 billion in damages.

2005 Hurricane Katrina in the United States

Hurricane Katrina hit the Gulf Coast of the U.S. in 2005. It wreaked havoc in the coastal areas and affected the politics of the entire United States. The Department of Health and Human Services estimated that after Hurricane Katrina, over 65% of the general welfare was provided by sources other than the government. The affected residents' faith in their government was shaken and they turned to faith- and community-based organizations for help.

1. The ____________________ contributed to a political change in the country because ____________________

____

2. The ____________________ contributed to economic difficulties because ____________________

3. The ____________________ contributed to a physical change of the landscape because ____________________

B. Read the passage. Then fill in the information.

Drought in Ethiopia

Ethiopia is an African country which suffers from long-term recurring droughts. Most parts of the country receive little or irregular rainfall. Subsistence farming, which is the main occupation of Ethiopians, also suffers due to the lack of water for crops. Because of this, the women and girls in a family have to spend their days fetching water from faraway places. The girls have to put a stop to their education at an early age. Also, the water they fetch is usually contaminated because of the lack of proper sanitation facilities. People drinking it or using it for crops get sick. Many children die from serious water-related diseases such as cholera and diarrhea. The economy also suffers as crops fail and food prices soar.

Humanitarian organizations like the United Nations Children's Fund (UNICEF) helped by providing food and water but their help was only short-term. Although Ethiopia has large groundwater reserves, this water remains deep under the surface in underground caverns and is hard to reach. New wells have been drilled in some areas, but the demand for water far exceeds the supply, and people from nearby areas flock to the communities where the wells are located. This puts a strain on the already limited supply of water and makes it hard to reduce the impacts of the drought.

1. **Social Impact**

   a. ______________________

   b. ______________________

2. **Economic Impact**

   a. ______________________

   b. ______________________

3. **Ways to Deal with Droughts**

   a. ______________________

   b. ______________________

4. **Problems in Dealing with Droughts**

   a. ______________________

   b. ______________________

7

Natural Resources

There are three types of resources available in nature: renewable, non-renewable, and flow resources. Their distribution around the world greatly depends on the Earth's physical features and natural processes.

A. Match each type of natural resource with its definition. Circle the correct example. Then identify the natural resources and their types.

Types of Natural Resources

Flow Renewable Non-renewable

_______________ Resource

a resource that can be regenerated or replenished if used responsibly

e.g. **fish / silver**

_______________ Resource

a resource that cannot be replaced once it is used up because it takes millions of years to form

e.g. **water / fossil fuels**

_______________ Resource

a resource that must be used at the time and the place where it occurs or it will be lost

e.g. **wind / gold**

Natural Resources

trees oil tides solar energy

1. 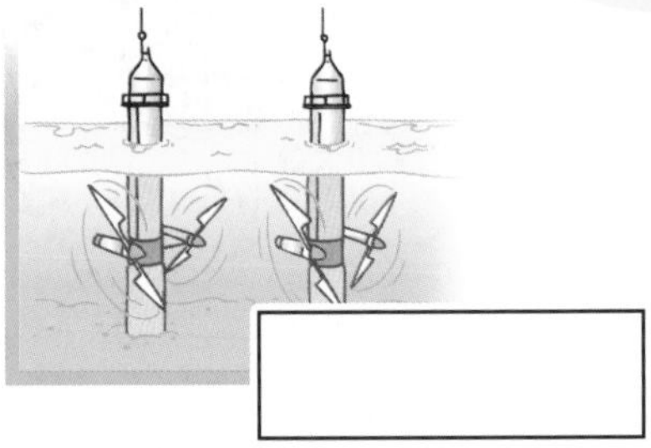

The gravitational forces of the sun, the moon, and the Earth result in the rise and fall of sea levels, from which energy can be harnessed to produce electricity.

It is a _______________ resource.

2. 

This resource is mostly found undersea or in areas where bodies of water once existed and where layers of mud covered the remains of organic matter. It is extracted by pumps from underground.

It is a _______________ resource.

3. 

This is when radiant sunlight and the sun's heat are harnessed to form useful power. Its amount and intensity depend on location, weather, and climate conditions.

It is a _______________ resource.

4. 

This resource is most abundant in forests. It takes many years before they can be used to make paper and furniture, and be used in the construction of houses.

It is a ______________ resource.

B. Read the passage. Then answer the questions.

Natural Resources in Brazil and Malaysia

Many countries are rich in natural resources; among them are Brazil and Malaysia.

Brazil is a large country in South America, with the Equator running across its north. It contains extremely rich mineral resources including iron ore, bauxite, tin, and gold. It also has huge petroleum and natural gas reserves offshore. Brazil's climate is mostly tropical with lots of rainfall, so about three-fifths of Brazil is covered by forests, and timber is among the most abundant resources of the country. Also, with its various river systems and plentiful rainfall, hydro power provides 71% of the country's electricity. Agriculturally, Brazil is one of the largest producers of coffee, sugar cane, and oranges.

Malaysia lies at latitude 2º 30' N and longitude 112º 30' E. Its rich mineral resources include tin, iron ore, bauxite, and copper. Petroleum and natural gas are its most valuable resources, with massive reserves located offshore. Malaysia has a tropical climate, which favours forest growth. About two-thirds of Malaysia is covered by forests, providing huge resources of timber. Malaysia is also among the world's leading producers of rubber and palm oil. The country's electricity is mostly produced by petroleum, though the abundant rainfall and the many rivers on steep terrain are great potentials for hydro power.

1. Regarding natural resources, how are Brazil and Malaysia similar?

____

____

2. What physical features and natural processes give rise to these similarities?

____

____

8

Mining of Natural Resources

Humans have been extracting natural resources all around the world for different purposes. However, there are both advantages and disadvantages to the process of their extraction, as in the case of large-scale mining.

A. Fill in the blanks to complete the paragraphs.

erosion trees political chemicals
extracting roads government habitat
rights minerals sedimentation harm

Mining is the process of extracting 1.____________ , both metallic and non-metallic, and other geological materials that occur naturally in the earth.

The process of 2.____________ minerals depends on where they are located. For example, mining in the depths of a rainforest involves cutting down large areas of 3.____________ and building 4.____________ to and from the sites before the minerals can be extracted. This causes 5.____________ loss for the wildlife in the area.

Excavation of mines causes soil 6.____________ , through which rock particles are carried in river water and results in 7.____________ downstream. 8.____________ used in some mining processes contaminate rivers, kill aquatic plants and animals, and threaten the health and lives of people in the area.

So, while mining may generate revenue for the 9.____________ and create jobs in a country, it also causes long-term 10.____________ to the environment and the people living there. Moreover, it may give rise to 11.____________ tension as different parties, such as the government, corporations, and residents, argue over land 12.____________ and the advantages and disadvantages of mining, as in the case of gold mining in the Amazon Forest.

B. Identify the types of impacts of gold mining and circle the correct words to complete the information.

Gold Mining in the Yanomami Territory

The Yanomami live in northern Brazil and southern Venezuela. With a population of around 32 000, they are the largest isolated tribe in South America. For many years, their territory has been invaded by gold prospectors and miners and they have suffered greatly from the impact of gold mining.

Impacts of Gold Mining

Social Political Environmental Economic

_______________ Impact

- **Forests / Mountains** on floodplains were cleared and riverbanks were blasted away, resulting in the loss of wildlife habitats.
- Mercury used in the process of gold mining and other **nutritious / toxic** materials generated during the mining process contaminate important water sources.

_______________ Impact

- The Yanomami hunt, fish, and gather fruits from the rainforest. The damage done to the forest and water sources through gold mining has greatly **increased / reduced** their main food and water supply.
- People living in the area are exposed to the toxic mine tailing and become sick. Miners also transmit malaria and other diseases to the Yanomami, who **have / do not have** immunity to the diseases. During the 1980s, 20% of the Yanomami died because of the invasion of gold prospectors and miners and the diseases they brought with them.

_______________ Impact

- The **prices / supply** of basic goods such as rice and beans have increased tremendously.

_______________ Impact

- In Brazil, conflicts arose between the Yanomami and the gold prospectors. The government had to step in to **protect / expel** the miners from the Yanomami territory. New laws have been put in place to **encourage / combat** illegal gold mining, but most of them are not enforced to their full extent.

9

Water as a Natural Resource

Water is one of the most precious natural resources on Earth. Plants and animals cannot survive without water. However, for many people around the world, getting fresh water is an everyday challenge, and millions of people are dying because of the lack of fresh water supply.

A. Identify the various uses of water. Then write an example for each with the help of the picture.

About 71% of the Earth's surface is covered in water. The total supply of water on Earth today is the same as millions of years ago, and it will be the same millions of years from now. This is because water is continually recycled through the water cycle.

We use water for different purposes in our everyday lives.

Uses of Water

Transportation
Recreation
Agriculture
Household Purposes
Generating Power

1. ____________________

e.g. ____________________

2. ____________________

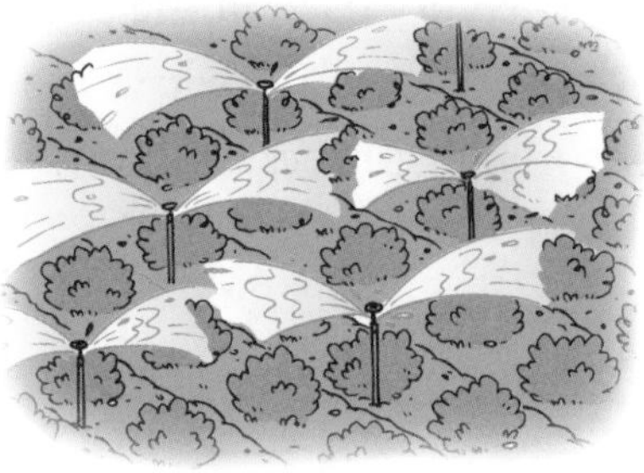

e.g. ____________________

3. ____________________

e.g. ____________________

4. ____________________

e.g. ____________________

5. ____________________

e.g. ____________________

B. Read the paragraphs and the bar graph. Then answer the questions.

Although there is an abundance of water on Earth, only less than 3% of all the water is fresh water, which most living things rely on to survive. Among this 3%, two-thirds are trapped in glaciers, snow caps, and untapped groundwater reserves. It takes a long time for water that is not fresh to be recycled through the water cycle to become fresh again, so it is important to conserve fresh water to meet the huge demands of people around the world.

Many countries are experiencing water scarcity due to fast-growing populations, resulting in an increased demand for water. The problem is intensified by prolonged droughts resulting from climate change, water pollution because of various human activities such as mining and farming, and unsustainable water management. Water is so scarce that it is harming people's health and well-being, and even causing death. The scarcity also hampers economic development and, very often, causes conflicts in these countries.

Renewable Freshwater Resources in 2015

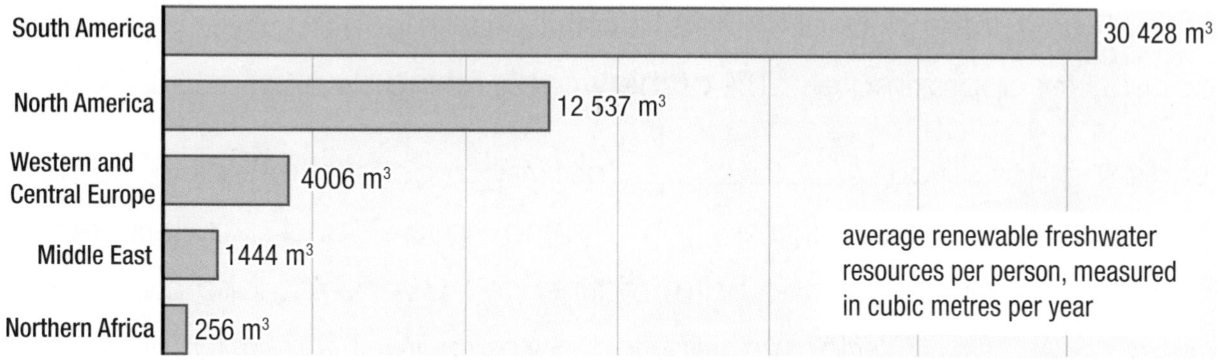

1. Which problem do you think contributes most to water scarcity?

   ____

2. Which two parts of the world had the least amount of renewable freshwater resources in 2015?

   ____

3. How many cubic metres of freshwater resources per person did North America have in 2015? Do you think the people living there should use water sustainably? Explain.

   ____

   ____

Impact of Overfishing

The fishing industry in countries around the world depends on sustainable fishing practices. Unsustainable practices of overfishing have devastating environmental, social, and economic consequences.

A. Unscramble the words and fill in the blanks to learn about overfishing.

Overfishing refers to fishing in a way that is not 1. ____________ (susabletain). This means that the rate of fishing is so high that there is not enough time for fish stocks to recover or 2. ____________ (bulidre).

Illegal and unreported 3. ____________ (ishfing), which occurs across all types of fisheries in both national and international waters, contributes much to overfishing as it accounts for approximately 20% of the world's fishing 4. ____________ (tchca).

Overfishing has serious 5. ____________ (netivega) consequences. Chemical and solid waste discharged from fishing boats and trawlers cause 6. ____________ (llutionpo) and harm marine life. Overfishing also disrupts the ocean 7. ____________ (doof) chain and poses a great threat to the natural balance and 8. ____________ (heahtl) of ocean ecosystems.

Overfishing also has 9. ____________ (cisoal) and economic impacts. Many people around the world depend on the ocean's ability to produce fish for food and for 10. ____________ (jbos). The decline in fish stocks greatly affects those who depend on fish as their main source of protein in their 11. ____________ (dtei). In addition, overfishing depletes fisheries, which results in unemployment and affects many people's livelihoods. Canada is one of the countries affected by overfishing in the 1990s. The collapse of the Atlantic cod fishery during this period had negative social and economic consequences in Canada.

B. Read the passage. Then answer the questions.

Moratorium on Atlantic Cod Fishing

The Collapse of the Atlantic Cod Fishery in Canada

Cod fishing was once a thriving industry in the communities along the Atlantic coast of Canada. New technologies and improved equipment in the 1950s and 1960s allowed fishermen to fish extensively in both inshore and offshore waters.

However, in the 1990s, after 500 years of overexploitation, the Atlantic cod stock dwindled and was almost completely depleted. A moratorium on cod fishing, which led to the largest industrial closure in Canadian history, was imposed in 1992 by the federal government, banning all cod fishing activities. The industry collapsed and this seriously affected the socio-economic structure of Atlantic Canada, with Newfoundland suffering the most from the impact. Over 35 000 fishermen and workers in the industry from over 400 coastal communities lost their jobs and their livelihoods.

The federal government helped the people affected by providing income assistance and new job training. Some of them took the alternative of working in invertebrate fisheries such as lobster, crab, and shrimp; others left the fishing industry or moved to live in other parts of the country.

Today, studies show that the recovery of the Atlantic cod stock is slow but promising.

1. What caused the depletion of the Atlantic cod stock in Canada?

____

____

2. Why did the federal government declare a moratorium on cod fishing in 1992?

____

____

3. The moratorium brought about great socio-economic changes to the Atlantic communities. If you were a decision maker in the federal government, would you have imposed the moratorium? Why?

____

____

11

Using Natural Resources

The use of natural resources helps improve our quality of life. However, the extraction and overexploitation of natural resources, including diamonds, often poses great challenges to society and the environment. People around the world are making every effort to resolve these issues.

A. Fill in the blanks. Then match the practices with the descriptions. Write the letters in the boxes.

serious
negative
organizations
extraction
reduce

As the problems arising from the extracting and use of natural resources have become more and more serious, governments, non-governmental orginization and groups, as well as individuals around the world, are promoting or practising different ways to reduce, if not eliminate, the various negative impacts of overexploiting the Earth's resources.

Ways to Lessen the Impact of Using the Earth's Resources

1. Ethical Consumerism [c]
2. Fair Trade [d]
3. Energy-saving Strategies [b]
4. Sustainable Practices [a]

A This is the practice of using the Earth's available resources responsibly, such as reusing and recycling materials.

B This includes the use of energy-efficient appliances that can perform the same functions and provide the same results with the use of less energy.

C This is the practice of buying things that are produced without harming or exploiting humans, animals, and the environment, and boycotting those that are produced otherwise.

D This is a social movement aiming to ensure that disadvantaged producers are paid fair prices for their products so that they can be self-sustained and live better lives.

B. Read the passage. Then answer the questions.

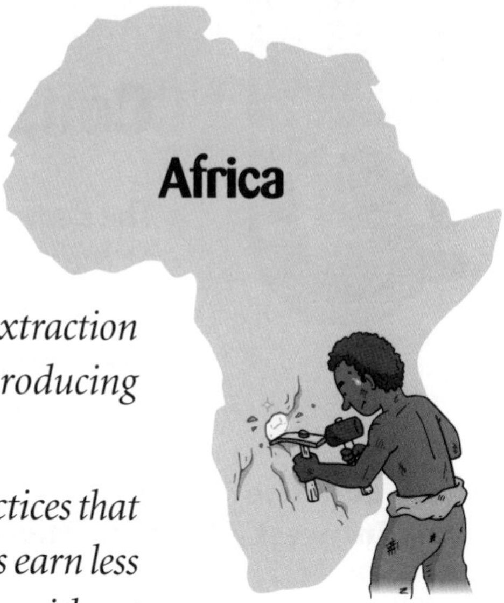

Blood Diamonds

Diamonds are among the most valuable and most sought-after natural resources in the world. However, the extraction of diamonds has devastating impact on the diamond-producing communities.

Some diamonds are mined using violent and inhumane practices that exploit workers, including child labourers. Diamond diggers earn less than a dollar a day, work in extremely dangerous conditions without any safety equipment, and have little or no training or proper tools for mining. The diamonds mined in this way are often known as blood diamonds or conflict diamonds. The mining of blood diamonds has severe environmental and social impacts, including deforestation, soil erosion, and the relocation of entire communities in poor countries. Moreover, the profits from these illegally-traded blood diamonds have often been used to fund civil conflicts and wars in African countries.

The global diamond industry has worked with the United Nations and non-governmental organizations to eliminate the trade of blood diamonds. The Kimberley Process Certification Scheme, an international diamond certification system, was adopted in 2003 to prevent conflict diamonds from entering the legitimate diamond market. About 80 countries that are involved in the diamond trade have participated in this scheme. They have committed to not producing blood diamonds and to trade diamonds only with member countries. They have also committed to investing the revenues from diamond trading in the development of infrastructure in diamond-producing communities.

1. How do you think "blood diamonds" got their name?

____

____

2. Do you think the Kimberley Process Certification Scheme can effectively eliminate the trade of blood diamonds? Explain.

____

____

Conserving Natural Resources

The Earth provides us with an abundance of natural resources. However, at the rate that humans are exploiting them, some resources will soon be depleted. We have to use natural resources sustainably to ensure that they will still be available for future generations.

Circle the correct words and fill in the blanks to learn about the Rainforest Alliance. Then answer the question.

Sustainable practice is encouraged by various groups and organizations around the world to protect the Earth's natural resources. Among these not-for-profit organizations is the Rainforest Alliance.

Rainforest Alliance

Type of Organization
- **business / non-profit**
- **governmental / non-governmental**

Goals
- to conserve biodiversity in some of the world's most vulnerable **cities / ecosystems**
- to ensure sustainable livelihoods

How to Achieve the Goals

Transforming Land-use Practices

impact waterways sustainable certifies protection deforestation pesticides

The Rainforest Alliance promotes 1. ____________ agriculture, which is the practice of growing crops to meet the needs of the present generation without compromising the future generations' ability to meet their needs.

Agriculture is responsible for 70% of the world's 2. ____________ . Clearing vast areas of forests for agriculture deprives the Earth of vital forest resources and leads to soil erosion. Residues of 3. ____________ and harmful chemical fertilizers used on farms are discharged into nearby water bodies, contaminating sources of fresh water, which is another precious natural resource.

To conserve these resources, the Rainforest Alliance encourages farmers to supply food locally, and take into account the 4. ____________ of their farming activities on the environment. It provides them with the necessary training on methods to increase their yield while maintaining the land they work on. The farmers also learn important ways of protecting 5. ____________ and maximizing the recycling of waste produced from farming. The Rainforest Alliance 6. ____________ farms that practise sustainable agriculture. Its certification is built on the three main pillars of sustainability – environmental 7. ____________ , social equity, and economic viability.

Transforming Business Practices

certified plantations earnings seal sources

To ensure that farmers practising sustainable agriculture get their fair share of 8. ____________ , the Rainforest Alliance encourages businesses to use raw materials or ingredients in their products that originate from 9. ____________ farms. With its efforts, many businesses are selling products with 10. ____________ from certified farms. In 2012, a major coffee house in the United States started sourcing all of its beans from Rainforest Alliance Certified farms at fair prices. A world leading tea company committed to having all its tea 11. ____________ certified by 2015. Now, there is an increasing number of products in the market that carry the green frog 12. ____________ on them, which is a label to show that they are either from Rainforest Alliance Certified farms or have been made with ingredients from these farms.

Transforming Consumer Behaviour

In what way do you think consumer behaviour is transformed? How does this contribute to conserving natural resources?

____

____

____

____

SCIENCE

Ecosystems

- *The system of interaction between living and non-living things in an area is called an ecosystem.*
- *Ecosystems can be any size, with smaller ecosystems found inside larger ones.*

The dry weather, the soil, the plants, and the animals here, including myself, are the components of a desert ecosystem.

A. Read the paragraph. Then match the words in bold with their meanings.

An **ecosystem** is a natural area where living and non-living things interact with each other. For the living members of an ecosystem, or **community**, it is their **habitat**, providing everything they need to live. Many different **species** of **organisms** can live in an ecosystem, but their **populations** vary, depending on their role.

1. The number of members of a species within an ecosystem — community
2. A particular type of organism — species
3. A living thing — organisms
4. The natural home of an organism — population (~~organisms~~)
5. A place where organisms interact with each other and their environment — ecosystem
6. The organisms, both animal and plant, within an ecosystem — Habitat

B. Fill in the blanks to complete the definitions. Fill in the missing letters and check the correct answer to complete the diagram of interactive ecosystems. Then draw a representative picture in each circle.

animals landforms ecosystem atmosphere

Biosphere: the 1. ________________ that encompasses the entire Earth, including all land surface, water, and the 2. ________________ , as well as the living things within it

Biome: a large area of Earth defined by similar plants, 3. ________________ , weather patterns, and its 4. ________________ , such as a **tropical rainforest**

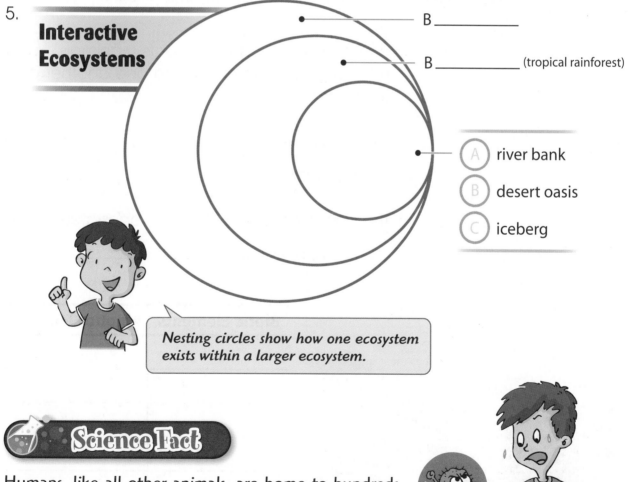

5.

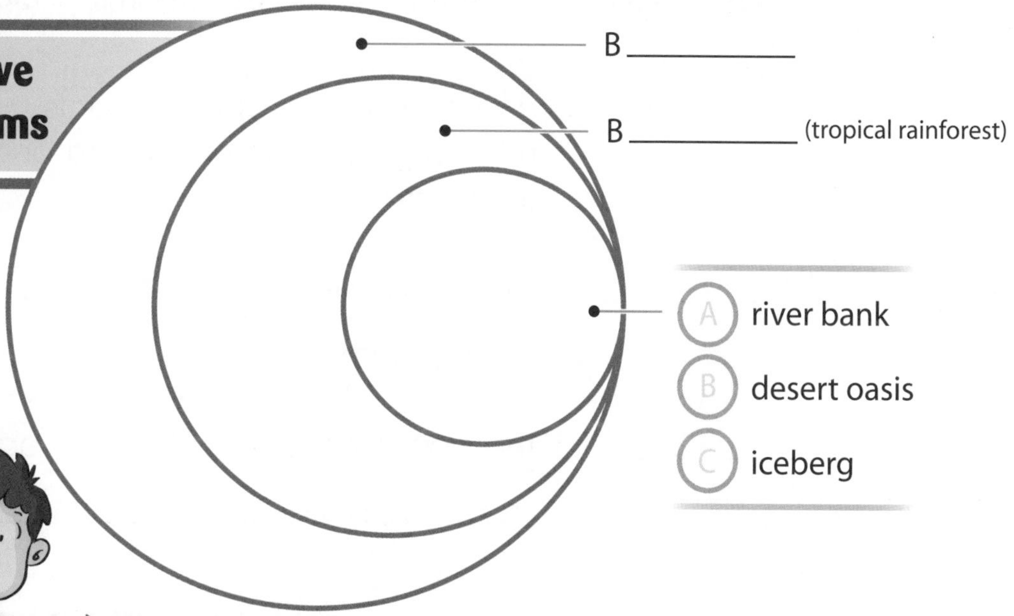

Nesting circles show how one ecosystem exists within a larger ecosystem.

Science Fact

Humans, like all other animals, are home to hundreds of different kinds of bacteria and other microorganisms. We are walking ecosystems.

Biotic and Abiotic Elements in Ecosystems

I'm a biotic member.
I'm an abiotic member .
We live well with each other.

- Living or having lived members of an ecosystem are called biotic, and non-living or never having lived members are called abiotic.
- Biotic or abiotic members of an ecosystem affect each other.

A. Fill in the blanks. Then identify five biotic and five abiotic elements of the ecosystem shown.

abiotic　water　ecosystem　microorganisms　biotic

1. ____________________ : a habitat in which plants, animals, and microorganisms interact with one another and their surroundings

2. ____________________ : the living elements of an ecosystem, such as plants, animals, and ____________________

3. ____________________ : the non-living elements of an ecosystem, such as soil, air, and ____________________

4.

Biotic Elements	Abiotic Elements

B. Each sentence describes a relationship between two elements of an ecosystem. Highlight the biotic elements blue and the abiotic elements yellow. Then describe their relationships.

1. Humans cannot live more than three or four days without water.

   Relationship: ____________________

2. Tiny wild berries are a major food source for the lumbering black bear.

   Relationship: ____________________

3. Wind is one of the forces responsible for soil erosion.

   Relationship: ____________________

4. The beaver builds its shelter, a partially submerged lodge, out of logs harvested from trees in its own habitat.

   Relationship: ____________________

5. Snakes and other reptiles use the warmth of the sun to raise their body temperatures after a cool night.

   Relationship: ____________________

6. For a typical meal, the "cleaner fish" cleans the gills and teeth of other bigger fish, which, in turn, become cleaner.

   Relationship: ____________________

Science Fact

The most unique animals and plants on Earth are found in ecosystems that developed far from neighbouring ecosystems, such as the Galapagos Islands.

Galapagos Iguana

3

Food Cycle

- *The food cycle is made up of producers, consumers, and decomposers.*
- *Different models have different ways of showing relationships within the food cycle.*

A. Trace the arrows to complete the food cycle. Then fill in the blanks with the given words.

fungi decomposer nutrients omnivore
plant primary consumer herbivore producer food

Food Cycle

1.

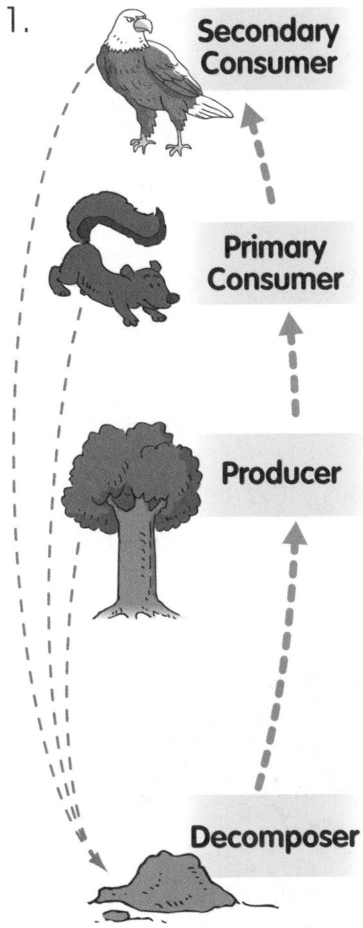

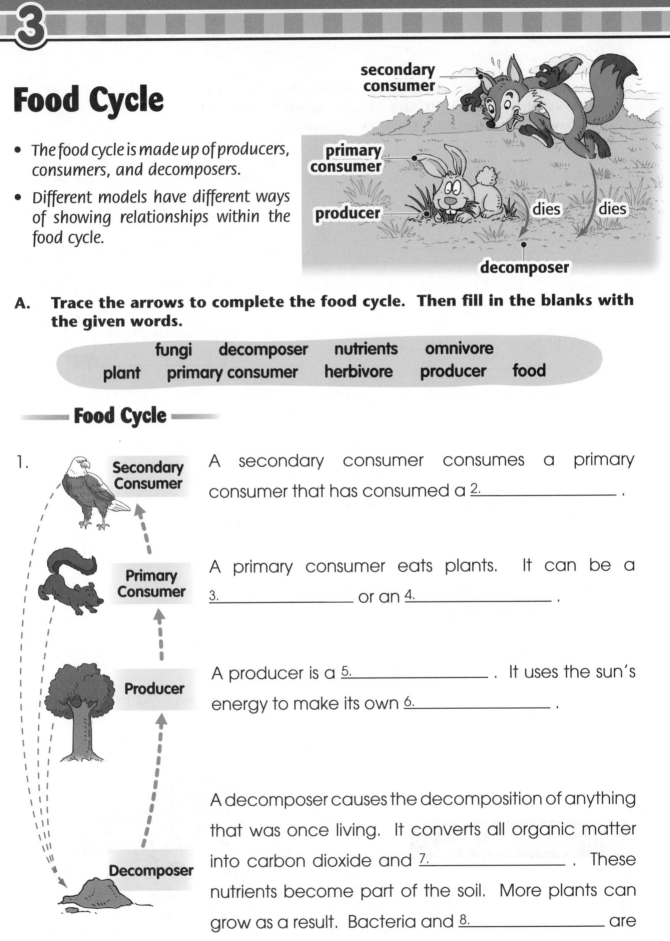

A secondary consumer consumes a primary consumer that has consumed a 2.________________ .

A primary consumer eats plants. It can be a 3.________________ or an 4.________________ .

A producer is a 5.________________ . It uses the sun's energy to make its own 6.________________ .

A decomposer causes the decomposition of anything that was once living. It converts all organic matter into carbon dioxide and 7.________________ . These nutrients become part of the soil. More plants can grow as a result. Bacteria and 8.________________ are primary decomposers.

B. Construct a food cycle with one of the food chains below. Check the food chain. Then add a decomposer to complete the cycle.

Food Cycle

(A) zooplankton → krill → seals

(B) grass → zebra → lion

(C) leaf → dragonfly → frog → snake

C. Match each model with its name. Write the letters. Then answer the questions.

1.

- **A** **food web**
- **B** **food cycle**
- **C** **food chain**
- **D** **energy pyramid**

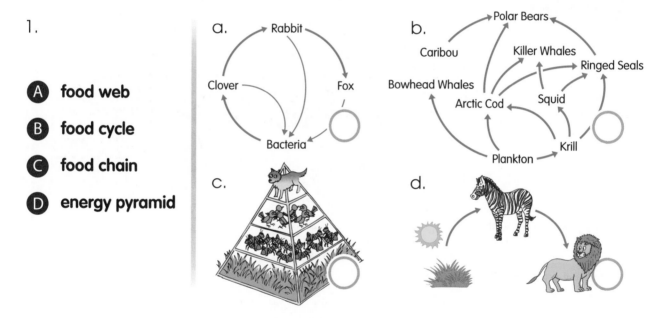

a.

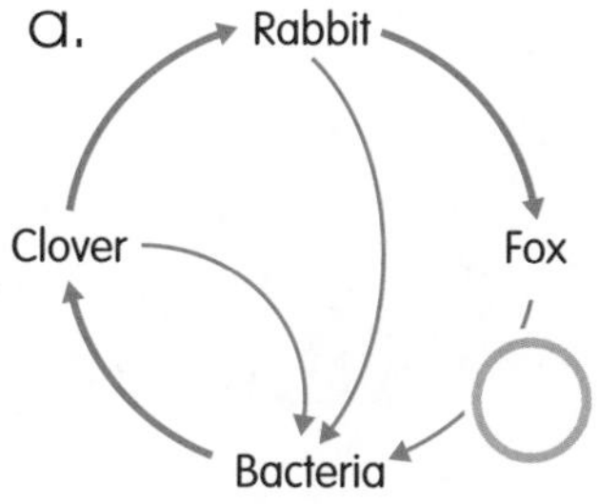

b.

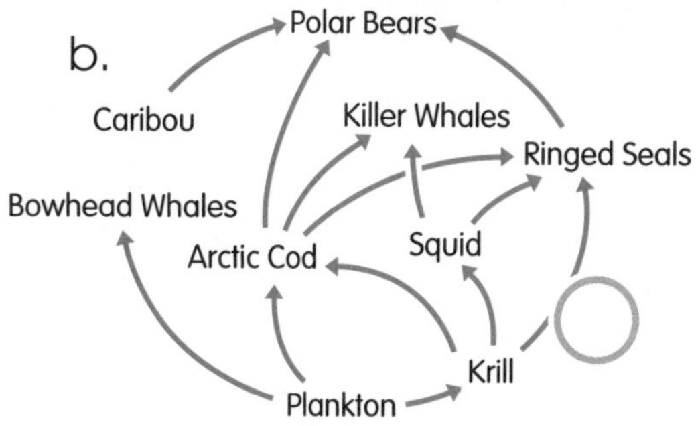

c.

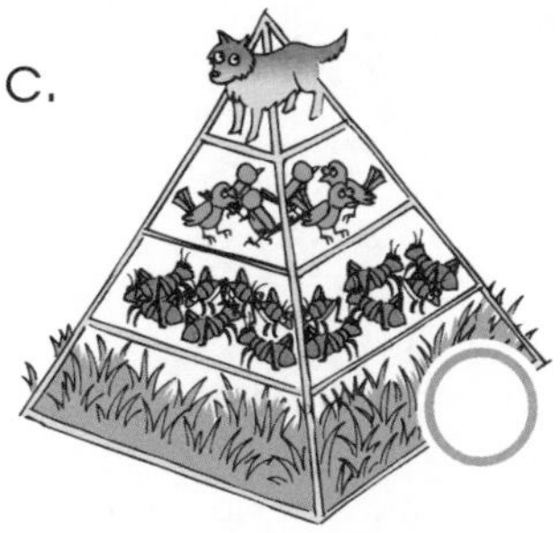

d.

2. Which model would you use to show

   a. a straight-line relationship from the food source to the food consumer? ____________

   b. how members of different food chains depend on each other? ____________

Science Fact

Food chains are usually not very long because some of the food energy is lost from one link to another.

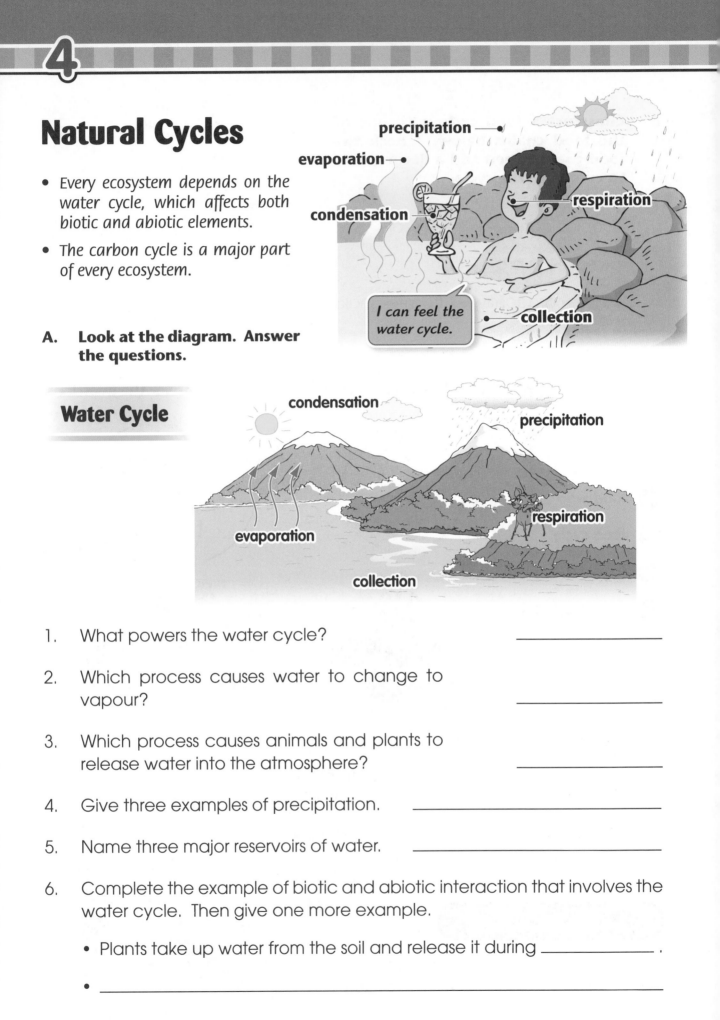

Natural Cycles

- Every ecosystem depends on the water cycle, which affects both biotic and abiotic elements.
- The carbon cycle is a major part of every ecosystem.

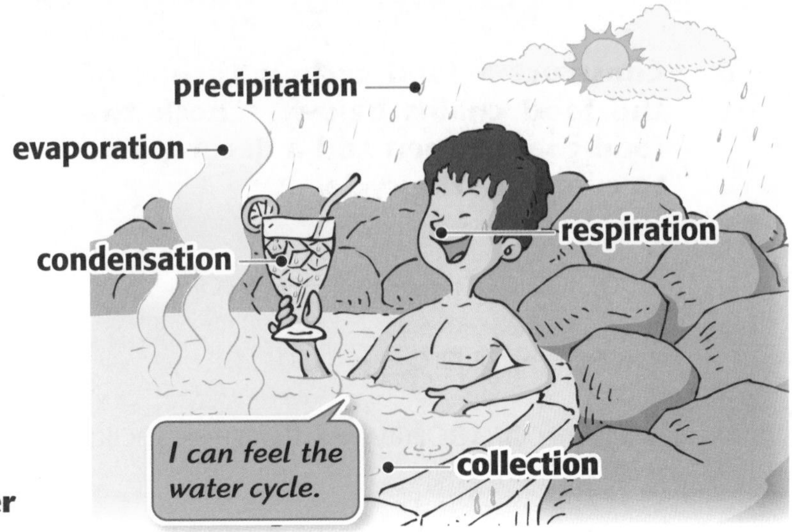

A. Look at the diagram. Answer the questions.

Water Cycle

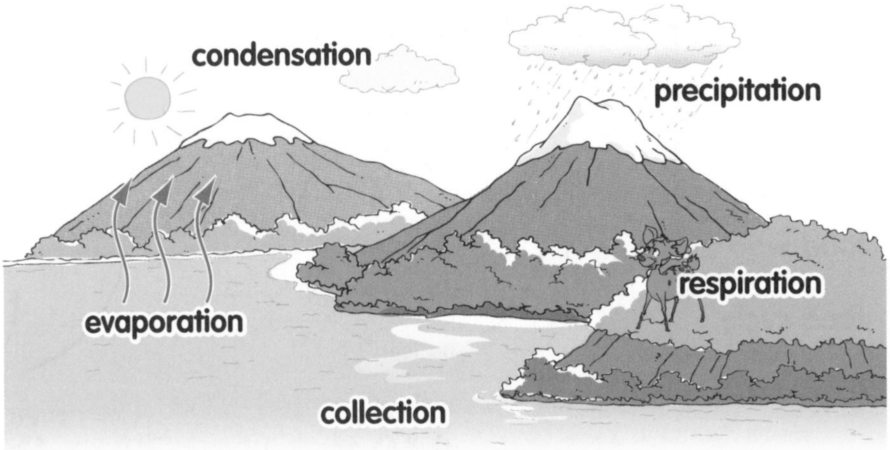

1. What powers the water cycle? ____________

2. Which process causes water to change to vapour? ____________

3. Which process causes animals and plants to release water into the atmosphere? ____________

4. Give three examples of precipitation. ____________________

5. Name three major reservoirs of water. ____________________

6. Complete the example of biotic and abiotic interaction that involves the water cycle. Then give one more example.
   - Plants take up water from the soil and release it during ____________ .
   - ________________________________

B. Read the passage and complete the carbon cycle with the words in bold.

Carbon, the fourth most common element on Earth, is found within every cell of every living thing, as well as water, rocks, soil, and air. Pairing up with oxygen, it cycles through the ecosystem in a number of ways.

Animals release carbon dioxide into the atmosphere through **respiration**. Plants use this carbon dioxide during **photosynthesis**; it helps them make food for themselves. Forests of trees use so much carbon dioxide that they are known as **carbon sinks**, as are oceans, which use up far more carbon dioxide than they release.

The carbon from dead animals and plants is released into the earth through **decomposition**. They may be stored there for millions of years, when they may be released as carbon dioxide from a volcano. The coal, oil, and natural gas we extract from the earth is millions-of-years-old carbon. Lots of carbon dioxide is released during the **combustion** of **fossil fuels**.

Carbon Cycle

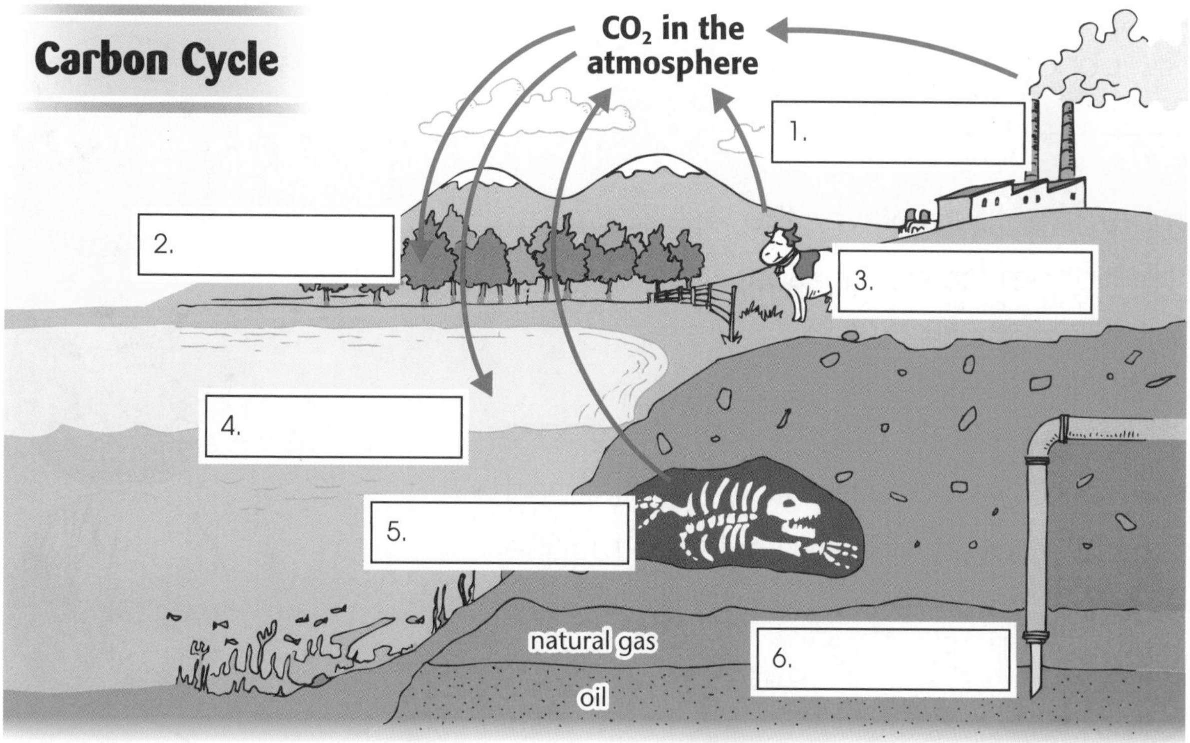

Science Fact

All the carbon on Earth now is all the carbon there ever has been and ever will be.

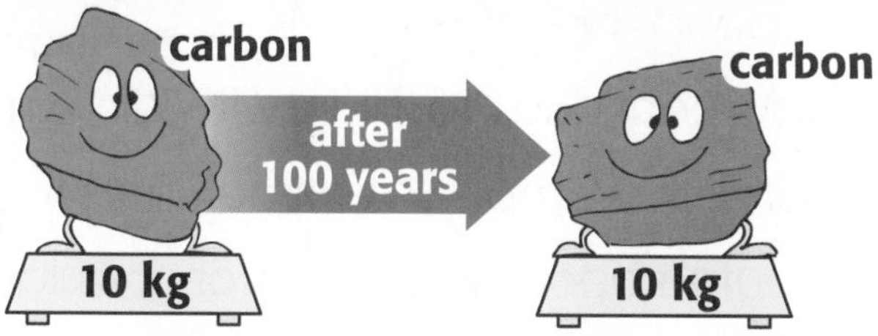

Succession and Adaptation

I'm sure there was a pond here before.

- *Succession is the change that happens when one habitat is replaced by another.*
- *Adaptation is the ability of plants or animals to change to better suit their environment.*

A. Read the paragraph. Complete the descriptions with the given words and draw lines to match them with the pictures.

Pond Succession

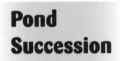

Sometimes succession is quickened by events, either natural or human-caused, such as drought, floods, and fires. Succession can cause habitat loss for animals and plants.

debris emergent marsh inhabit

As a pond develops, animals come to 1.__________ the pond. •

As more creatures arrive, the 2.__________ on the bottom increases. Some submergent vegetation appears. •

3.__________ plants appear on the edges of the pond. As pond plants grow, die, and decompose, layers of debris build up to raise the pond. •

Emergent plants grow across the floor. Then the pond becomes a 4.__________ . The marsh continues to fill in with dirt and debris to form a swamp. Over time, the swamp may dry out to become a forest or grasslands. •

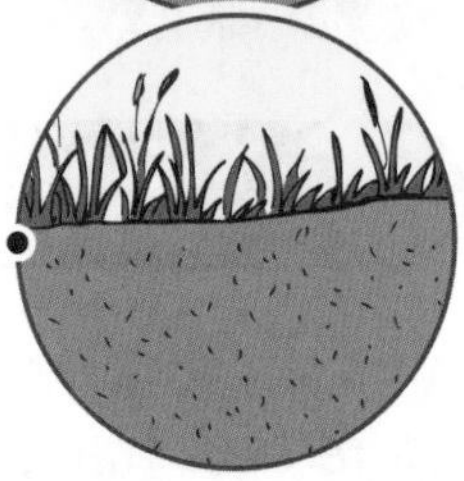

B. Match each term with its definition. Write the word on the line.

succession adaptation extinction competition species diversity

1. ______________ the most drastic event to happen when a species cannot adapt to a changed environment and cannot survive

2. ______________ this is when two or more species put pressure on the same limited elements of an ecosystem to fulfil their needs for living

3. ______________ where, through change in an ecosystem, one habitat is replaced by another

4. ______________ the assortment of different species of organisms in an ecosystem, which goes up and down with the process of succession

5. ______________ this must take place in order for an organism to stay in an environment that is changing

C. Try the experiment showing fast-motion succession.

Experiment – Fast-Motion Succession

Materials

- *a tray with high edges*
- *soil*
- *water*

Steps:

1. Pat the soil into the tray, leaving depressions for a small pond and adjoining streams.
2. Slowly sprinkle water over the soil. Let the "rain" fall, filling up the streams and pond.
3. Continue to sprinkle even after they are full. "Sediment" from run-off and erosion will gradually fill the pond.

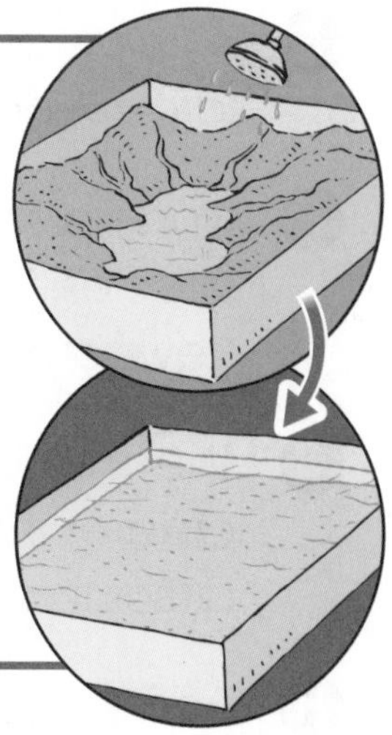

Science Fact

Geological time is much slower than the time we are used to. Your lifetime is but a wink in the time an ecosystem might go through one succession.

Human Activity

- *Human activity can negatively impact ecosystems.*
- *There are things we can do to reduce, and even reverse, negative impacts on ecosystems.*

A. Underline the factors involved in harming the ecosystems.

Problems

(A) Air pollution from factories and cars causes acid rain, a form of precipitation that harms forests and other plants.

(B) Construction and logging practices can increase sediment in nearby streams, suffocating fish and destroying spawning grounds.

(C) It may take hundreds of years to replace groundwater that has been depleted due to overuse.

(D) Chemical fertilizers from agriculture may leach into lakes and rivers.

(E) A dam built along a river drastically changes the ecosystem, flooding large areas of land and forcing its inhabitants to leave or die off.

(F) Non-native species introduced into an ecosystem can become invasive species, where native plants or animals cannot compete with the newcomer.

(G) The manufacturing of goods creates industrial waste that is difficult to dispose of.

(H) Transportation pollution is a serious problem. Most of the food we eat has been transported hundreds of kilometres to reach us.

B. Match the solutions with the problems mentioned in part A. Write the letters on the lines.

Solutions

There are alternatives to activities that cause ecosystem destruction. We have to solve the problems creatively.

1. The town of Remington passed a law restricting construction and protecting vegetation near stream banks. ______
2. BeeCome Farms adopts organic farming practices. Their eco-friendly ways attract more pollinating bees and have less of an impact on the natural ecosystem. ______
3. The Wests do most of their grocery shopping at the local farmers' market. They care about where things they buy come from. ______
4. Margaret always uses recycled items, and her friends enjoy her homemade gifts. ______
5. Sand City is doing environmental impact studies on all possibilities before deciding how to provide power for its growing population. ______
6. The Forest family are using a water-saving device after they found out how much water was used every time the toilet was flushed. ______
7. A&M Company gives staff a reward if they walk to work or take environmentally friendly modes of transport. ______
8. At the airport, Lydia was not allowed to bring home the plants she bought while travelling. ______

Science Fact

Land conservation is one way of protecting ecosystems from human activities.

Structures

Stop copying my design!
PRO

- *Structures are things with a definite size and shape. Human-made structures are based on structures found in nature.*
- *Structures can be made of one or many parts, and can be classified as being solid, frame, or shell.*

A. Find the similarities between the natural and human-made structures. Match the structures that are similar. Then give one more example.

Natural Structures	Human-made Structures
mosquito mouthpart •	• fishing net
spiderweb •	• needle
kangaroo pouch •	• bowl
honeycomb •	• baby frontpack
tooth •	• brick wall
bird wings •	• spear tip
nest •	• airplane wings
________________ •	• ________________

B. Write whether each of the following is a solid, a frame, or a shell structure.

1. ________________ is a framework that supports other parts of the structure. A skeleton is a framework.

2. ________________ is protective; it blocks entry or exit.

3. ***________________ is mostly matter. If it is made of more than one part, the parts are stacked or piled close together.***

C. Determine whether the objects are solid, frame, or shell structures.

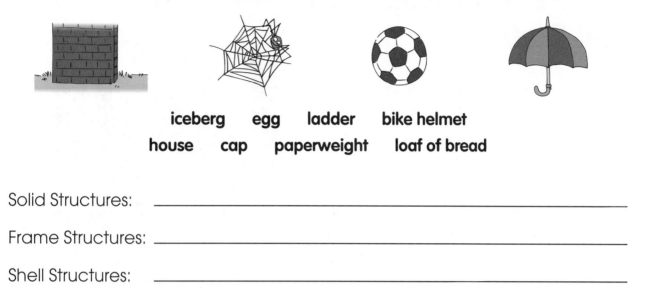

iceberg egg ladder bike helmet
house cap paperweight loaf of bread

Solid Structures: ______________________

Frame Structures: ______________________

Shell Structures: ______________________

D. For each box, think of an object that is created by combining the two structures.

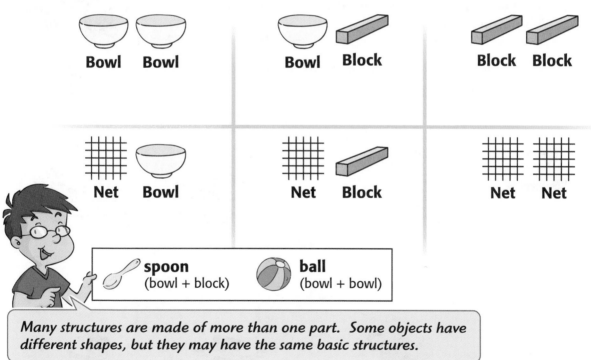

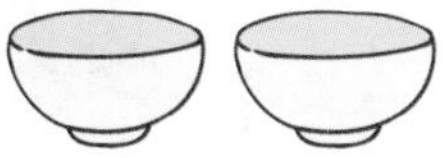

Bowl Bowl

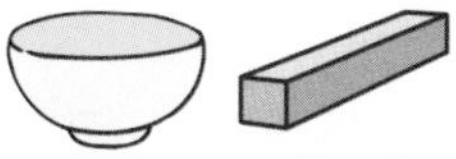

Bowl Block

Block Block

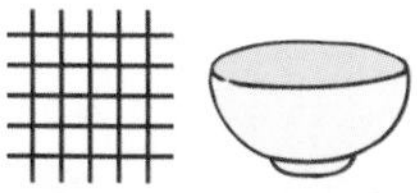

Net Bowl

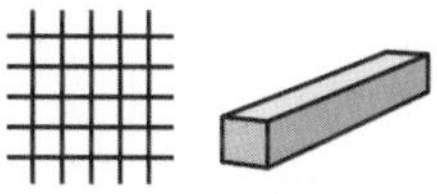

Net Block

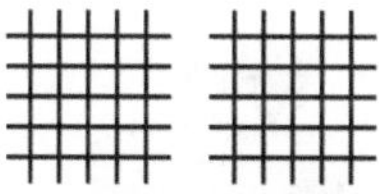

Net Net

spoon
(bowl + block)

ball
(bowl + bowl)

Many structures are made of more than one part. Some objects have different shapes, but they may have the same basic structures.

Science Fact

At more than 6000 kilometres long, the Great Wall of China is the world's largest human-made structure.

Centre of Gravity and Stability

I think my centre of gravity should be somewhere around my tummy.
Mark Your Centre of Gravity
Oh! I'm sorry!

- *Stability is the capacity a structure has for staying upright.*
- *The stability of a structure depends largely on its centre of gravity.*

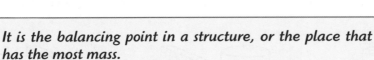

A. Check the correct definition. Label each picture as stable or unstable. Then mark the centre of gravity on each picture.

1. Centre of Gravity:

   (A) ***It is the balancing point in a structure, or the place that has the most mass.***

   (B) It is the balancing point in a structure, or the place that has the least mass.

2. a.

__________ __________

b.

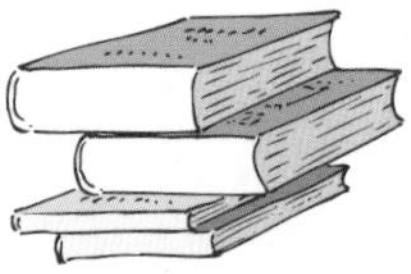

__________ __________

c.

__________ __________

d.

__________ __________

B. Redesign these structures so that they have better stability. Draw the new structures.

A structure performs its function best if it is stable.

a glass of lemonade with a fruit skewer

a triple-decker bus

C. Do the experiment about the centre of gravity. Then answer the question.

Experiment – Finding Changes in the Centre of Gravity

Materials

- *a cereal box*
- *scissors*
- *marker*
- *paper clips*

Steps:

1. Cut out a big circle from the cereal box.
2. Find the point at which it will balance on your fingertip. Mark it with an X.
3. Attach a paper clip to the edge of the circle.
4. Find the point at which it will balance on your fingertip. Mark it with another X. Can you see that the centre of gravity changes?

What happens if you add another paper clip right beside the first one?

____

____

Science Fact

It is a fact that when we walk, we are starting out by "falling". That is, we become unstable with the first movement of our foot, and then adjust our centre of gravity as we move our body over our foot.

Forces on Stable and Unstable Structures

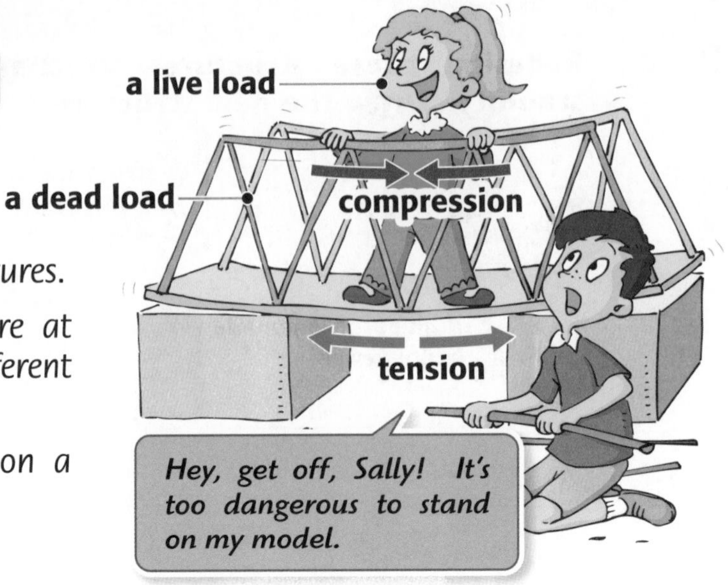
a live load
a dead load
compression
tension
Hey, get off, Sally! It's too dangerous to stand on my model.

- *Different types of forces act upon structures.*
- *A force can be applied to a structure at different magnitudes and from different directions.*
- *The point of application of a force on a structure is the point of contact.*

A. Complete the passage about forces that act upon structures.

live torsion shear dead
compressive load tensile

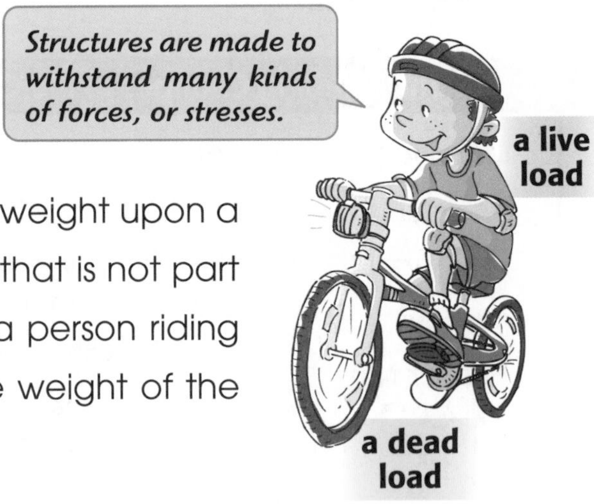
Structures are made to withstand many kinds of forces, or stresses.
a live load
a dead load

External Force

A 1. ______________ is an external force of weight upon a structure. A 2. ______________ load is one that is not part of the structure itself, like the weight of a person riding a bicycle. A 3. ______________ load is the weight of the structure itself, in this case, the bicycle.

Internal Force

An internal force can be one that pushes or pulls. A compression force occurs when a load, either live or dead, pushes upon a structure. The structure's ability to carry a load is its 4. ______________ strength. A train track must have enough compressive strength to withstand a train's weight as well as its own. A pull is called a tension force. A rope swing is a structure that must have the 5. ______________ strength to withstand the pull of a child's weight on the end.

Two other internal forces are shear and torsion. 6. ______________ force is where different parts of the structure press in opposite directions, while 7. ______________ force is the twisting of an object in opposite directions.

B. Read the following sentences. Circle the correct words.

1. Baby Bear's chair did not have enough compressive / tensile strength to hold Goldilocks.
2. Goldilocks was a live / dead load on the Three Bears' chairs.
3. Goldilocks was a tension / compressive force on both their chairs and their beds.
4. Rapunzel let down her long, braided hair, and then the Prince applied tension / compressive force as he climbed up her tower.
5. The old witch used torsion / shear force to punish Rapunzel by cutting her hair short.

C. Draw an arrow at the point of application to indicate the direction and magnitude of force.

Drawing Arrows to Indicate Force

Direction: The arrows show the direction of force.

Size: The larger magnitude of force, the larger the arrows.

Placement: The arrows are placed at the point of application of force.

Science Fact

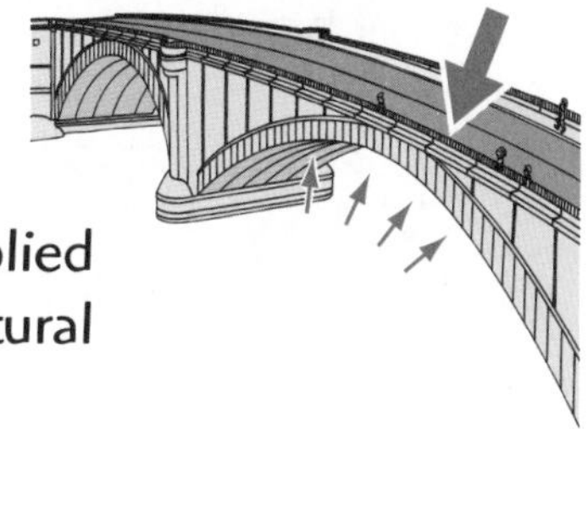

An eggshell is surprisingly strong when compressive force is applied to the ends. Humans have imitated this shape in the architectural arch, which holds up many bridges and buildings.

Materials and Design

- *Every structure has a function, and the materials used to make a structure affect its ability to perform that function.*
- *Certain factors must be considered when choosing materials to build a structure.*

Mom, let's buy this wool scarf for Grandma. Wool is soft and has good insulating properties. It'll keep Grandma warm all winter.

A. Timothy is making props. What properties should he look for in the materials for making the props below? Help him check the correct properties.

1. **sunset**
   - (A) colour
   - (B) water resistance
   - (C) strength

2. **staircase**
   - (A) elasticity
   - (B) environmental impact
   - (C) strength

3. **stage make-up**
   - (A) flexibility
   - (B) water resistance
   - (C) energy efficiency

4. **fake sword**
   - (A) elasticity
   - (B) fire resistance
   - (C) hardness

5. **costumes**
   - (A) hardness
   - (B) decomposability
   - (C) appearance

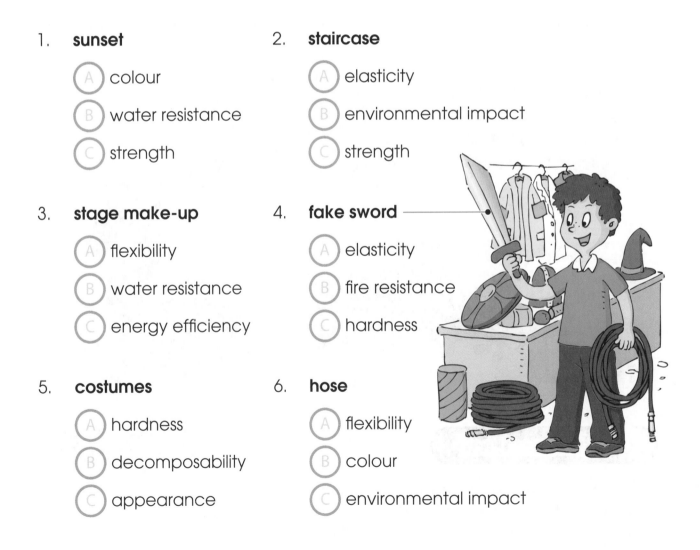

6. **hose**
   - (A) flexibility
   - (B) colour
   - (C) environmental impact

B. Fill in the blanks with the correct words.

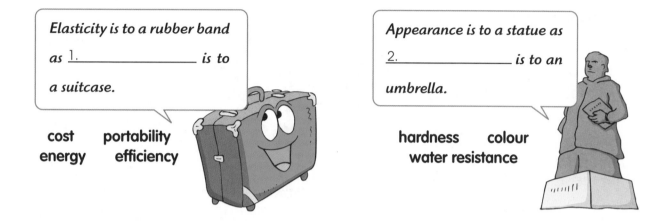

Elasticity is to a rubber band as 1. ____________ *is to a suitcase.*

cost portability
energy efficiency

Appearance is to a statue as 2. ____________ *is to an umbrella.*

hardness colour
water resistance

C. Complete the chart by writing what materials would be used to make these human-built structures. Then write one factor that would be considered by the builder when choosing the materials.

Building	Material	Factor Considered
skyscraper	concrete	strength
tree house		
hamster cage		
bus shelter		
tent		
laptop		

Materials

e.g. plastic
glass
concrete
metal
wood

Factors Considered

e.g. flexibility
hardness
energy efficiency
cost
portability
strength
water resistance

Science Fact

The silk of a tiny spider is one of the strongest materials in the world. For its diameter and weight, it is stronger than steel. For general toughness and elasticity, it beats out anything humans have made.

The Particle Theory of Matter

- *The particle theory of matter describes what makes up all matter.*
- *Particles of matter behave in different ways, depending on the state of the matter.*

gas
Particles can move from place to place.
liquid
solid
Particles are densely packed together.
Particles of liquids can move freely but are confined to a container.

A. Unscramble the letters to complete the statements about the Particle Theory of Matter. Then write "true" or "false" for each statement.

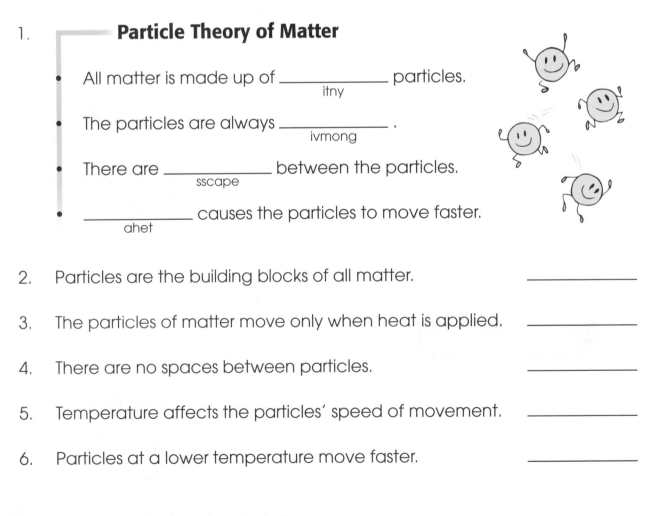

1. **Particle Theory of Matter**

   - All matter is made up of ______________ particles.
     (itny)
   - The particles are always ______________ .
     (ivmong)
   - There are ______________ between the particles.
     (sscape)
   - ______________ causes the particles to move faster.
     (ahet)

2. Particles are the building blocks of all matter. ______________

3. The particles of matter move only when heat is applied. ______________

4. There are no spaces between particles. ______________

5. Temperature affects the particles' speed of movement. ______________

6. Particles at a lower temperature move faster. ______________

B. Read about the behaviour of the particles in different states of matter. Write what state the matter is in. Then continue the pattern by drawing the particles to complete the diagrams.

____

The particles are so close together that they can barely move.

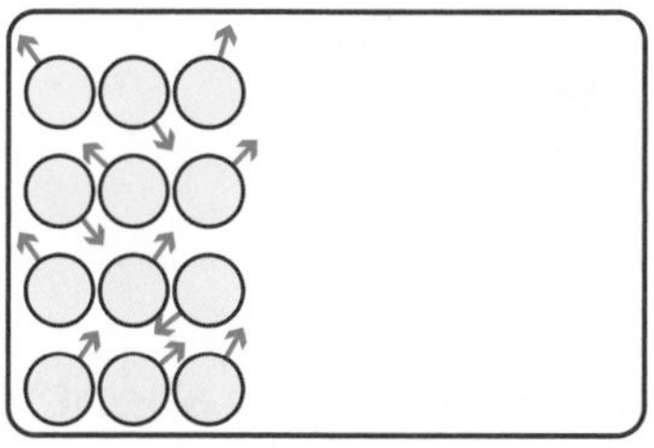

____

The particles are spread farthest apart and move in all directions, filling any container they are in.

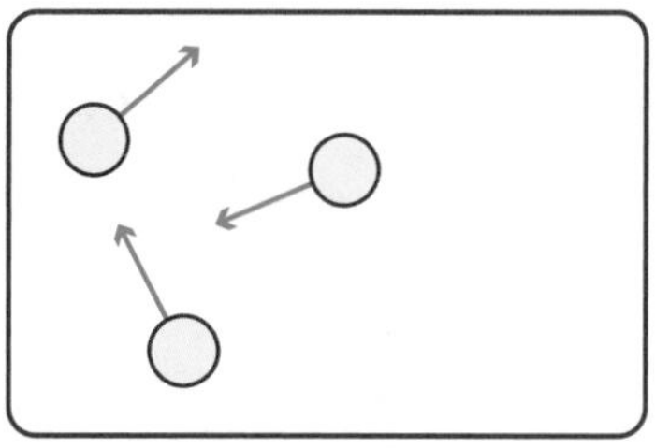

____

The particles remain together, though they are far enough apart to slip past each other.

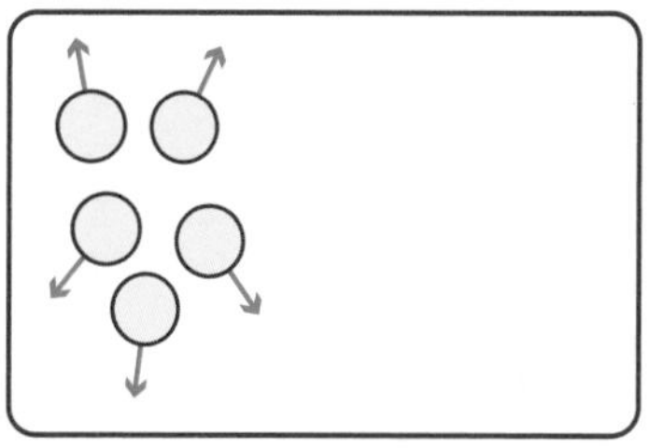

C. What happens to particles of water in different states? Complete the diagram by drawing the missing particles. Then fill in the blanks.

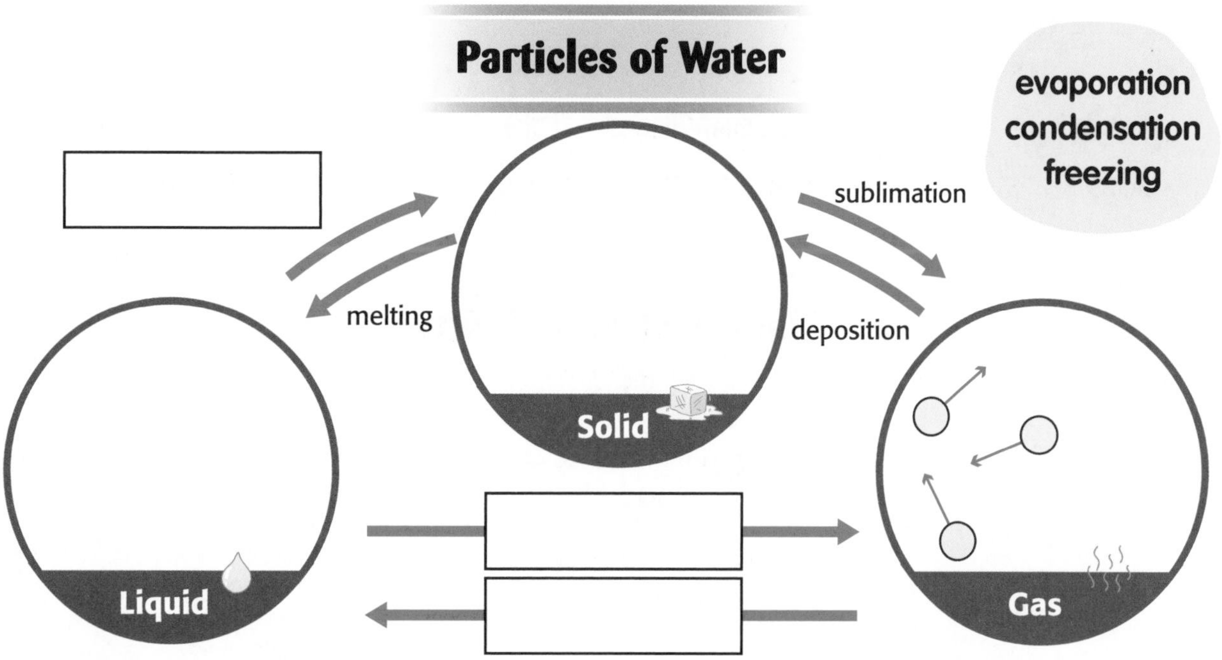

The Greek philosopher Democritus was the first to theorize that matter was made up of tiny particles.

12

Pure Substances and Mixtures

- *All matter is either a pure substance or a mixture.*
- *Most matter is either a mechanical mixture or a solution.*

Oh no! You mixed them up!
It's a mechanical mixture. I can seperate them easily if you like.
RICE
beans

A. Circle the correct words to complete the sentences giving the facts about the two different types of matter. Then complete the chart with the words in bold.

1. A **pure substance** is matter that is made up of identical / different particles.

2. A **mixture** is matter that contains particles from two / twenty or more pure substances. It is either a **mechanical mixture** or a **solution**.

Classification of Matter

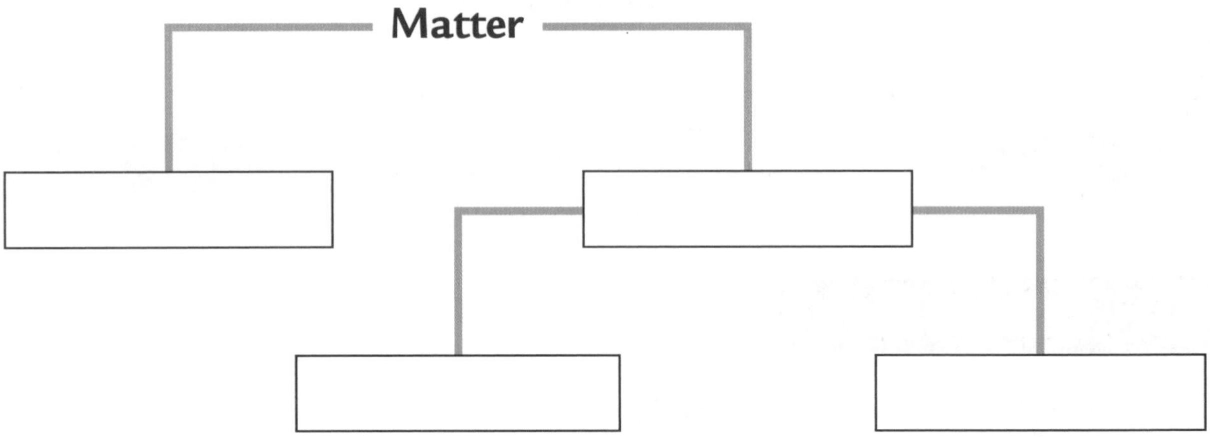

B. Identify whether each is an example of a pure substance or a mixture. Write "ps" or "m" on the line.

1. Cocoa is made from more than one kind of particle. ______
2. All particles that make a diamond are identical. ______
3. Regardless of where it is found, the melting point of carbon is 4000°C. ______
4. Oxygen, nitrogen, and a few other substances make up air. ______
5. Milk is made up of fat, and many other components. ______
6. Aluminum is a solid with a shiny, silvery appearance. ______
7. Brass is made from copper and zinc. ______

C. Label each substance as being a mechanical mixture (mm) or a solution (s).

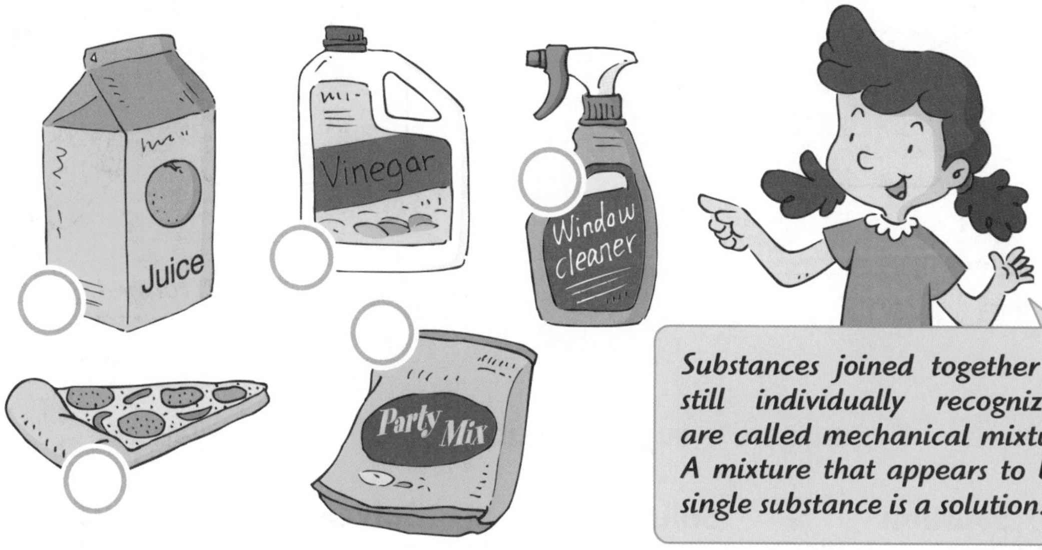

Substances joined together but still individually recognizable are called mechanical mixtures. A mixture that appears to be a single substance is a solution.

Science Fact

In ordinary language many things are called pure. Pure honey! Pure soap! Pure silk! In chemistry, though, scientists use the definition of "pure" that is explained by the particle theory of matter. So, to a chemist, there is no pure soap, honey, or silk.

All about Solutions

- A solution is a substance formed when one substance (solute) has been dissolved in another (solvent).
- A solute is the part of a solution that is dissolved in another substance.
- A solvent is the part of a solution that dissolves another substance.

Can I have a glass of solution made of carbon dioxide and water?
MENU
Pop = Solution
Solute
carbon dioxide
Solvent
water
Do you mean you want a glass of pop?

A. Fill in the blanks to complete the descriptions. Identify the missing solute or solvent of each solution and its state of matter with the help of the given substances. Then write the solution type.

1. ## Making a Solution

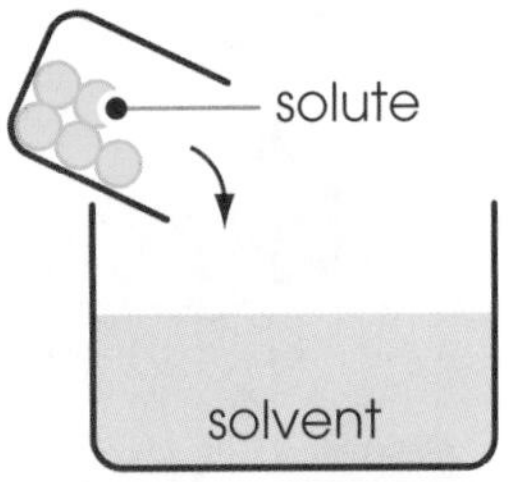

solute
solvent

Dissolve the ____________ in the solvent.

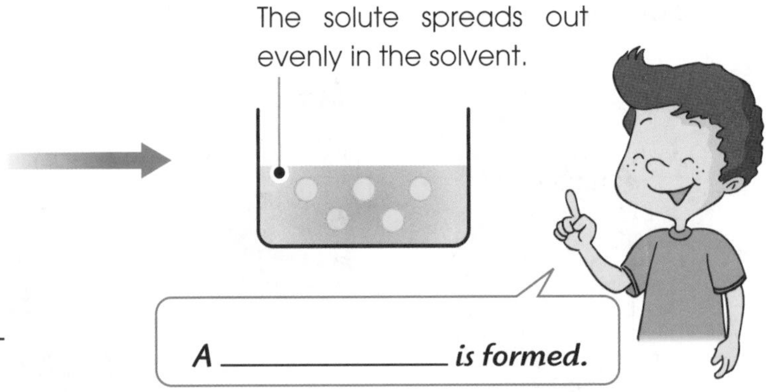

The solute spreads out evenly in the solvent.
A ____________ is formed.

2. oxygen sugar water salt zinc water

Solution	Solute	Solvent	Solution Type
pop	carbon dioxide (gas)		gas – liquid
salt water		water (liquid)	solid – liquid
vinegar	acetic acid (liquid)		liquid – liquid
brass		copper (solid)	
air	nitrogen (gas)		
maple syrup		water (liquid)	solid – liquid

B. Fill in the blanks and label the diagrams with "saturated" or "unsaturated".

When a solvent has dissolved the greatest amount of solute that it can, it is a 1. ______________ solution. An 2. ______________ solution is one that is capable of dissolving more solute.

3. ______________ 4. ______________ 5. ______________ 6. ______________

C. Match each definition with the correct word.

concentration •	• a low concentration of dissolved substance in a solvent
dilute •	• a solution that can still dissolve more solute
solvent •	• a solvent that has dissolved all the solute it can
solute •	• ability to dissolve
solubility •	• unable to dissolve
insoluble •	• amount of solute dissolved in a solution
saturated •	• substance that dissolves in a solution
unsaturated •	• dissolves another substance

Science Fact

Water is known as the universal solvent, as it is capable of dissolving more solutes than any other substance.

Separating Mixtures

- *Mixtures can be separated into their different substances by using different methods.*
- *The physical properties of substances in a mixture determine how they can be separated.*

I know! You separate the nails from the sand by magnetism!
A Mixture of Sand and Nails

A. Name each method of separation. Then match it with its definition. Write the letter in the circle.

filtration magnetism distillation evaporation density

1.  ______________ ○
2.  ______________ ○
3.  ______________ ○
4. 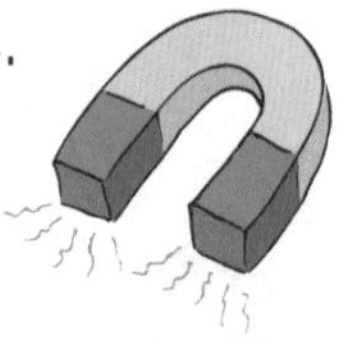 ______________ ○
5.  ______________ ○

Ⓐ the evaporation, and then condensation, of a liquid in order to separate the substances of a solution

Ⓑ turning a liquid into a gas to separate it from another substance in the mixture

Ⓒ the use of a substance's greater mass per volume to separate it from other substances in a mixture

Ⓓ the separation of a larger substance from a smaller one using a filter that does not allow the larger substance to pass through

Ⓔ the use of a magnet to attract a substance, separating it from other substances in a mixture that are not attracted to the magnet

B. Look at each mixture. Name a physical property that can help determine a method of separation.

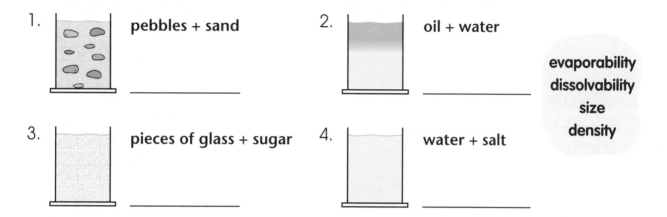

1. 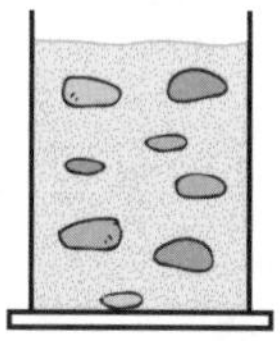 pebbles + sand ____________

2. 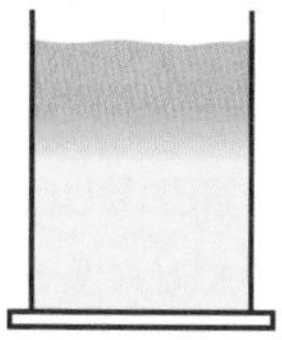 oil + water ____________

3. 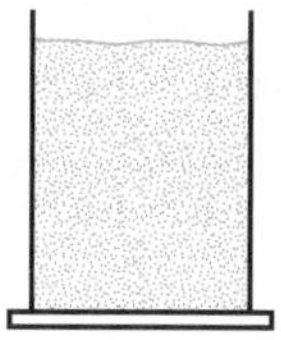 pieces of glass + sugar ____________

4. 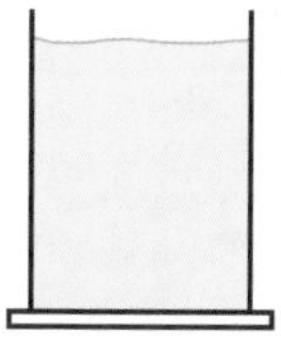 water + salt ____________

evaporability
dissolvability
size
density

C. Write the method of separation that is being used for each mixture.

1. 

____

2. 

____

3. 

____

4. 

____

Science Fact

When evaporation is used to separate water from a dissolved solid, such as salt or sugar, the solid substance often appears in the form of a crystal. Each crystallized solid has its own unique geometrical shape, which helps scientists identify it.

Solutions, Mixtures, the Environment, and You

- Negative impacts on the environment occur when certain solutions and mixtures are used and/or disposed of improperly.
- Some solutions and mixtures being created are harmful to the environment.

SUN
BLEACH
Sally, this is a useful solution, but it's extremely dangerous. We have to handle it carefully.

A. Match the descriptions with the solutions and mixtures that are found in the house. Write the letters in the circles.

1.

Ⓐ This may contain turpentine, which helps remove oil-based materials.

Ⓑ This contains solutions that make it one of the most hazardous household products that can be bought at the supermarket.

Ⓒ This solution is used to whiten things, but it is extremely dangerous and should not be mixed with other chemicals.

2. Ⓟ This solution lowers the freezing point of water. It turns into an acid in the body; drinking even a small amount of it could be fatal.

Ⓠ This may contain mixtures and solutions that are able to help control pests in a garden and should be chosen on the basis of their toxicity.

Ⓡ Made from tree resins, this dangerous fluid is used as a solvent to break down oil-based paint. It must be deposed of at an authorized facility.

Ⓢ Companies are beginning to produce these decorative products with low volatile organic compounds, and they should be chosen over those that are more toxic.

B. Fill in the blanks with the words in the diagram to complete the passage. Then answer the questions.

Acid Rain Formation

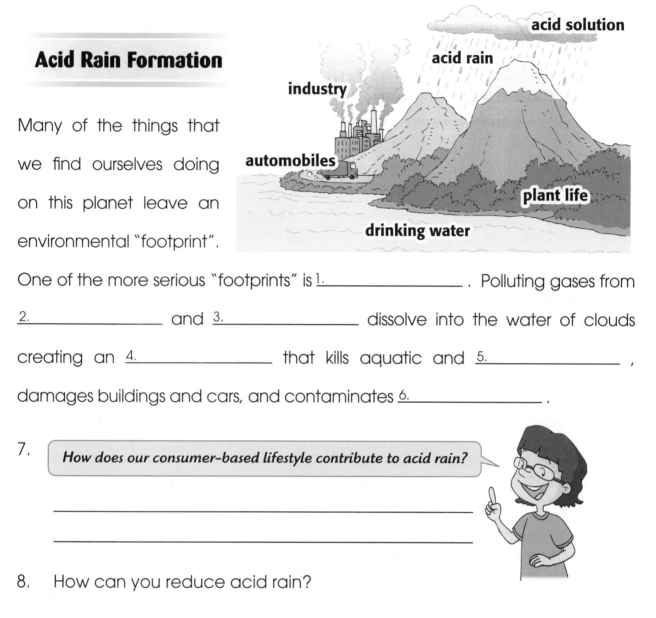

Many of the things that we find ourselves doing on this planet leave an environmental "footprint". One of the more serious "footprints" is 1. ______________. Polluting gases from 2. ______________ and 3. ______________ dissolve into the water of clouds creating an 4. ______________ that kills aquatic and 5. ______________, damages buildings and cars, and contaminates 6. ______________.

7. *How does our consumer-based lifestyle contribute to acid rain?*

____

____

8. How can you reduce acid rain?

____

____

Science Fact

Be environmentally friendly and use lemon juice – a natural cleaning substance – to clean your house. Lemon juice can be used to dissolve soap scum and hard-water deposits. The lemon peel can be placed in the garbage disposal to freshen the drain and the kitchen.

16

Heat and the Particle Theory of Matter

- *Heat, also called thermal energy, is the energy in the particles of a substance.*
- *Temperature is a measurement of the heat energy of an object at a given time.*
- *We use the particle theory of matter to explain heat energy.*

A. Fill in the blanks with the help of the clues. Then colour the thermometers and draw particles in the beakers.

1. **The Particle Theory of Matter**

- All substances are made of ______________ (not big) particles.
- The particles are always ______________ (going everywhere).
- The more heat energy a substance has, the ______________ (not slower) the particles' motion.

2. ***Beaker A contains a liquid that has more heat energy than the liquid in beaker B. The temperature of the liquid in beaker B is 20°C.***

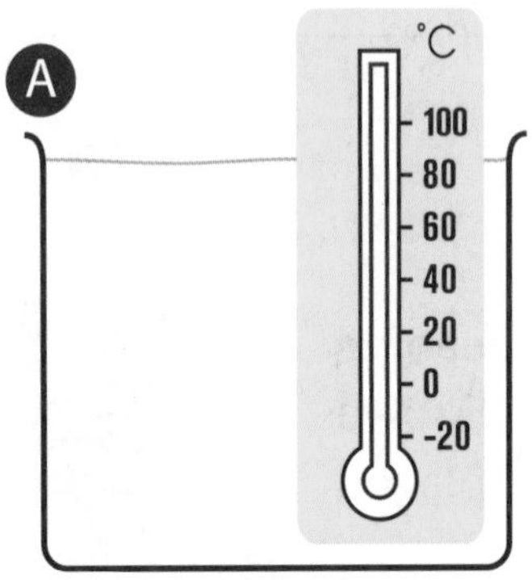

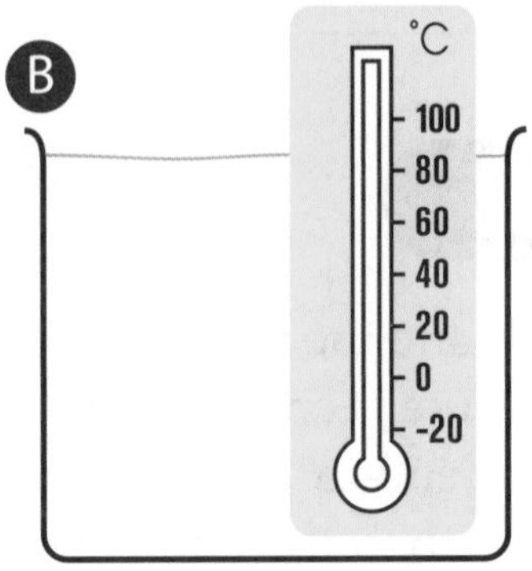

B. Put the substances in order from the one that has the most heat energy per cubic centimetre to the one that has the least. Write 1 to 5.

C. Check the correct endings to complete the sentences.

Heat is

1. (A) a form of energy.
   (B) a form of light.

2. (A) a result of the growth of particles in a substance.
   (B) a result of the vibration of particles in a substance.

3. (A) measured with a thermometer.
   (B) measured with a spring scale.
   (C) measured with an equal arm.

4. (A) never transferred from one substance to another.
   (B) something that is transferred from one substance to another.
   (C) sometimes transferred from one substance to another.

Science Fact

Heat energy always flows from the substance with more heat energy to the substance with less heat energy.

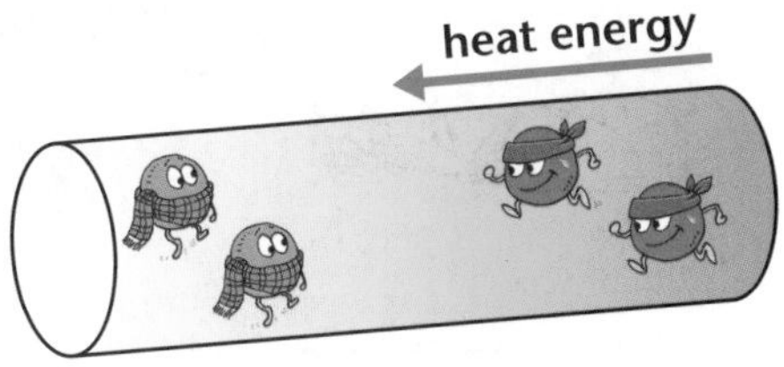

17

Heat and Volume

Look! The crack is much bigger than before!
July
Sam, don't worry. In winter, the concrete contracts, moving the edges slightly further apart. When it is summer, the crack will not be as big.

- *Most substances that gain heat expand in volume, while substances that lose heat contract.*
- *Unlike any other substances, when water changes state to become ice, it expands.*

A. Fill in the blanks with "more" or "less".

1. A particle of liquid water has ____________ energy than a particle of evaporated water.
2. Fast-moving particles take up ____________ space than slow-moving particles.
3. Particles in a hot liquid take up ____________ space than the particles of the same liquid when it is cold.
4. Particles of evaporated water take up ____________ space than particles of liquid water.
5. The particles of a solid have little energy and require ____________ space than a liquid with more energy.

B. Decide whether each picture is an example of substance expanding or contracting. Write "expand" or "contract" on the line.

1.

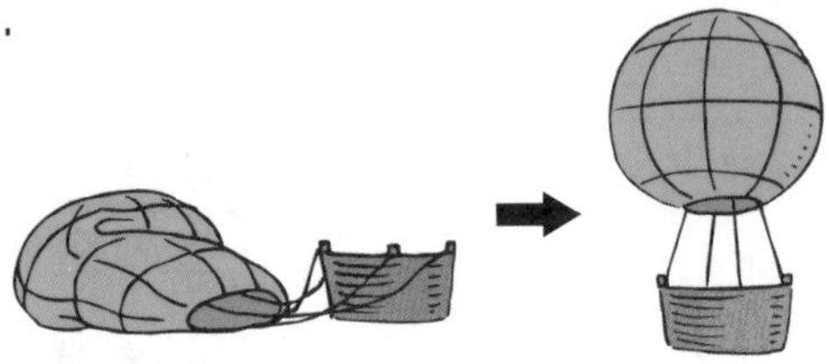

____

2.

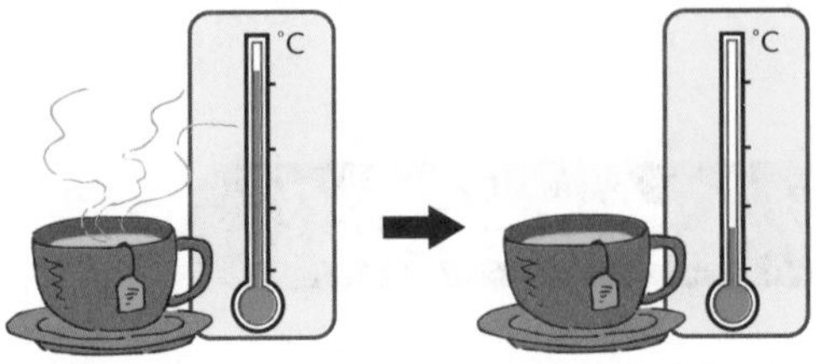

____

C. Help Mr. Cowan label the models of the water's particles to show their unique response to freezing. Write "water" or "ice" on the lines.

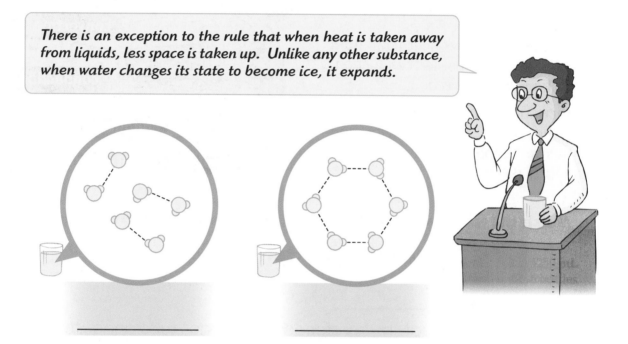

There is an exception to the rule that when heat is taken away from liquids, less space is taken up. Unlike any other substance, when water changes its state to become ice, it expands.

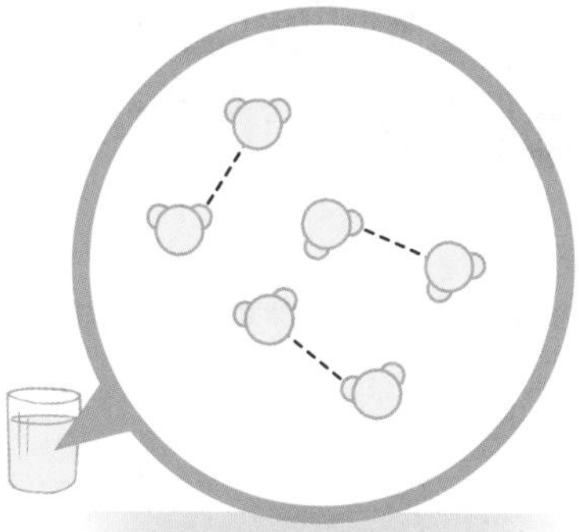

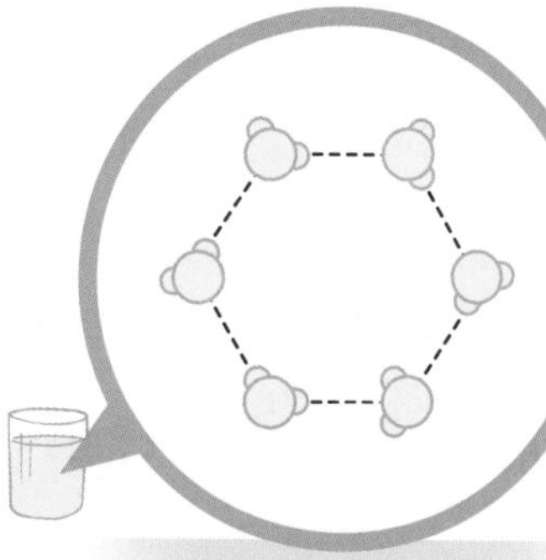

______________ ______________

D. Use the particle theory to explain why a tightened lid on a jar is easier to remove when heated.

____

____

____

____

____

Science Fact

Can you guess why popcorn pops? A kernel pops when heated because the liquid inside the kernel turns to gas. The gas particles take up more space than the liquid particles do.

18

The Transmission of Heat

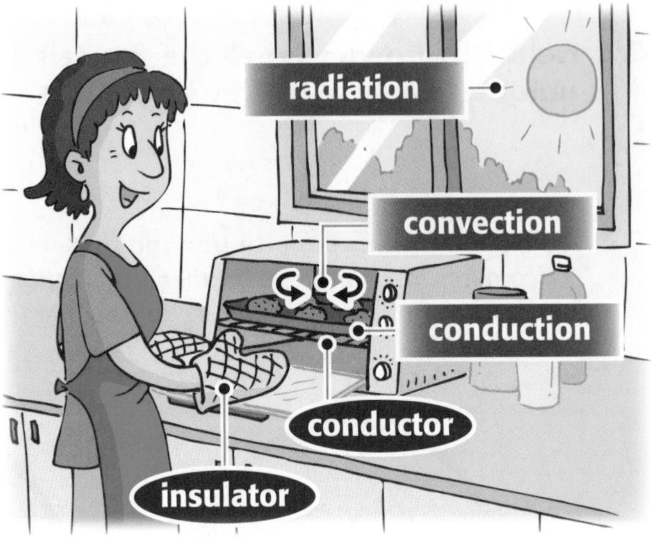

- *There are three ways heat flows from one substance to another: conduction, radiation, and convection.*
- *A thermal insulator is a substance that has low heat conductivity, and a thermal conductor has high heat conductivity.*

A. Match the words with the definitions. Then check the correct examples.

radiation convection conduction

1. 

____

Heat is transferred from one substance to another through direct physical contact when both substances are conductors of heat.

(A) a hot pan on the oven

(B) a wet shirt under the sun

2. 

____

Heat is transferred when warm and less dense gas or liquid moves upward to make way for cold and denser gas or fluid.

(A) a spoon in a cup of hot chocolate

(B) the vegetable drawers at the bottom of a refrigerator

3. 

____

Heat travels through air (or space), from an object that radiates heat to another that absorbs it.

(A) food heated in a microwave

(B) hot water in a kettle

B. Decide whether the method of heat transfer is conduction, radiation, or convection.

1. A metal spoon used to stir a hot mixture becomes hot itself. ____________
2. A campfire warms campers even if they are sitting three metres away from it. ____________
3. Eric must use an oven mitt to hold the handle of his cast iron pot. ____________
4. Emperor penguins huddle to stay warm in some of the coldest weather conditions on Earth. ____________
5. The hot water in a kettle rises to the top, only to cool and sink once more. ____________

C. For each object, write whether the material it is made with should be a thermal insulator (TI) or thermal conductor (TC).

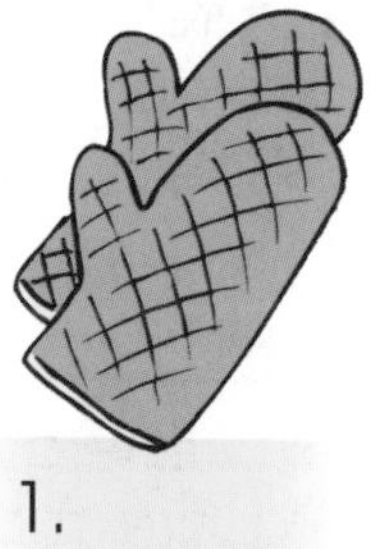
1.

2.

3.

4.

Science Fact

Snow is an excellent thermal insulator. A blanket of snow can protect tender plants, as well as buried pipes, against harsh winter temperatures.

Heat and How It Is Produced

During digestion, the chemical energy stored in food is released into my body. I can use the energy to stay warm, to grow, or to move my muscles.

- *There are many different sources of heat energy available.*
- *Some sources are non-renewable, meaning they can be used up, while others are renewable.*

A. Name the major heat producers.

Major Heat Producers

Chemical Energy **Mechanical Force** **Electrical Energy**
Nuclear Energy **Solar Energy** **Geothermal Energy**

1. ____________________

This produces heat through a push or pull that can cause friction and results in faster-moving particles.

2. ____________________

Coal-burning and hydroelectric generating stations are major producers of one of our main sources of heat: electricity.

3. ____________________

It takes advantage of the intense heat found within the Earth. Some parts of the world use this renewable heat source more than other parts of the world.

4. ____________________

When atoms are split, energy is released. While there are many advantages of using this source of heat energy, there are many unsolved, and perhaps, unsolvable disadvantages.

5. ____________________

This form of energy is released when fuels such as wood and natural gas are burned. The same thing happens when we eat food, an important fuel for our bodies. But in this case, the heat is produced through the process of digestion.

6. ____________________

A form of radiant energy, this is one of the most obvious natural sources of heat available to us. Electromagnetic waves carry this heat source the great distance it needs to travel to reach Earth.

B. Write which type of energy produces the heat in each of the following.

1. 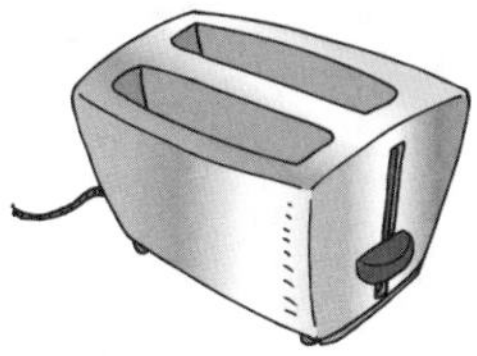

2. 

3. 

4. 

5. 

C. Write "T" for the true sentences and "F" for the false ones.

1. Chemical energy from fossil fuels is non-renewable. ______
2. Food is a source of heat only if it is cooked before eating. ______
3. Geothermal heat originates in the Earth's oceans. ______
4. Radiant energy travels by electromagnetic waves. ______
5. The sun is a form of electrical energy. ______
6. A geyser, a heat source coming from the Earth, is a source of geothermal energy. ______
7. Friction, from a mechanical force, can be a source of heat energy. ______

Science Fact

Electrical energy is one of the largest producers of heat in our homes, and the sources of heat are usually intended for something else!

I'm an example of an unintended heat producer.

The Greenhouse Effect

- The greenhouse effect occurs naturally – the Earth's atmosphere captures the sun's heat and warms the land and air within.
- The greenhouse effect is intensified when more greenhouse gases are released into an atmosphere. This can cause an unnatural rise in the Earth's temperature.

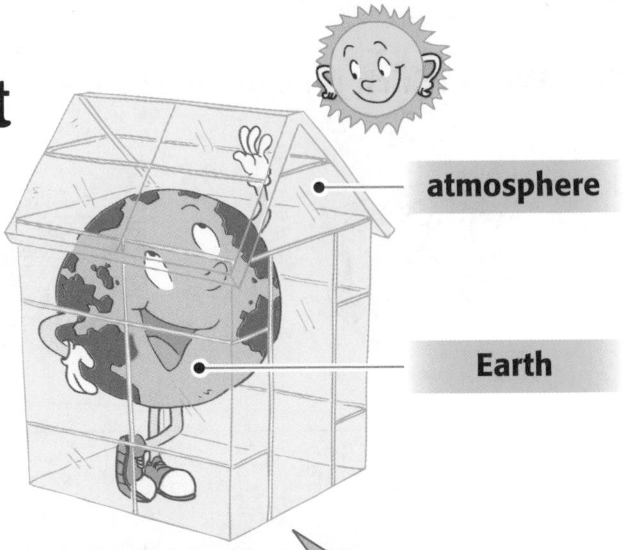
atmosphere
Earth

The greenhouse effect is useful because trapping some energy keeps the temperatures on our planet mild and suitable for living things.

A. Fill in the blanks to complete the diagram.

The Greenhouse Effect

sun's rays
atmosphere
trapped
Earth
radiation
greenhouse

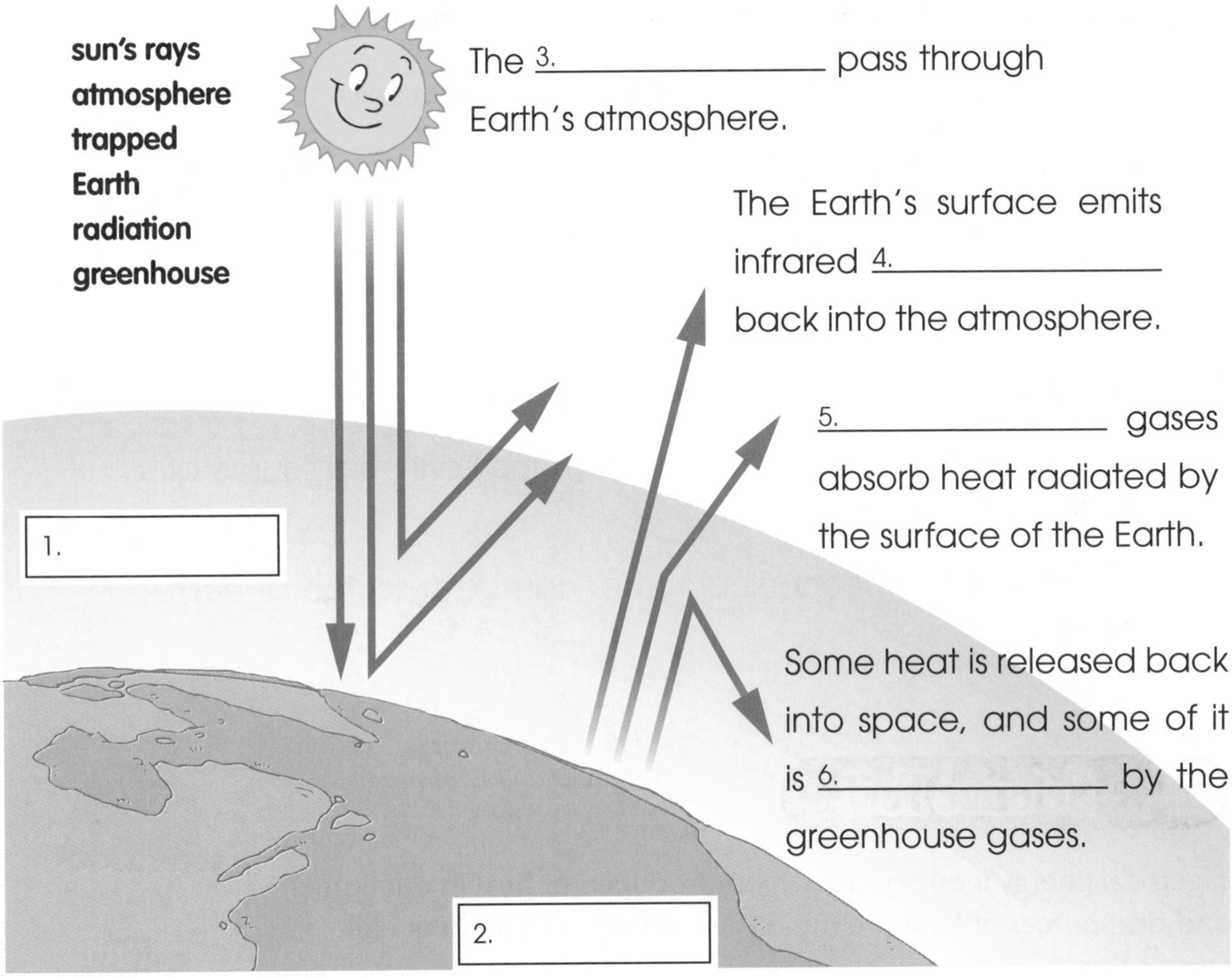
The 3. ______ pass through Earth's atmosphere.
The Earth's surface emits infrared 4. ______ back into the atmosphere.
5. ______ gases absorb heat radiated by the surface of the Earth.
Some heat is released back into space, and some of it is 6. ______ by the greenhouse gases.
1.
2.

B. Fill in the missing letters to complete the names of the greenhouse gases. Then check the sources of the greenhouse gases.

water vapour   ozone   methane   carbon dioxide   nitrous oxide

Common Greenhouse Gases

- c__________ d__________
  - produced naturally when animals breathe
  - product of fossil fuel combustion
  - product of forest fires
- m__________
  - produced when garbage decays
  - product of the digestive process of livestock and manure
- o__________
  - occurs naturally
- n__________ o__________
  - product of fossil fuel combustion
  - emitted through the use of certain fertilizers and industrial processes
- w__________ v__________
  - occurs naturally

Sources of Greenhouse Gases

- (A) cooking
- (B) burning fossil fuels
- (C) decaying organic matter
- (D) agricultural livestock
- (E) during the process of photosynthesis
- (F) plant and animal respiration
- (G) volcanoes
- (H) deforestation
- (I) watering lawns

C. Write the correct answers.

1. *The increase in greenhouse gases in the atmosphere causes Earth's average temperature to __________ (rise/fall).*

2. ________________ (Ozone/Methane) is a greenhouse gas emitted by agricultural livestock.

3. A significant amount of water vapour is released into the atmosphere through plant and animal ________________ (respiration/decomposition).

Science Fact

Methane, the second most important greenhouse gas, can be used as a fuel to generate electricity through a gas recovery system.

ANSWERS

1 Exponents

1. 3 x 3 x 3 x 3 x 3 x 3 x 3 x 3
2. 4 x 4 x 4 x 4 x 4
3. 8 x 8 x 8 x 8 x 8 x 8 x 8
4. 12 x 12 x 12 x 12
5. 9 x 9 x 9 x 9 x 9 x 9
6. 7 x 7 x 7 x 7 x 7 x 7 x 7 x 7
7. 3 8. 6 9. 2 ; 2 ; 2
10. 7 11. 4 12. 8
13. 11 ; 11 ; 11 ; 11
14. 3 15. 5 ; 3 16. 7 ; 5
17. 22 ; 10 18. 13 ; 6 19. 39 ; 2
20. 1 ; 100 21. 64 22. 3^4 ; 81
23. 7^3 ; 343 24. 5^5 ; 3125 25. 9^3 ; 729
26. 2^6 ; 64 27. 1^8 ; 1
28. 5^4 ; 5 x 5 x 5 x 5 ; 625
29. 7^6 ; 7 x 7 x 7 x 7 x 7 x 7 ; 117 649
30. 2^8 ; 2 x 2 x 2 x 2 x 2 x 2 x 2 x 2 ; 256
31. $2^2 \times 5^3$ 32. $4^3 \times 6^2$ 33. 5×9^4
34. $1^2 \times 8^4$ 35. $2^4 \times 7^5$ 36. $3^6 \times 8^3$
37. 27 ; 1296 a. >
125 ; 32 b. <
1024 ; 343 c. >
729 ; 4096 d. >
38. > 39. < 40. <
41. > 42. < 43. >
44. 5 ; 25 ; 2 ; 625 ; 625 ; perfect square
45. 8 x 8 ; 64 ; 64 ; 3 ; 262 144 ; 262 144 ; perfect cube
46. 2 ; 2401 ; 2401 ; perfect square
47. 3 ; 19 683 ; 19 683 ; perfect cube
48. A: 8 ; 15 ; 415 ; 67
itself
B: 1 ; 1 ; 1 ; 1
If the exponent of a power is 0, then the answer will be 1.

2 Squares and Square Roots

1. From 1^2 to 10^2: 1, 4, 9, 16, 25, 36, 49, 64, 81, 100
2. 7 3. 6 4. 9
5. 2 6. 10 7. 4
8. 1 9. 9 10. 6
11. 9 12. 4 13. 5
14. 4 15. 9 16. 1
17. 4 18. 4 ; 4
19. 7 ; $49 = 7^2$ 20. 64 ; $8^2 = 64$
21. 625 ; $25^2 = 625$ 22. 49 ; $7^2 = 49$
23. 81 ; $9^2 = 81$ 24. 100 ; $100 = 10^2$
25. 144 ; $144 = 12^2$ 26. 15 ; 225
27. 20 ; $20^2 = 400$ 28. 11 ; $11^2 = 121$
29. 256 ; $\sqrt{256} = 16$ 30. 289 ; $\sqrt{289} = 17$
31. 21 ; $21^2 = 441$ 32. 8 ; $\sqrt{64} = 8$
33. 400 ; $20^2 = 400$ 34. 6 ; 36
35. 3^2 ; 9 36. 8^2 ; 64 (square units)
37. 256 ; 16 38. $\sqrt{144}$; 12 (units)
39. 289 ; 576 40. 64 ; 225
17 ; 24 8 ; 15
41.

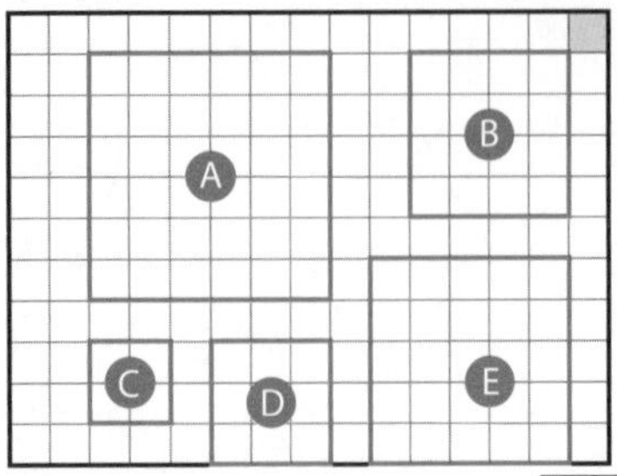

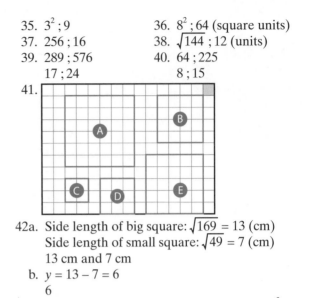

42a. Side length of big square: $\sqrt{169} = 13$ (cm)
Side length of small square: $\sqrt{49} = 7$ (cm)
13 cm and 7 cm
b. $y = 13 - 7 = 6$
6
43. Area of a small square: 576 ÷ 4 = 144 (cm^2)
Side length of small square: $\sqrt{144} = 12$ (cm)
12

3 Factors and Multiples

1. ①②③⑥
①②③ 4, ⑥ 12
6
2. ①③ 5, 15
① 2, ③ 4, 6, 8, 12, 24
3
3. ① 2, ⑦ 14
① 3, ⑦ 21
7
4. ①②③④⑥⑫
①②③④⑥ 9, ⑫ 18, 36
12
5. ①②④ 8
①②④ 5, 10, 20
①②④ 7, 14, 28
4
6. ①②③④⑥ 8, ⑫ 16, 24, 48
①②③④ 5, ⑥ 10, ⑫ 15, 20, 30, 60
①②③④⑥ 8, ⑫ 16, 24, 32, 48, 96
12
7. 1, 2, 4, 8 ; 8 8. 1, 2, 4, 5, 10, 20 ; 20
9. 1, 2, 3, 4, 6, 12 ; 12 10. 1, 2, 4 ; 4
11.

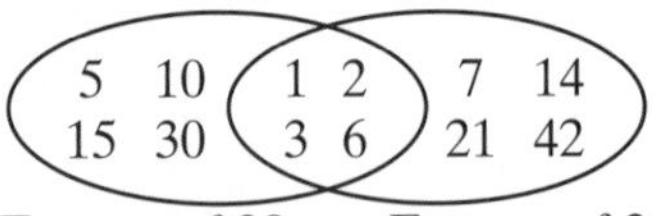

; 6

12. Factors of 28 Factors of 35

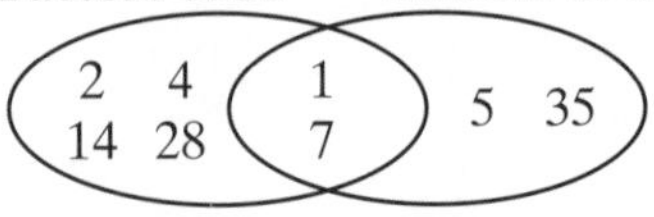

; 7

13. Factors of 12 Factors of 20

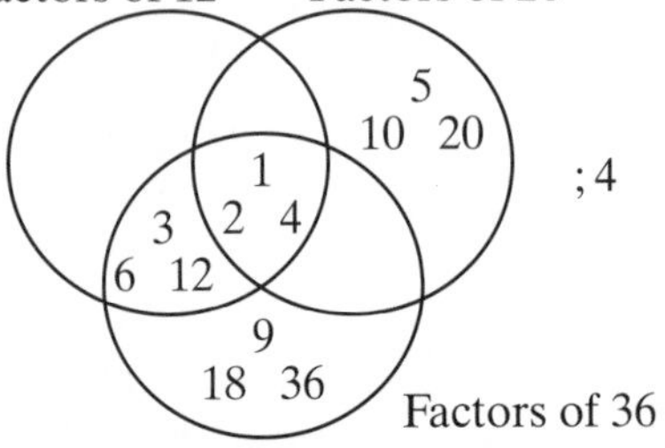

; 4

14. Factors of 10 Factors of 45

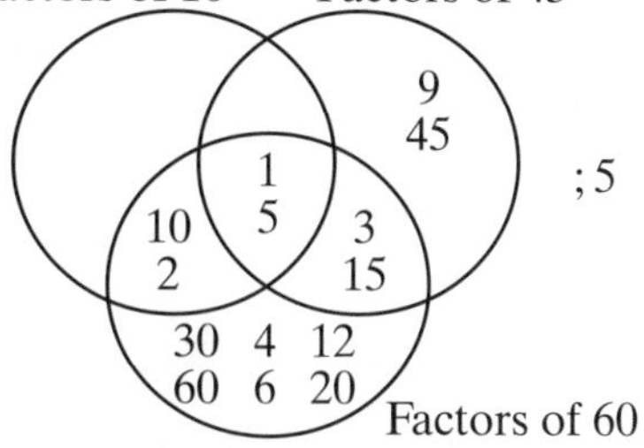

; 5

15. Make a legend to mark the multiples of the numbers.
 a. 30, 60, 90 ; 30
 b. 12, 24, 36, 48, 60, 72, 84, 96 ; 12
 c. 20, 40, 60, 80, 100 ; 20
16a. 10, 20, 30, 40, 50, 60, 70, 80, 90, 100
 b. Each multiple goes up by 10 each time.
 c. 110, 120, 130, 140, 150
17. 4, 8, 12, 16, 20, 24, 28, 32, 36, 40, 44, 48
 6, 12, 18, 24, 30, 36, 42, 48, 54, 60, 66, 72
 12
 12, 24, 36, 48
18. 3, 6, 9, 12, 15, 18, 21, 24, 27, 30, 33, 36
 4, 8, 12, 16, 20, 24, 28, 32, 36, 40, 44, 48
 5, 10, 15, 20, 25, 30, 35, 40, 45, 50, 55, 60
 6, 12, 18, 24, 30, 36, 42, 48, 54, 60, 66, 72
 7, 14, 21, 28, 35, 42, 49, 56, 63, 70, 77, 84
 L.C.M.: 12 ; 30 ; 42 ; 35
19. 4, 8, 12, 16, 20, 24
 6, 12, 18, 24
 12
20. 1, 2, 3, 6, 9, 18
 1, 2, 3, 4, 6, 12
 6 ; 3 ; 2

4 Integers

1. -3 ;
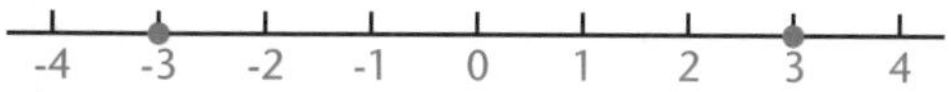

2. +6 ;
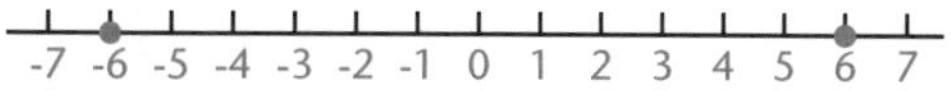

3. -7 ;
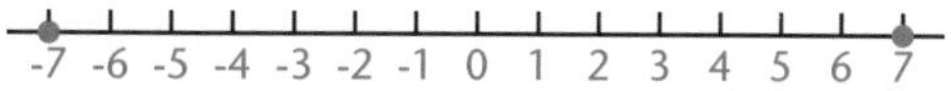

4. -2 ;
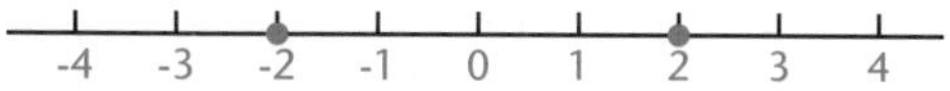

5. +5 ;
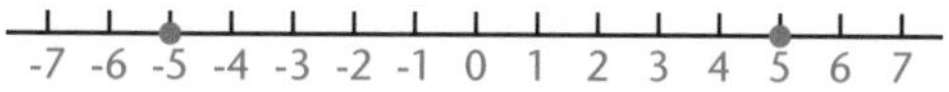

6. -8 ;

7. +5°C 8. +2 kg 9. +3 cm
10. -$273 11. +$4/h 12. +18 km^2

13. < ;
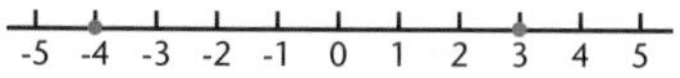

14. > ;
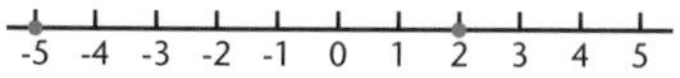

15. < ;
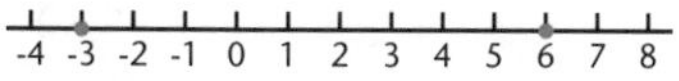

16. > ;
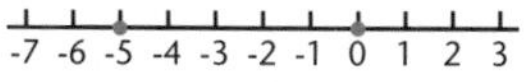

17. +5
18. -3
19. -2
20. 0
21. -4, -2, +6, +8
22. -5, -3, +2, +5
23. -9, -7, -1, 0
24. -11, -8, +3, +12
25. -4, -2, 0, 4
26. -15, -9, -6, -3
27. 7
28. -1 ;
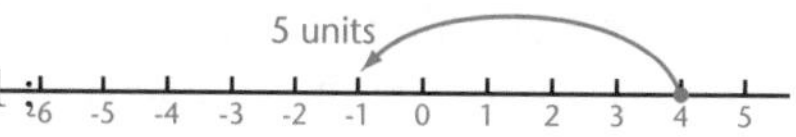

29. 3 ;
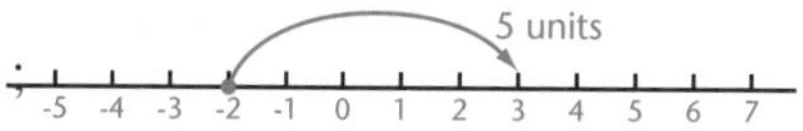

30. 4 31. -12 32. -9
33. 6 34. -1 35. -6
36. -7 37. -3
38a. 5 b. 2 points c. -1 point
39. No. The team needs 5 more points.
40. -4 41. 6 42. 11
43. -5 44. 9 45. -3
46. -8 47. 0 48. -6
49. 5
50. Wednesday: 4°C ; 1°C ; -3°C
 Thursday: -6°C ; -11°C ; -3°C

5 Ratios and Rates

1a. 2 ; 5 b. 2:10 c. 5:10
 d. 10:17
2a. 7:6 b. 8:7 c. 5:16
3. Colour 5 circles green and 6 rectangles red.
 5:6
4. Colour 3 triangles and 3 squares red, 3 stars blue, and 2 stars yellow.
 3:3
5.

Marbles	Ratio	Ratio (New)
green : blue	3:2	3:6
red : green	4:3	5:3
blue : all	2:9	6:14
red : all	4:9	5:14

6. 6 ; 10
7. 8 ; 28
8. $\frac{4}{3}$
9. $\frac{3}{5}$

(Suggested answers for questions 10 to 19)
10. 2:6 11. 2:4 12. 15:4
13. 2:5 14. 3:2, 12:8 15. 2:5, 8:20
16. 16:10, 32:20 17. 2:5, 20:50
18. 4:5, 24:30 19. 2:14, 6:42
20. 9 21. 2 22. 1
23. 2 24. 6 25. 18
26. 1:3 ; 9 27. 2:5 ; 9 28. 5:2 ; 7
29. 5:3 ; 6 30. 5:8 ; 3 31. 7:3 ; 6
32. height:base = 2:3
 2:3 = 18:27
 The length of the base is 27 cm.

33. Tom's candies:my candies = 4:5
4:5 = 28:35
Tom has 28 candies.
34. 13.73 km/h
35. $0.59/chicken ball
36. 9 pages/day
37. 5 bicycles/h
38. 42 ; 66 words/min ; Check B
39. 76.52 km/h ; 64.88 km/h ; Check A
40. 81.5 g/day ; 78.5 g/day ; Check A

6 Fractions

1a. $\frac{15}{35}$
b. $3 ; \frac{6}{15}$
c. $4 ; \frac{20}{24}$

2a. $\frac{4}{5}$
b. $2 ; \frac{4}{5}$
c. $5 ; \frac{1}{4}$

(Suggested answers for questions 3 to 6)

3. $\frac{1}{3}$
4. $\frac{2}{8}$
5. $\frac{8}{15}$
6. $\frac{2}{5}$
7. $\frac{5}{10} ; \frac{4}{10}$

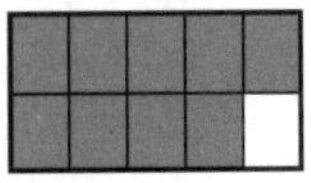

$; \frac{9}{10}$

8. $\frac{15}{20} ; \frac{2}{20}$

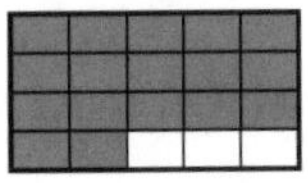

$; \frac{17}{20}$

9. $\frac{6}{10} ; \frac{7}{10}$
10. $15 ; \frac{4}{20} ; \frac{19}{20}$
11. $9 ; \frac{16}{30} ; \frac{25}{30} ; \frac{5}{6}$
12. $\frac{20}{36} + \frac{7}{36} ; \frac{3}{4}$
13. $\frac{4}{14} + \frac{5}{14} ; \frac{9}{14}$
14. $\frac{15}{20} + \frac{16}{20} ; 1\frac{11}{20}$
15. $\frac{9}{18} + \frac{17}{18} ; 1\frac{4}{9}$
16. $\frac{1}{2} + \frac{7}{10} ; 1\frac{1}{5} ; 1\frac{1}{5}$ kg
17. $\frac{5}{6} + \frac{1}{2} ; 1\frac{1}{3} ; 1\frac{1}{3}$ kg
18. $10 ; \frac{5}{10} ; \frac{2}{5}$
19. $30 ; \frac{25}{30} ; \frac{22}{30} ; \frac{1}{10}$
20. $\frac{1}{2}$
21. $\frac{1}{6}$
22. $\frac{1}{3}$
23. $\frac{1}{2}$
24. $\frac{1}{4}$
25. $\frac{1}{5}$
26. $\frac{9}{10} - \frac{1}{2} ; \frac{2}{5} ; \frac{2}{5}$ km
27. $\frac{9}{10} - \frac{1}{6} ; \frac{11}{15} ; \frac{11}{15}$ km/min
28. $\frac{5}{8} ; \frac{5}{8} ; 15 ; 1\frac{7}{8}$
29. $\frac{5}{6} + \frac{5}{6} + \frac{5}{6} ; 20 ; 3\frac{1}{3}$
30. $2\frac{2}{3}$
31. $\frac{6}{7}$
32. $2\frac{2}{5}$
33. $1\frac{1}{3}$
34. $2\frac{1}{4}$
35. $2\frac{6}{7}$
36. $3\frac{1}{2}$
37. $1\frac{3}{4}$
38. $\frac{3}{5} \times 7 ; 4\frac{1}{5} ; 4\frac{1}{5}$ L
39. $\frac{11}{12} \times 8 ; 7\frac{1}{3} ; 7\frac{1}{3}$ kg
40. $\frac{5}{6} \times 8 ; 6\frac{2}{3} ; 6\frac{2}{3}$ h

7 Decimals

1. 3 ; 2.8 ; 2.8 ; 2.804
2. 12 ; 11.5 ; 11.55 ; 11.549
3. 4 ; 4.1 ; 4.07 ; 4.068
4. 26 ; 25.8 ; 25.8 ; 25.802
5.

sum	difference	sum	difference
$\begin{array}{r} 18 \\ +\ 8 \\ \hline 26 \end{array}$	$\begin{array}{r} 18 \\ -\ 8 \\ \hline 10 \end{array}$	$\begin{array}{r} 17.620 \\ +\ 8.193 \\ \hline 25.813 \end{array}$	$\begin{array}{r} 17.620 \\ -\ 8.193 \\ \hline 9.427 \end{array}$

6.

sum	difference	sum	difference
$\begin{array}{r} 24 \\ +\ 9 \\ \hline 33 \end{array}$	$\begin{array}{r} 24 \\ -\ 9 \\ \hline 15 \end{array}$	$\begin{array}{r} 24.300 \\ +\ 9.087 \\ \hline 33.387 \end{array}$	$\begin{array}{r} 24.300 \\ -\ 9.087 \\ \hline 15.213 \end{array}$

7. 13.0 ; 5 ; 15
8. 8.76 ; 4 x 2 = 8
9. 3.24 ; 5 x 1 = 5
10. 18.17 ; 8 x 2 = 16

11. $\begin{array}{r} 22.4 \\ \times\ 1.8 \\ \hline \boxed{1792} \\ \boxed{2240} \\ \hline \boxed{40.32} \end{array}$
12. $\begin{array}{r} 1.76 \\ \times\ 3.7 \\ \hline \boxed{1232} \\ \boxed{5280} \\ \hline \boxed{6.512} \end{array}$
13. $\begin{array}{r} 8.7 \\ \times\ 3.1 \\ \hline 87 \\ 2610 \\ \hline 26.97 \end{array}$

14. $\begin{array}{r} 14.6 \\ \times\ 0.5 \\ \hline 7.30 \end{array}$
15. $\begin{array}{r} 1.06 \\ \times\ 4.3 \\ \hline 318 \\ 4240 \\ \hline 4.558 \end{array}$
16. $\begin{array}{r} 13.4 \\ \times\ 0.8 \\ \hline 10.72 \end{array}$

17a. 82.46 x 1.6 ; 131.936 (km)
b. 82.46 x 2.3 ; 189.658 (km)
c. 82.46 x 3.5 ; 288.61 (km)
d. 82.46 x 4.7 ; 387.562 (km)

18. 7.2 ; 6 ; 7
$\begin{array}{r} 7.2 \\ 58\overline{)417.6} \\ 406 \\ \hline 116 \\ 116 \\ \hline \end{array}$

19. 15.5 ; 32 ÷ 2 = 16
$\begin{array}{r} 15.5 \\ 208\overline{)3224.0} \\ 208 \\ \hline 1144 \\ 1040 \\ \hline 1040 \\ 1040 \\ \hline \end{array}$

20. 1.92 ; 12 ÷ 6 = 2
$\begin{array}{r} 1.92 \\ 625\overline{)1200.00} \\ 625 \\ \hline 5750 \\ 5625 \\ \hline 1250 \\ 1250 \\ \hline \end{array}$

21. 14.4 ; 22 ÷ 2 = 11
$\begin{array}{r} 14.4 \\ 15\overline{)216.0} \\ 15 \\ \hline 66 \\ 60 \\ \hline 60 \\ 60 \\ \hline \end{array}$

22. 24.7
23. 5.37
24. 4.2
25. 5.48
26. 6.5
27. 8.56
28. = 3.9 x 4
= 15.6
29. = 7.5 – 2.5
= 5
30. = 5.98 – 2.1
= 3.88
31. 10.5
32. 6.25
33. 9.28
34. 7.68
35. 6.3
36. 47.882

37. A ; 1.65
38. B ; 28.35
His average speed was 28.35 km/h.

8 Fractions, Decimals, and Percents

1. $\frac{35}{100}$; 0.35 ; 35%
2. $\frac{28}{100}$; 0.28 ; 28%
3. $\frac{52}{100}$; 0.52 ; 52%
4. $\frac{66}{100}$; 0.66 ; 66%
5. $\frac{42}{100}$; 0.42 ; 42%
6. $\frac{50}{100}$; 0.5 ; 50%
7. 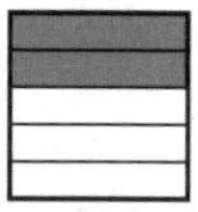
8. 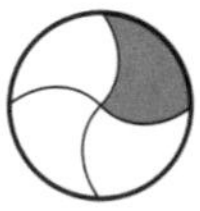
9. 

10a. 48% b. 80% c. 215%
d. 27.9% e. 8.2% f. 105%
11a. 0.52 b. 0.154 c. 2
d. 0.005 e. 0.089 f. 0.07
12. 0.3 ; 30% 13. 0.5 ; 50% 14. 0.75 ; 75%
15. 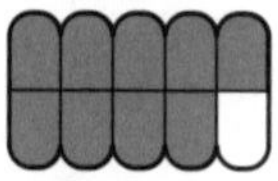
90%
16. 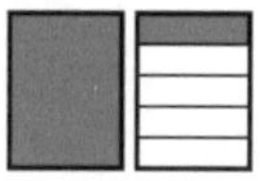
1.2
17. 30 ; 30 18. $\frac{18}{100}$; 18% 19. $\frac{64}{100}$; 64%
20. $\frac{75}{100}$; 75% 21. $\frac{95}{100}$; 95% 22. $\frac{60}{100}$; 60%
23. 0.16 ; 16 ;

```
   0.16
50)8.00
   50
   300
   300
```

24. 0.36 = 36% ;

```
   0.36
25)9.00
   75
   150
   150
```

25. 0.85 = 85% ;

```
   0.85
20)17.00
   160
    100
    100
```

26. $\frac{6}{25}$
27. $\frac{13}{25}$ 28. $\frac{39}{50}$ 29. $\frac{83}{100}$
30. $\frac{9}{25}$ 31. $\frac{31}{50}$
32.

	Fraction	Decimal	Percent
circle	$\frac{3}{10}$	0.3	30%
parallelogram	$\frac{2}{5}$	0.4	40%
triangle	$\frac{3}{4}$	0.75	75%
square	$\frac{7}{20}$	0.35	35%
rectangle	$\frac{9}{25}$	0.36	36%

33. Jason's cup: $\frac{4}{5}$ = 80%
George's cup: 0.7 = 70%
Tim's cup: 75% ; Jason
34. 1 – 0.25 – 0.1 = 0.65 ; 0.65 = $\frac{65}{100}$ = $\frac{13}{20}$
$\frac{13}{20}$ of the buttons are red.
35. English: $\frac{19}{20}$ = 95% ; Math: 89% ;
History: 0.92 = 92% ; Science: $\frac{23}{25}$ = 92% ;
He did the best in English.

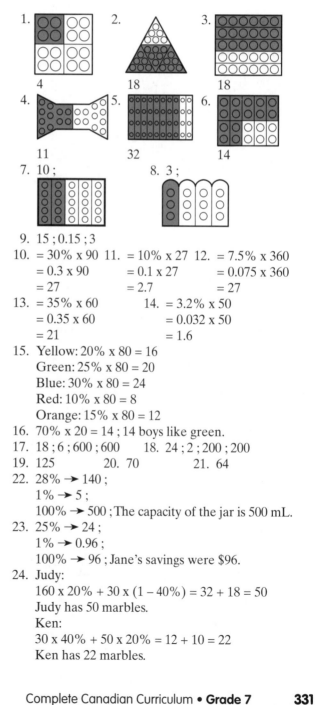

9 Percents

1. 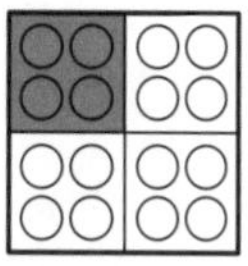
4
2. 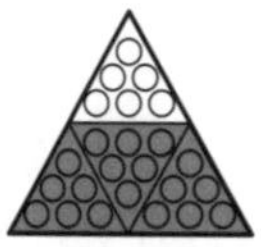
18
3. 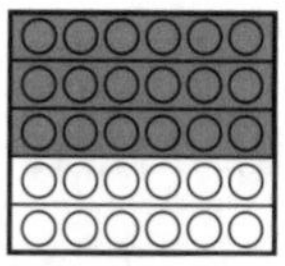
18
4. 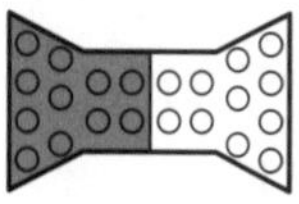
11
5. 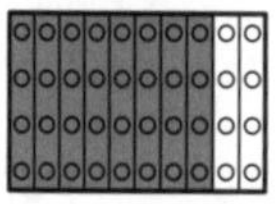
32
6. 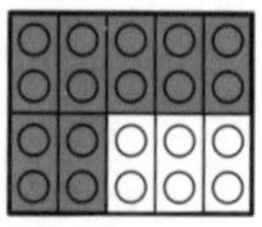
14
7. 10 ; 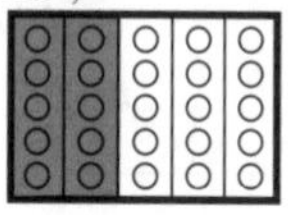
8. 3 ; 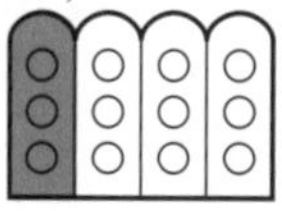

9. 15 ; 0.15 ; 3
10. = 30% x 90
= 0.3 x 90
= 27
11. = 10% x 27
= 0.1 x 27
= 2.7
12. = 7.5% x 360
= 0.075 x 360
= 27
13. = 35% x 60
= 0.35 x 60
= 21
14. = 3.2% x 50
= 0.032 x 50
= 1.6
15. Yellow: 20% x 80 = 16
Green: 25% x 80 = 20
Blue: 30% x 80 = 24
Red: 10% x 80 = 8
Orange: 15% x 80 = 12
16. 70% x 20 = 14 ; 14 boys like green.
17. 18 ; 6 ; 600 ; 600 18. 24 ; 2 ; 200 ; 200
19. 125 20. 70 21. 64
22. 28% ➔ 140 ;
1% ➔ 5 ;
100% ➔ 500 ; The capacity of the jar is 500 mL.
23. 25% ➔ 24 ;
1% ➔ 0.96 ;
100% ➔ 96 ; Jane's savings were $96.
24. Judy:
160 x 20% + 30 x (1 – 40%) = 32 + 18 = 50
Judy has 50 marbles.
Ken:
30 x 40% + 50 x 20% = 12 + 10 = 22
Ken has 22 marbles.

Sam:
160 x 45% + 50 x 48% = 72 + 24 = 96
Sam has 96 marbles.
Tina:
160 x (1 – 20% – 45%) + 50 x (1 – 48% – 20%)
= 56 + 16 = 72
Tina has 72 marbles.

25. 96 x 25% = 24
Pamela will get 24 marbles from Sam.

26. No. of red marbles Judy has:
50 x 70% = 35
No. of red marbles Erica gets from Judy:
35 x 80% = 28
Erica gets 28 red marbles from Judy.

10 Angles

1a. ℓ_1 and ℓ_2

b. ℓ_5 and ℓ_6

c. ℓ_3 and ℓ_4

d. ℓ_7 and ℓ_8

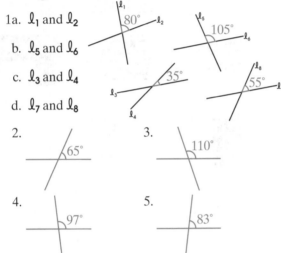

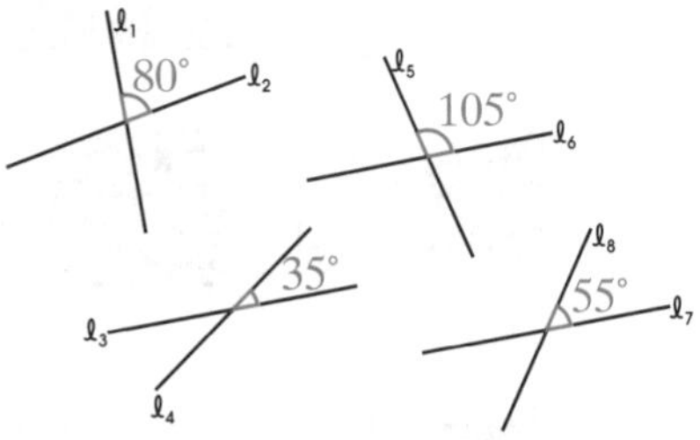

2.

3.

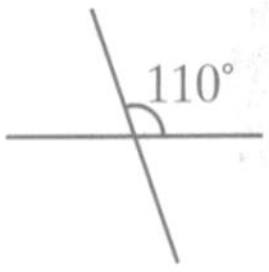

4.

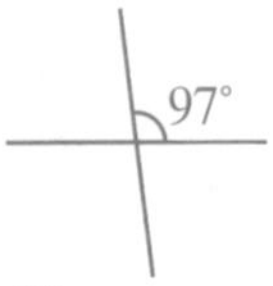

5.

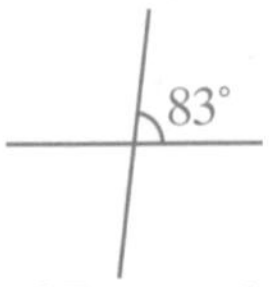

6. IJ ; w ; y

7. QR ; a and e ; d and f

8. AB ; m and p ; o and q

9.

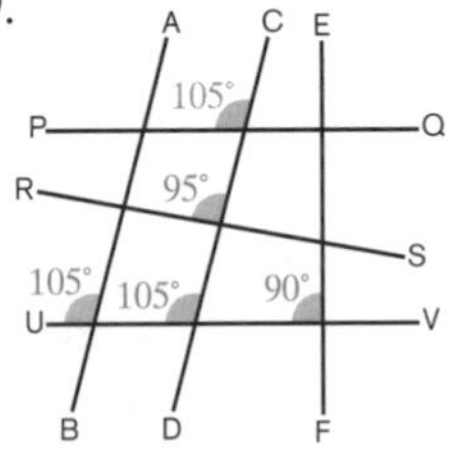

PQ ; UV
AB ; CD

10.

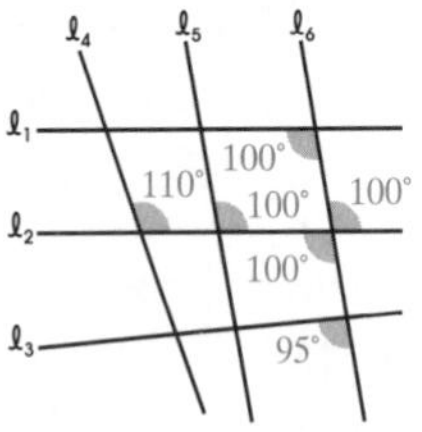

$\ell_1 // \ell_2$
$\ell_5 // \ell_6$

(Suggested answers for questions 11 to 13)

11.

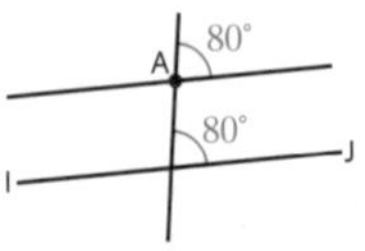

80°

12.

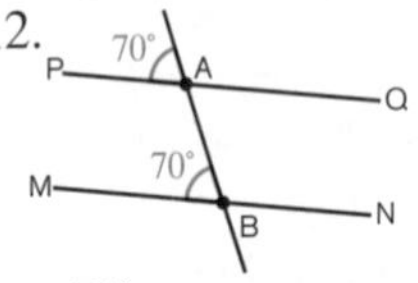

70°

13.

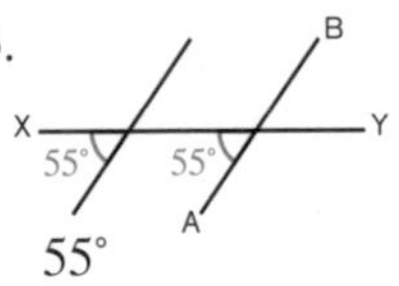

55°

14. perpendicular

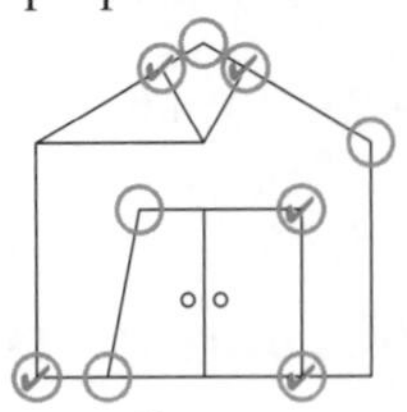

15.

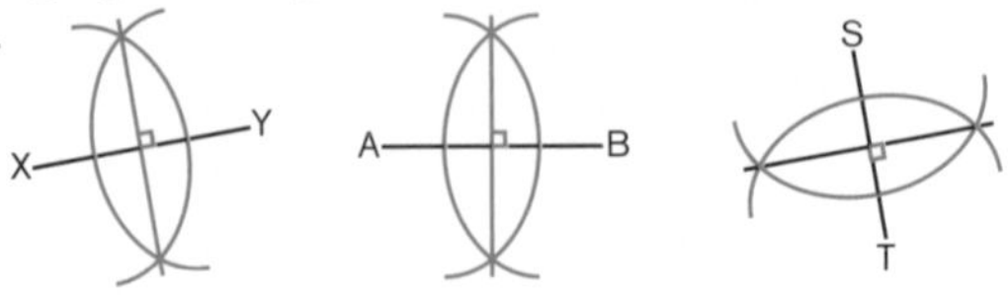

16.

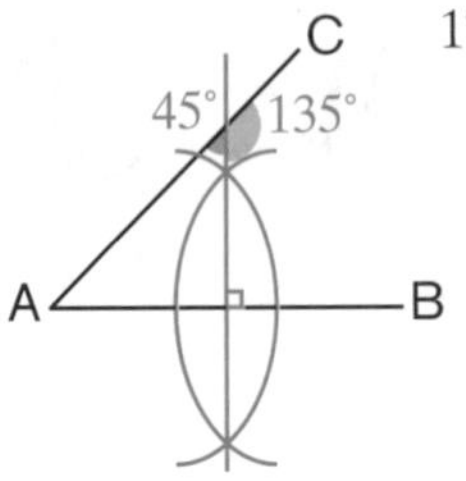

45° ; 135°

17.

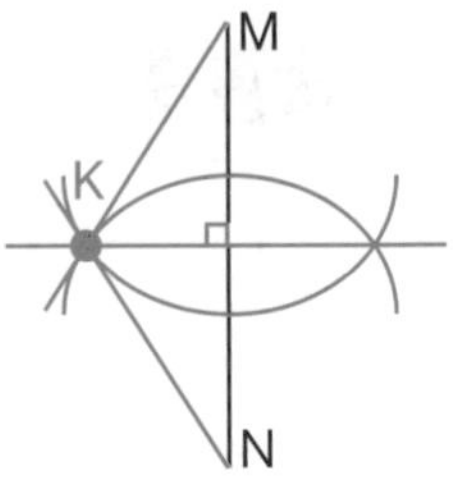

45°, 45°, and 90° ; isosceles

11 Angles and Lines in Shapes

1. F
2. F
3. T
4. T
5. F
6.

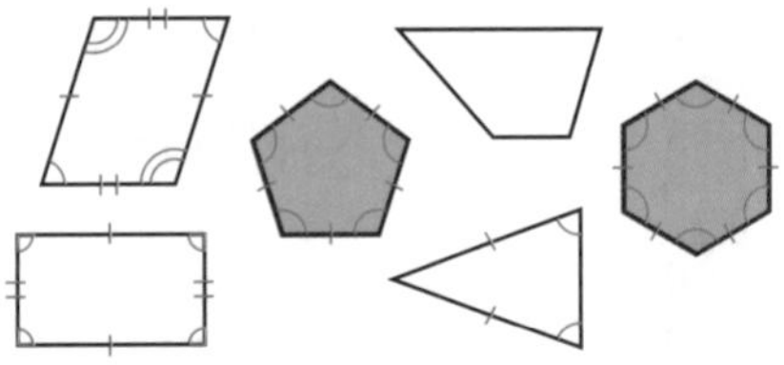

7.

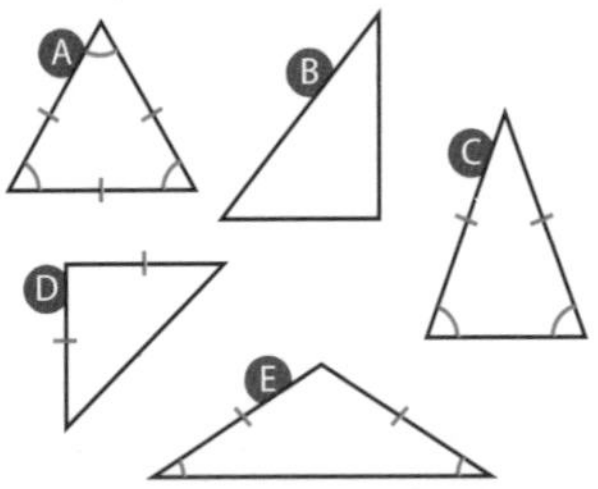

A: acute triangle, equilateral triangle
B: right triangle, scalene triangle
C: acute triangle, isosceles triangle
D: right triangle, isosceles triangle
E: obtuse triangle, isosceles triangle

8.

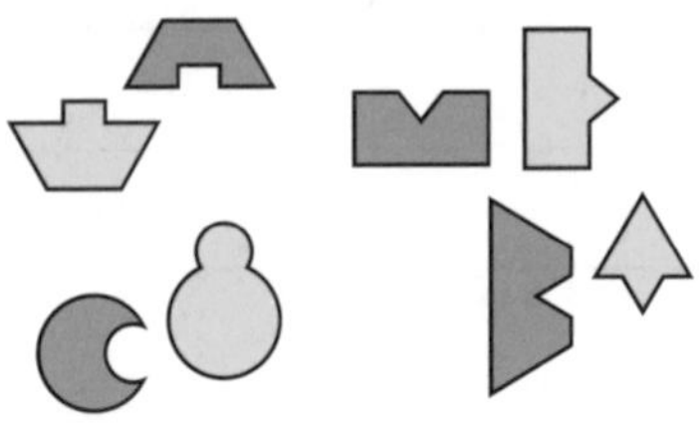

9. ✘ 10. ✘ 11. ✔
12. ✔ 13. ✘ 14. ✔
15. $a + 60° + 65° = 180°$
$a = 55°$
16. $m + 30° + 90° = 180°$
$m = 60°$
17. $3y = 180°$
$y = 60°$
18. $2r + 38° = 180°$
$2r = 142°$
$r = 71°$
19. $a + 57° + 90° = 180°$
$a = 33°$
$b = 67°$ (isos. △)
$c + 67° + 67° = 180°$
$c = 46°$
20. $3a = 180°$ (equil. △)
$a = 60°$
$42° + 100° + b = 180°$
$b = 38°$
21.

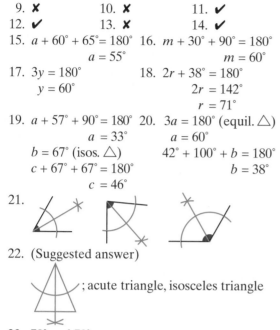

22. (Suggested answer)

; acute triangle, isosceles triangle

23. 70° and 70°

12 Congruent and Similar Figures

1. Sides: PQ ; QR ; PR
Angles: ∠P ; ∠Q ; ∠R
≅
2. Sides: DE ; BC = EF ; AC = DF
Angles: ∠D ; ∠B = ∠E ; ∠C = ∠F
≅ △DEF
3. Sides: AB = XW ; BC = WY ; AC = XY
Angles: ∠A = ∠X ; ∠B = ∠W ; ∠C = ∠Y
≅ △XWY
4. side-angle-side
5. angle-angle-side
6. side-side-side
7. angle-angle-side
8. side-angle-side
9. angle-side-angle
10.

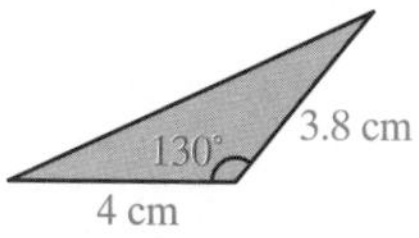

side-angle-side

11.

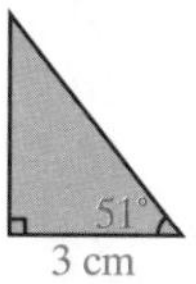

angle-side-angle

12.

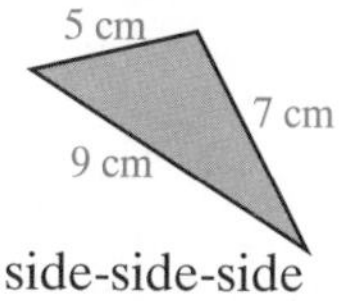

side-side-side

13. DE ; ∠E ; 68° ; EF ; 4 units ;
△DEF ; angle ; side
14. IJ = LM = 6 cm ; IK = LN = 8 cm ;
JK = MN = 11 cm ;
So, △IJK ≅ △LMN by side-side-side.
15. PQ = ST = 7 cm ; ∠P = ∠S = 90° ;
∠Q = ∠T = 44° ;
So, △PQR ≅ △STU by angle-side-angle.
16. Circle △ABC and △LMN.
∠B = ∠M = 65° ; ∠C = ∠N = 48° ;
BC = MN = 6 units ;
△ABC ≅ △LMN ; angle-side-angle
17.

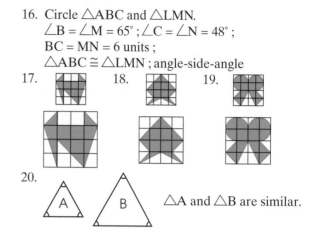

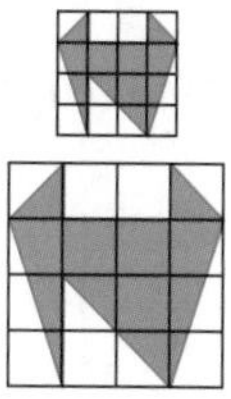

18.

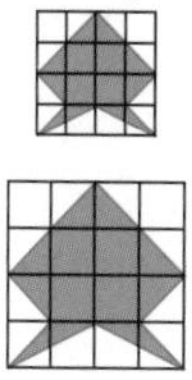

19.

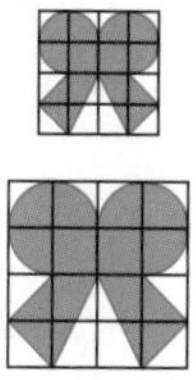

20.

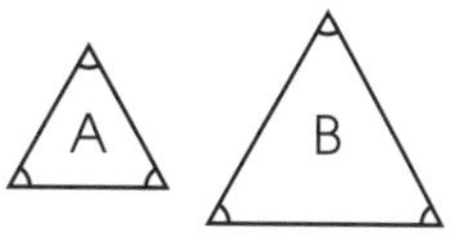

△A and △B are similar.

13 Solids

1.

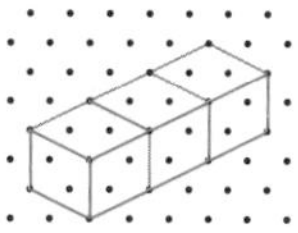

2.

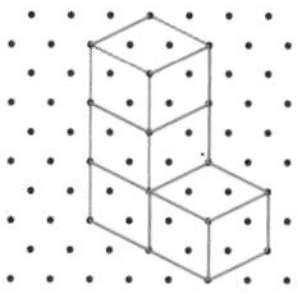

3.

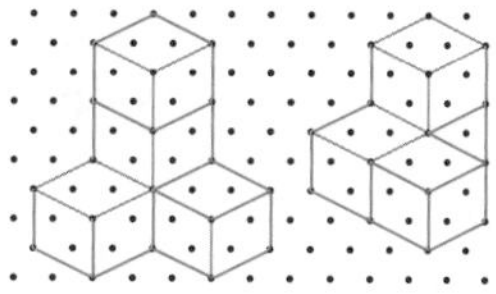

4.

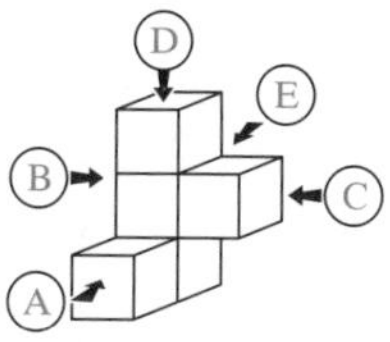

5.

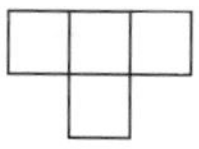

; B

6.

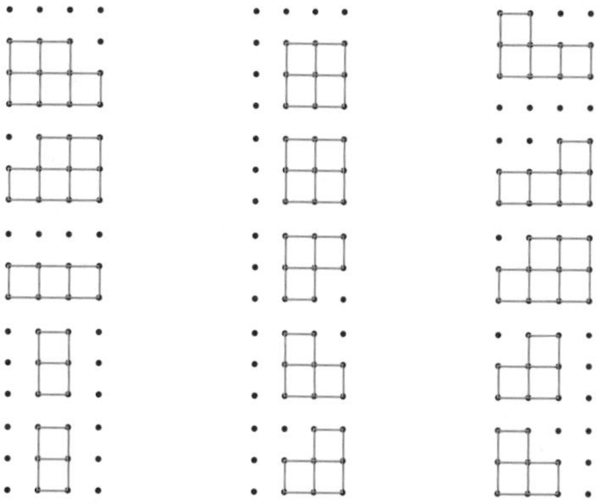

7.

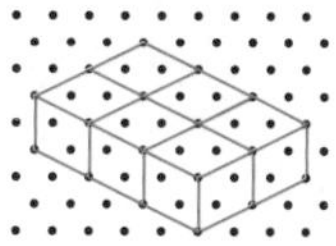

8.

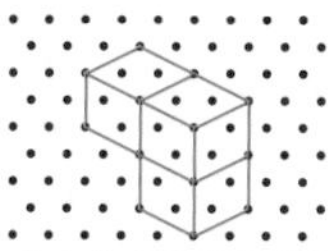

9.

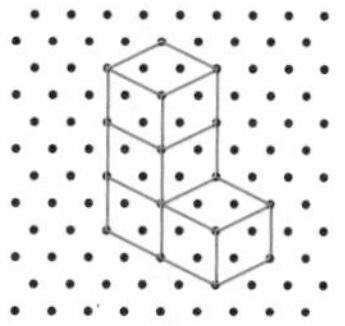

10.

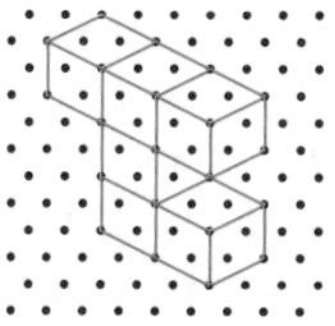

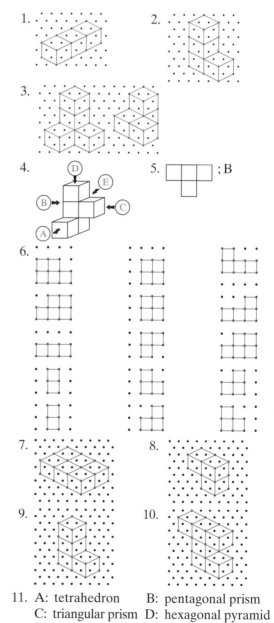

11. A: tetrahedron B: pentagonal prism
C: triangular prism D: hexagonal pyramid

12. 8 ; 18 ; 12 ;
2 ; 6 ;

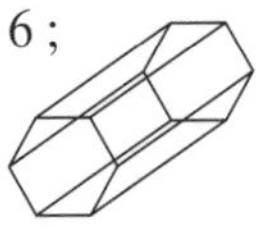

hexagonal prism

13. 9 ; 16 ; 9 ;
1 ; 8 ;

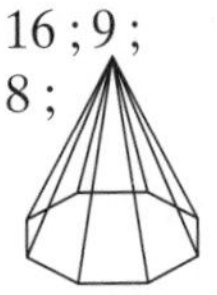

octagonal pyramid

14.

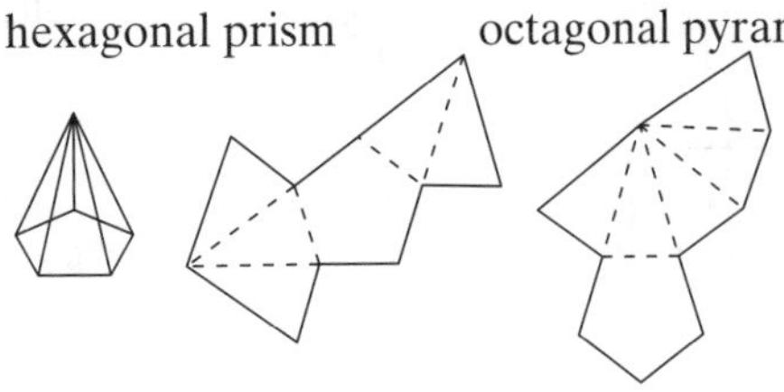

14 Area

1.

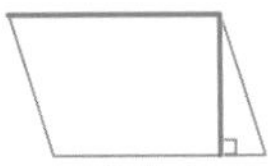

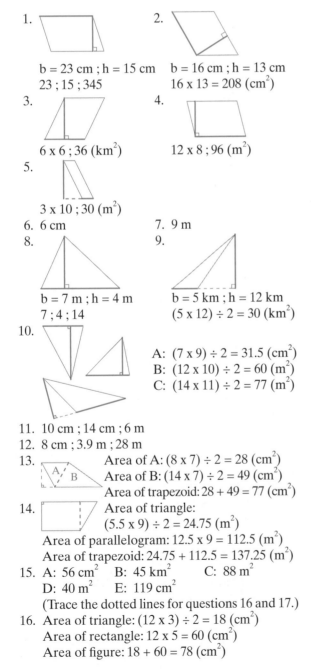

b = 23 cm ; h = 15 cm
23 ; 15 ; 345

2.

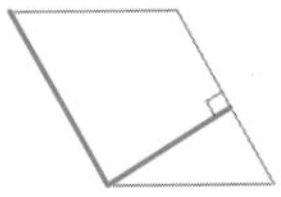

b = 16 cm ; h = 13 cm
16 x 13 = 208 (cm^2)

3.

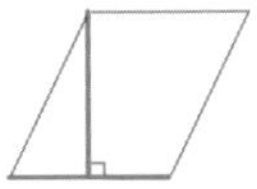

6 x 6 ; 36 (km^2)

4.

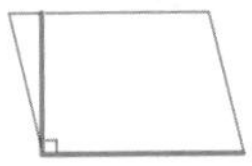

12 x 8 ; 96 (m^2)

5.

3 x 10 ; 30 (m^2)

6. 6 cm

7. 9 m

8.

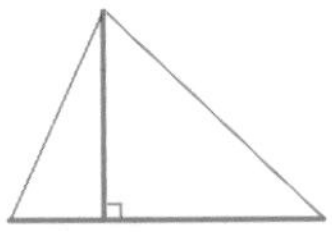

b = 7 m ; h = 4 m
7 ; 4 ; 14

9.

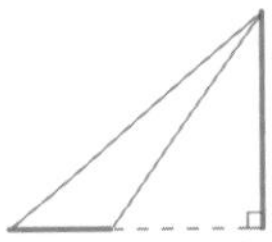

b = 5 km ; h = 12 km
(5 x 12) ÷ 2 = 30 (km^2)

10.

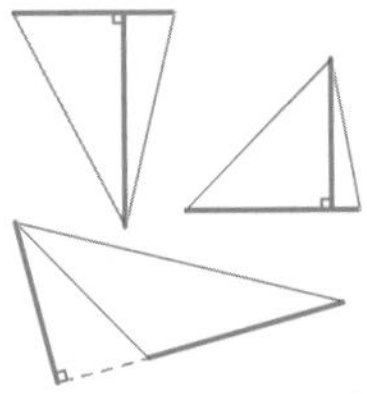

A: (7 x 9) ÷ 2 = 31.5 (cm^2)
B: (12 x 10) ÷ 2 = 60 (m^2)
C: (14 x 11) ÷ 2 = 77 (m^2)

11. 10 cm ; 14 cm ; 6 m

12. 8 cm ; 3.9 m ; 28 m

13.

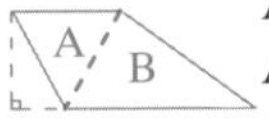

Area of A: (8 x 7) ÷ 2 = 28 (cm^2)
Area of B: (14 x 7) ÷ 2 = 49 (cm^2)
Area of trapezoid: 28 + 49 = 77 (cm^2)

14.

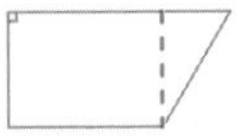

Area of triangle:
(5.5 x 9) ÷ 2 = 24.75 (m^2)
Area of parallelogram: 12.5 x 9 = 112.5 (m^2)
Area of trapezoid: 24.75 + 112.5 = 137.25 (m^2)

15. A: 56 cm^2 B: 45 km^2 C: 88 m^2
D: 40 m^2 E: 119 cm^2
(Trace the dotted lines for questions 16 and 17.)

16. Area of triangle: (12 x 3) ÷ 2 = 18 (cm^2)
Area of rectangle: 12 x 5 = 60 (cm^2)
Area of figure: 18 + 60 = 78 (cm^2)

17. Area of trapezoid:
(6 x 7) ÷ 2 + (3 x 7) ÷ 2 = 31.5 (m^2)
Area of parallelogram: 6 x 2 = 12 (m^2)
Area of figure: 31.5 + 12 = 43.5 (m^2)

18. A: 93 m^2 B: 162 m^2
C: 32.5 m^2 D: 52 m^2

19. (Suggested answer)

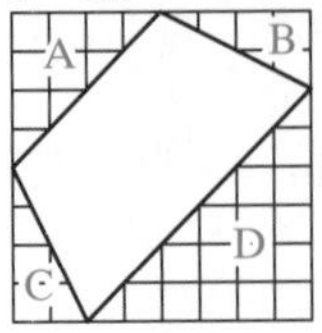

Area of A: (4 x 4) ÷ 2 = 8 (cm^2)
Area of B: (4 x 2) ÷ 2 = 4 (cm^2)
Area of C: (2 x 4) ÷ 2 = 4 (cm^2)
Area of D: (6 x 6) ÷ 2 = 18 (cm^2)

Area of trapezoid:
8 x 8 – (8 + 4 + 4 + 18) = 30 (cm^2)

15 Surface Area

1. A: 8 x 3 ; 8 x 12 ; 3 x 12 ;
48 ; 192 ; 72 ;
312

B: 2 x 7 x 2 + 2 x 7 x 10 + 2 x 2 x 10
= 28 + 140 + 40
= 208 (m^2)

C: 2 x 20 x 4 + 2 x 20 x 50 +2 x 4 x 50
= 160 + 2000 + 400
= 2560 (cm^2)

D: 2 x 11 x 6 + 2 x 11 x 5 + 2 x 6 x 5
= 132 + 110 + 60
= 302 (cm^2)

2.

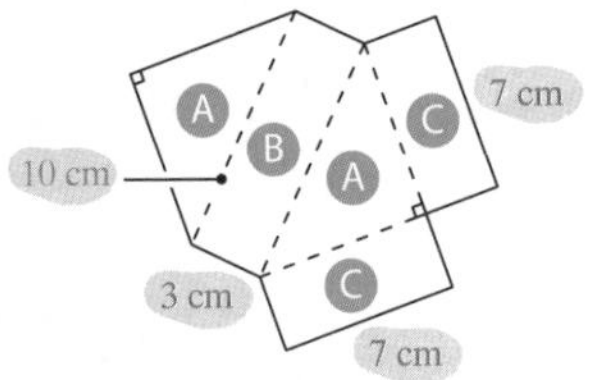

2Ⓐ = (7 x 7) ÷ 2 x 2 = 49 (cm^2) ;
1Ⓑ = 10 x 3 = 30 (cm^2) ;
2Ⓒ = (7 x 3) x 2 = 42 (cm^2) ;
49 + 30 + 42 = 121 (cm^2)

3.

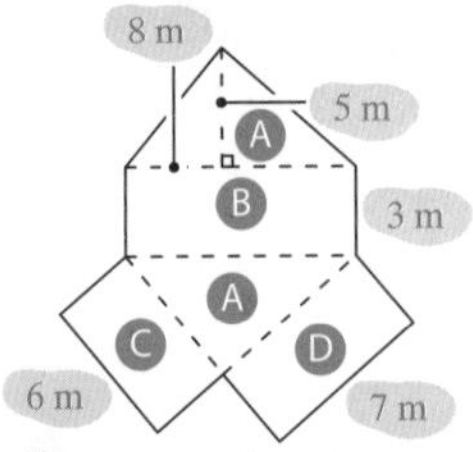

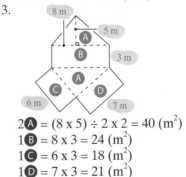

2Ⓐ = (8 x 5) ÷ 2 x 2 = 40 (m^2)
1Ⓑ = 8 x 3 = 24 (m^2)
1Ⓒ = 6 x 3 = 18 (m^2)
1Ⓓ = 7 x 3 = 21 (m^2)
40 + 24 + 18 + 21 = 103 (m^2)

4.

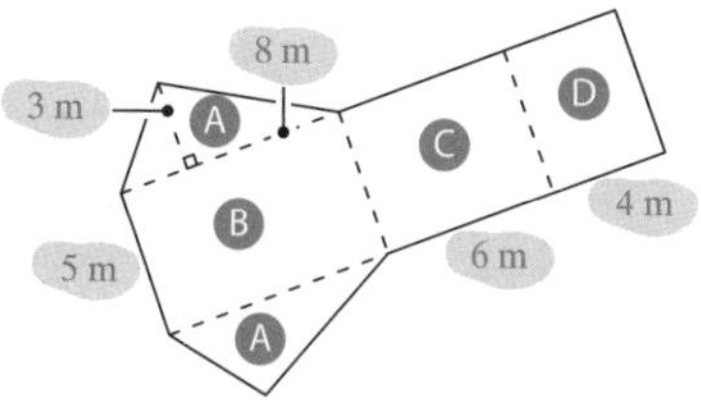

2Ⓐ = (8 x 3) ÷ 2 x 2 = 24 (m^2)
1Ⓑ = 8 x 5 = 40 (m^2)
1Ⓒ = 6 x 5 = 30 (m^2)
1Ⓓ = 4 x 5 = 20 (m^2)
24 + 40 + 30 + 20 = 114 (m^2)

5. 9 x 5 + 6 x 2 + 9 x 2 + 10 x 2
= 45 + 12 + 18 + 20
= 95 (cm^2)

6. 12 x 3 + 4 x 5 + 12 x 5 + 10 x 5
= 36 + 20 + 60 + 50
= 166 (m^2)

7a. 1625 cm^2 ; A   b. 518.4 cm^2 ; C

8.

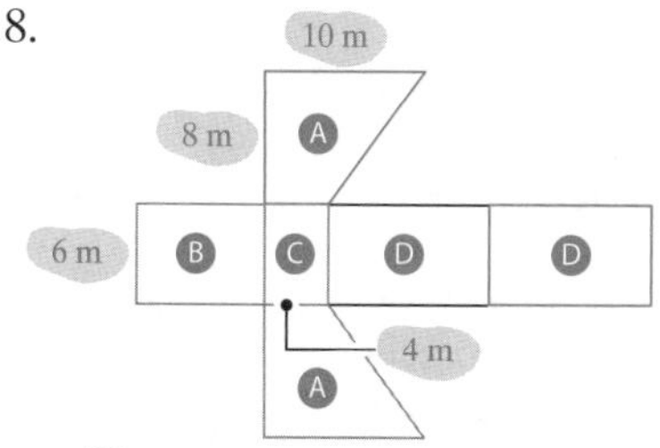

2Ⓐ = (4 x 8 ÷ 2 + 10 x 8 ÷ 2) x 2 = 112 (m^2)
1Ⓑ = 8 x 6 = 48 (m^2)
1Ⓒ = 6 x 4 = 24 (m^2)
2Ⓓ = (10 x 6) x 2 = 120 (m^2)
Total: 112 + 48 + 24 + 120 = 304 (m^2)

9.

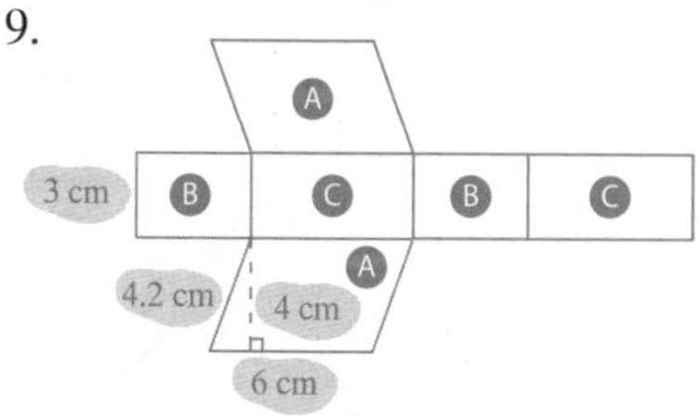

2Ⓐ = (6 x 4) x 2 = 48 (cm^2)
2Ⓑ = (4.2 x 3) x 2 = 25.2 (cm^2)
2Ⓒ = (6 x 3) x 2 = 36 (cm^2)
Total: 48 + 25.2 + 36 = 109.2 (cm^2)

10. A: 324 cm^2 B: 344 cm^2 ; A

16 Volume

1. 20 ; 6 ; 120
2. 63 x 12 ; 756 (cm^3)
3. 150 x 6 ; 900 (cm^3)
4. 1050 x 12 ; 12 600 (cm^3)
5. A: 60 x 11 ; 660 (cm^3)
   B: 500 x 18 ; 9000 (cm^3)
   C: 3.15 x 4.2 ; 13.23 (m^3)
   D: 2.16 x 0.5 ; 1.08 (m^3)
6. 3.67 m
7. 3.6 cm
8. 2.37 m
9. A: 27   B: 0.2
   C: 12.5   D: 0.5
10. A: 108 cubes   B: 360 cubes
    C: 200 cubes   D: 16 896 cubes
11. Area of base: (3 x 5) ÷ 2 + (7 x 5) ÷ 2 = 25 (m^2)
    Volume: 25 x 2 = 50 (m^3)
12. Area of base: 8 x 15 = 120 (cm^2)
    Volume: 120 x 6 = 720 (cm^3)
13. Area of base:
    (0.5 x 0.9) ÷ 2 + (1.3 x 0.9) ÷ 2 = 0.81 (m^2)
    Volume: 0.81 x 0.5 = 0.405 (m^3)
14. Area of base: (10 x 8.7) ÷ 2 x 6 = 261 (cm^2)
    Volume: 261 x 10 = 2610 (cm^3)
15. Area of base:
    (2 x 4) ÷ 2 + (5 x 4) ÷ 2 + 4 x 2 = 22 (cm^2)
    Volume: 22 x 3 = 66 (cm^3)
16. Area of base:
    (12 x 3) ÷ 2 + (12 x 8) ÷ 2 + (6 x 8) ÷ 2 = 90 (cm^2)
    Volume: 90 x 5 = 450 (cm^3)

17A: 6000   B: 6510 mL   C: 5250 mL

18A: 6   B: 7 bottles   C: 6 bottles

19. Volume of 40 pebbles: 3.6 x 40 = 144 (cm^3)
    Vase A holds: 6000 – 144 = 5856 (mL)
    Vase A can now hold 5856 mL of water.
20. Volume of gift box:
    6000 + 6510 + 5250 = 17 760 (cm^3)
    Thickness of gift box:
    17 760 ÷ (40 x 40 ÷ 2) = 22.2 (cm)
    The thickness of the gift box is 22.2 cm.

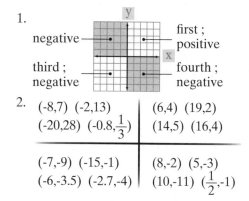

17 Coordinates

1.

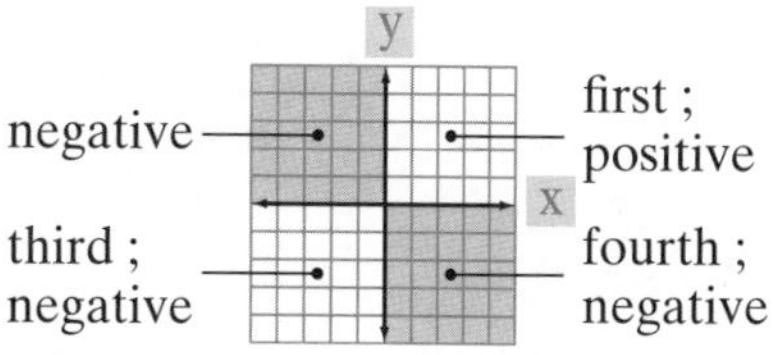

2.

(-8,7) (-2,13) (-20,28) $(-0.8,\frac{1}{3})$	(6,4) (19,2) (14,5) (16,4)
(-7,-9) (-15,-1) (-6,-3.5) (-2.7,-4)	(8,-2) (5,-3) (10,-11) $(\frac{1}{2},-1)$

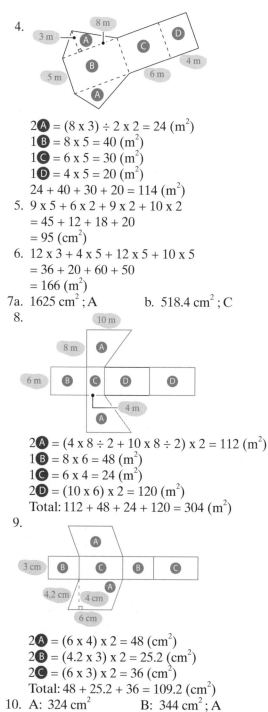

3.

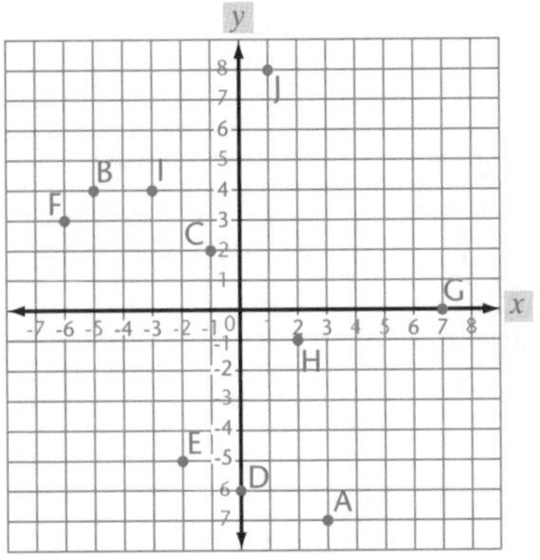

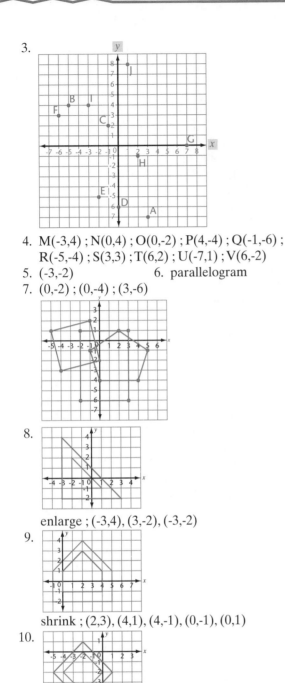

4. M(-3,4) ; N(0,4) ; O(0,-2) ; P(4,-4) ; Q(-1,-6) ; R(-5,-4) ; S(3,3) ; T(6,2) ; U(-7,1) ; V(6,-2)
5. (-3,-2)
6. parallelogram
7. (0,-2) ; (0,-4) ; (3,-6)

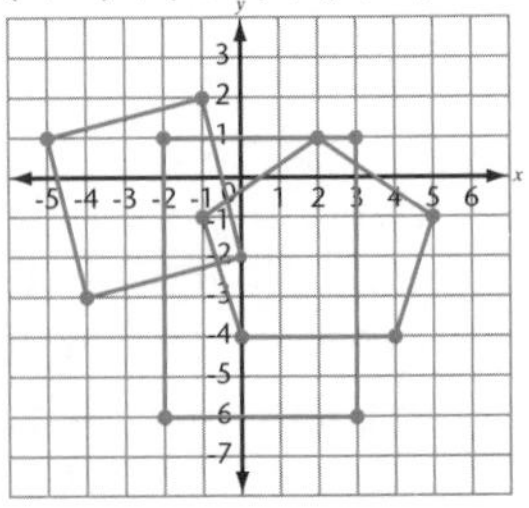

8.

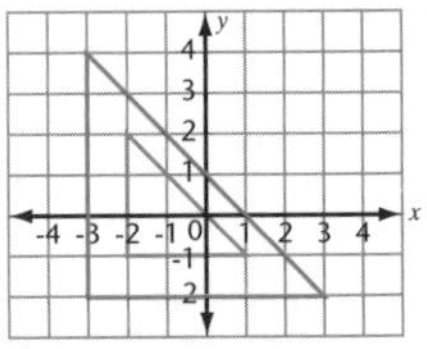

enlarge ; (-3,4), (3,-2), (-3,-2)

9.

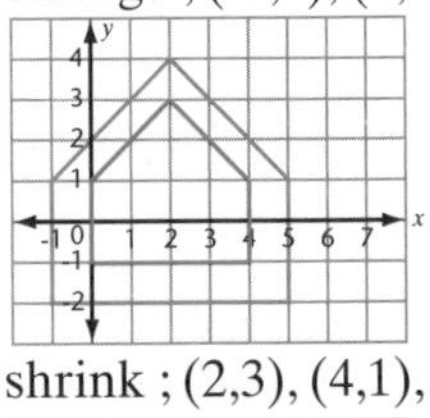

shrink ; (2,3), (4,1), (4,-1), (0,-1), (0,1)

10.

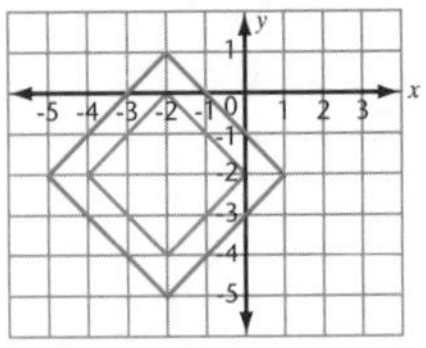

enlarge ; (-2,1), (1,-2), (-2,-5), (-5,-2)

11-12.

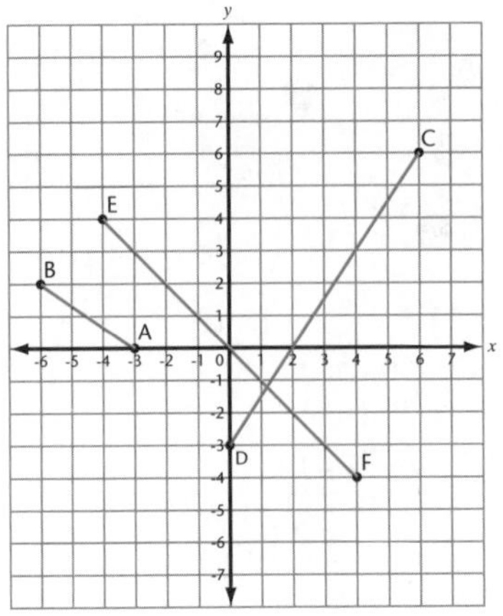

(-6,2) ;
(0,-3) ;
(4,-4)

13. No
14. Yes
15. (Suggested answer) (0,-3), (2,0), (4,3)
16. Three points on the line EF are (-4,4), (-3,3), (-2,2). The x and y values of each coordinate are the opposite of each other.

18 Transformations

1a. translation b. rotation c. reflection
d. rotation e. translation
2. Translation Image: D, E, H
Reflection Image: A, C
Rotation Image: B, F, G
3.

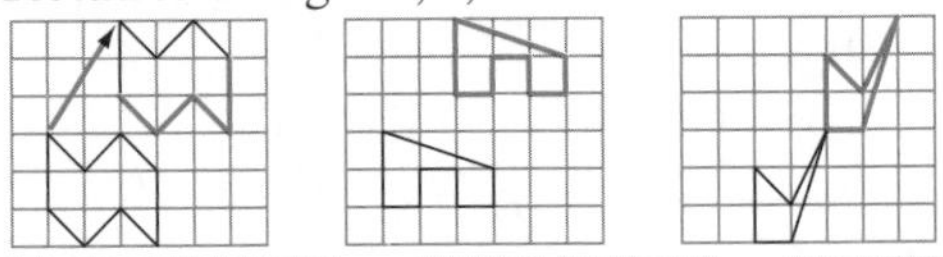

4.

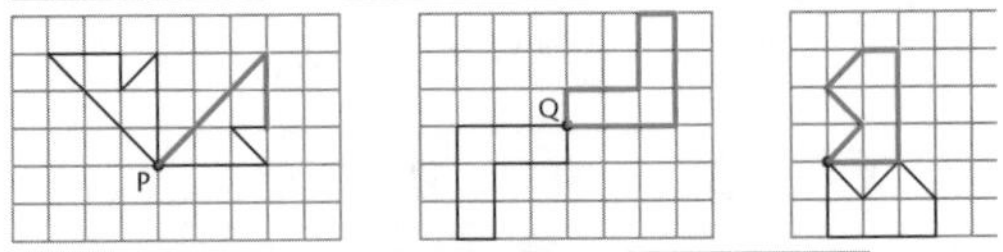

5.

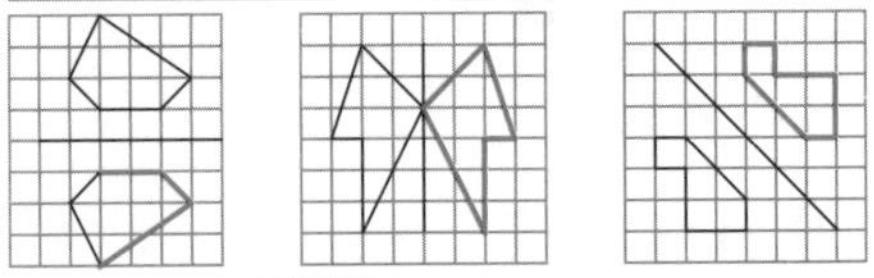

6.

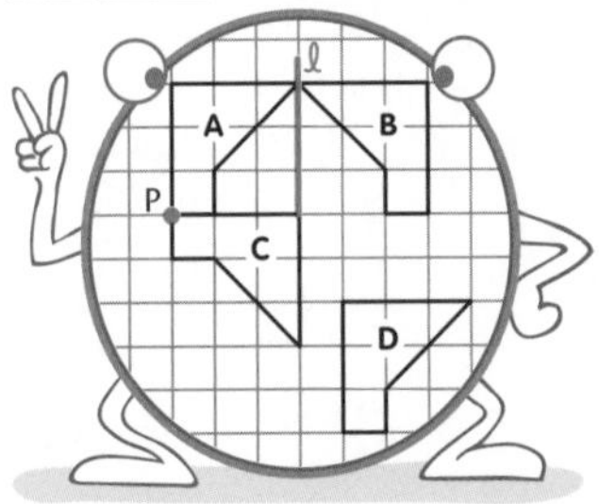

Flip figure A in line ℓ to get image B. ;
Rotate figure A 90° at point P to get image C. ;
Translate figure A 4 units right and 5 units down to get image D.

7. 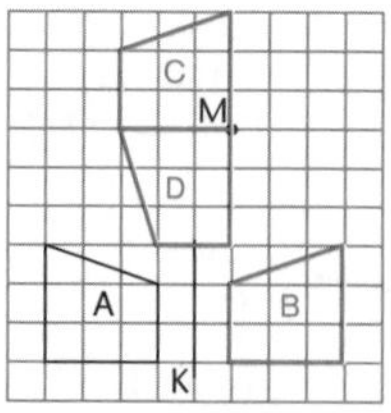

8. 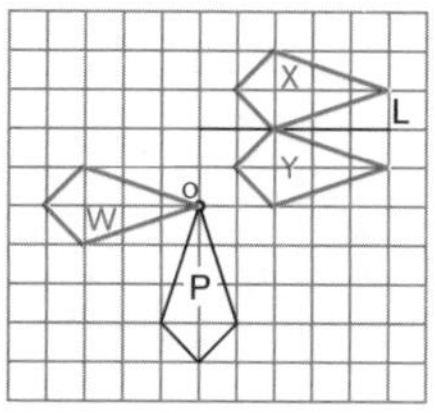

9. Translate A 1 unit right and 4 units up. Then reflect it in line ℓ. ;
Reflect A in line ℓ. Then translate it 1 unit left and 4 units up.

10. Rotate M $\frac{1}{4}$ clockwise about point K. Then translate it 1 unit left and 5 units up. ;
Translate M 5 units left and 1 unit down. Then rotate it $\frac{1}{4}$ clockwise at point K.

11. ✔ 12. ✘ 13. ✘

14. 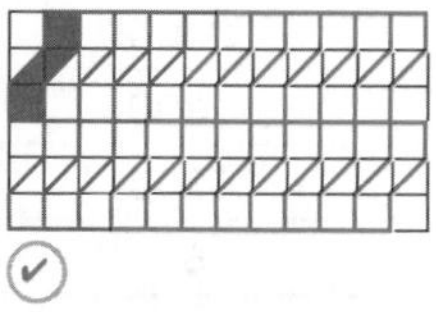

15. 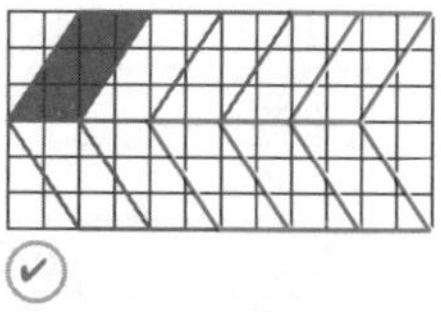

16. 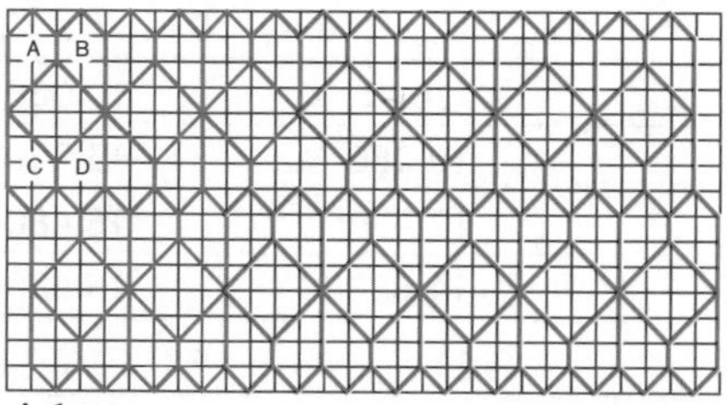

right ;
A & B is reflected in a horizontal line along the bottom to make C & D. ;
Figure A, B, C, D, and the square forms a decagon. The decagon is translated 4 units right to make its way across and translated 1 unit right and 7 units down to make its way down.

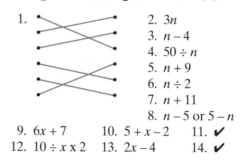

5.  ;
5 ; 5 ; 5, 10, 15, 20, 25... ; 5 ;

6. Descriptions: 1 ; 1 ; 3 ; 8 ; 5 ; 8
Multiples of 8: 16 ; 24 ; 32 ; 40 ; 48
Pattern rule: 8 ; 5 ; 8 ; 5

7. 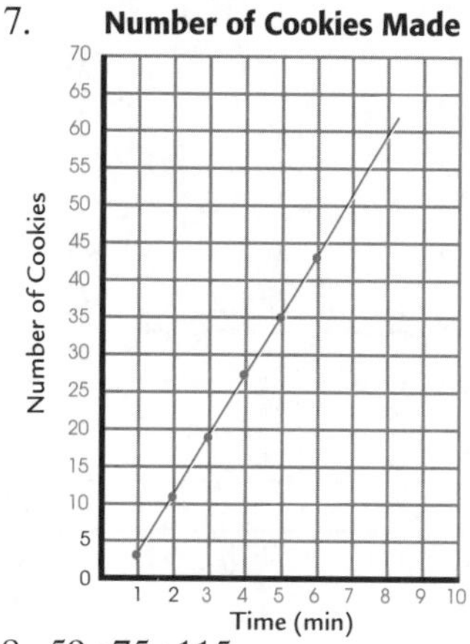

8. 59 ; 75 ; 115
9. 9 min ; 11 min
10a. Output: 16 ; 19
Descriptions: increases ; 3 ; 3 ; 1 ; 3
Pattern rule: 3 ; 1
b. 46 ; 58 ; 73 ; 106
11a. Output: 19 ; 23
Descriptions:
- Each output number increases by 4 each time.
- Compare the output number with multiples of 4. Each output number is 1 less than 4 times the input number.

Pattern rule:
Output number = 4 x Input number – 1
b. 79 bones

19 Patterning

1. Circle the first three terms.
a. 3 b. 3 c. 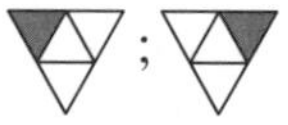
2. Circle the first four terms.
a. 4 b. 2 c. 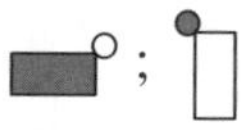
3. 4AKM ; 4 ; 4, 8, 12, 16, 20... ; 4 ;
M ; K ; M ; 4
4.  ; 2 ; 2 ; 2, 4, 6, 8, 10... ; 2 ;

20 Algebraic Expressions (1)

1. 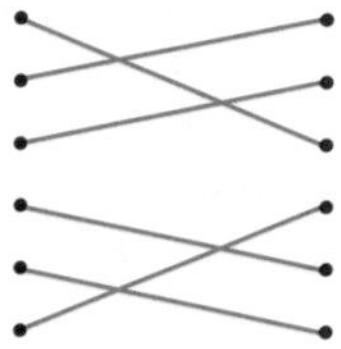
2. $3n$
3. $n - 4$
4. $50 \div n$
5. $n + 9$
6. $n \div 2$
7. $n + 11$
8. $n - 5$ or $5 - n$
9. $6x + 7$ 10. $5 + x - 2$ 11. ✔
12. $10 \div x \times 2$ 13. $2x - 4$ 14. ✔

15. ✔ 16. $3m$ 17. $(3 + n)

18. $(3k) 19. $\$(\frac{3k}{2})$

20a. $(24 + 2y)$°C b. $(24 + 3y)$°C

21. $(24 - y)$°C 22. $(108 - 2p)$ mL

23. $(2p + 5)$ mL

24. $7 + 8 = 15$
$8 \div 2 = 4$

25. $4(3) - 5 = 7$
$9 + \frac{3}{2} = 10\frac{1}{2}$

26a. 17 b. 1 c. 2

27. 2
1 ; 8(1) + 2 ; 10
2 ; 8(2) + 2 ; 18
3 ; 8(3) + 2 ; 26
4 ; 8(4) + 2 ; 34

28. 0 ; 0 – 0 ÷ 2 ; 0
1 ; 1 – 1 ÷ 2 ; 0.5
2 ; 2 – 2 ÷ 2 ; 1
3 ; 3 – 3 ÷ 2 ; 1.5
4 ; 4 – 4 ÷ 2 ; 2

29.

n	\$(4 + 7n)	n	\$(6n – 4)	n	\$(12 – 2n)
1	\$11	1	\$2	1	\$10
2	\$18	2	\$8	2	\$8
3	\$25	3	\$14	3	\$6
4	\$32	4	\$20	4	\$4

30. Jenny's savings increases by \$7 each week. ; Erica's savings increases by \$6 each week. ; Stella's savings decreases by \$2 each week.

31. \$(46 + 53) = \$99

21 Algebraic Expressions (2)

1. By car: 50 ; 100 ; 150 ; 200
By airplane: 120 ; 240 ; 360 ; 480

2. 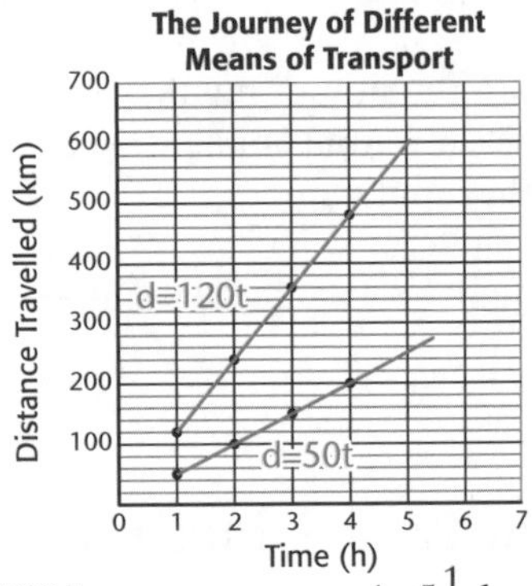

3. 300 km 4. $5\frac{1}{2}$ hours

5. The airplane travels at a constant speed of 120 km per hour.

6. Karen's Earnings: 14 ; 18 ; 22 ; 26 ; 30 Mike's Earnings: 18 ; 20 ; 22 ; 24 ; 26

7. 

8. \$54 ; \$38

9. Yes. The intersection point represents the week in which the children earned the same amount.

10. I prefer Karen's earning pattern because her earning is always greater than Mike's after the first 3 weeks.

11. 4 ; $(4(s + 200))$ m ;

s	A (4s)	B (4(s + 200))
400	1600	2400
500	2000	2800
600	2400	3200
700	2800	3600

12a.

y	A (480 + 2400y)	B (480 + 3200y)
3	7680	10 080
4	10 080	13 280
5	12 480	16 480
6	14 880	19 680

b.

y	A (480 + 2000y)	B (480 + 2800y)
3	6480	8880
4	8480	11 680
5	10 480	14 480
6	12 480	17 280

13. $20m$; \$(6 + 90% x 20m) ; \$(16 + 80% x 20m)

14.

Number of Visits	General \$(20m)	Silver \$(6 + 90% x 20m)	Gold \$(16 + 80% x 20m)
1	\$20	\$24	\$32
2	\$40	\$42	\$48
3	\$60	\$60	\$64
4	\$80	\$78	\$80

15. 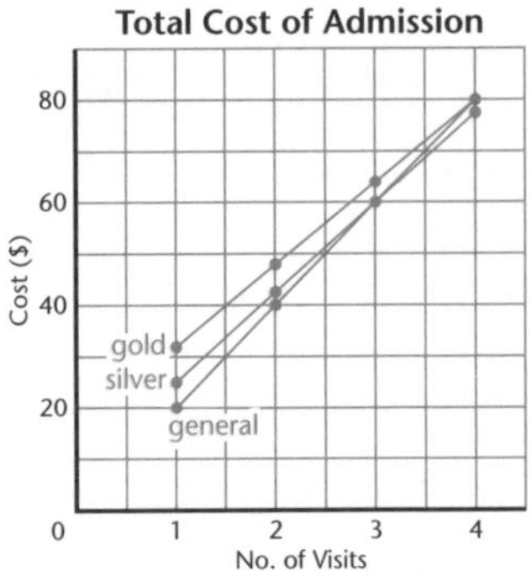

16. Jane should choose the silver membership because it has the lowest total cost.

22 Equations

1. 
2. 
3. 
4. $\div$; y ; 3
5. $-$; 21 ; 20
6. y ; + ; 34
7. $3y = 18$
8. $\frac{1}{6}y = 9$
9. 4
10. 36
11. 7
12. 40
13. 2
14. 35

15-18. (Individual checking)

15. 7 ; 7 ;
    14

16. $t \div 2 \times 2 = 15 \times 2$;
    $t = 30$

17. 4 ; 4 ;
    14 ;
    14 ;
    7

18. $3m + 2 - 2 = 8 - 2$
    $3m = 6$
    $3m \div 3 = 6 \div 3$
    $m = 2$

19. Check B ;
    $7x = 546$
    $\frac{7x}{7} = \frac{546}{7}$
    $x = 78$; 78

20. Check C ;
    $4x + 20 = 68$
    $4x + 20 - 20 = 68 - 20$
    $\frac{4x}{4} = \frac{48}{4}$
    $x = 12$; 12

21. Check A ;
    $2x + 17 = 89$
    $2x + 17 - 17 = 89 - 17$
    $\frac{2x}{2} = \frac{72}{2}$
    $x = 36$; 36

22. Check A ;
    $6(y - 1) = 54$
    $\frac{6(y-1)}{6} = \frac{54}{6}$
    $y - 1 + 1 = 9 + 1$
    $y = 10$; \$10

23-24. (Individual answers)

25-26. (Individual checking)

25. x ;
    x ; 3 ; 25
    $2x + 3 - 3 = 25 - 3$
    $\frac{2x}{2} = \frac{22}{2}$
    $x = 11$; \$11

26. Let y be the number of treats in a small tub.
    $\frac{y + 112}{2} = 92$
    $\frac{y + 112}{2} \times 2 = 92 \times 2$
    $y + 112 - 112 = 184 - 112$
    $y = 72$
    There are 72 treats in a small tub.

23 Data Management (1)

1. discrete
2. continuous
3. continuous
4. continuous
5. discrete
6. primary data
7. secondary data
8. primary data
9. biased ; unbiased ; biased
10. unbiased ; biased ; biased
11. census
12. sampling
13. sampling
14. sampling
15. census
16. census

17.

Temperature (°C)	Tally	Frequency
11 – 15	||	2
16 – 20	卌	5
21 – 25	卌 ||	7
26 – 30	卌 ||||	9
31 – 35	卌 ||	7

18. 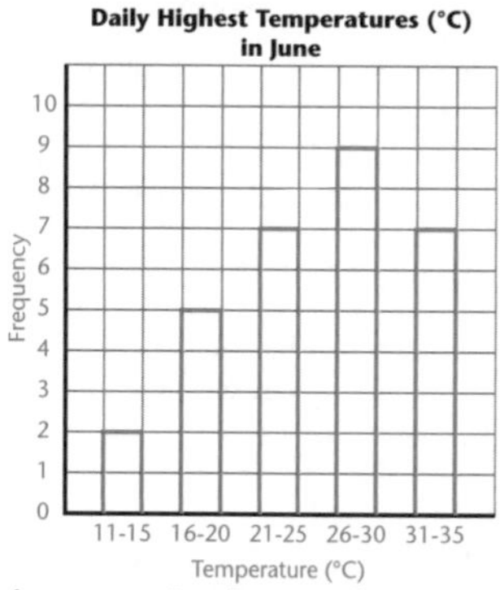

19. It is a set of primary data which is discrete.
20. The range is 26°C – 30°C.
21. No. Because he will get the indoor temperature.

22a. 33 b. 6 c. 18 – 65

23.

Stem	Leaf
13	0 5 6 9 9
14	2 2 7 8 9
15	0 2 3 4 5 5 7 7 8 8 8 9 9
16	0 1 1 2 2 4 4 4 4 7
17	0 2

24. 130 – 172 cm
25. 11 children
26. It is a set of secondary data because it was collected by someone other than Daven.

24 Data Management (2)

1. 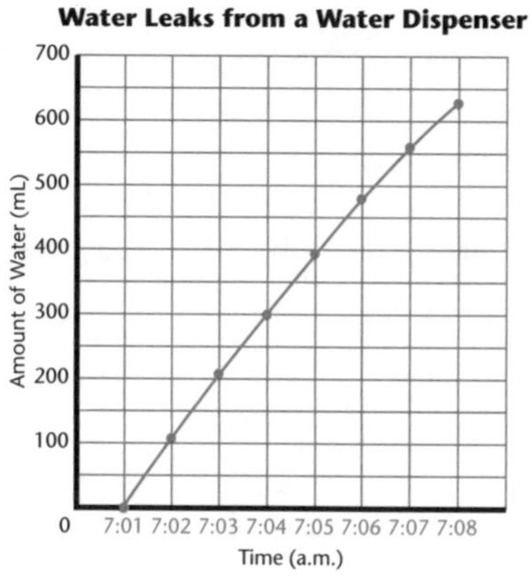

2. 7:01 – 7:02
3. No. The amount of water leaking starts at 105 mL in the first minute and decreases by 5 mL every minute.
4. The amount of water leaking decreases. The amount of water collected at 7:09 a.m. is 700 mL.
5. 132° ;
   $\frac{5}{30} \times 360° = 60°$;
   $\frac{1}{30} \times 360° = 12°$;
   $\frac{2}{30} \times 360° = 24°$;
   $\frac{9}{30} \times 360° = 108°$;
   $\frac{2}{30} \times 360° = 24°$;

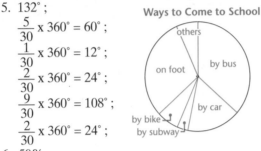

6. 50%
7. (Individual answer)
   (Individual examples for questions 8 to 10)
8. line graph 9. bar graph 10. circle graph
11. Check A
12. He should present graph A. Because it makes the plant seem to have a more dramatic growth.
13. 670 ; 820 ; 970 14. 31 seconds
15. The line graph is the most appropriate to show the data because it is a set of continuous data measured over a period of time.

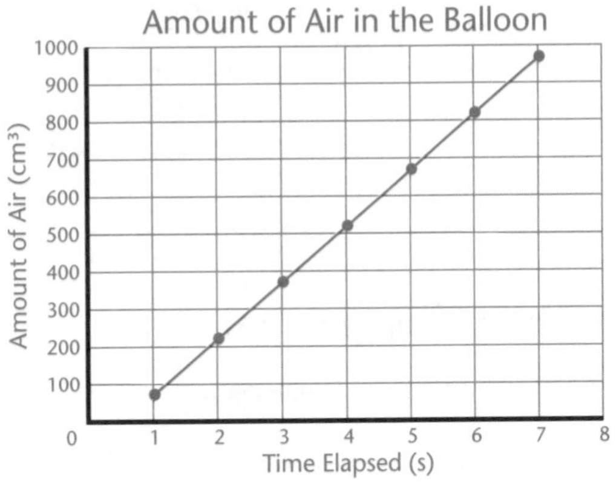

16. (Suggested answer)
    The amount of air in the balloon increases as time elapses. Therefore, the line goes upward.

25 Mean, Median, Mode

1. (Suggested answers)
   mean: the average of a set of data; add all the values and divide by the number of values
   median: the middle value; put the values in order and find the middle value
   mode: the value that appears the most
2. mean ; 69 3. mode ; 64 ; median ; 68
4. She should use the median because it is the highest amount.
5. He should use the mode because the value is 20.
6. 11 computers ; 11 computers ;
   6 computers and 11 computers
7. 6 ; 10 ; 19 8. 122 ; 123 ; 124
9. 119 ; 116 ; 137 10. Mrs. Jenkin's class
11. the mode
12.

Stem	Leaf
14	0 3 5 6 7
15	0 2 2 4 4 4 8 9
16	2 2 3 3 9
17	0 5

13. 155.9 cm ; 154 cm ; 154 cm
14. 17 ; 18 marbles ; 18 marbles
15. 17 marbles ; 17.5 marbles ; 20 marbles
16. 18 x 8 = 144 ; 144
17. 15.1 x 5 = 75.5 ; 75.5
18. 75.5 – 14.7 x 4 = 16.7 ; 16.7

26 Experimental Probability

1. $\frac{7}{10}$; $\frac{3}{10}$ 2. $\frac{22}{50}$; $\frac{28}{50}$
3. 20 ; $\frac{5}{20}$; $\frac{9}{20}$; $\frac{6}{20}$ 4. 15 ; $\frac{6}{30}$; $\frac{9}{30}$; $\frac{15}{30}$
5a. $\frac{135}{280}$, 0.48, 48% b. $\frac{64}{280}$, 0.23, 23%
c. $\frac{199}{280}$, 0.71, 71%
6a. $\frac{15}{85}$, 0.18, 18% b. $\frac{46}{85}$, 0.54, 54%
c. $\frac{24}{85}$, 0.28, 28% d. $\frac{40}{85}$, 0.47, 47%
7a. $\frac{5}{25}$; $\frac{6}{25}$ b. 3 ; 5 ; 4 ; 2 ; 5 ; 6
c. $\frac{13}{25}$
8. 87% ; 79% ; 67% ; 82% ; 94%
9. Geography 10. Science
11. Maples: 0.42 ; 0.47 ; 0.12
    St. Jacobs: 0.44 ; 0.29 ; 0.26

12. St. Jacobs
13. Possible relative frequency of winning:
$\frac{19}{48} = 0.4$, $\frac{20}{48} = 0.42$, $\frac{21}{48} = 0.44$, $\frac{22}{48} = 0.46$,
$\frac{23}{48} = 0.48$
The Maples have to win at least 4 more games.
14.

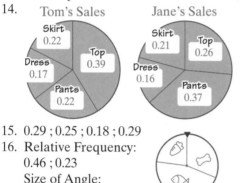

15. 0.29 ; 0.25 ; 0.18 ; 0.29
16. Relative Frequency:
0.46 ; 0.23
Size of Angle:
111.6° ; 165.6° ; 82.8°

17. Bone: 31 times, Fish: 46 times, Carrot: 23 times

27 Theoretical Probability

1a. 12 b. $\frac{3}{12}$ c. $\frac{2}{12}$
d. $\frac{9}{12}$
2a. 20 b. $\frac{2}{20}$ c. $\frac{15}{20}$
d. $\frac{18}{20}$ e. $\frac{17}{20}$
3a. $\frac{9}{30}$ b. $\frac{8}{30}$ c. $\frac{11}{30}$
d. $\frac{2}{30}$ e. $\frac{11}{30}$ f. $\frac{28}{30}$
g. $\frac{20}{30}$
4a. $\frac{1}{3}$ b. $\frac{2}{3}$ c. $\frac{1}{6}$
d. $\frac{3}{6}$ e. $\frac{3}{6}$
5a. $\frac{1}{26}$ b. 0 c. $\frac{2}{26}$
d. $\frac{1}{26}$
6. Probability: 0.36
Prediction: 10 ; 0.54 x 100 = 54 ; 0.36 x 100 = 36
7a. Box A b. 6 red balls
8. (Individual answers for tally and relative frequency)
Theoretical Probability: $\frac{1}{8}$; $\frac{3}{8}$; $\frac{1}{4}$; $\frac{1}{4}$

9. (Individual answer)
10. dots: 800 x $\frac{1}{8}$ = 100 (times)
wavy lines: 800 x $\frac{3}{8}$ = 300 (times)
stripes: 800 x $\frac{1}{4}$ = 200 (times)
checkers: 800 x $\frac{1}{4}$ = 200 (times)
It will land on dots 100 times, wavy lines 300 times, stripes 200 times, and checkers 200 times.
11. Let y be the no. of times she needs to swing.
$\frac{3}{8}y = 150$; $y = 400$
She will have to swing the paper clip about 400 times.

28 Applications of Probability

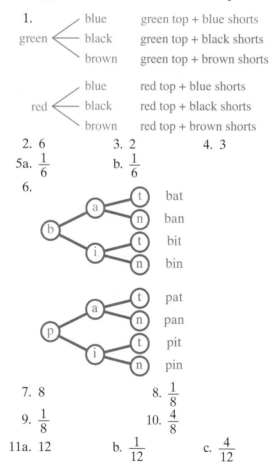

1.
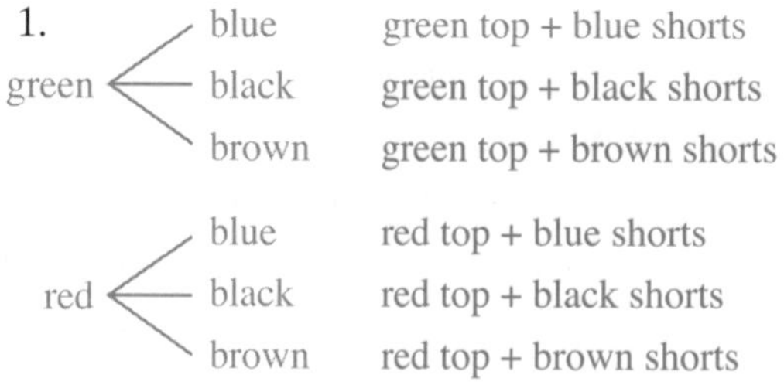

2. 6 3. 2 4. 3
5a. $\frac{1}{6}$ b. $\frac{1}{6}$
6.
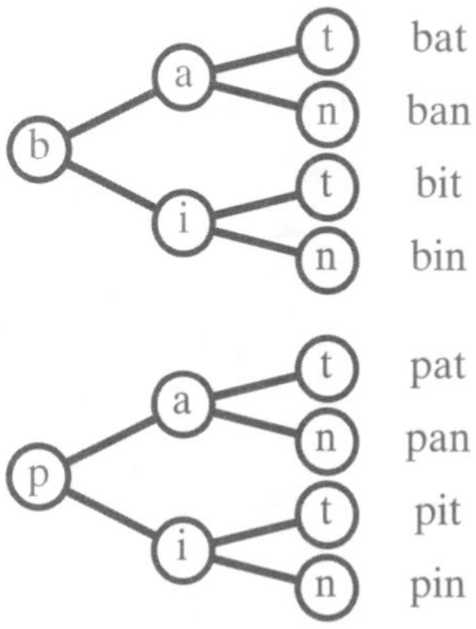

7. 8 8. $\frac{1}{8}$
9. $\frac{1}{8}$ 10. $\frac{4}{8}$
11a. 12 b. $\frac{1}{12}$ c. $\frac{4}{12}$

12. **Flavour — Topping — Outcomes**

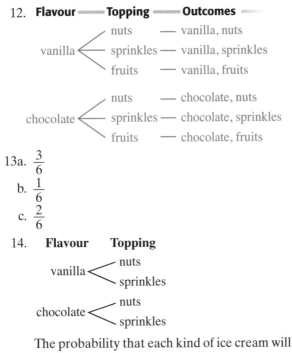

vanilla
- nuts — vanilla, nuts
- sprinkles — vanilla, sprinkles
- fruits — vanilla, fruits

chocolate
- nuts — chocolate, nuts
- sprinkles — chocolate, sprinkles
- fruits — chocolate, fruits

13a. $\frac{3}{6}$

b. $\frac{1}{6}$

c. $\frac{2}{6}$

14. **Flavour** **Topping**

vanilla
- nuts
- sprinkles

chocolate
- nuts
- sprinkles

The probability that each kind of ice cream will be chosen is $\frac{1}{4}$. The probability of choosing a vanilla ice cream cone with sprinkles will be greater.

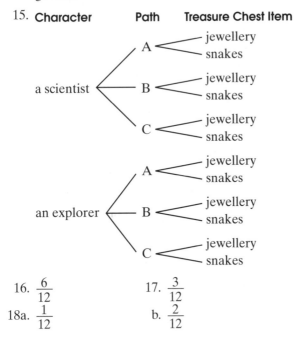

15. **Character** **Path** **Treasure Chest Item**

a scientist
- A
  - jewellery
  - snakes
- B
  - jewellery
  - snakes
- C
  - jewellery
  - snakes

an explorer
- A
  - jewellery
  - snakes
- B
  - jewellery
  - snakes
- C
  - jewellery
  - snakes

16. $\frac{6}{12}$

17. $\frac{3}{12}$

18a. $\frac{1}{12}$

b. $\frac{2}{12}$

1 New Year's Resolutions

A. (Suggested answers)
1. improve
2. promise
3. secular
4. consciously
5. constructive

B. (Individual writing)

C.
1. has
2. represents
3. was
4. has
5. is ; are
6. include
7. want
8. Has
9. makes

D.
1. Either of the two resolutions is made by me.
2. Neither the girls nor Bosco thinks that making resolutions is useless.
3. Working out, as well as reading, is a way to release stress.
4. Mrs. Bauer, together with her students, volunteers to help out after school.
5. Either Angie or Carl is going to be the first to tell us the resolutions.
6. Everybody, including all the teachers, is going to the New Year Camp.

2 The Three Roses: a Czech Folktale

A.
1. It was strange for the woman to have found a palace in the woods because she had never heard of any palace in the woods before.
2. (Individual answer)
3. (Suggested answer)
The wizard asked the girl to cut off his head so he might reveal to her his true form as a handsome young man.
4. (Individual answer)
5. (Individual answer)

B.
1. ✘
2. ✔
3. ✔
4. ✘
5. ✘
6. ✔
7. ✔
8. ✘
9. ✔

C.
1. had heard ; asked ; wanted
2. was not ; had fallen
3. appeared ; had picked
4. had given ; took
5. had cut ; changed

D. (Individual writing)

3 Mythical Creatures from the World of Fantasy

A.
1. half human, half horse
2. human with goat-like features
3. eagle with a lion's body
4. part man, part fish, swordfish spear growing out of his head
5. has a lion's head, a turtle's shell, a scorpion's sting, and bear's legs
6. part wolf, part whale

B.
1. active
2. passive
3. passive
4. active
5. passive
6. active
7. active

C.
1. Professor Rayner delivered a lecture on mythical creatures.
2. Nina Kirwan wrote *Exploring the World of Fantasy*.
3. I drew that picture of a unicorn flying in the sky.
4. Mr. Reid's class staged the Inuit legend.
5. The students made all the costumes and props for the play themselves.

D. 1. We were told to do a project on Greek mythology.
2. The famous painting *The Rebirth of the Phoenix* was stolen.
3. A statue of the Ogopogo was built in a park in Kelowna.
4. The island nation of Iceland is inhabited by elves and fairies.
5. A picture of Nessie has been sent to the press.

4 Facebook – Are You Revealing Too Much?

A. 1. F
2. T
3. F
4. F
5. F
6. T

B. (Individual writing)

C. 1. PSP
2. G
3. I
4. G
5. PTP
6. PTP
7. G
8. I
9. PSP

D. 1. to spend ; noun
2. to be put; adjective
3. to read ; noun
4. to find ; adverb
5. to develop ; adverb
6. to have ; noun

E. (Individual sentences)
1. visiting
2. participating
3. written
4. to create
5. to help

5 "My Olympic Hero" Speech Competition

A.

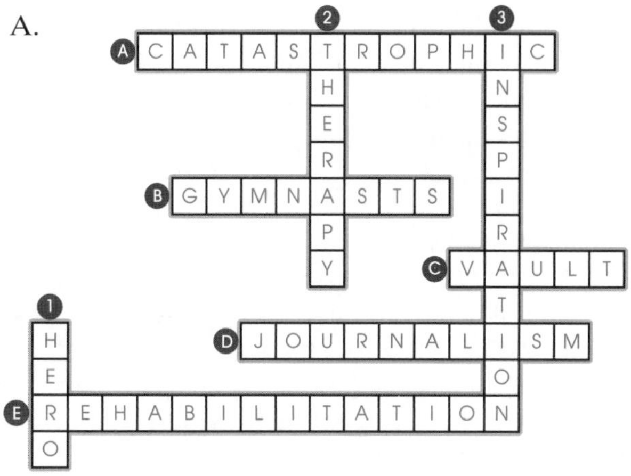

B. 1. COM
2. SUB
3. SUB
4. OBJ
5. OBJ
6. COM
7. SUB
8. COM

C. Sang Lan also began to realize that she could achieve her Olympic dream in other ways. For example, she was part of the Beijing Olympic Games Bid Committee. In 2004, she carried the Olympic torch during the Athens Olympic Games torch relay. She also carried the torch through Beijing during the torch relay leading up to the 2008 games. In addition, she hosted a TV talk show in China about the games, called "Sang Lan Olympics 2008". Sang Lan dreamed of representing China in the 2008 Paralympic Games as a ping-pong player, but this dream was not realized as her hands cannot grasp properly. Though Sang Lan cannot participate in any Olympic Games as an athlete, she plans to continue to be involved in future Olympics.

D. (Individual writing)

6 Family "Memoirs" – the Gift of a Lifetime

A. (Individual answers)
B. (Individual answer)
C. 1. is making
2. has taken
3. will bind
4. can also be added
5. would be
6. can buy; can think
7. would not have been; had not brainstormed
8. was made; is treasured
9. could not say
10. would be regarded; has ever received
D. (Individual sentences)
1. infinitive
2. gerund phrase
3. past participle phrase
4. gerund phrase
5. infinitive phrase
6. present participle phrase

7 Superstitions around the World

A.

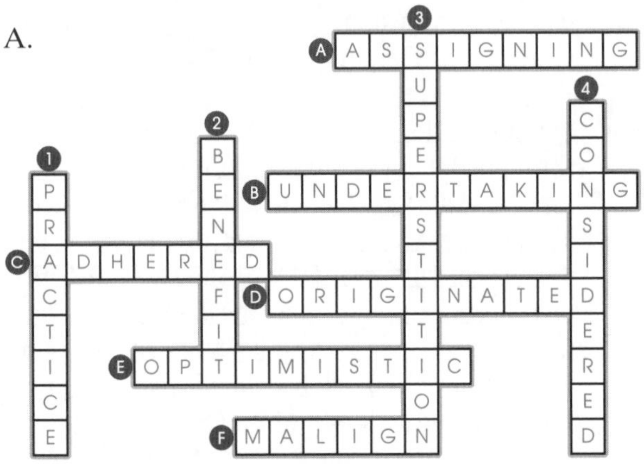

B. 1. very common
2. strange and insulting
3. so superstitious; somewhat difficult
4. awfully silly
5. quite upset; big black
6. Objective and scientific
C. (Individual writing)

D. 1. ✔
2. ✔
3.
4. ✔
5.
6.
7. ✔
E. (Individual writing)

8 Muhammad Yunus and the Grameen Bank

A. 1. F
2. T
3. T
4. F
5. F
6. T
7. T
8. F
9. T
B. 1. P
2. I
3. P
4. P
5. I
6. I
7. P
C. (Suggested answers)
1. The Elders is a group of very widely respected world leaders.
2. The Elders contribute quite greatly to solving some very tough global problems.
3. The Elders are very generously sponsored by a group of founders.
4. Nelson Mandela worked quite actively in fighting for freedom and equality in African countries.
5. The Elders respond very quickly to conflict situations around the world.
D. (Individual writing)

9 The New 7 Wonders of the World

A. (Suggested examples)
The Seven Wonders of the Ancient World ; the Great Pyramid of Giza
The Seven Natural Wonders of the World ; Mount Everest
The Seven Wonders of the Medieval Mind ; Stonehenge
The Seven Underwater Wonders of the World ; Lake Baikal
The Seven Wonders of the Modern World ; CN Tower
The Seven Forgotten Natural Wonders ; Niagara Falls
The Seven Forgotten Modern Wonders ; the Eiffel Tower
The Seven Forgotten Wonders of the Medieval Mind ; Mont Saint-Michel
The New 7 Wonders of the World ; Machu Picchu

B.
1. ADJ
2. ADV
3. ADV
4. ADV
5. ADV
6. ADJ
7. ADV
8. ADJ

C.
1. of the Mayan culture
2. in the Mayan language
3. at the site
4. at the centre
5. in 2007
6. with 91 steps
7. of its four sides
8. for astronomical purposes

D. (Individual writing)

10 Harmful Microorganisms

A.
1. Pathogens are disease-producing microorganisms.
2. Salmonella is a bacterium that causes food-borne infection.
3. Noroviruses are found in faecal-contaminated water and cause food-borne infection.
4. Staphylococcus aureus are bacteria that produce toxins said to be the most common cause of food poisoning.
5. SARS is a serious and highly infectious form of viral-borne pneumonia.

B.
1. Pathogenic microorganisms are harmful because the diseases they cause may be fatal.
2. When meat is left at room temperature for many hours, the bacteria in it may multiply and contaminate the meat.
3. Illness caused by noroviruses is characterized by nausea, vomiting, and diarrhea.
4. Pathogens can evolve rapidly to avoid being detected by our immune system.
5. Most bacteria are harmless and a few are even beneficial, but some can cause infectious diseases.
6. Although influenza is often confused with the common cold, it is a more severe disease caused by a different kind of virus.
7. At human body temperature, flu viruses can remain infectious for a week but at 0°C, they can last for more than 30 days.
8. When we cough, we have to cover our mouth to avoid the spread of flu viruses.

C. (Suggested answers)
1. cook food thoroughly to destroy harmful germs
2. If we do not handle food properly
3. food poisoning can still occur

11 The Science of Dreams

A.
1. B
2. B
3. A
4. B

B.
1. ✔
2. ✘
3. ✘
4. ✔
5. ✔
6. ✔
7. ✔
8. ✘
9. ✔
10. ✔
11. ✘

C. Whenever you mention déjà vu to your friends, there will surely be one or two among them that tell you they have had this experience before.

Déjà vu means "already seen" in French. It refers to an uncanny feeling that you have experienced a new situation before.

When I was very young, I had this dream. I came to a temple on a beach. There was an open area built with concrete in front of it. I saw many old people sitting at big round tables. Although they were having a feast, I couldn't hear any sound. Then I saw a Chow-chow tied to a pole. I went over and played with it for a while. After I played with the dog, I turned around and found that all the old people were gone. I was all alone!

Many years later, I went on a trip with my family to an island in Southeast Asia. The tour guide took us to a beach. There I saw a temple with a concrete open area in front. It gave me the creeps the moment I saw it because it was the first time I had been to that island, but everything was exactly the same as in my dream, even the colours of the temple! The only difference was that there were no old people around. Do you know what the weirdest thing was? There was a Chow-chow tied to a pole near the temple!

12 Chindogu: Strange Inventions We Can Actually Use

A.
- a prototype must have been made
- inventions cannot be for real use
- must be tools for everyday life
- humour must not be the only reason for creating the items
- items must have the inherent spirit of anarchy
- items are not for sale
- items are not propaganda
- items are never taboo
- items cannot be patented
- items must be without prejudice

B.
1. why there are so many inventions
2. that measure when the user has fallen into a deep sleep
3. who may be having a nap during lunchtime
4. whose books have been translated into many different languages
5. to whom the prize was awarded
6. when these two great inventors first met in history
7. in which the design contest is held
8. where the exhibition was held
9. that we encounter in our daily lives
10. that has been voted The Strangest Invention of the Year

C. (Individual answers)

13 Totem Poles

A.
1. There are very few totem poles built prior to the 1800s still around today.
2. European settlers discouraged Aboriginal groups from continuing with their traditions.
3. Trees used for making totem poles on the island of Hokkaido, Japan are smaller in size than those found in the Pacific Northwest.
4. Anthropologists refer to wooden figures found in these places as "ancestor figures", "greet figures", "talismans", or "tikis" instead of totem poles.
5. Totem poles are sacred objects and cannot be made by just anyone.

B.
1. CP
2. CX
3. CX
4. S
5. CPX
6. CP
7. S

C. (Suggested examples)
1. The Royal British Columbia Museum in Victoria, B.C. has one that is dated pre-1400s!
2. Totem poles are sacred objects and cannot be made by just anyone.
3. Some totem poles record clan lineage, while others are in fact historical records of the community.
4. Totem poles can also be found in other parts of the world, although they are a little different.
5. Even if you have not had the good fortune of seeing them in person along the Pacific Northwest, you have probably seen them on television.

6. Totem pole construction declined in the early 1900s as European settlers discouraged Aboriginal groups from continuing with their traditional ways.
7. Their totem poles are smaller because the sources of wood are much smaller trees than those found along the Pacific Northwest, and they are not painted.

14 One More Reason to Save the Rainforest

A. (Suggested answers)
Paragraph 1: the rainforests' role
Paragraph 2: what rainforests are to animals and what we get from them
Paragraph 3: what "superfoods" are and who uses/wants them
Paragraph 4: what the acai berry is, what it does, and how to consume it
Paragraph 5: what the yerba mate is, what it does, and how to consume it
Paragraph 6: what the cupuassu is, what it does, and how to consume it
Paragraph 7: what we should do to protect these "superfoods", both those that exist and those yet to be discovered

B. 1. majority
2. kilograms
3. derived
4. antioxidants
5. dioxide
6. benefits
7. medicines
8. biodiversity
9. ecosystems
10. popular
11. variety
12. superfoods
13. subtropical
14. contain

C. (Individual sentences)
1. dwellers
2. unknown
3. herbal
4. gentler
5. original
6. discover

15 The Endangered Tibetan Antelope

A. 1. chiru, Tsod, Zanglingyang
2. wild goats and sheep
3. cold alpine meadows and deserts, mainly the Tibetan Plateau
4. less than 75 000
5. 80 to 85 centimetres high at the shoulder
6. slightly smaller than males
7. grey to reddish-brown with white underside ; black markings on face and legs in winter (males only)
8. slender, curving black horns (males only), can survive extremely cold conditions (-40°C)
9. plants and grasses

B. 1. lives
2. deserts
3. graze
4. slender
5. their
6. secret
7. degrees
8. prices
9. poachers
10. sell
11. despite

C. (Individual writing)

16 One Laptop Per Child

A. 1. Computers can enrich our learning experience by increasing global communication, so we can get more information and learn more.
2. The OLPC project was set back as a result of competition from competitors who, in fear of losing business, started manufacturing their own low-cost computers.
3. (Individual answer)

B. 1. 4
2. 2
3. 2
4. 3 ; 7
5. 2
6. 7
7. 1
8. 5
9. 6

C. 1. XO was unveiled at the World Summit on the Information Society held in Tunisia in November 2005.
2. Inspired by the OLPC project, the Brazilian government started to investigate the use of laptops in education.
3. I came across an article about the features of XO in the computer magazine Today's Technology.
4. Mr. Negroponte aimed to eliminate poverty in developing countries through the One Laptop Per Child project.
5. Daisy told me her family has bought a new computer, so she can do research on the Internet for our English project.
6. This laptop has a maximum memory capacity of 5 GB.

17 Yummy International Desserts

A. Baklava: Middle-East and Mediterranean countries ; a sweet, sticky dessert made of layers of phyllo pastry, honey, and pistachio nuts
Trifle: England ; custard, fruit, jam, and bits of sponge cake or biscuits thrown in a bowl in layers and topped with whipped cream
Gulab Jamon: South Asian countries ; balls of cake soaked in sweet rose water syrup
Crêpes Suzette: France ; thin pancakes rolled in a sauce of orange juice, sugar, and liqueur

B. (Individual answer)

C. 1. Rachel has a sweet tooth**:** she likes all kinds of desserts.
2. We ordered three desserts**:** cheesecake topped with blueberries, raspberries, and strawberries**;** yogourt parfait with layers of yogourt, fruit, and granola**;** crepe filled with bananas, fresh cream, and chocolate sauce.
3. The world-famous restaurant expects one thing from the new pastry chef**:** creativity.
4. Have you heard of this saying**:** "A world without ice cream is a world in darkness"?
5. The four-judge panel for the dessert competition includes**:** Mrs. Emily Miller, Principal of the French Culinary Academy**;** Mr. Ryan Cann, Executive Chef of North Windsor Hotel**;** Ms. Hannah Evans, Chief Editor of *Fine Cuisine Magazine***;** Mr. Logan Ramos, former winner of the competition.
6. We need these ingredients to make waffles**:** flour, sugar, eggs, milk, and baking powder.
7. This is the first cake I made**:** a chocolate shortcake topped with sweetened strawberries and whipped cream.

D. 1. The souffle at this restaurant **(**I don't remember its name**)** is excellent. You must give it a try.
2. The article **"**How to Make Award-Winning Desserts**"** has given us useful information.
3. Simply Delight **–** a cozy café in downtown Toronto **–** offers a fantastic assortment of desserts and special drinks.
4. **"**Wow, this is the most scrumptious lemon meringue pie I've ever had!**"** exclaimed Josh.
5. Valeria is learning to make chocolate éclair **–** a favourite dessert of everyone in her family.
6. This Japanese chef uses nori **(**dried seaweed**)** in many of his desserts.
7. Tiramisu **–** an Italian dessert made with coffee and mascarpone cheese **–** is loved by many.
8. Elmo gave the brownie a big bite **(**he would have put the whole piece into his mouth if he could**)** and was already reaching for the last piece on the plate.

18 After the "Boom"

A. 1790:
Alexander MacKenzie described the oil sands in his chronicles.
1870:
Fort McMurray was established as a Hudson's Bay Company trading post.
1896:
Gold was discovered in a river near Dawson City.
1930s:
Abasands Oil exploited the oil sand resources.
1960s:
The search for Klondike gold in Dawson City was over.
1967:
The Suncor plant opened in Fort McMurray.
1978:
The Syncrude consortium mine opened in Fort McMurray.

B. (Individual answer)

C. 1. heating
2. stemming
3. worried
4. purposeful
5. hierarchy
6. employed
7. referred
8. visualized
9. speculative
10. terrifying
11. receiver
12. reindeer
13. hurries
14. development

D.

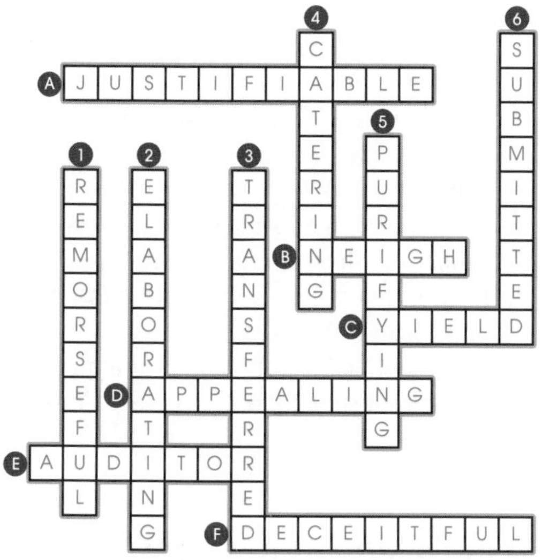

19 From St. Laurent to the Smithsonian

A. 1. 80 kilometres north of Winnipeg, Manitoba
2. the lake monster Manipogo, a legendary white horse, and UFO sightings
3. about 1200 people
4. Mitchif (a mixture of Cree/Salteaux, French, and English)
5. Coulee

B.

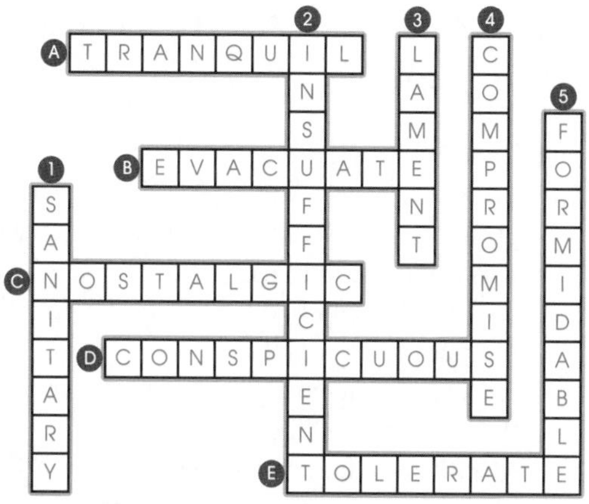

C. (Suggested answers)
1. courageous ; daring ; fearless
2. limit ; confine ; contain
3. band ; hoop ; circle
4. quiver ; tremble ; shudder
5. astonishing ; marvelous ; wonderful
6. stop ; quit ; end

D. (Suggested words)
lives – resides
see – witness
huge – giant
legendary – mythical
snake – serpent

20 The Making of a Sea-faring Legend

A. 1. (Individual answer)
2. They are about frightening sea creatures.
3. (Individual answer)

B. (Individual writing)

C. 1. M
2. S
3. S
4. P
5. S

D. (Individual writing)

21 The Academy Awards: Oscar's Big Night

A. (Individual answers)

B. (Suggested answers)

1. Holding the Oscar in his hands, the winner was too excited to say a word.
2. Seeing the celebrity exiting the limousine, the people got excited.
3. To create suspense, the presenter paused before announcing the winner.
4. Months in advance, people registered for the bleacher seats outside the theatre.

C.

1. The Academy Awards ceremony, the greatest event in show business, is held annually.
2. The Oscar, a gold-plated statuette, is presented to every Academy Award winner.
3. James Cameron, a Canadian-American director and screenwriter, won the Best Director Award for *Titanic,* released in 1997.
4. The Oscar, one of the most recognized awards in the world, is a symbol of achievement in the film industry.

22 A Story of What Kids Can Do

A.

1. ✔
2. In his first book, Craig Kielburger wrote about the injustices against children in various South Asian countries.
3. Craig founded "Leaders Today" with his elder brother Marc.
4. ✔
5. Craig received a Doctorate in Education from Nipissing University.
6. Craig Kielburger believes that world peace has to begin with the children.

B.

1. without
2. because
3. to
4. because/since
5. although
6. before
7. after
8. and
9. think
10. except
11. if
12. although
13. because/since

C.

1. Craig Kielburger always thinks of freeing children around the world from enslavement.
2. Craig Kielburger's achievements in fighting for child rights can be proven by the distinctions he has received.
3. "Leaders Today" organizes programs to train young people as leaders.
4. You do not need volunteer experiences to join the group.
5. All new volunteers will have to attend the orientation tomorrow at noon.

D. (Suggested answers)

1. Child labour has existed in some countries for a long time.
2. Although not invited, Craig would meet with world leaders and demand that they stop child labour.
3. To achieve world peace, it is essential to ensure children's rights.
4. I think that young people have the power to better the world.
5. Free The Children has built more than 500 schools in China, Kenya, Sri Lanka, etc.

23 The Truth about Carbs

A. (Suggested answers)

1. Weight will be lost quickly but will be regained just as fast. Ill health could also be an effect.
2. Blood sugar levels rise.
3. The cells use the sugar as their energy source.
4. Refined food products containing "bad" carbs are widely marketed and readily available.
5. Home entertainment systems and computers are more affordable and common.

B.

1. To live healthy lives, we must choose our food wisely and work out regularly.
2. Carbohydrates provide the energy we need to work and play in our everyday lives.
3. This book focuses on and gives detailed explanations of the benefits of low-carb diets.
4. Dietitians promote proper eating habits and participate in research.

C. 1. Classified as a simple carb, lactose is found mainly in dairy products.
2. Although easily digested, carbs from refined foods are not recommended by dietitians.
3. As a carbohydrate found in plants, fibre is not digested by our bodies.
4. Like a sponge, insoluble fibre absorbs water to help move solid waste out of our bodies.

24 Your Carbon Footprint

A. Paragraph 1: what a "carbon footprint" is
Paragraph 2: why we must be aware of our "carbon footprint" ; effects of one's carbon footprint
Paragraph 3: the two types of carbon footprint
Paragraph 4: five best ways to reduce our carbon footprint
Paragraph 5: ways to reduce our secondary footprint
Paragraph 6: what carbon "offset" schemes are

B. (Suggested writing)
1. Global warming has numerous negative effects.
2. Saving energy in our daily lives is easy.
3. We can all help reduce the amount of waste that goes to landfills.

C. (Individual writing)

25 The Biofuel Controversy

A. 1. Biofuels are used in place of gasoline to reduce carbon emissions.
2. Mass production of biofuels will result in an increase in food crop prices.
3. 200 kilograms of corn can feed someone for a year.
4. The Tata Nano is not powered purely by non-carbon fuels.
5. Forests will be cut down to provide land needed for the production of plants for biofuels.

B. Dear Editor: salutation
Paragraph 1: introduction
Paragraph 2: body
Paragraph 3: body
Paragraph 4: conclusion
Sincerely: closing

C. (Individual writing)

26 A Letter from Sammy in Mali

A.

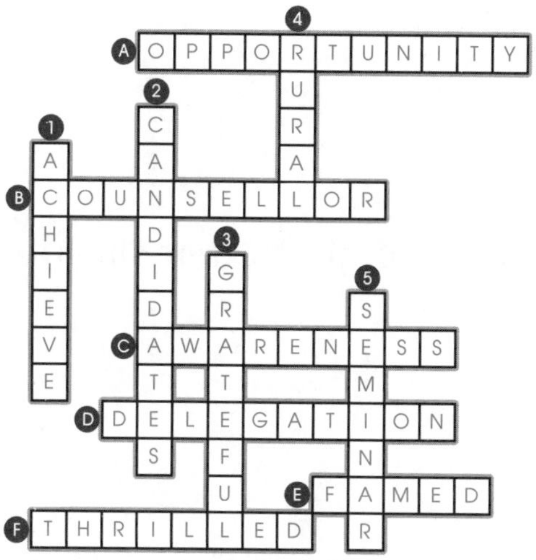

B. 1. Hi Kiyoka
2. Love,
3. (Suggested answers)
a. I hope you're doing well.
b. I'll never forget it.
c. I'm so excited.
4a. See the postmark on this letter?
b. Can't wait to show Worokia my own country.
c. Will write again soon.
5a-c. There is no subject.

C. (Individual writing)

27 The Elements of Fiction

A. 1. Plot: the story you wish to tell, answers the question, "What's happening?"
2. Conflict: the struggle between two people or between a person and something else
3. Characters: the people who act out the plot
4. Setting: the place and the time in which the plot takes place
5. Theme: the underlying meaning of the story
6. Point-of-view: the way the story is narrated
7. Style: the language the author uses to deliver the story

B. (Individual writing)

C. (Individual writing)

28 Who Will Be Next on the Moon?

A. 4
3
1
5
2
6

B. (1 and 2 – Individual answers)
3. (Suggested answers)
The Chinese Lunar Exploration Program is run by China's space agency and involves explorations by un-manned robotic vehicles and human missions. Chang'e 1 and 2 analyzed the moon in preparation for Chang'e 3. Chang'e 3 deployed an unmanned lunar rover in December 2013. The program has three more unmanned Chang'e missions in mind, after which the manned space program will commence around 2025.

C. (Individual writing)

1 Daily Life in Early Canada

A. king
seigneurs:
1. church
2. grain
3. disputes
habitants:
4. taxes
5. labour
6. harvest

B. (Individual answers)

2 The Expulsion of the Acadians

1. Acadia
2. Treaty
3. France
4. allegiance
5. Charles Lawrence
6. deported
7. Britain
8. Thirteen Colonies
9. They refused because the Acadians were originally from France.
10. He was afraid that if war ensued between Britain and France, the Acadians would fight for France instead of Britain.
11. The Acadians moved to Louisiana and established a strong Cajun community.

3 Seven Years' War

A.
1. Britain
2. fur trade
3. Algonquin
4. Quebec
5. bilingual
6. The French and Indian War and the War of the Conquest
7. Britain and France both wanted to conquer North America.

B.

1. It was important because Quebec was located along the St. Lawrence River. The river was used to send supplies and reinforcements to French colonies. If the British captured Quebec, the French would be depleted of their resources.
2. It was a turning point because after the battle, Britain won more victories against France, eventually winning the war.
3. (Individual answer)

4 The Royal Proclamation and the Quebec Act

The Royal Proclamation:
First Peoples ; France ; rights ; settlement
Quebec Act:
Quebec ; Catholics ; colonists ; revolution

1.

The Royal Proclamation	Quebec Act
October 7, 1763	1774
the First Peoples	the French
the colonists in the Thirteen Colonies	the colonists in the Thirteen Colonies

2. It recognized First Peoples' rights by giving them the land that was rightfully theirs.
3. The Quebec Act allowed the French inhabitants to practise their faith and allowed them to have representation in the colony.
4. They contributed by favouring the First Peoples and the French inhabitants over the colonists. The Royal Proclamation and the Quebec Act both put limitations on the colonists.

5 Displacement: the Loyalists

A. 1. American Revolutionary War
The Patriots
The Loyalists
2. The colonies were angry about paying taxes and about being unable to occupy lands to the west. They also wanted national independence.
3. They were displaced because they were forced to leave their homes and properties and move elsewhere.
4. The war changed the lives of the Loyalists. They were persecuted and lost all of their possessions. They had to move away and find new homes.

B. Similarities: A ; D ; E
Differences: B ; C ; F
(Individual answer)

6 Interactions

A. 1. trading
2. fur
3. unlicensed
4. transported
5. skills
6. compete
7. populations
8. needed
9.

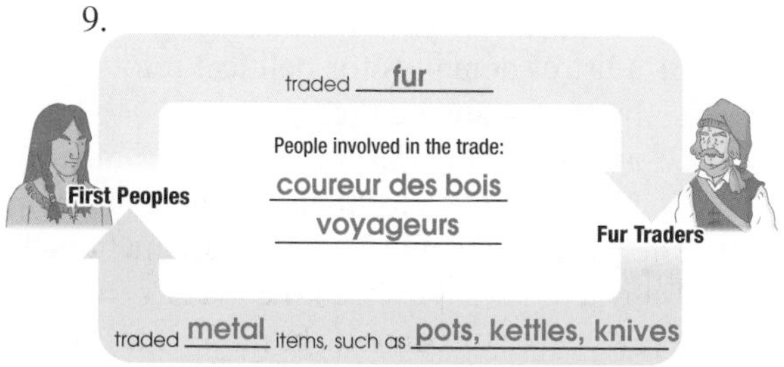

10. (Individual answer)

B. (Individual answer)

7 Challenges in Immigration

A. 1. People immigrated from Britain because of the Industrial Revolution, which was affecting employment opportunities. In Ireland, the Great Famine left people sick and starving. They moved to Canada looking for better lives.
2. The immigrants struggled on their way to North America. On the ships, they got sick and some of them died. When they arrived in Canada, they struggled to adapt to the harsh Canadian climate.
3. (Individual answer)

B. 1. disease
2. treat
3. quarantine
4. healthy
5. organizations
6. blamed

(Suggested answer)
Positive:
The cholera epidemic compelled the government to establish public health organizations.
Negative:
The cholera epidemic made people turn against immigrants, blaming them for the disease.

8 The Timber Trade

A. 1. timber
2. Ottawa River
3. economic
4. pine
5. export
6. The timber industry contributed to the colonies' population and economic growth.
7. France imposed a blockade that prevented Britain from accessing wood from the Baltic region.
8. (Individual answer)

B.

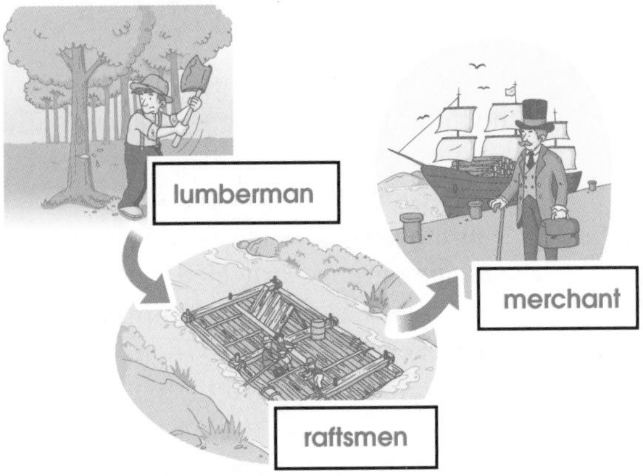

C. (Suggested answer)
The timber trade created jobs, which attracted people to move to Upper and Lower Canada.

9 War of 1812

1. The United States
2. Britain
3. The First Peoples
4. Upper Canada
5. Lower Canada
   War of 1812
   Began in: June, 1812
   Ended in: December, 1814
   Cause:
   The United States did not like Britain stopping them from trading in Europe. Britain tried to stop trade between France and the United States.
   Parties Involved:
   The United States, Britain, Upper Canada, Lower Canada, and the First Peoples
   Outcome:
   The war ended with the Treaty of Ghent on December 24, 1814. The treaty presented a status quo.
6. It means that it restored the status of both the United States and Britain to the way it was before the war.
7. (Suggested answer)
   Resisting American occupation meant stopping the United States from gaining Canadian land. Canada is as large as it is today because it kept the United States from occupying its territory.

10 Important Personalities

A. Richard Pierpoint:
was offered the chance of freedom in return for fighting for Britain in the American Revolutionary War ; rewarded with a land grant in the Niagara Region
Laura Secord:
learned of the plans for a surprise attack by the American army ; became a celebrated war heroine after her death

B. 1. T
2. F
3. T
4. F

C. (Individual writing)

11 The Rebellions

A. 1. ethnic
2. British
3. suppressed
4. Patriotes
5. oligarchic
6. gain
7. debt
8. refuge
9. A: wealthy British merchants who dominated the Legislative Council
   B: a list of demands for political reform sent by Papineau and the Patriotes
   C: an elite group that ran the government in Upper Canada for their own personal gain
10. The British held more power than the French. They actively suppressed the French culture.
11. They were discontent because the ruling power took advantage of their position to favour themselves. This negatively affected the common people.

B. Lord Durham suggested that Upper Canada and Lower Canada be unified into one nation.

12 The Province of Canada

A. 1. united into one political entity
   2. elected by the public
   3. internal affairs
   4. based on ethnic division

B. 1. Executive Council ; Legislative Council
   2. It was unfair because Lower Canada had to help pay Upper Canada's debt and had the same representation in the government although they had less debt and a larger population.
   3. The Act impacted the French Canadians negatively. In Lower Canada, they were a majority but after the union, they became a minority. The Act also tried to squash their culture and assimilate them into the British culture.

1 Natural Processes and Landforms

A. 1. Plate Tectonics
tectonic ; collide ; mountain ranges ; Himalayas
2. Deposition
sediments ; water ; delta ; shallow ; rock ; Grand Canyon ; pressure

B. 1. Mechanical: Rocks are physically broken up.
Chemical: Chemical reactions break down the bonds that hold rocks and minerals together.
Organic: Rocks are broken up by plants and animals.
2. Weathering breaks down rocks, changing and reshaping the landform. The rock pieces are then carried away by water or wind and deposited in another place through erosion, changing or building the landform there.

2 Land and Water

A. A: stream
B: boundary
C: saturated ; aquatic
D: land
E: mouth

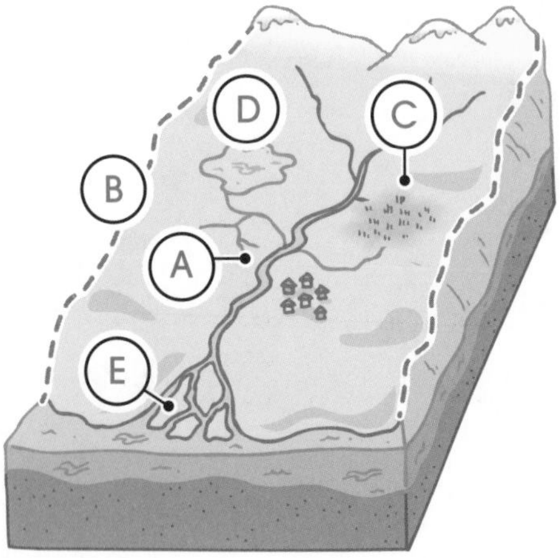

B. depth ; downhill ; fast ; wider ; loses ; decreases ; fertile ; mouth
(Suggested answers)
1. The wide plains of Punjab cause the Indus River to slow down while becoming wider and less deep.
2. The Indus River brings rich sediments down to the plains of Punjab, allowing for the creation of alluvial terraces.

3 Climate Patterns

A. 1. Latitude ; Equator ; higher
2. Elevation ; sea level ; temperatures
3. Closeness to Water ; cooler ; longer
4. Ocean Currents ; raise ; cool

B. 1. Moscow
2. 56°N ; 56°N
3. Although the two cities lie on the same latitude, Glasgow is closer to the ocean than Moscow, so it is warmer in winter. The warm ocean currents passing nearby also help raise Glasgow's winter temperatures.

4 Natural Vegetation

A: Boreal Forest ; Northern ; short ; coniferous
B: Tropical Rainforest ; equatorial ; abundant
C: Temperate Grasslands ; north ; drought ; grasses
D: Tundra ; snow ; shrubs
(Suggested countries)
C ; Uruguay
A ; Canada
D ; Russia
B ; Brazil

5 Impact of Human Activities

A. 1. electricity ; C
2. wood ; D
3. irrigate ; A
4. Factories ; B

B. Rhodesian government:
We think the construction of the dam is a must to service the electricity needs of nearby communities.

Residents of Zambia and Zimbabwe:
The construction of the dam certainly benefits us. We can have a constant supply of electricity and this improves our lives!

Indigenous Tonga people:
The construction of the dam forced us to leave our home. We are relocated to different areas and have to suffer frequent droughts and infertile soil. It has disrupted our lives severely and the compensation was minimal!

The rescue team in Operation Noah:
The construction has severe negative impacts on wildlife. We have to rescue and relocate the animals suffered from flooding and habitat loss immediately!

6 Impact of Natural Disasters

A. 1. The 2005 Hurricane Katrina in the United States contributed to a political change in the country because people lost faith in the government when it did not help them as much as they expected.
2. The 2011 Japan Tsunami contributed to economic difficulties because it caused $235 billion in damages.
3. The 2013 Pakistan Earthquake contributed to a physical change of the landscape because the tremors resulted in the formation of a small island.

B. (Suggested answers)
1a. Girls have to stop their education to collect water from faraway places.
b. Because of the lack of proper sanitation facilities, people who drink or use water for crops get sick.
2a. Crops fail and incomes of farmers are greatly reduced.
b. Food prices soar as food becomes scarcer with the failure of crops.
3a. Humanitarian organizations provided food and water for the short-term.
b. Wells have been drilled.
4a. Underground water reserves are too deep to reach.
b. The demand for water exceeds the supply and people flock to the communities where the wells are located.

7 Natural Resources

A. Renewable ; fish
Non-renewable ; fossil fuels
Flow ; wind
1. tides ; flow
2. oil ; non-renewable
3. solar energy ; flow
4. trees ; renewable

B. 1. Both Brazil and Malaysia have rich mineral, timber, hydro, and agricultural resources.
2. Both countries lie close to the Equator, have a tropical climate with lots of rainfall, and have many rivers.

8 Mining of Natural Resources

A. 1. minerals
2. extracting
3. trees
4. roads
5. habitat
6. erosion
7. sedimentation
8. Chemicals
9. government
10. harm
11. political
12. rights

B. Environmental Impact:
Forests ; toxic
Economic Impact:
prices
Social Impact:
reduced ; do not have
Political Impact:
expel ; combat

9 Water as a Natural Resource

A. (Suggested examples)
1. Household Purposes ; washing dishes
2. Agriculture ; irrigating farmland
3. Generating Power ; producing hydroelectricity
4. Transportation ; transporting cargo
5. Recreation ; swimming

B. 1. (Individual answer)
2. Middle East and Northern Africa had the least amount of renewable freshwater resources in 2015.
3. 12 537 m^3 ; (Individual answer)

10 Impact of Overfishing

A. 1. sustainable
2. rebuild
3. fishing
4. catch
5. negative
6. pollution
7. food
8. health
9. social
10. jobs
11. diet

B. 1. 500 years of overexploitation of the Atlantic cod stock caused its depletion.
2. The federal government declared a moratorium on cod fishing because the Atlantic cod stock dwindled near the point of complete depletion.
3. (Individual answer)

11 Using Natural Resources

A. extraction ; serious ; organizations ; reduce ; negative
Ways to Lessen the Impact of Using the Earth's Resources:
1. C
2. D
3. B
4. A

B. 1. (Suggested answer)
They got their name because the revenues from these diamonds had been used to finance civil wars and conflicts, claiming millions of lives.
2. (Individual answer)

12 Conserving Natural Resources

non-profit ; non-governmental ; ecosystems

1. sustainable
2. deforestation
3. pesticides
4. impact
5. waterways
6. certifies
7. protection
8. earnings
9. certified
10. sources
11. plantations
12. seal

(Individual answer)

1 Ecosystems

A. 1. population
2. species
3. organism
4. habitat
5. ecosystem
6. community

B. 1. ecosystem
2. atmosphere
3. animals
4. landforms
5. (Suggested drawings)

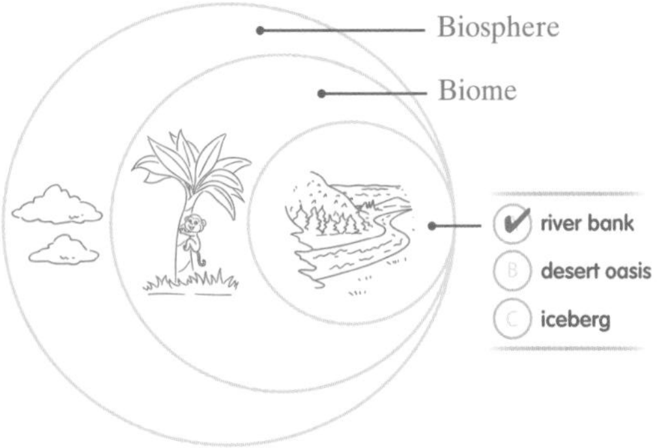

2 Biotic and Abiotic Elements in Ecosystems

A. 1. ecosystem
2. biotic ; microorganisms
3. abiotic ; water
4. (Suggested answers)
Biotic Elements:
tree ; deer ; grass ; bird ; bacteria
Abiotic Elements:
sun ; water ; air ; mountain ; soil

B. Highlight these words blue:
Humans ;
berries ; black bear ;
beaver ; trees ;
Snakes ; other reptiles ;
cleaner fish ; other bigger fish
Highlight these words yellow:
water ;
Wind ; soil ;
sun

1. biotic & abiotic
2. biotic & biotic
3. abiotic & abiotic
4. biotic & biotic
5. biotic & abiotic
6. biotic & biotic

3 Food Cycle

A. 1.

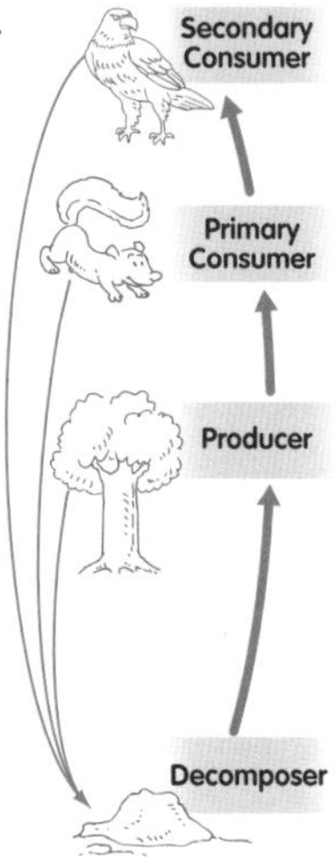

2. producer
3. herbivore
4. omnivore
5. plant
6. food
7. nutrients
8. fungi

B. (Suggested drawing)
C ;

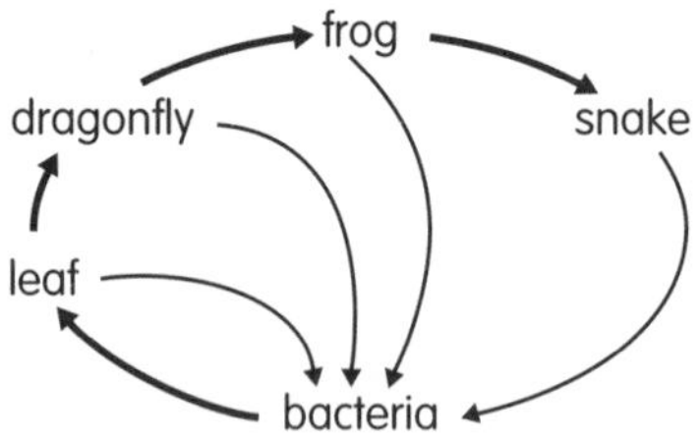

C. 1a. B
b. A
c. D
d. C
2a. food chain
b. food web

4 Natural Cycles

A. 1. the sun
2. evaporation
3. respiration
(Suggested answers for questions 4 and 5)
4. rain, snow, and hail
5. oceans, lakes, and rivers
6. respiration
(Individual example)

B. 1. combustion
2. photosynthesis
3. respiration
4. carbon sinks
5. decomposition
6. fossil fuels

5 Succession and Adaptation

A.
1. inhabit
2. debris
3. Emergent
4. marsh

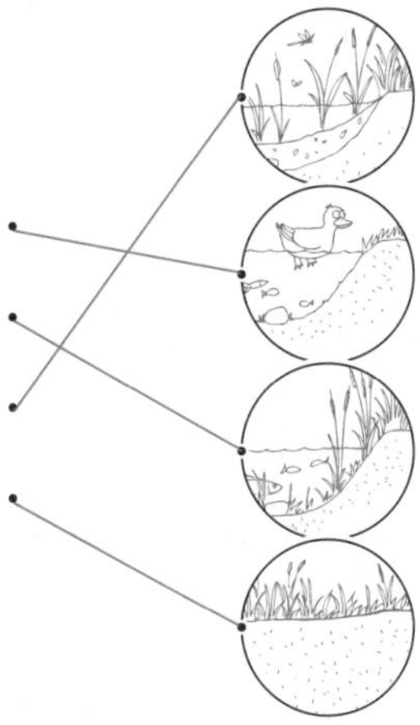

B. 1. extinction
2. competition
3. succession
4. species diversity
5. adaptation

C. (Individual experiment)

6 Human Activity

A. (Underline these factors.)
A: Air pollution ; acid rain
B: Construction and logging practices
C: overuse
D: Chemical fertilizers
E: A dam ; flooding
F: Non-native species ; invasive species
G: manufacturing of goods ; industrial waste
H: Transportation pollution

B. 1. B
2. D
3. H
4. G
5. E
6. C
7. A or H
8. F

7 Structures

A.

mosquito mouthpart	fishing net
spiderweb	needle
kangaroo pouch	bowl
honeycomb	baby frontpack
tooth	brick wall
bird wings	spear tip
nest	airplane wings
(Individual answer)	(Individual answer)

B. 1. A frame structure
2. A shell structure
3. A solid structure

C. Solid Structures:
brick wall, iceberg, paperweight, loaf of bread
Frame Structures:
spiderweb, umbrella, ladder, house
Shell Structures:
soccer ball, egg, bike helmet, cap

D. (Individual answers)

8 Centre of Gravity and Stability

A. 1. A
2a. 
unstable ; stable
b. 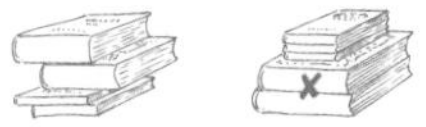
unstable ; stable
c. 
stable ; unstable
d. 
stable ; unstable

B. (Individual drawings)
C. The centre of gravity moves closer to the side where the paper clips are placed.

9 Forces on Stable and Unstable Structures

A. 1. load
2. live
3. dead
4. compressive
5. tensile
6. Shear
7. torsion

B. 1. compressive
2. live
3. compressive
4. tension
5. shear

C.

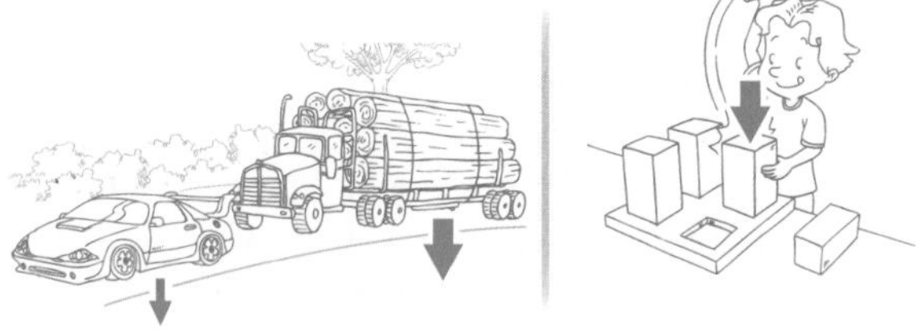

10 Materials and Design

A. 1. A
2. C
3. B
4. C
5. C
6. A

B. 1. portability
2. water resistance

C. (Individual answers)

11 The Particle Theory of Matter

A. 1. tiny ; moving ; spaces ; Heat
2. true
3. false
4. false
5. true
6. false

B. Solid Gas Liquid

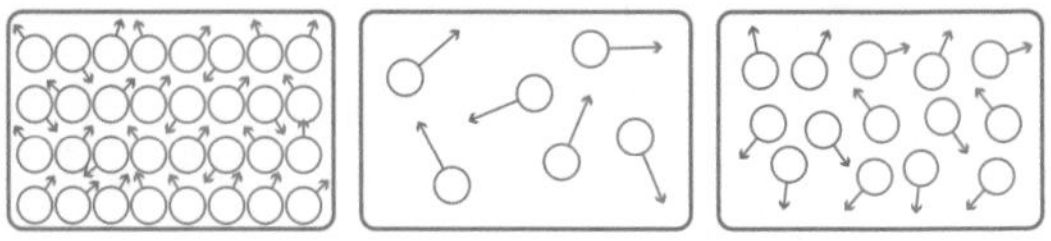

C.

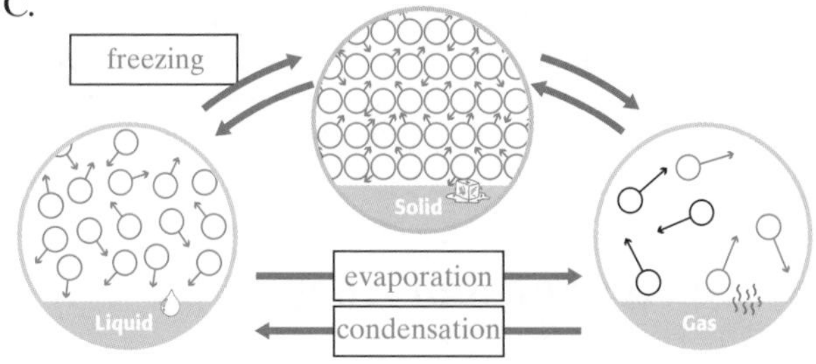

12 Pure Substances and Mixtures

A. 1. identical
2. two

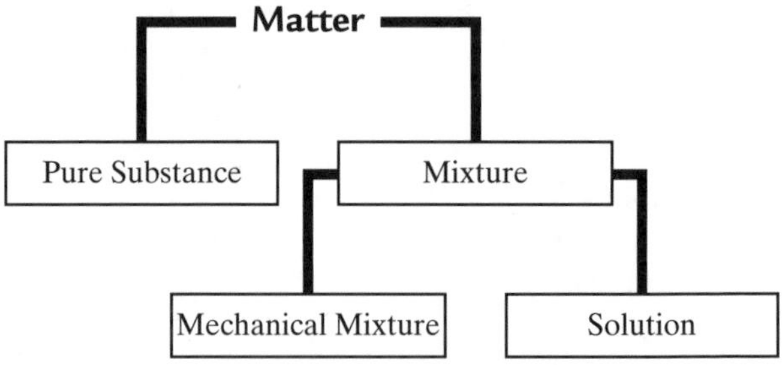

B. 1. m
2. ps
3. ps
4. m
5. m
6. ps
7. m

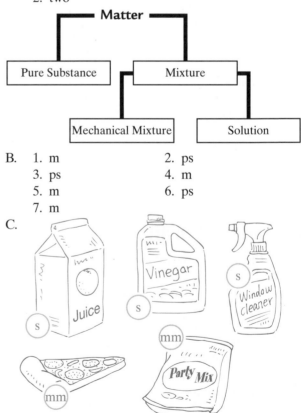

C.

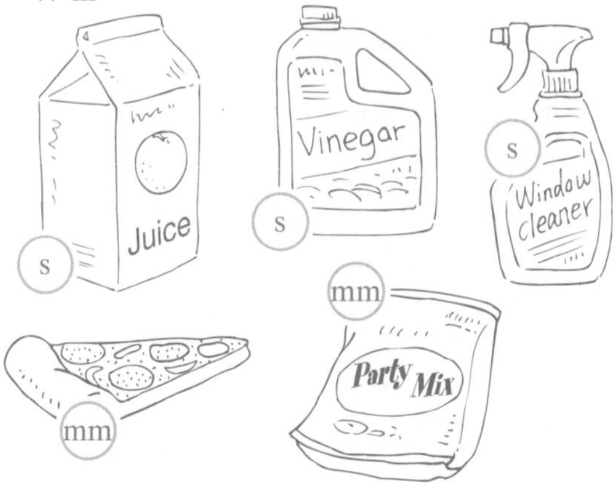